Metamorphosis through Conscious Living

Metamorphosis through Conscious Living:

A Transpersonal Psychology Perspective

Edited by

Lindy McMullin, Regina U. Hess and Marcie Boucouvalas

Cambridge Scholars Publishing

Metamorphosis through Conscious Living:
A Transpersonal Psychology Perspective

Edited by Lindy McMullin, Regina U. Hess and Marcie Boucouvalas

This book first published 2017

Cambridge Scholars Publishing

Lady Stephenson Library, Newcastle upon Tyne, NE6 2PA, UK

British Library Cataloguing in Publication Data
A catalogue record for this book is available from the British Library

ISBN (10): 1-4438-5361-5
ISBN (13): 978-1-4438-5361-3

This book is formatted according to the requirements of Cambridge Scholars Publishing, UK. The style of the American Psychological Association's (*Publication Manual of the American Psychological Association,* 6th edition, 2010) has been adopted **only** for the references in the endnote section.

As a compilation of contributions by international authors who adhere to either American English or to British English, especially with regard to spelling, it was decided to retain the writer's original voice; therefore, the book contains chapters written in the respective spelling of each author.

TABLE OF CONTENTS

ACKNOWLEDGEMENTS

The editors wish to thank the international transpersonal authors for their contribution to this book that highlights the XVI EUROTAS conference that took place in Crete, 1-5 October 2014. We honour the land and the people of Hellas. We wish to thank all those who participated, supported and helped in the organization of the conference. Special appreciation and acknowledgements go out to Ingo Jahrsetz for his choice of Crete as the perfect place for the conference, Frances Vaughan and Zana Marovic for their special support, and the members of the scientific committee including Jure Biechonski, Marcie Boucouvalas, Ingo Jahrsetz, Les Lancaster, David Lukoff, Vladimir Maykov, Lindy McMullin, Sangeetha Menon and Steven Schmitz. We thank our publishers, Cambridge Scholars Publishing, for their trust, and in particular Sam Baker for reaching out to us, Victoria Carruthers, Amanda Millar, Sophie Edminson and Courtney Blades for their support. As in any endeavor of this nature, however, there are the invisible and sometimes inaudible ones, those whose presence silently offers both inspiration and support. Although too numerous to mention, for the most part you know who you are and we are most grateful.

Including the readers, we understand that all together we have membership in a greater whole—*Ubuntu*—and aim to contribute to further community building with this volume.

Finally, we wholeheartedly welcome comments and dialogue from all.

FOREWORD

ROSEMARIE ANDERSON AND LES LANCASTER

The theme of this book and the 2014 European Transpersonal Association (EUROTAS) Conference it represents is *metamorphosis*, an ancient Greek word meaning change (*meta*) in form (*morph*). The 2014 EUROTAS Conference organizers understood metamorphosis to mean the transformation of self, society, and world culture. In a stroke of brilliance, they organized the conference on the island of Crete near Knossos, the cradle of European civilization some 1500 years prior to the rise of the Indo-Europeans that later held sway in mainland Greece in Athens, Corinth, Sparta, and Troy. The Minoans (approximately 3000 B.C.E. to 1450 B.C.E.) were a peace-loving, goddess-based culture, composed largely of mixed-blood, dark-skinned people from the surrounding Mediterranean coastline, primarily from the north coast of Africa and the Near East. They crossed the Mediterranean Sea by ship first as traders and then as settlers, for the fertile land and available water in Crete were accommodating to crops and its relatively isolated location secure from the aggressive cultures along the great river beds of the ancient world.[1, 2] Locating a conference on metamorphosis in the cradle of European civilization, as well as beginning and ending the conference with rituals reminiscent of the ancient Greek mysteries, brought together the forces of sacred geography and transformation in one historic, international conference. This book offers chapters based on conference presentations by transpersonal psychologists from around the world and extends this metamorphosis to you, the readers.

At this juncture of our nearly fifty-year history as a field, transpersonal psychology is faced with a dilemma—and some think a crisis. Since the founding of *The Journal of Transpersonal Psychology* in 1969 by Anthony Sutich, transpersonal psychology has pioneered the study and personal exploration of alternative states of consciousness, parapsychological phenomena, "ultimate values, unitive consciousness, peak experiences, B-values, ecstasy," … and "the sacralization of everyday life…".[3] Sutich was supported by Abraham Maslow (1969) and others who often gathered in Sutich's home in Palo Alto, California. Today, the study of consciousness, neurocontemplative science, and research into mindfulness, compassion, intuition, spiritual experience, and even *sunyata* have blossomed in psychology and throughout the human sciences, including medicine and the health sciences. As a field, our historic subject matter has "gone mainstream". Given these developments, it is legitimate to ask about the role transpersonal psychology might play now and as it moves beyond its Golden Jubilee. Are others now doing what we hoped to do and perhaps even doing it better because of university and research foundation support and more adequate funding? Perhaps our mission is complete. Or, is our purpose as transpersonal researchers, therapists, healthcare specialists, and practitioners clearer than ever? We think the latter.

As we both have said on various occasions, including our own keynotes at this conference,[4, 5] the critical feature that makes research, scholarship, and practice *transpersonal* is *engagement with the Sacred*, the sacred other that lives both within and beyond us as individuals and unique cultures. Our research practice, professional practice, and contemplative practice are embedded in that Sacred whether we like it or not. What makes transpersonalists different from others is that we affirm the sacred mystery at the core of our world and our experience, and strive to incorporate it into our scholarly work and professional practice. Our approach differs in this critical regard from most of those studying spiritual topics in other branches of psychology and the human sciences, for whom explanations tend towards the biological and who employ methods that emphasize detachment. Indeed, the study of topics firmly embedded in sacred paths for centuries, such as compassion, mindfulness, and unitive states, has become a Trojan horse for those who would see these expressions of human endeavor locked into a reductive framework. Therefore, these developments actually serve to sharpen the delineation between the discipline of transpersonal psychology and other approaches. Our discipline eschews explanations that package the Sacred in, for example, neo-phrenological visions of the brain. Instead, transpersonal psychology insists that the very way in which the researcher frames a research question and chooses a methodology determines whether or not the research journey becomes a sacred encounter.

The transpersonal approach is distinctive in placing the potential metamorphosis of all those involved in scholarship, research, and professional practice as a core value. Of course, we will always be in need of clearer and more astute methods and models that embed the Sacred in our professional and personal practice. Over time, how we discern and integrate the Sacred in our professional and personal lives is inevitably a matter of choice and we will no doubt differ in our choices and practices now and in the future. What would it mean for transpersonal researchers with differing epistemological stances to recognize the sacred other in the conduct of research? What would it mean for transpersonal therapists and other healthcare specialists to safeguard the impulse of the sacred other in their clients and themselves in the conduct of treatment without jeopardizing their professional licensure to practice? To answer these questions and many others, we are all in this together – and hopefully in dialogue together. This book represents a critical phase of that dialogue.

There are many contrary positions and opinions taken in this book. Some of them differ from ours or represent topics or interests we might not have thought imaginable. All this is good, showing healthy levels of discussion and debate. The very nature of the field is diverse. The imaginative, radical people drawn to the field in the past, present, and future will ensure diversity and future thinking. No one needs to worry that we transpersonalists are going to run out of ideas or start agreeing with each other soon. Radical thinking and creativity are "signatures" of the field. This book follows in the now long-standing tradition set in motion by Anthony Sutich[6, 7] and Abraham Maslow[8] of proposing courageous and creative ideas.

In dialogue with others, let the crescendo towards new paradigm scientific and professional methods and models that honor the Sacred begin within transpersonal psychology. This book leads the way forward.

Bibliography

[1] Geldard, R. G. (1989). *The traveler's key to ancient Greece: A guide to the sacred places of ancient Greece.* New York, NY: Knopf.
[2] Scully, V. (1979). *The earth, the temple, and the gods: Greek sacred architecture* (Rev. Ed.). New Haven, CT: Yale University Press.

[3] Sutich, A. (1969). Some considerations regarding transpersonal psychology. *The Journal of Transpersonal Psychology, 1*(1), 11-20.
[4]Anderson, R. (October, 2014). *Research in a sacred world.* Keynote address, 2014 EUROTAS Conference, Crete, Greece. Available: www.youtube.com/watch?v=meZ3Imv51QY
[5] Lancaster, L. (October, 2014). *A compromise too far: Mindfulness and the challenge of the sacred.* Keynote address, 2014 EUROTAS Conference, Crete, Greece. Available: www.youtube.com/watch?v=eDunH5mova0
[6] see 3
[7] Sutich, A. (1976). The emergence of the transpersonal orientation: A personal account. *The Journal of Transpersonal Psychology, 8*(1), 5-19.
[8] Maslow, A. (1969). The farther reaches of human nature. *The Journal of Transpersonal Psychology, 1*(1), 1-9.

INTRODUCTION

THE XVI EUROTAS CONFERENCE

LINDY MCMULLIN

Crete is the island of the cave, the palace temple and the labyrinth and by tradition the birthplace of Nikos Kazantzakis, El Greco and Eleftherios Venizelos. Crete has always retained its radiance in its belief of the unity of life. Mycenaean art renders this experience of unity in the seal of c.1500 BC, in which the goddess holds the double-bladed axe next to the tree of life. Maria Gimbutas[1] (2001) suggests the axe evolved from the double wings of the Neolithic butterfly with the soul and butterfly as *psyche.*

The butterfly is the transformed figure of the caterpillar that has gone through its process of metamorphosis. From crawling on the earth to flying through the air, nature gives a perfect picture of harmony and balance that comes through unity, in the form of the butterfly. The process of metamorphosis is not an easy process or to be taken lightly. The butterfly lays eggs on a leaf. When the egg hatches, a caterpillar emerges that begins to eat the specific leaf on which it was born, eating and eating until it grows, shedding its outside skin numerous times. When the caterpillar ceases growing, it forms itself into a chrysalis and begins to undergo major changes; dormant cells called imaginal cells in the body of the caterpillar begin a process of creating new form and structure. At first the caterpillar's immune system attacks these imaginal cells, regarded as threats. The cells continue to multiply, however, and connect with each other until they start forming clusters and clumps. As they resonate at the same frequency, passing information back and forth, they no longer act as discrete individual cells but as a multi-cell organism that eventually emerges as a butterfly. The pattern inherent in the process of metamorphosis is a process of disintegration. The caterpillar grows its imaginal discs whilst developing inside its egg, portraying evolution as a predetermined certainty. Whilst disintegration is in process, so is transformation unseen to the naked eye. The re-integration of order within chaos is a guarantee before the birth of the butterfly taken to symbolize a different state.

Accordingly, conscious of the impending global crisis and with symbolic intention, the organization of the XVI EUROTAS conference was undertaken by SYNTHESIS, the Hellenic Association for Transpersonal Psychology and Research. Focus was on uniting the world of transpersonal psychology and for the first time in history, three main transpersonal organizations ATP, EUROTAS, and ITA came together in Crete in October 2014. SYNTHESIS closed in 2015 but the vision that maintained the flame lit during the EUROTAS conference is still in process. Metamorphosis never ends as it is an ongoing process, that brings with it reflective understanding, hope, compassion and a desire to build strong foundations for a global renaissance.

The mission of the conference was to help facilitate a metamorphosis both for the country of Greece and the field of transpersonal psychology through the coming together of transpersonal professionals and interested people from around the world in community and open sharing. Evident was a deep desire to contribute to a healthy renewal, regeneration, and transformation of the state of being in the world. At the core of this transpersonal vision was the idea of metamorphosis, the ability of individuals and organizations to transcend the limited sphere of mind associated with the ego and to learn to live in ways that incorporate a richer and more interconnected consciousness.

Transpersonal psychology brings together profound lessons from mythic and mystical systems of thought with the rigor of psychological science to address these issues, re-visioning what has been taken for granted. Transpersonal Psychology suggests both an ancient and new vision of reality that honors all spiritual and religious traditions. It also acknowledges the possibility of going beyond a limited awareness of everyday life to enable some to experience reality in ways that transcend the human perspective[2].

Michael Washburn[3] describes the dangerous odyssey of self-knowledge as an essential part of attaining humanness. Through building, developing and expanding self-capacities for spirituality, wisdom, creativity, connectedness, love and compassion, there is an implicit value in human experience. This process in turn connects experience to existential meaning, purpose, identity, narrative, spirituality, relationships and participatory action[4].There are assumptions underpinning Transpersonal

Psychology that realities of human experience transcend the material and personal, complementing the idea that a higher state of being will incorporate a transformation of humanity and the world. This system of belief in human potential brought the organization of the XVI EUROTAS conference into a transpersonal field of potentiality and possibility. Drawing on ritual and symbolic significance, a very particular conference symbol (the emblem of a bird in flight on the disc of Phaistos) was chosen that would demonstrate the essence of unity and collaborative learning to take place at the Pilot Beach Hotel in Chania.

The disc of Phaistos, discovered in 1908 in southern Crete, apparently dating from about ca.1700-1500BC, provided a foundation from which to extract the essential aspects of being. Found by the Italian archaeologist Luigi Pernier in the treasure room of the ruins of the palace in Phaistos, it is a two-sided, circular clay tablet, imprinted on both sides, with symbols in spiral pattern that have been named Linear A. The disk containing a total of 242 distinct symbols broken into 61 groups is made of high quality clay, like that used for Minoan "egg-shell" cups. Both faces of the disc have a spiral line incised from the periphery to the center, with a regularity of the spiral on side A missing from that of side B. Many of the symbols are pictures of clearly recognizable objects, imprinted with stamps. Three basic scripts were used in ancient Crete between the third and the late second millennium BCE: Hieroglyphic, Linear A and Linear B. All Linear A texts from the Protopalatial period come from the ruins of the first palace at Phaistos and have not been deciphered until recently. Dr Gareth Owens, a linguist researcher with the Technological Educational Institute of Crete, recently proposed that the disk be read in a spiral direction from the outside rim to the inside. Using scripts from Minoan Linear A and Mycenaean Linear B from ancient Greece, he claims that some words could mean pregnant mother or goddess, concluding that the disk may render a prayer to a Minoan goddess.[5]

On side A, a total of five cases depict a bird in flight, possibly an eagle apparently holding a snake in its talons. This emblem from the disc was extracted and chosen to convey the process of metamorphosis in the collaborative synthesis between The European Transpersonal Association (EUROTAS), the International Transpersonal Association (ITA), and the Association for Transpersonal Psychology (ATP). It signaled the beginning of a new cycle and metamorphosis within the associations and flight to new horizons. The conference brought two hundred and fifty people together from 35 countries from around the world, to follow lectures, seminars and workshops within the framework of empirical science. In an endeavor to acknowledge the significance of the disc, a trip to the ruins of Phaistos was organized as well as an array of cultural events.

Marcie Boucouvalas[6] suggests that transpersonal development represents transformations or lasting changes of consciousness that restructure a world view or state of being in the world, and that an array of disciplines—including those at the macro level—are awakening to the call. Questing consciousness must journey into the depths of psyche where both masculine and feminine aspects of psyche must unite. The transition from the goddess in Crete to a masculine representation of god, suggests that the feminine archetypal figure was dealt a sharp blow in the past. Holding this thought in mind, the XVI conference paid homage to the balance between feminine and masculine, by choosing an equal number of key note speakers. Credit was given to ritual in the form of Lyre music, Hermes' gift to Apollo known to embody the *Cista Mystica*. The symbols of sacred marriage were present in the opening ceremony of the conference. These gifts were given back to the Mother Goddess of Crete, calling for a deeper commitment to the psycho-socio-cultural and spiritual dimensions of human experience. Homage was paid to Athena, Hermes, Phoebus Apollo, Phoebe Artemis and Hestia, goddess of the hearth in the inaugural speech that invited the flame of consciousness to be lit in service to humanity and science. In this unique way, the conference was given to the land of Greece and its peoples as well as to Gaia in the hope that humanity recognizes the need to counter balance and engage the scientific community.

The XVI EUROTAS conference aimed at raising consciousness and so it has fulfilled its goal with this book that highlights some of the work undertaken at the conference. It was a privilege to organize such a historic event and with great humility I honor the great voices that resound in the pages of this book. It is my sincere wish that this is just the beginning of an even greater cycle in re-visioning the future of the transpersonal, worldwide.

Bibliography

[1] Gimbutas, M. (2001). *The living goddesses.* Berkeley, CA: University of California Press.
[2] Mann, R. D. (1984). *In the light of consciousness: Experiences in transpersonal psychology.* Albany, NY: State University of New York Press.

[3] Washburn, M. (2003). *Embodied spirituality in a sacred world*. New York, NY: State University of New York Press.
[4] Hoffman, L. (2009). General overview. Retrieved from http://www.existential-therapy.com /General_Overview.htm.
Maykov, V. (2005). The transpersonal tradition in Russian culture. *The International Journal of Transpersonal Studies*, *24*, p. 78.
[5] Howard, J. (2014, 28 October). Scientists finally crack the code of the ancient 'Phaistos Disk'. The Huffington Post. Retrieved from www.huffingtonpost.com/2014/10/28/ancient-cd-rom-phaistos-disk.
[6] Boucouvalas, M. (1999). From transpersonal psychology to a multi-disciplinary transpersonal orientation. *The Journal of Transpersonal Psychology, 31*(1), 27-39.

Voices of the EUROTAS Council of Elders

Anne Baring
Ashok Gangadean
Judith Miller
Lindy McMullin
Marcie Boucouvalas
Pier Luigi Lattuada
Tanna Jacubocz-Mount
Vitor Rodrigues
Zana Marovic

Note: These reflections do not represent all those who contributed their voices to the EUROTAS Council of Elders, but to those who responded to a request to forward their contribution in writing.

Abstract

We present here the first "Council of Elders" that took place in Crete during October 2014 at the Global XVI EUROTAS (European Transpersonal Association) Conference, held in collaboration with the Association for Transpersonal Psychology (ATP) and the International Transpersonal Association (ITA) and organized by Synthesis (the then-Greek Transpersonal Association), thus uniting all these organizations in the effort. Tanna Jakubowicz-Mount was the mother of this idea, supported by Vitor Rodrigues. In her words: "the Spirit of Times is calling on us all, to centre our wisdom and healing powers, to convey a message with powerful resonance that may contribute to global healing, and shift planetary awareness to a higher dimension. We are at a crucial point in modern history. We have never faced such a big Economic, Ecological,

Humanitarian, Geopolitical and Spiritual crisis. The global economy is in collapse and the ability of the planet to support life, is breaking down. We still have a choice! It is up to us to use this crisis as an opportunity to shift human consciousness and bring about global change". The Council of Elders is a step towards this direction, bringing together some of the most experienced professionals within EUROTAS and trying to benefit from their knowledge and wisdom. In so doing, we are in touch with the spiritual traditions of Humankind honouring its elders but also gathering their contributions to the enlarged society. The texts below are the product of this initiative.

Keywords: council, elders, EUROTAS, global, wisdom

The Role of an Elder

Motto: An Elder is the one who transforms life experiences into heart wisdom

Vitor Rodrigues and Tanna Jakubowicz-Mount

The Spiritual Traditions of our Planet do have a sense of respect for the Elders within communities. This is no surprise as for thousands of years, Elders have been both the keepers of memory and the guardians of wisdom; both their own and the product of generations before them. They knew about life, education and preserving harmony in society. They knew about the culture they belonged to, the relationship it had with the cycles in Nature and the way humans could dance with them. Keepers of the past and gatherers of experience were in the best position to also ponder about the future in at least two ways: what to do within their societies, and what their societies could and should do, within the greater Cosmos. In the Native American tradition, Elders are placed in the highest position of honour a tribe can offer its members. Traits generally associated with Elders are: knowledge, wisdom, counselling skills, a loving heart, compassion, willingness to teach, even temperedness, patience, and willingness to take on responsibility. The Elders hold communities together by making space for different, even opposing points of view. Also the wisdom of women and their eldership was once revered very highly within indigenous societies.

Moving into Eldership Time reminds one of the Hindu Sannyasa, which is a renunciation stage where people transcend limited identification with self, family, race, religion, and nation and instead become citizens of the World and the Universe. This is a time for devotion to spiritual instruction and noble service.

This Stage of Integrity is a time for the altruistic community, where service often comes in the form of civic and environmental service; giving back to the family, clan, and community through mentoring and spiritual midwifery. The spiritual Elder heralds the next phase of human and global development.

Anne Baring

I think that in the course of our lives we, as Elders, can clearly see that what is now taking place beneath the surface of our culture is a spiritual awakening on a planetary scale. This awakening is beginning to heal the long-established split in our psyche and in our culture between spirit and nature, between the Masculine and Feminine Archetypes. We are increasingly engaged in a process of transformation – of our values, our beliefs, our patterns of behaviour – that is connecting us with a deeper ground and creating a new vision or paradigm of reality utterly different from the old one. The recovery of the Feminine invites a reorientation of consciousness: receptivity not only to the events occurring in the external world but an inner receptivity to the long-ignored voice of the soul. It is helping us to relate to the deep cosmic source of our psychic life and draw up the living waters from those depths. It immeasurably deepens and broadens our perspective on our presence on this planet, giving deeper meaning to our lives. Slowly but surely, it is changing everything.

The focus of the Feminine is on relationships of all kinds. We can see the growing influence of the Feminine in the expansion of the environmental movement; in the determination of women in every culture to free themselves from their long oppression and subservience and encourage their increased participation in society; in many new approaches to healing both psyche and body. It is reflected in the mounting revulsion for our weapons of mass destruction; in compassion for the helpless victims of our addiction to war; in the engagement of hundreds of thousands of people in the work of helping both the planet and the victims of poverty, hunger and disease. These different channels of influence are creating new perspectives on life, new ways of connection that bring together body, soul, mind and spirit.

As part of this emerging process, the young desperately need help and support in developing new ways of thinking, new strategies for action. The future is in their hands. In my contribution to the meeting I spoke of an educational initiative started a few years ago by a friend in Scotland called "Inspire — Aspire: Global Citizens in the Making; Transforming Inspiration into Aspiration." It was originally a programme designed for children aged 10-18 in the Commonwealth Nations to help them to develop their ideas about what kind of future they would like to see and what kind of contribution they would like to make to bringing it into being, choosing a mentor whose words and actions have inspired them. Hundreds of thousands of children have now completed this programme and it is now spreading to countries all over the world. This is an example of how change can come about and how ideas can inspire the next generation to value their lives and the contribution they can make to the wellbeing of all.

Why the TransPersonal awakening of our cultures is our highest priority!

Ashok Gangadean

It is now clear that TransPersonal Literacy and Intelligence brings us to the Source of all our worldviews, cultures, religions and forms of life.

This Primal Source Field is named differently in our great philosophical, spiritual and religious traditions through the ages. Whether invoked through Tao, Aum, Yahweh, Allah, Brahman, Sunyata (Emptiness), Christ, God, Spirit or the Foundational Energy Field of all the Sciences…the collective wisdom of our planet through the ages has recognized that this Source Field is the generative Source of our diverse scriptures, worldviews, enlightenment teachings, indeed, of all worldviews, narratives, ideologies, religions and disciplinary forms of life.

This consensus teaching of our great wisdom endowment reveals that we humans become Whole Persons when we access the Source Code of Life and re-centre our lives and cultures in the Source Field which is the Sacred Space of ((Infinite Presence)). Our great planetary awakening teachings concur that the Fundamental Source Field is boundless, hence trans-finite, and as such this Infinite Presence must be the generative source of all possible worldviews, narratives, disciplines and forms of life.

Furthermore, our Wisdom Endowment is the sacred space of TransPersonal Intelligence and Cultural Life. This global Source Intelligence also recognizes that we humans are lodged in deep and chronically entrenched patterns of personal and cultural dysfunctions and pathologies when we are alienated from Infinite Source (Infinite Presence) which nevertheless surrounds us and sources our lives and cultures in every way. In this light our Source (TransPersonal) wisdom is clear that pre-Sourced mental and cultural patterns are the primary source of human dysfunctions, chronic fragmentation, polarization, and wide-ranging forms of human and cultural violence.

Our more awakened and evolved Self cannot come forth and blossom in such pre-Sourced cultures and worldviews which are dominated by ego-mental or monocentric mental practices and forms of life. This pre-Sourced "self" is not the mature Human and is lodged in cultures of monologue which are severed from Source Life. In this context the depth of "TransPersonal" awakening is our personal and inter-personal evolutionary shift from dysfunctional monologue to non-violent cultures of Deep Dialogue where we mature as awakened Persons.

Our global wisdom teaches that the awakened Human who lives the Source Intelligence is a Dialogue Person-- an ((I===Thou)) Human--who lives and experiences the deep connectivity of the Primal Field of Reality. This is the space of awakened Reason, moral consciousness, human compassion, love, respect across borders and the sacred meeting space of diverse worlds. This is where we find deep Unity in sacred Diversity. The awakened TransPersonal Human is a Dialogue Being.

Whether the Teachings of Buddha, or the Yoga Science of Krishna or the Logos-in-the Flesh Teachings of Jesus, to mention a few preeminent Source Code pioneers- it is clear that the Literacy of Global Wisdom reveals that we cannot mature as awakened Whole Humans within monocentric cultures where our mental patterns objectifies everything it touches and produces: cultural spaces of "I===It". The "self" or "person" in such "I===It" cultures is not yet a fully evolved Person who embodies the highest Moral Law and Awakened Rational Life. The "ego-mental" self is thus a pre-Sourced self and the TransPersonal Self is the Human who has awakened and entered the TransPersonal Intelligence of Life in Presence. This is the TransPersonal Culture.

Our collective Wisdom is clear that our wide-ranging human dysfunctions, pathologies and forms of violence trace to our pre-Sourced forms of life and cultures. And our maturation to becoming Whole Persons, living the deep dialogical intelligence of TransPersonal Presence, is the highest form of human activism, which gets to the source of wide-ranging crises facing humanity today. This is why our personal and cultural evolution to the non-violent Dialogic and TransPersonal Intelligence is highest urgency for healing our cultures, our worlds, our personal lives.

Spiritual Warriors – A necessity for our time

Judith S. Miller

Like most Elders in our circle, I believe that the beginning of the 21st century is a very challenging time for humanity. As advanced technology and jetliners make our world smaller, we are pushed to examine ourselves in relation to all that is around us – both near and far.

What form should such examination take? Many of us directly engage with individuals, activities, and energies in other parts of the world. We eagerly learn from indigenous peoples, shamanic cultures, and Eastern traditions.

An important question, however, has to do with the stance we take within our own culture, our own environment, our own tradition, and our own people? My experience is that many Westerners look beyond their own borders for inspiration. And once finding inspiration in some distant place, they then attempt to bring it home.

As a developmental, transpersonal psychologist, I believe that a healthy connection to our Western culture and mystical roots is exceedingly important. When you live out of your authentic self, your ground, your being, your identity, is penetrated by the sacred. Sociological cross-cultural research also tells us that erosion of a strong cultural and spiritual identity leads to a self-image that loses its definition and becomes more fragile. We become thwarted in our development if we deny an essential part of our being.

My message for this council is that I believe it is time to pay more attention to what is at "home." Rather than totally dismissing our Judeo-Christian tradition as one that is mired only in hypocrisy, dualism, and historical violence, we must open ourselves to the original mystical sacred ground that is the foundation of Western spirituality. Additionally, we must examine the Western core values and strengths of who we are individually and collectively, while exploring where our culture and tradition may have lost its way.

We are a mixture of light and shadow. The place and culture, in which we were born, where we now live, are mixtures of light and shadow. Only by thoroughly investigating these energies, will we gain authentic awareness of ourselves and the paradigm in which we function.

The prevailing worldview in Western culture during the early 21st century is postmodernism. This serves as a "super theory" or paradigm for interpreting human experience. Postmodernism holds the view that there is no absolute truth, because everything is relative and determined by individual perceptions.

Clearly, it has arisen as a reaction against pre-modernism when the church was the ultimate authority, governing every aspect of a person's life. It also counters the modern worldview that holds that nothing is true unless it can be verified by the scientific method.

Many of us who are active in the transpersonal field have been significantly impacted by the Postmodern worldview. This is understandable – popular culture, academia, psychology and modern intellectual thought supports it. Postmodernism reflects our cultural norms and also the transpersonal values of multiculturalism and diversity.

At the same time, when we think about the postmodern concept of relativism (where the only things real are peoples' perceptions), we must consider how this argues against the Absolute. And if there is no Absolute, then there is no God, there is no sacred, there is no spiritual ground.

Today, more than at any other time, it is critically important for us to understand that Western institutions and the postmodern worldview cannot eradicate darkness in people or in society. Opening one's soul to the Divine is the only way.

At the same time, it is not easy to personally explore and confront the contradictions and splits in our own worldview, the worldview of popular culture, and the worldview of our colleagues and friends in the transpersonal field.

If we are to become the spiritual warriors that I believe we are meant to be, we must do this. And in so doing, we will be able to lead lives that are God-directed rather than ego directed. Then and only then, will we know that living one's true nature means to be one with each other and God.

The monk and mystic Thomas Merton (1915-1968) said: "We stumble and fall constantly, even when we are enlightened. But when we are in true spiritual darkness, we do not even know that we have fallen."

It is a privilege to be part of the Council of Elders, a tapestry of Hope in the 21st Century

Lindy McMullin

The Elders pave the way for change, and often this task is not easy. When global systems collapse, fear grows and this fear must be faced with the Wisdom of the Ages and the experiences we have, to ease the delivery of a new way of thinking. A Changing Perception is my new project, aimed at educating the young in Mindfulness Practice, Leadership and Communication Skills in Athens Greece.

If we address the needs of the new generation, aiming to bring about a balance between technology and spirituality, we can certainly offer our wisdom to birth Conscious Living. There is a great need to bring boundaries into place where we understand the complementarity of dualism, able to move beyond and into the union of diversity. The youth inherit the planet from us, but it is the solemn duty of the Council of Elders to bring back the sacred in this world of fast lane living that is threatening human existence.

Crisis is a challenge for breakthrough and the focus needs to be on the potential we have inside of us, to facilitate a balanced birth of new ideas. As science progresses, it gives us ways in which to truly ponder on the nature of existence and the Transpersonal Perspective needs to become part of Global Change. A new Education System needs to address problems parents are facing as well as incorporate the process of self-development within relationships and the dynamics involved in parenting. Children need to explore ways in which they can expand their awareness of the environment, and understand that self-esteem can no longer be reliant only on the outside world but is an aspect of self-development, that incorporates looking at feelings and finding ways to face these feelings in a harmonious manner.

I believe firmly that it is not only the welfare of the planet that is at stake, but it is the welfare of Self that needs to be addressed, to bring about a new world view and paradigm shift. We need to become aware that as we evolve, we need to prepare the new generation to bring balance – the balance we could not bring but know of. It is our duty as Elders to give them hope for a new tomorrow. I am honoured to be a member of the Council of Elders.

Marcie Boucouvalas

Transpersonal psychology can be thought of as the heartbeat and heartthrob of a greater transpersonal multi-disciplinary movement, especially since it focuses on the whole human species in all its nuances. What potential awaits, however, when we remember the importance of the transpersonal voices in disciplines that deal with the macro context—such as sociology, anthropology, ecology, business-entrepreneurship, and many others. In order to effect a transpersonal way of being on our planet the attention to group, organizational, and societal dynamics in which such disciplines are engaged is essential. Moreover, what about the extragalactic orientations as well as the micro worlds? Transcending any insularity becomes an imperative. I envision transpersonal efforts (including conferences) with such collaborative initiatives.

As others have also emphasized, from inception the transpersonal movement has been on the vanguard of initiatives that have now migrated to mainstream interests. Can we once again blaze trails? I think so. Staying vigilant with regard to the forthcoming second scientific revolution is worthy of pursuit, especially since embodied within is a worldview that the transpersonal orientation embraces. A key question to address becomes: For what areas of the transpersonal is the current scientific paradigm useful and for what might it be limiting? Just think of what it might be like to move beyond the concern that some academics face in working with mainstream psychology regarding the "respectability" of one's research to initiating an epistemological and ontological orientation to inquiry catalysed and supported by a new scientific revolution.

Pier Luigi Lattuada

First of all I hope that this one will not be “just one more Circle” but one that can send a real message and offer something real to the world.

Many of us here spoke about indigenous traditions or ancient traditions. Well, in Brazil the ancient traditional healer uses a specific word, which is AXÈ.

AXÈ is the sacred force of LIFE. There is something that you see in the eyes of the shaman…something that you see when you “avatar”, when you say: “I see you”…what you see and what you feel in that moment is the AXÈ.

I don t know why, but life brought me back to Brazil since 1982 and it’s been a learning journey since that first moment when I was 27 years old. What I learned in Brazil working with shamans and in contact with all kind of ancient traditions – yes, because Brazil is like a planet where there are so many different traditions, including also the ones focused on the “plants of power” – what I’ve learned is that we can reduce all these realities to the word AXÈ.

And the AXÈ blossoms from the eyes, comes out from the gesture when we are in the Art. But to “be in the art” means to work in the Transpersonal field, to be in contact with the Essence, with the Oneness, it’s easy to say but it’s very hard to do, it’s a work that must be done every day.

As I wish to share the word that I feel inside me with the people present at our conference and with our community, I say “Dare”; we have to dare more and more and more in order to be, to understand and be in contact with the circle of the ancient tradition.

We have to dare more and more. I experienced that this has a price, everything has a price, and I think that all of us here know what I mean.

In my case, in 30 years of living and experiencing Brazil, I have been in jail, I had an accident, my first marriage ended, and it was an actual struggle for many years; I observed all those things that happen to us and all the problems, are proportional to our awareness and to our compassion.

The more we dare to stay in the art and the more we dare to let the ego go, the least problems we have in our life, so: "to dare more", is my witness.

Alchemy of Love

Tanna Jakubowicz-Mount

As far as I can see, we are at the most crucial point of modern history. We have never faced such a big economic, ecological, humanitarian, geopolitical and spiritual crisis. Global economy is in collapse and the ability of the planet to support life is breaking down.

We are in the midst of a real culmination of two world orders struggling- the old order of separation and violence with the new order of unity and love. The old order is breaking down because it was based on a wrong assumption: on Ego delusion of separation of men and Universe. The guards of the old order are mobilizing their forces to keep the division of the world and their spheres of influence and profit. The threat, armies and war are created to overcome economic crisis and depopulate mankind. Maybe we cannot take responsibility for political and economic changes, but surely we can assist people in times of transition. We can foster consciousness evolution towards a new level of existence- emergence of sustainable global civilization.

I believe the root cause of the world crises is what I call 'the original sin of humanity'- the disconnection from the primordial ground of life. After ages of ignorance we have ended up with a large wound in heart and a huge vacuum in the soul of humankind.

The wounded heart and hole in our soul seek healing and replenishment from outside, through symbolic substitutes such as money, status and power- this fuels the politics of expansion and exploitation. Homo Separatus, deceived and disconnected, spiritually homeless and hungry, suffering from deep solitude, fear, despair, scarcity, greed and violence is devouring the Earth alive! My deepest concern is that so much human energy is turned against Life on this Earth. My burning question is: how can we reverse this process?

From 'Many Pieces' to 'One Peace'

During the Holistic Centre Gathering at the 50th Anniversary of Findhorn I heard the saying: We are the nurses of an old dying world and the midwives of humankind renewed and a new world.

Imagine that the world is a patient going through a spiritual emergency process. It might be the dark night of the soul, the most chaotic and fearful process of death and rebirth.

I call this process Alchemy of Love, because I believe that personal and transpersonal love has the most healing, transformative and unifying power:

I perceive our patient as one who is willing to undergo profound transformation into wholeness and oneness but is threatened by the demons of separation, greed and violence. Cut off from sources of life, the patient doesn't feel life force flowing, and deprived of Divine Feminine - mother energy, doesn't feel love within. Lack of love and connection causes Ego to replace real quality nourishment with artificial imitations.

So I believe that what the world really needs is the stream of unconditional love to nourish the hungry soul and heal the wounded heart. How can we deliver the essence of love to millions of hungry souls? Can we dissolve our hearts into the pure nectar of love and feed the world? Can we assist our patient in a process of reintegration to then journey towards transcendence?

I believe that if many of us awakened healers would radiate their love to the world, our patient would progress in transformation.

We also need to apply love by creating the space of safety and trust for reintegration of all scattered pieces of people's psyche and soul. The most important is to reclaim and reconcile conflicted parts like the victim and persecutor within, so we don't cast our shadows onto the world, causing conflicts and wars.

The great power of love is needed to align human consciousness with Wholeness. This is the process of evolving and metamorphosis from Homo Separatus having a disconnected, fragmented, polarized psyche to Homo Holos becoming one with the boundless, universal field of Light-Love-Life-giving energy. We need to reconnect with the Source of Life for Humanity to survive!

How to do it – My vision: INDRA-net

I propose to develop INDRA-net, the International Direct Radiant Action – a cross-cultural, multi-faith, long term project for international networking. The power of this action lies in the fact that it comes from people as they engage in actions on behalf of life itself.

The proposal includes the introduction of initiation rites and ceremonies for people to tap directly into the Source. A main aim is to incorporate more life-serving rituals and ceremonies into the following areas of people's lives: (a) Birth and upbringing, (b) Family life, (c) Education, (d) Community life, (e) Cycles of Earth-Life ceremonies. I appeal to transpersonal practitioners from various countries to become involved in such a service for the community. Let us bring forth our spiritual, healing powers to focus on meeting people's needs for connection, community, compassion, selfless love, trust and meaning. So all of us can come back home relieved of fear and solitude, belonging to the Earth and the Universe, and acting together for the common good.

Vitor Rodrigues

I see that many people in the Transpersonal Movement are getting more sophisticated and more self-demanding in their quest for Spirituality. They also become less naïve about what spirituality really is all about and what it means to go beyond personal centring. They became more available to inspiration from, and service to, the higher worlds of being. However I believe that, as the Dalai Lama acknowledged, we must be able to also speak the language of Science and to use it, because such is the language our modern world is sensitive to. In the same way, we should struggle for Science to again become a quest for Truth, as in recent years it has become a mere servant of economic interests and, therefore, a source of many untruths.

I am a witness, as are many, of the way our modern rulers and economic powers still drive the world in a feverish consumerism, drying out the possibilities of our planet to sustain Humanity and marching towards ecological catastrophe. They don't seem to know how to stop. We should strive towards new values and a new definition and approach to what is a sustainable and rich world. To me, it is obvious that a growing number of local initiatives (such as eco-villages, learning communities, or open source technologies) are moving towards alternative ways of being in society, of using and renewing resources of energy, water, food or minerals and of dealing with each other. I hope they will surpass and leave behind many governments and companies. However, we have the responsibility of proposing and thinking creatively about new humankind; one that will value Culture – also the Culture of the individual – as the main richness and as something we don't lose when we share but that increases by sharing. If I produce something beautiful, like an artistic masterpiece, and then replicate it and share it (books are an excellent example, the same way paintings are), I don't lose the product but many can benefit from it. This is generally true for cultural products, general knowledge or wisdom. In the same way, supreme values of human dignity, beauty, justice or love are markers of conscious development to be promoted and celebrated everywhere. They may replace the pervading ideas about what being a rich human being is all about. In the cultural world, sharing makes us all wealthier in limitless ways. Quite the opposite happens in the economic world where for me to be very rich implies that I hold in my hands a big portion of something others are deprived of. Richness is limited in the material world of objects but limitless in the cultural world. So let us assert boldly that Knowledge and Wisdom, Art and Culture, Spirituality and other products of human lives at their best, are the really important heritage of our species and that they are important because they are appreciated by conscious beings and promote consciousness growth. To me, it is obvious that the essence of humans is consciousness, as no one is human without it, no matter how beautiful, physically perfect or functionally capable one might be.

To me, the model of a future Humanity that can indeed thrive is an orchestra where everyone has a role and individuality but everyone fits into a major, harmonic whole. The bigger the orchestra, the bigger degree of instruments and choirs, the more it grows in power and beauty – and the better it can play major symphonies. As we come closer to this, we may be coming closer to developing a status that may help us become a conscious part of a bigger community where perhaps other humanities, from other worlds outside our own planet, might pertain. Being part of a major, cosmic community, seems to me only possible to humans who have learned to play together at the service of Beauty and larger symphonies, not to humans who keep playing against each other and even trying to steal each other's instruments or imposing their musical style or even specific plays as the only or the best ones. So let us be what we talk about and let us build our future according to larger views.

Towards global psychology and community

Zana Marovic

Being a transpersonal therapist in South Africa and working with clients from diverse cultures compelled me to face the fact that most of psychological training and practice reflects the Western paradigm and therefore is relevant only to a small percentage of the population.

I would like to call for a "big picture wisdom" that embraces global psychology – psychology that applies to all humans but retains cultural uniqueness. As we open the door to global psychology, indigenous psychology becomes a relevant addition to understanding people in their cultural context and assisting development of societal-wide compassion toward other cultures. Indigenous cosmology and concepts such as rationality, multilevel interconnectivity, spirituality, and ecological sacredness offer unique contributions and ancient wisdom that may be vital for addressing current global challenges.

The crucial task for establishing global psychology is to open the door on exploration of indigenous knowledge, engage in dialogue with shamans and traditional healers, as well as acknowledge and systematically incorporate indigenous wisdom and its unique perspective into current psychology training. The integration of transpersonal, African and other indigenous insights hold the promise to a wise way forward: one that promotes consciousness renewal and vision of global psychology and the community.

Conclusion

Coming together at the Council, we pondered on a major question. How to apply our transpersonal vision and experience to the world, which is in the process of spiritual emergency, and lead a new spiritual emergence; a woven tapestry of creative visions and idea?

Our talks had much in common. In virtually all of them there is an underlying idea that the solution to modern troubles and deep dangers facing humanity today, depends on our ability to bring back spirituality and a sense of the sacred into everyday life. There is also frequent emphasis on the importance of education of the young and on welcoming their contribution. Many of the elders seem to be extremely focused on the need to produce real contributions in ways that amount to daring to be "spiritual warriors"; facing both the darkness within as well as the world. Such a feat entails acknowledging the dangers of our present world state, such as pollution, war, greed, lust for power in economy and politics, general competition and separation amongst others, and to then propose solutions. Such solutions may be found in the ways we as representatives of the Transpersonal movement try to bring the wisdom of the ages into our world, respecting and welcoming Indigenous Wisdom amongst other. The texts above emphasise love and reassert the feminine as ways to restore and mend collective wounds; on welcoming and accepting Science as an important contribution in our world; on Alchemy or transformation of values and practices; on bringing back some rituals to normal human life and life cycles; on changing the way we see ourselves as separate and selfish humans, and open towards the Cosmos and other civilizations. This also implies being at the service of higher realms of wisdom and reality, no matter whether we call them Source, God, Whole, Life or AXE.

PART I:

A TRANSPERSONAL CALL FOR ACTION

CHAPTER ONE

WHY TRANSPERSONAL AWAKENING OF OUR CULTURES IS HIGHEST PRIORITY

ASHOK GANGADEAN[1]

Abstract

TransPersonal Intelligence is an evolutionary portal to the Source of our diverse worldviews, cultures, ideologies, disciplines, religions and forms of life. This Primal Source Field is named differently in our great philosophical, spiritual and religious traditions through the ages. Whether invoked through Tao, Aum, Yahweh, Allah, Brahman, Sunyata (Emptiness), Christ, God, Spirit or the Foundational Energy Field of all the Sciences...the collective wisdom of our planet through the ages has recognized that this Source Field is the generative Source of our diverse scriptures, worldviews, enlightenment teachings, indeed, of all worldviews and narratives. This consensus teaching of our great wisdom endowment reveals that we humans become Whole Persons when we access the Source Code of Life and re-center our lives and cultures in the Source Field which is the Sacred Space of ((Infinite Presence)). Our great planetary awakening teachings concur that the Fundamental Source Field is boundless, hence trans-finite thus TransPersonal. Our global wisdom teaches that the awakened Human who lives the Source Intelligence is a Dialogue Person--an ((I===Thou))[2] Human--who lives and experiences the deep connectivity of the Primal Field of Reality. This is the space of awakened Reason, moral consciousness, human compassion, love, respect across borders and the sacred meeting space of diverse worlds. This is where we find deep Unity in sacred Diversity. The awakened TransPersonal Human is a Dialogue Being. Source (Transpersonal) Intelligence, skills of Deep Dialogue and the cultivation of Global Consciousness are essential to the authentic cultivation and embodiment of Collective Intelligence as we face the evolutionary challenges of deep communication and finding consensus and synergy across borders.

Keywords: Collective Wisdom, Deep Dialogue, Global Consciousness, TransPersonal Intelligence

Preface

Note to readers: I feel moved in these introductory remarks to help orient the reader to a key notational innovation that I have developed over decades and found to be of the highest importance in dilating "narrative space" from our more familiar and customary conventions to a more "primal" or foundational Source Word which opens the way to TransPersonal discourse.

In the meditative journey of this essay we shall see that when we step back from being grounded in our more localized perspectives, worldviews, ideological orientations and dilate our rational consciousness into a more expansive and inclusive global light across and between diverse wisdom and spiritual teachings astounding patterns come to the fore which were not as readily accessible before. In this global light between First Teachings through the ages it becomes evident that our revered visionary teachers were in diverse ways seeking to open pathways to assist humanity in making a great dimensional crossing from more /egomental/ or /monocentric/ patterns of life, experience and culture to a more ((integral, holistic, dialogic)) pattern of awakened Life.

In this global light between diverse First Teachings through the ages it has become clear that the transpersonal and transformational medicine of our revered teachers has not been adequately tapped and realized. One striking finding is that our deeply institutionalized codes of life, experience and culture making have continued to dominate our individual and cultural lives and inscribed chronically entrenched barriers to seeing and making our all-important crossing into our ((Source Field)), which is vital for our personal and collective Well Being and Human Flourishing.

Our great Wisdom Teachings through the ages concur that our Primal Field of Reality is, and must be, an Infinite Force which is the Source of all life, all worlds, all narratives, cultures and worlds. And one astounding finding in this global light is that when we humans are alienated or severed from our ((Source Life)) we suffer existentially in abysmal ways. To be de-((Sourced)) is to live a dysfunctional life. So the greatest evolutionary challenge before us is to come to clarity that our current dominant patterns and codes of life alienate us from our ((Source Reality)) and hold us captive in pathological ways.

It is to address and bring into the open the vital dimensional difference between our customary life codes and forms of life on the one hand, and our genuine crossing into our long emerging ((Source Life)) that I have introduced innovative inter-dimensional "markers".

In this global light I have been using inter-dimensional markers for the past two decades in my presentations around the globe to help listeners and readers become aware of this vital shift in our mind operating processes: I use **"/…/"** , **"single brackets"** to call out when our "consciousness mother board" is lodged within an /egomental/ and /monocentric/ technology or "logistic" of thinking, experiencing, feeling, wording and living, in contrast and contradistinction to our more mature and evolved ((holistic, integral, dialogic)) patterns of ((life)): **"((…))" "double brackets"**.

Since "((…))" calls out our dimensional shift to ((Source Word)) and ((Source Life)), ((TransPersonal Realities)) it becomes clear that this ((Primal Source)) is the Source of all possible narratives, perspectives, worldviews, religions, cultures and disciplines. And one of the great disclosures of our ((Global Wisdom Teachings)) is that all "/…/" /egomental/ or /monocentric/ narratives are situated within and funded by the ((Source Infinite Word)). This global truth is rendered as **((…/…/…))** which shows that all /narratives/ are situated within the ((..)) foundational transpersonal ((space)).

Unfortunately, and understandably, when readers first encounter these innovative inter-dimensional markers- "/…/" and "((…)) it can be both strange, even annoying and confusing – sometimes even distracting one from the narrative flow and primary intended sharing. Accordingly, I felt moved to provide this orienting opening and to offer these advanced organizers to my readers to hopefully better process the challenge of crossing from /egomental/ mental patterns and codes to ((TransPersonal)) Life. We shall see that the "transpersonal" movement is at heart a shift beyond /egomental/ psyche and life to the more advanced and mature ((holistic= integral)) Psyche and Life in our Global Age.

If we continue to present the "transpersonal" within the /egomental space of language and culture the important "revolution" to ((TransPersonal)) loses its clarity and power.

I invite the reader to visit my primary website: www.awakeningmind.org where they will find many YouTube performances clarifying these markers.

Overview: Evolutionary Shift to Transpersonal Intelligence

It is now clear that TransPersonal literacy and intelligence bring us to the source of all our worldviews, cultures, religions and forms of life. This Primal Source Field is named differently in our great philosophical, spiritual and religious traditions through the ages. Whether invoked through Tao, Aum, Yahweh, Allah, Brahman, Sunyata (Emptiness), Christ, God, Spirit or the Foundational Energy Field of all the Sciences...the collective wisdom of our planet through the ages has recognized that this Source Field is the generative Source of our diverse scriptures, worldviews, enlightenment teachings, indeed, of all worldviews, narratives, ideologies, religions and disciplinary forms of life.

This consensus teaching of our great wisdom endowment reveals that we humans become Whole Persons when we access the Source Code of Life and re-center our lives and cultures in the Source Field which is the Sacred Space of ((Infinite Presence)). Our great planetary awakening teachings concur that the Fundamental Source Field is boundless, hence trans-finite, and as such this Infinite Presence must be the generative source of all possible worldviews, narratives, disciplines and forms of life.

Furthermore, our Wisdom Endowment is the sacred space of TransPersonal Intelligence and Cultural Life. This global Source Intelligence also recognizes that we humans are lodged in deep and chronically entrenched patterns of personal and cultural dysfunctions and pathologies when we are alienated from Infinite Source (Infinite Presence), which nevertheless surrounds us and sources our lives and cultures in every way. In this light our Source (TransPersonal) wisdom is clear that pre-Sourced mental and cultural patterns are the primary source of human's dysfunctions, chronic fragmentation, polarization, and wide-ranging forms of human and cultural violence.

Our more awakened and evolved Self cannot come forth and blossom in such pre-Sourced cultures and worldviews, which are dominated by ego-mental or monocentric mental practices and forms of life. This pre-Sourced "self" is not the mature Human and is lodged in cultures of monologue, which are severed from Source Life. In this context the depth of "TransPersonal" awakening is our personal and inter-personal evolutionary shift from dysfunctional monologue to non-violent cultures of Deep Dialogue where we mature as awakened Persons.

Our global wisdom teaches that the awakened Human who lives the Source Intelligence is a Dialogue Person- an ((I===Thou)) Human--who lives and experiences the deep connectivity of the Primal Field of Reality. This is the space of awakened Reason, moral consciousness, human compassion, love, respect across borders and the sacred meeting space of diverse worlds. This is where we find deep Unity in sacred Diversity. The awakened TransPersonal Human is a Dialogue Being.

Whether the Teachings of Buddha, or the Yoga Science of Krishna or the Logos-in-the Flesh Teachings of Jesus, to mention a few preeminent Source Code pioneers, it is clear that the Literacy of Global Wisdom reveals that we cannot mature as awakened Whole Humans within monocentric cultures where our dominant (pre-Sourced) mental pattern objectifies everything it touches and produces: cultural spaces of "I===It". The "self" or "person" in such "I===It" cultures is not yet a fully evolved Person who embodies the highest Moral Law and awakened Rational Life. The "ego-mental" self is thus a pre-Sourced self and the TransPersonal Self is the Human who has awakened and entered the TransPersonal Intelligence of Life in Presence. This is the TransPersonal Culture.

Our collective Wisdom is clear that our wide-ranging human dysfunctions, pathologies and forms of violence trace to our pre-Sourced forms of life and cultures. Our maturation to becoming Whole Persons, living the deep dialogical intelligence of TransPersonal Presence, is the highest form of human activism that gets to the source of wide-ranging crises facing humanity today. This is why our personal and cultural evolution to the non-violent Dialogic and TransPersonal Intelligence is highest urgency for healing our cultures, our worlds, our personal lives.

When we step back from our more localized cultural narratives, perspectives, worldviews and disciplinary orientations and dilate our hearts and minds into the more expansive and inclusive global space whence our diverse worldviews co-originate and co-arise, striking new patterns and insights come into relief that were not accessible before. When we dilate our rational and spiritual intelligence into the ((Source Field)) and gain access to the long emerging ((Logos Code)) that flows through all our diverse worldviews, religions, ideologies and cultures we move from monologue to ((deep dialogue)) and enter this Primal Common Ground of deep consensus, convergence, connectivity and synergy across and between worlds. This evolutionary crossing and maturation from cultures of "monologue" to awakened Cultures of Dialogue is the key to the cultivation of Collective Intelligence.

This Deep Dialogue literacy, technology and intelligence is what empowers us to rise together in ((Collective Intelligence)) across the deeply entrenched borders that divide our cultures and worlds. Gaining access to this ((Primal Logos Code)) through the rational arts of Deep Dialogue is thus key to cultivating genuine ((Collective Intelligence)) in this dilated global light. The ontological medicine of Deep Dialogue across and between worlds is vital for cultivating authentic ((Collective Intelligence)) and tapping the resources of ((Global Wisdom)) for our Global Age.

Source (Transpersonal) Intelligence, skills of Deep Dialogue and the cultivation of Global Consciousness are essential to the authentic cultivation and embodiment of Collective Intelligence as we face the evolutionary challenges of deep communication and finding consensus and synergy across borders. Thus, we cannot enter ((Transpersonal Intelligence)) within the divisive, fragmented and polarized spaces of monologue cultures, but must mature as mindful and awakened Humans in the arts of Deep Dialogue. We are not egosapiens, but LogoSapiens. And it is in mature dialogue cultures that we humans flourish.

In what follows I invite the reader first to take a journey together into the depths of the long emerging ((Source Code)) to experience how and why this collective Global Wisdom of the ages calls upon us with highest urgency to evolve into cultures of deep dialogue.

Why Awakened Source Literacy is the Heart of Transpersonal Intelligence

My lifework as a Logician and Ontologist has been focused for fifty years on pioneering deeper pathways into the Primal Logic of Logos that has been the moving passion of our most gifted and revered teachers (first philosophers, logicians, ontologists, awakening guides...) across the planet and through the ages. Awakening pioneers such a Buddha, Krishna, Moses, Jesus, Socrates, Lao Tzu...to name a few...have been calling humanity to go deeper into the Primal Code of Logos as our most urgent evolutionary priority in our maturation as Humans, as LogoSapiens. The diverse traditions of First Philosophy across the planet have all been seeking to tap and bring forth the Primal Code of the Field of Reality--of That Which is Primal and First – as our ultimate concern in our maturation and flourishing as Humans.

The term "First Philosophy" comes from Aristotle as he seeks to tap the Code of Being in recognition that this is First in the highest sense and all other fields, disciplines and aspects of human experience and culture flow from this Code of Primary Being. But this tradition of First Philosophy – the Call to What-is-First – ranges across the planet and through the ages in our highest and best pioneering teachers: The Call of Yahweh to Abraham and Israel = Humanity, the deep meditations on AUM in the founding of the Science of Yoga at the heart of the Vedas, the historic breakthrough of Buddha in breaking the egomental barriers and moving into the Primal Field of Emptiness (Sunyata) which is the Field of Reality and the Space of Dharma (=Honor Code: awakened moral compassion), the encounter of Moses at the Burning Bush (=Presence of Infinite Spirit), the founding of the European tradition of the quest for Logos (the Primal Source of Rational Light, Speech, Word) by Socrates, Plato, Aristotle...in birthing "Philo-Sophia" ...Love of Wisdom in the quest to Know Thy Self...In the classic birthing of Chinese First Philosophy by the genius of Lao Tzu in declaring that the Tao that is "named" is Not the TAO.

This is the unprecedented "global" turn (breakthrough, evolutionary advance, maturation, development, emergence...) in the quest for the Primal Word (Code, Logic, Field, Ontology...). My lifelong quest to uncover the deeper missing (yet ever present and presiding) **Primal Logic of the Word** across our great philosophical traditions and noble scriptures led me (called me, attracted me, guided me...) to gain deeper Global access to the emergent Code. The discovery that Moses, Socrates, Buddha, Krishna, Jesus, et al...were tapping the same ((Source Code))...the same Global Logic of Logos would be an evolutionary advance (research breakthrough) of the highest order.

I shall not (and cannot) develop these rich themes here on this occasion. These themes have been developed in my several volumes and countless public performances over decades. This has also been a primary focus on my Annual ((Reflection on Activities)) over the past decade and more. I bring this central theme of my research, scholarship, teaching and community development to the fore on this occasion because this breakthrough to the ((Primal Code)) is of supreme importance for our human enterprise, for every aspect of our human condition, and certainly for our rational enterprise and deepening our ((literacy)) and liberal arts cultures. Pause and ((imagine)) for a moment that such diverse revered teachers as Moses, Jesus, Buddha, Socrates, Krishna, Lao Tzu are pioneering pathways into this ((Primal Code of Logos)). Once we access this ((Code)) it is the most Simple, Evident and Obvious insight imaginable...so super simple and obvious that we cannot (dare not) "see" it. For once we see that the Primal Field is, and must be, Boundless...this ignites a flood of allied Code Insights that have been seen, corroborated, reaffirmed, celebrated... in widely diverse contexts by our great Teachers and Traditions across the planet. The Boundless Primal Field (of Reality) is thus Infinite, hence Infinitely One, hence the Primal Source of all possible worlds, words, scripts, narratives, perspectives, religions, scriptures, cultures, ideologies, disciplines, forms of life. Most of all...must be Infinitely HereNow. This Infinite Primal Field of Being (Primal Word, Code, Origin, Source, Existence...) CANNOT be displaced and pushed aside, even by the mightiest "egosapien". Our Teachers knew and saw that nothing could be or survive apart from this ((Source Field)) that directly holds and funds any and every iota of existence.

This is where I found it imperative as Logician and Ontologist to bring into the open an innovative notation to help us recognize and remember when we are lodged within /egomental reason/ and /language patterns/ and when we cross into the ((Code Script)) of the Rationally Awakened Life. My simultaneous introduction of these Code Markers: **"/.../" vs "((...))"** to bring to the fore the **dimensional shift** from /word/ to ((word)), from /code/ to ((code)) is of the utmost importance in finally seeing the ((Global Power)) of the ((Logos Code)). And this vital notational innovation ignited a flood of new ((insights)) into the long dormant ((Common Ground))... the ((Source Code)) of our great ((evolutionary pioneers)). And it is evident how our Teachers insisted that the ((Infinite Word)) cannot be /named/ or rendered within the /script/ of pre-Awakened mental praxis and literacy.

The Millennial Conflation of These Contrasting Dimensions of Life and Word

It became clear in my evolving research over decades that the **endemic conflation** of the contrasting dimensions of /language/ (script, literacy, word-power, mental practices...) and ((Language)) contributed to the chronic failure over millennia to receive and process the full ((Transformative Code Medicine)) of our Great Teachers. My innovative Notation is meant to de-conflate the contrasting dimensions between /word/ and ((Word)), between /code/ and ((code)) between /logos/ and ((Logos)), between /self/ and ((Self))... Thus, the introduction of **these Onto-Cultural Markers** is of supreme importance for our human enterprise. Our Code Pioneers were making an all-important and urgent call to humanity to ((up Script)) from /word/ to ((Word)), and not to /down-load/ their ((Code Teaching)) to /egomental codes/ and /language games/.

By bringing to the fore the vital shift in a **((Visible Font))** from /culture/ to ((Culture)), from /scripture/ to ((Scripture)), from /Buddha/ to ((Buddha))...for example, opened the way for everyday folks (such as students) to stand back from deeply entrenched mentation (= thought) patterns and ((see)) as never before the urgent ((Code Call)) of our evolutionary Awakening Teachers. The millennial conflation of these two dimensional of life and culture and literacy facilitated and enabled the **continued /default/ mode** of the evolutionary dominance and privileging of /Script/ and the displacement of ((Script)). Humanity has been stuck in this default mode of privileging (alleged) **self-sourced /Script/** as the primary and dominant /literacy regime/ in town. This is why our evolutionary ((markers)) to expose this fatal fallacy, calling it out for accountability and making it impossible for /Script/ to continue the deception of being /self-sourced/ is of highest importance in allowing the ((Source Medicine)) to take effect.

This breakthrough explicitation of the ((inter-dimensional)) shift and contrast between /word/ and ((Word)), /life/ and ((Life)), /ethics/ and ((Ethics)), /reason/ and ((Reason)), /truth/ and ((Truth)), /meaning/ and ((Meaning)), /scripture/ and ((Scripture)) dilates a long emerging evolutionary upgrade (maturation) in our human journey.

We can see across the planet that the pre-Evolved "conflation" of the /language/ and ((Language)) has been a monumental barrier to our Rational Health and Ontological Well Being. This endemic "conflation" made it too easy, perhaps inevitable, to continue to "download" ((Script)) to /script/, the ((Word of God)) to /word of god/. The "default" script invariably collapsed to "/...((...)).../" – swallowing the ((Source Word)) into the /egomental/ language games. When ((Buddha Speaks)) his "speech" is downloaded into our everyday common sense, familiar language, our *lingua franca*: "/...((x)).../", and the ((Source Code Medicine)) is lost. ((God)) becomes down-sized to /god/. Instead we have been called by our ((Code)) pioneers to **((cease and desist))** in this pandemic addiction and called urgently to ((Up-Script)) and rise to ((Code)). This shift has been seen by our great Teachers as a ((Life)) and /Death/ issue. This is why making the ((dimensional shift)) highly ((visible)) to the public and ((user friendly)) is of highest importance in gaining the ((Literacy)) of being ((Human)). This is why so much of my creative life has been focused here.

To sum up: gaining direct ((access)) to the ((Source Code)) is Life and Death for us, as our ((Teachers)) have insisted. This shift to ((Source Life)) is our maturation as Whole Persons...as ((I===Thou)) beings...as ((LogoSapiens)) and this is the ((litcracy)) of Collective Intelligence. This is the literacy and technology of Deep-Dialogue.

Once we truly de-conflate the two dimensions of Literacy and Intelligence astounding new insights abound. We can see that "/.../" language development is an important stage in human evolutionary development. This is a vital stage in our evolutionary development: to use language to convey /information/ and use /words/ to describe or represent the /world/ and build /culture/ is a necessary early stage of rational = human development. We ARE as we "script".

This "/.../" stage of evolutionary development is endemic across the planet in all our cultures. It includes the mental or consciousness practices, the level of "lens" development and capacity, the "hermeneutical" or interpretation powers, the stage of "meaning", language capacity, experience capacity, communication practices, mind operating processes, etc. All of these go together and are incorporated into "/.../" language and life development.

This level of "language" and "mentation" development is naturally endemic, pandemic across the planet in the life of the people. It is a **generic /language game/** across cultures and worlds: it is an "equal opportunity" evolutionary Pre-((Code)) stage of development, pervasive in our human condition. Simply put, it is the habit of **"talking about"** any given "X". This /informational/ or /representational/ stage of language, literacy and mentation is vital in our early development and survival. But, as our great ((Code)) teachers have taught, we humans must evolve (mature, grow) in our Rational Intelligence (Language Capacity) and gain direct access to the ((Source Code)) that funds and makes it possible to have /words/, /worlds/, and /language/ and /talk about it/. I call this stage of human development: /egomental/ or /monocentric/ life. It would be a ((fatal mistake)) to remain stuck at this stage that tends to act and live as if /words/ are /self-sustaining/ and not always held, supported and sustained by ((Source Field)).

In other ((Words)): our ((Code)) Pioneers saw clearly that any form of life that, in effect, is severed (alienated, eclipsed, split...) from ((Source

Field)) is lodged in dysfunction which matures into human pathologies and patterns of violence. It invariably inhibits our full maturation as ((Persons)) and inhibits ((Well Being)) and ((Human Flourishing)).

The ((Code Intelligence)) makes clear that no /word/, no /human/, no /event/, no /world/, no /narrative/, no /discipline/, no /language/, no /culture/... could survive for a moment if severed from ((Source Field of Reality)). We cannot "ego" apart from ((Source Code)), we cannot use language, have experience, be alive, think, feel, say "I", reject ((Source)), deny "God"...whatever...without the continuous direct funding of ((Source Field)).

In ((fact)) we "humans" can NEVER actually sever funding relations with ((Source Field)), BUT we can create /stories/, we can create /barriers/, /defenses/, /cave culture spaces/, /religions/, /academies/, /ideologies/, /worldviews/, /institutions/.../political patterns/, /disciplines/... that perpetually displace, eclipse, cover up ((Source Code Reality)) that holds us, feeds us, funds us and make all these mythologies and forms of life possible.

This means that /monocentric/ cultures or narratives or lives that act **as if** /self-sourced/ and self-sustaining are in bad ((Faith)). There is an inherent OntoRational self-deception and cover-up at the heart of any and all such forms of life. In ((Biblical)) terms this is the condition of ontological /sin/ - the self-created breach and break and alienation from ((Source)), and in ((Meditative Science)) terms this is /samsara/- being caught on a self-perpetuating and inter-generational karmic cycle of ignorance, delusion, self-deception, sophistry due to the severance from ((Source Code Reality)) whether ((named)) ((AUM, God, Brahman, Christ, Allah, Emptiness, Logos, Sophia, Tao, Reality, The Primal Field, Presence...)) This is the heart of what our revered ((Source Code Pioneers)) saw, diagnosed and addressed with powerful Code Medicine.

This, for example, is the essence of what Buddha discerned in his enlightenment – the source of human dysfunction and suffering and mal praxis. This is what ((Jesus)) sacrificed for – taking on our /sin/ that we may be liberated. This is the essence of Lord Krishna's ((Yoga Technology)): helping /Arjuna/ see that his life and culture and meaning and ethics imploded because of this /samsara/ breach. And ((Source Code)) empowers us to see across borders that the deep onto-diagnostic and /sin/ and /samsara/ are alternate names for the same medical crisis: ((SinSara)).

Briefly put: **Every /x/ is ((x))**: We are always already situated within ((...)) = the ((Primal Source Field of Infinite Presence)). And any and every "word" /x/ gets its being and voltage from ((..)), from ((x)). Thus, ((Source Word: Logos)) provides the ((voltage)) for any item whatever, and sources every sign or word: "/pen/" dilates when Sourced into "((pen))" /pen/ is a packaged, objectified /entity/ within the mono-centric language games; but ((pen))...((seen and uttered)) within the ((Source Word Zone)) ignites with boundless ((fractal meaning)): this ((pen)) is mightier than the /sword/. And so with every "word": monocentric self-sourced /words/ are anemic in ((meaning)) while any such "word" spoken or expressed from the ((Source Semantic Field)) ignites with boundless ((meaning)) and ((truth force)). This, for example, is what Descartes discovered when he left /I/ and entered ((I am)).

Any /scripture/ magnified and lights up in ((meaning and Source Code Power) when processed as ((scripture)); and so on. This ((Source Code)) dilation and re-location is true of every "x" in existence. Thus, /English/ matures into ((English)) when authentically ((Code Sourced)), and so on. **And here we find a Primal Law: ((Every /x/ is ((X)))): = ((.../x/...)).** Thus when we say **"/I/"**, our Code Teachers recognized, we cannot avoid **((/I/)).**

This is a monumental disclosure: our evolutionary journey is from /I/ to ((I am)). This ((I am)) is ((I===Thou)) =We are ((Dialogue Beings))...and this is where ((Collective Intelligence)) ignites and manifests. This is where we can reach ((common ground)) and ((consensus)) across /borders/. This captures and sums up the heart of our diverse ((global enlightenment)) teaching: our so-called "High Self": Source Self, Awakened Self, Evolved Self...is always already intimately ((close)), and the greatest awakening journey is to dilate from /I/ to ((I am)). And the classic pathway to open this maturation space from the artificially /objectified/ "self" lodged and constituted in its /ego identity/ is to let go...(stand back, detach, open deeper source space...) dilate and ignite deeper ((Self Identity)) is ((Source Code Onto- Semantic Field)). This evolutionary journey from /self/ to ((Self)) is the adventure into ((Awakened Rational Life)). This is our ((educational enterprise)).

This is an astounding "game" changer. The clarification in ((Global Light)) that the emergent ((Source Code)) is and must be the same ((Logos Code)) for our diverse great Teachers, indeed, of all our worldviews, cultures, scriptures, disciplinary narratives...has astounding implications for our evolutionary journey, not to mention our liberal arts enterprise. This dilation to the ((Logos Code)) as the ((Source Code)) for such diverse pioneers as Moses, Buddha, Krishna, Socrates, Jesus...makes ((evident)) the Rational Common Ground of the global truth-force of these teachings.

For example, the rational validity of the Code Teaching of ((Jesus)) is not that he is "Son of God" and therefore his teachings are universally valid. It is rather that ((Jesus)) as the ((Logos in the Flesh)) ...as the ((Embodied Christ Code)) = ((...)) is bringing through the ((Source Code)) of Awakened Reason which reveals that we Humans are ((I...Thou)) Sacred Beings, not /I...It/ entities that can be /objectified/. ((Persons)) are ((Dialogue Beings)) and when we upScript to this Christ Code we enter the space of Deep Dialogue Compassion, Rational Intelligence and Moral Life. In this respect the ((Honor Code)) is the ((Source Code)) that our Moral Teachers were dilating and tapping.

Again, the Yoga Technology that Lord Krishna is teaching – the AUM Code – calls upon folks to let go of the dysfunctional /egomental/ patterns of life and culture and rise = Up((Script)) to the AUM Zone, which is the sacred space of ((I Thou)) Moral Flow. So ((Yoga)) is not /Yoga/. And a moral pioneer such as Gandhi...living this AUM Script and Gospel ((Script)) is assisting humanity in the all-important evolutionary advance from /ethics/ to ((Ethics)), from /truth/ to ((Truth Force)).

The validity of Buddha's ((Four Noble Truths)) for all humans is not from the authority of "Buddha" as an "Enlightened Teacher"...but from the Objectivity of the ((Source Code)) the ((Logos Code)) which is the Moral Dharma (Law) of ((I...Thou Compassion)). The essence of Buddha's breakthrough ((Medicine)) is that we are not self-sourced /atomic entities/ but liberated Persons (beyond /entities/) in ((Buddha Zone)) the ((LogoSphere)). So, too, for Socrates and his quest for the ((Logos)) and the Rational Light...

These are prominent examples. My decades of research and scholarship takes us through the evolution of these amazing traditions and great innovative teachers as this unfolds through the centuries into the 21st century. Once we have access to the missing ((Global Logos Source Code)) we are able to detect profound ((Patterns)) and key missing ((Links)) across borders as the centuries unfold. For example when we fast- forward to Descartes' ((Meditations)) we can now see clearly that when he pressed his "doubt" experiment to the limit he saw he could call into /doubt/ any /thought/ or /proposition/ in the prevalent /cultural mental spaces/. And when he boldly crossed into the ((I am)) in quest of ultimate "foundations" of Rational Life...we can see that he left the /egomental/ culture space and crossed into the ((Logos Zone)). His breakthrough ((I am)) cannot be down-scripted to /I am/ as scholars who conflated ((Language)) and /language/ invariably did. But a competent ((meditative reading)) of Descartes' ((Meditations)) makes clear that Descartes was pioneering a dimensional shift into ((Source Code)), the Source of ((Rational Light)).

Concluding Summary

These meditative reflections seek to dilate deeper rational space and gain unprecedented access to the long emerging and still missing ((Source Code)) that is the key to Awakened ((Transpersonal Life)). I suggest that gaining access to this all-important ((Source Code)) is our highest priority now in our continuing evolutionary maturation as Transpersonal Humans.

Bibliography

[1] Margaret Gest Professor of Global Philosophy
(Haverford College, U.S.A.)

[2]Although Martin Buber in his classic book ***I and Thou*** (first published in German during 1923 as *Ich and Du*. Berlin: Schoken Verlag) introduces an analogous distinction between two contrasting forms of human relationships – "I and It" versus "I and Thou". I take this distinction to another ((dimension)) with my global Source Narrative. When I use my notation of /I…It/ vs ((I===Thou)) this brings out as never before that "/…/"mind, life and culture space is /I…It" whereas the dimensional shift to ((...)) TransPersonal ((space)) is ((I===Thou)). Without my innovative inter-dimensional ((…/…/…)) we lose the power of this shift if both are mis-taken within the /…/ space.

Furthermore, over two decades ago I formed a ((Global Dialogue Institute)) and introduced the term ((deep-dialogue)) to contrast with /monologue/ to clarify and reveal that ((deep dialogue)) is the ((I===Thou)) dimensional shift to ((TransPersonal Space)). This is developed in depth in my ((Seven Stages of Deep Dialogue)) at my website www.globaldialogueinstitute.org

CHAPTER TWO

THE GREAT CHALLENGE OF OUR TIME: AWAKENING TO THE FEMININE

ANNE BARING

Abstract

In the first part of this chapter I will look at the powerful mythologies and beliefs which have structured our present view of reality. In the second part I will explore the transformation of this view through the process of awakening to the Soul and the Feminine. The greatest challenge of our time is not political or economic. It is about the rescue of the soul and healing the split between spirit and nature deeply embedded in the patriarchal religions and in modern science. A new planetary awareness is currently emerging which recognises the essential unity of all aspects of life. A new cosmology is being born which challenges scientific reductionism with a new vision of our profound relationship with an intelligent and living universe. As this deep soul-impulse gathers momentum, the marriage of our rational mind with our long neglected soul is beginning to change our perception of reality. This invites us to recognise we have a role to play in the service of the planet and ultimately the Cosmos, to know ourselves in our innermost nature as cosmic beings, incarnated here for a purpose, aware of our fundamental unity.

Keywords: Feminine, myth, nature, spirit, soul, transformation

In the first part of this chapter I will look at the historical and psychological factors which I believe have led to our present perilous situation and the great challenge of our time. In the second part I will explore what awakening to the Feminine involves.

We are living in a time of momentous evolutionary change which is seeing the breakdown of old structures and the arduous birth of a new worldview and an emerging planetary as opposed to a national perspective. The scientific discoveries of the last 100 years—the thrilling expansion of our knowledge about the universe, the sub-atomic world, the geological formation of the earth and the neurophysiology of the brain— have shattered the foundation upon which our culture was built just as the discoveries of Copernicus and Kepler shattered the medieval view of reality. Yet we cling to the belief we can master and exploit the earth's resources for the sole advantage of our species; that technological progress will bring us all we need and desire.

Einstein said that with the splitting of the atom everything has changed save our mode of thinking and thus we drift towards unparalleled catastrophes. How do we change our mode of thinking? It may help to look far back into the past to understand how our present mode of thinking has come into being.

The first necessity for changing our mode of thinking is to jettison the current secular belief that the universe is without life, meaning or purpose and to recognise we live in a universe that is alive, conscious and the unseen ground of our own consciousness.

One of the greatest problems we have inherited is the fact that the patriarchal religious tradition rests on a fundamental dissociation between spirit and nature. The concept of deity in Judaism, Christianity and Islam contains no feminine dimension: nature was not included in their image of spirit. All three religions ruthlessly eliminated the animistic belief that spirit was present in nature. Today, we are faced with the devastating effects of this absence of nature and the feminine archetype in our concept of spirit. There is minimal respect for nature; no relationship with the life of the planet; no apparent awareness we are destroying the habitat that sustains us—a habitat that was once held to be sacred and worshipped as the Great Mother, as it still is in Indigenous cultures.

Awakening to the Feminine means moving towards a new image of spirit that embraces nature and all planetary life. It means recovering a very ancient understanding that the cosmos has a soul, and intelligence, and that spirit is immanent in every particle of matter: every stone, flower, tree and blade of grass.

Few people are aware that, as explained in my book, *The Myth of the Goddess*, the Great Mother was worshipped for at least 25,000 years before patriarchal civilisation developed and the cosmos was imagined as a Mother from whose womb all life emerged.[1] In the Neolithic era and in the great civilisations of the Bronze Age the whole cosmos was imagined as a living being: an organic, sacred and living whole. This world was seen as an epiphany or showing forth of an unseen source or ground which breathed it into being, animating and sustaining it. Everything was infused with divinity because each and all were part of a living, breathing, connecting web of life animated by spirit. People felt they lived within a Sacred Cosmic Order.

From around 2,000 BC we enter an era of huge social and political change that I have named the Solar Era. The sun rather than the moon becomes the primary celestial body. With the rise of the patriarchal religions the Great Father replaces the Great Mother and two immensely powerful mythologies become the primary influence on the social, political and religious history of the West, right up to the present time.

The principle myth that dominates the Solar Era is the battle between light and darkness, good and evil, originating in Persia with Zoroaster and reflected in countless images of a hero fighting a dragon. This polarising mythology led ultimately to the battle to conquer and subdue nature in the service of man. The former emphasis on relationship was replaced by the drive for power and dominance. Despite its spectacular cultural and technological achievements, this 4,000 yearlong era has been dominated by war, conquest, territorial expansion and the creation of gigantic empires.

Set in the context of the psyche however, this story can be understood to reflect the nascent ego's struggle for autonomy in relation to the immense power of the matrix of nature and instinct out of which it was emerging and which, in mythology, is symbolised by the dragon. The ego's great fear was of being swallowed by the jaws of the dragon, falling back into the apparent unconsciousness of nature—into dissolution and oblivion. Because of this struggle, the ego and the developing conscious mind – identified with the solar hero – became increasingly split off from the feminine matrix out of which it was emerging. The ego's struggle for autonomy was tantamount to matricide and it destroyed the possibility of maintaining a relationship with the Feminine.

Our problems today arise from the fact that over the last four millennia, our conscious mind has become detached from the older matrix of the psyche out of which it has evolved; detached from any sense of *relationship* with planetary and cosmic life. As time went on, it has become more and more inflated and omnipotent until its detachment is now complete and it no longer has any relationship with or awareness of the psychic depths from which it has emerged; no relationship with nature or the cosmos. Like Icarus, it has flown too close to the sun.

The second immensely powerful myth that dominates this era from c. 700 BC is the story of the Fall of Man as told in the Book of Genesis, and the expulsion of our primal ancestors, Adam and Eve, from the Garden of Eden. In this myth, the image of deity changes from Great Mother to Great Father. The Great Mother is demoted into the human and flawed figure of Eve. Divine Immanence is lost. The emphasis is henceforth on the transcendence of spirit. Earth is no longer the locus of the divine but becomes a place of exile and punishment for primordial sin. Man is given dominion over the earth but he is exiled from the divine order. He lives in a world contaminated by the fall and subject to sin, suffering and death.

From a modern psychological perspective, this myth can be said to describe the birth of consciousness and the painful separation of the ego from the deeper matrix of the psyche but, understandably both at the time and subsequently, it was interpreted as literal fact and divine revelation. It became the foundation of Christian doctrine and the reason why we needed a Redeemer. The radical change of consciousness which it reflects tore us out of nature— symbolised by the Garden of Eden—and led to pathological symptoms of anxiety and the compensatory desire for power and security resulting from a profound experience of dissociation, separation and loss: symptoms similar to those a child exhibits when it has lost its mother.

I believe it has had a disastrous effect on the human psyche and on western civilisation as a whole. It led to deep feelings of sexual guilt and to a virulent misogyny because all women were inevitably identified with Eve whose act, in taking the apple from the serpent, was believed to have brought sin, death and suffering into the world.

With hindsight, we can now understand that the emergence of the ego and the conscious mind from the older matrix of instinct was a tremendous evolutionary achievement but it was won at the expense of the former *instinctive* sense of relationship with the earth. Henceforth worship was directed away from the earth towards the transcendent Father in heaven; all rituals of relationship with nature and the Great Mother or Great Goddess were ruthlessly suppressed. All pagan temples were destroyed, including the great temple of Eleusis that had existed for three thousand years.

Why did this tremendous archetypal shift of emphasis from Creator as Mother to Creator as Father happen? I believe it happened because at this stage in the evolution of consciousness, the fragile ego needed the support of the transcendent masculine image of deity to help it emerge from the matrix of instinct, to strengthen and focus it, to develop into what we now call our conscious rational mind. Hence it defined a male image of deity. However, the effects of this shift of emphasis and the loss of the feminine archetype were catastrophic: the feminine archetype, associated with nature, soul, body and matter, was split off from spirit. Thinking was dissociated from feeling. Nature and the Earth were no longer sacred. Nature was effectively de-souled. Man was identified with spirit and mind. Woman was identified with nature and the body. Woman became subject to Man, giving rise to the misogyny that still afflicts us today. Body was dissociated from mind and mind from soul. From AD 418 Church Doctrine taught that sexual intercourse transmitted the Original Sin of the fall.[i]

Western civilization developed on the foundation of this fundamental dissociation between spirit and nature, creator and creation. Over the millennia, this dissociation effectively destroyed the ancient recognition of the presence of spirit in the natural world and opened the way to its ultimate exploitation. The feminine archetype, once personified by the image of the Great Mother and the Great Goddesses of earlier civilizations and with the deep instinctive sense that the world was part of a Sacred Cosmic Order, was relegated to the unconscious. Our current worldview rests on the premise of our separation from and mastery of nature, where the resources of the planet are unthinkingly plundered to serve the ever-growing numbers and needs of our species. Our most urgent task is to heal the split between spirit and nature and to reconnect our conscious, rational mind with the feminine matrix of our psyche that the psychiatrist C. J. Jung called our primordial soul.

---

[i] St. Augustine's Doctrine of Original Sin was incorporated into Church Law in AD 418.

Immersed in the fascination with science and technology and the belief in limitless growth, we have forgotten our profound *relationship* with the planet. Technological progress; scientific advance; the acquisition of wealth and political and corporate power have become the supreme goals. The human mind has virtually replaced God: it no longer recognises a dimension of reality beyond the material universe, nor any form of consciousness transcendent to its own. It has lost all awareness of the soul.

Jung warned us about this situation with these words:

> As at the beginning of the Christian Era, so again today we are faced with the problem of the general moral backwardness of our species which has failed to keep pace with our scientific, technical and social progress.[2]

Having survived three devastating totalitarian regimes in the last century, which between them killed over 100 million people, we are now faced with a fourth—the threat of an Islamist Caliphate taking root in the Middle East and extending along the shores of North Africa as far as Morocco, potentially even worldwide. Christians are under assault in more than a hundred countries. Thousands of Muslims are dying horrifically at the hands of fellow Muslims. Jews are threatened by the same hatred that led to the Holocaust: a hatred that would like to see the State of Israel wiped from the map. We see young warriors slaughtering men, women and children in the name of Allah, glorifying depravity in the name of the God of Compassion. Despite the teachings of all religions about the sanctity of life, we can see that humanity as a whole is still morally unconscious, still fatally drawn to follow psychopathic leaders. Jung commented on these psychoses:

> God's powers have passed into our hands. The powers themselves are not evil, but in the hands of man they are an appalling danger—in evil hands.[3]

How can we understand our own nature better than we do at present? The image of the dragon can be understood to personify the immense power of our unconscious primordial instincts in relation to our still fragile conscious mind. These instincts, ensuring or promoting our survival, have directed our habits of behaviour for countless millennia and now, unrecognised and untransformed, threaten our species with extinction.

When aroused by fear, trauma, religious zeal or territorial ambition, these primordial instincts can burst through the fragile defences of the conscious mind, taking possession of it and causing it to act as predator, attacking whosoever it designates as its prey. A psyche possessed by these primordial instincts loses all sense of morality and the evolutionary achievement of a conscious reflecting mind. It is not generally understood that, because of their immense age and power, these instincts can easily overpower or take possession of the conscious mind. It is no good killing the dragon. We have to learn how to create a relationship with it, using the sword of insight to become conscious of where our instincts can drive and possess us—whether as individuals, nations or religious groups—if we are to have a hope of surviving as a species.

With nuclear fission, tremendous power was put into our hands, power that we were in no sense morally equipped to handle. The belief that matter is 'dead' rather than alive with spirit, allowed us to split the atom and develop a dangerous technology which, since 1945, has left lethal residues of radioactivity on the earth from some 2,000 nuclear explosions as well as the accumulating plutonium waste from nuclear reactors, some elements of which can last for 500 million years. It has driven us to create ever more dangerous weapons with which to perpetuate our addiction to war. It has given terrifying power to enemies such as the Jihadists of Islamic State. From the perspective of the great spiritual teachers of humanity, we have created a truly demonic technology but the imprinting of our survival instincts, serving our perceived needs for defence, may prevent us from recognising this.

The Buddha and Christ, two of the greatest teachers of humanity, showed us the way to raise these primordial instincts to the awakened state. These great teachers did not ask for belief and worship but opened the way to the further evolution or transformation of human consciousness —still unconsciously in bondage to primordial instincts—into the awakened and enlightened state they themselves embodied.

Awakening to the Feminine

Now I will turn to the second part of this chapter and what awakening to the Feminine involves. In its deepest archetypal sense, what does the word 'Feminine' mean? As I have defined it in my book, *The Dream of the Cosmos,* it stands for a totally different perspective on life, a totally different paradigm of reality and for the values which reflect and support that paradigm. It stands for a new and conscious relationship with the earth and the cosmos and the arduous creation of a new kind of civilisation which honours that relationship and those values. Awakening to the

Feminine invites the recognition that we live within a Sacred Order and that we have a responsibility to the cosmos to protect the life of this planet and all the variety of resources it embraces instead of exploiting them for the benefit of our species alone. Awakening to the Feminine would fulfil Einstein's wish that we change our mode of thinking.

I think the first trigger for this awakening was Rachel Carson's seminal book, *Silent Spring*, published in 1962. But the second and most powerful trigger was the astronauts' landing on the moon in July 1969 which gave us the breathtaking view of Earth seen from space. Five hundred million people watched the Apollo landing and listened to Neil Armstrong's famous words, "… one small step for man, one giant leap for mankind". In the space of a few hours, our planetary eyes expanded to cosmic eyes. For the first time we became visually aware of the exquisite beauty and fragility of our blue planet and knew it was our home in the vastness of the starry cosmos.

Despite the enormous problems that confront us I think that something comparable to an annunciation and a birth is taking place in our world, announcing a new phase in the evolution of human consciousness: a slow awakening to a unified vision of reality and a connected universe.

Awakening to the Feminine invites us to listen to the long-ignored voice of the soul that speaks below the threshold of consciousness—speaks to us through dreams and visions, through our deepest instincts and intuitions and through the depressions that afflict so many of us and that are rooted in loss of soul and the withdrawal of spirit from nature. Many symptoms of distress such as depression and serious mental and physical illness can be seen as the ultimate effects of this long-standing disconnection.

Awakening to the Feminine means defining a new image of spirit: moving beyond an image of a creator god who is separate and remote from his creation towards an understanding that creative spirit is immanent in every aspect of life on this planet. Divine Mind is not something separate from us. We are co-inherent with it, participants in it.

It also means addressing the view of death currently promoted by scientific materialism. Some years ago, psychiatrist Elisabeth Kübler-Ross, who for many years had worked with the dying, wrote: "Death is the final stage of growth in this life. There is no total death. Only the body dies. The self or spirit, or whatever you may wish to label it, is eternal."[4]

The role of the Feminine is to reunite what has been separated through the oppositional paradigm that has dominated the Solar Era: the masculine with the feminine; this world with the invisible dimensions of the cosmos; the rational with the trans-rational. Through the near-death experience recounted by thousands of individuals, and the huge body of recorded evidence about our survival that now exists, we are being made aware of the immortality of the soul and the existence of our subtle or soul body. This is helping to dismantle the firewall that reductionist science has constructed in its insistence that there is only material reality and that the death of the physical brain is the end of consciousness. The apparent finality of death may be the greatest of our illusions.

The metaphysical traditions of both East and West have long taught that we are living within subtle fields of reality which are imperceptible to our 'normal' level of consciousness and the instruments so far devised by science. These metaphysical traditions tell us that our lives are woven into a cosmic tapestry whose threads connect us not only with many dimensions of reality but with multitudes of beings inhabiting those dimensions. Beyond the present confines of our sight a limitless field of consciousness interacts with our own.

The greatest challenge of our time is not political or economic. It is, in the deepest sense, about the rescue of the neglected dimension of soul and about healing the split between spirit and nature that is so deeply embedded in the three patriarchal religions. We are all engaged in a process of transformation manifesting as a new planetary consciousness which recognises we are part of an immense invisible web of life, known in Indian cosmology as the *Net of Indra*. A new cosmology is being born; a new vision of our profound relationship with an intelligent and living universe. This emerging paradigm gives us hope that we may rescue this planet from our predatory and exploitive habits in time to counteract the danger of destroying not only a million more species, but our own as well. As this deep soul-impulse gathers momentum, the marriage of our rational mind with our long neglected soul is beginning to change our perception of reality.

This gives us hope for the future. If we can recover the forgotten values intrinsic to the lunar era of the Great Mother without losing the priceless solar attainment of a strong and focused conscious mind, together with all the extraordinary discoveries we have made and the incredible skills we have developed, we could heal both the fissure in our soul and our raped and vandalised planet. It is a tremendously challenging, dangerous and creative time to be alive.

Bibliography

[1] Baring, A., & Cashford, J. (1992). *The myth of the goddess: Evolution of an image.* London & New York, NY: Penguin Books Ltd.
[2] Jung, C.G. (1964). *Civilization in transition* CW10 (par. 585). London, England: Routledge & Kegan Paul.
[3] Jung, C.G. CW 10 (par. 879) London, England: Routledge & Kegan Paul.
[4] Kübler-Ross, E. (1975). *Death: The final stage of growth* (p. 166). Englewood Cliffs, NJ: Prentice-Hall Inc.

CHAPTER THREE

TRANSPERSONAL REVOLUTION

PIER LUIGI LATTUADA

Abstract

When I start taking responsibility for myself, and stop delegating changes, then my very personal revolution begins. In this chapter I try to demonstrate that the history of humanity is the history of First Attention--that is to say of an imprisoned vision maker, of that same crisis in which it wishes to move. We state we are close to an epochal leap in consciousness; more and more people are about to notice the cage and are ready to step into the Second Attention, [1] daughter of an informed observation and able to recognize the identifications that imprison us in judgment. We will come to understand that the leap from First to Second Attention is directly connected to the mastery of our vital energy and to the passage from repression to transformation. We will analyze the Paradigm of Faith and the Paradigm of Reason. We will suggest a further mode, the awakening to a new consciousness.

Keywords: crisis, First Attention, revolution sacredness, Second Attention

For those who rightly turn up their noses at the term revolution, recalling all the violent outbreaks aimed at the upheaval of the established order that ended up making things worse; to the more sophisticated, who want to keep in mind that the etymological meaning of the Latin word *revolutus*, participle of *revolver*, that is to say turn again, indicates, rather than a change, a turning back. Accordingly, I feel the need to give the following explanation.

By using expressly the term revolution I wish to point out two aspects: the first refers to a radical overturn of conscience rather than society, of the paradigm through which daily human experience unfolds; the second aspect indicates a recovery, a re-birth of a new respectful attitude towards the eternal recurrence typical of the living, of that intrinsic cyclic nature of the vital process that we named Law of Transformation or Metamorphosis, rather than a return to the past.

To those who ask themselves what is the meaning of transpersonal, we could answer, simplifying, that its dimension begins one minute after remaining with your eyes closed and in silence, within oneself.

If we remain in the presence of ourselves we can easily notice that inner experience is of a nature, that is to say it goes beyond I, our conscious personality, and it conciliates logic and analogy, dominion and sharing within the pure being, here and now, in aware observation and beyond judgment. In silence and with our eyes closed, it becomes obvious inside us that, as Wilber[2] reminds us: "Your self identity, in other words, depends entirely upon where you draw that boundary line."

When I say, "*This is what I am*", at the same time I'm stating that *"I am not that"*, I am drawing a borderline and I am placing myself on one side of it. On the contrary, when I do not draw a limit, I realize there is no limit. I simply am. Paradoxically, this understanding takes me back home and allows me to find myself again. It invites me to start a journey, to take responsibility for myself, to stop delegating change and to begin my very personal revolution--a Revolution.

However, let us look at what is happening nowadays.

Crisis

Nowadays the common perception is to live in times of crisis. Consensual reality strengthens this belief impending over us, with its economic data: the loss of jobs, the stagnation of growth, the decrement of production, youth discomfort and the suicide of entrepreneurs oppressed by taxes. The international scenario shows us an even more disconcerting panorama: the winds of war blow at the doorway of Europe, tens of thousands of desperate people cut through water to knock on the doors of the idealized first world, the fundamentalist threat terrorizes and produces deaths in the Arab countries spreading its obscurantist influence worryingly throughout habitants of a continent on its knees, such as Africa. Where fundamentalism is not yet a threat, hunger, epidemics, tribal wars and ignorance do the job. The first world is squashed by power lobbies; at the top of the world a spider web of political-financial-masonic plots seems to reign, woven by a small group of omnipotent families.

Culture has been degraded to consumer products; what has value does not sell; the market reigns supreme over the choices of private investors and public administrators.

In conclusion, many matters apparently talk of crisis.

On the level of Reality, on the stage of our post-modern age, the drama of decay is represented, a show that has reached a record of replicas. Wherever we look, our premiere, clouded by judgment, grasps the seeming Reality just described.

I will try to demonstrate that the history of humanity is the history of the First Attention; that is to say of an imprisoned vision, maker of that same crisis in which it wishes to move. We state that we are close to an epochal leap in consciousness; more and more people are about to notice the cage and are ready to step into the Second Attention,[3] daughter of an informed observation and able to recognize the identifications that imprison us in judgment.

We will come to understand that the leap from First to Second Attention is directly connected to the mastery of our vital energy and to the passage from repression to transformation. However, let us consider what history has to offer.

The Paradigm of Faith

The main light in the darkness of irrationality has been represented for many centuries by religion. With the birth of religion, mankind began to look for meaning to existence. Since then, the history of humanity coincided with the history of explanations, that is to say judgments, which human beings tried to give to themselves and their surrounding nature. Rudiments of paradigms began a declination of knowledge.

The ecstatic mind of the shaman realized the direct experience of the Divine recognizing divinities and demons in nature, living in the world and bending the world to their own will. They could only adapt to the supernatural trying to gain its sympathy, through ceremonies and sacrifices. The explanation was laid in the myth through which the world was organized. The *mythological paradigm* reigned supreme for millennia during which through the "participation mystique" the soul of the world dialogued directly with the soul of the living; the Goddess reigned in a dimension enchanted by the numinous force of the Gods.

After, the "crisis of the Neolithic", God was placed in heaven and became unique. The great monotheistic religions were born as well as the great philosophical systems that explained the world through unifying principles. In the Western world, since the birth of Christ until the Renaissance, the history of explanation coincided with the history of the Church. Humankind was not really allowed to question because all the answers were already given and the Church was the only custodian and interpreter. The *paradigm of faith* led humanity through the darkness of consciousness until the Middle Ages.

Then came a reform claiming the restitution of consciousness to mankind, an expression of a process meant to be the birth of science; a historic compromise was necessary for the Church to allow mankind to investigate nature: Descartes was forced to deal only with *res extensa*, matter, and had to leave the *res cogitans*, consciousness, to the Church. The subject was separated from the object, Gods were alienated from human beings and the world was disenchanted.

In the modern world, investigation substituted the indigenous, and measurement, the ecstatic experience. The ecstatic, magic and disquieting charm of the Shaman was definitively pushed back into the reassuring womb of reason. Nature stopped being animated by protecting and terrifying divinities to become a place of domination, control and submission.

Historians place the birth of the modern Self between two crucial events (as Tarnas[4] reminds us) during that extraordinary century and a half that goes from Leonardo, Colombo, Luther and Copernicus to Shakespeare, Montaigne, Bacon, Bruno and Galileo, passing through Giotto, Michelangelo, Donatello and Raphael, among others. The two events are: the *Oratio de Homini Dignitate* by Pico della Mirandola (1486) and the *Discours de la Methode* by Descartes (1637).

The Paradigm of Reason

Three centuries of science went by, ingrained in the *Cartesian paradigm*. During these centuries matter was the only reality, and consciousness was a ghost, an artifact to be excluded and considered as insignificant. According to Newton, physical objects whose motion was regulated by mechanic cause-effect laws populated the world, which unfolded in absolute space and time. Every physical reaction had to have a physical cause explainable objectively. Scientific, measurable and verifiable truths substituted absolute metaphysical truths. Thus, the modern scientific method gave an extraordinary impulse to technological progress, which due to the discovery of electricity, mechanics, the invention of the telephone, of cinematography, radiography etc., led humanity into the era of cyber space, space shield, genetic engineering and magnetic resonance. The gradual and unrelenting success of rational thought over the ecstatic mind, produced the final triumph of the culture of domination, based on the expropriation and exploitation of nature; this was at the expense of the ancient culture of sharing, based on harmony with the laws of nature and the direct experience of unity of the living.

The expulsion of the yearning for ecstasy of the collective consciousness carried out by the rational mind, produced the arrival of *compulsory sexual morality* (as Reich defines it[5]) in consciousness. As a consequence, the consolidation of the culture of contempt towards natural laws, the introduction of guilt in relation to pleasure, control and enslavement of nature for personal profit, the loss of the sense of sacredness of existence, the denial of inner experience in favor of intellectual experience, the tyranny of control over trust, of thought over imagination and of reasoning over intuition and so on, occurred, resulting in the unbridled competition of human beings with other human beings, typical of the modern age.

The modern human being, empowered by those achievements, finds it obvious that technological and cultural progress proceed alongside with the increase of the control exercised by human beings on the natural world. The logic of control has increasingly entered the mind of mankind imposing an authoritarian regime rigidly determined by the codes of reason. Intense emotions, altered states of consciousness, erotic passion, the ecstatic experience of nature, the imaginary, listening and silence are considered by conventional wisdom as “not serious” issues, as strange, exotic and sometimes even dangerous and sinful matters. The logic of control, daughter of the *compulsory morality*, imprisoned the individual within the obsession for the full and the terror for the empty. Ours is a full culture, dramatically unbalanced towards the external side. Not doing is experienced as leisure, closing your eyes as sleeping, silence as sadness, solitude as discomfort, taking care of oneself as disease and going slow as inefficiency. Moreover, as Grof[6] reminds us, the largest triumphs of this science, such as nuclear energy and space rocketry, cybernetics, computers and modern bacteriology, have become dangers for life itself and daily nightmares.

Awakening

To a discerning eye, the paradigms of faith and reason, as they have been delineated for millennia, show us the rope. Our hero, free from the cage of the mind, realizes that the problems are neither faith nor reason, but rather the way through which the mind of the small man inside us appropriated them. The problem resides in the borderlines, or better said, in who draws them, the ordinary mind, which dominated by fear and thirst for power, mystified faith with the belief that made reason the dictator.

The world became prey to many small men and women, dictators, all of them with their own beliefs, truer than the neighbor's, waved around like a flag, wielded like a sword, smuggled as faith, elevated to unquestionable dogma, used as a crutch for their moral smallness and to feed their inner emptiness.

Therefore, in the eyes of our hero, the current struggle to overcome the crisis, the political and economic strategies of restoration of public administration accounts, the austerity measures and the re-launch of production, seem as useless as the vision and behavior that created them in the first place. Remindful of Einstein's warning, which points out the impossibility to overcome a problem by using the same mind that created it in the first place, our hero might be suggesting awakening from the great collective dream of Reality. From outside the cage, he sees that the show is coming to its end, that the curtain is falling, that the lights are about to turn on; in short, the actors will take their stage clothes off and exit backstage; everyone, actors and spectators, will meet in the streets, squares, gardens, buildings, seas, mountains, woods, rivers or lakes of Real Life. Ready to accustom our eyes to the real light and to see with clear, empty and awake eyes, willing to understand that we are not dealing with a crisis but rather with an awakening, with a revolution rather that a standstill.

A Further Mode

"Whatever you have the chance to do, do it, whatever dream you can dream, begin. Audacity brings genius, magic and power in one's Self, start now",[7] said Murray.

Paradoxically, by leaving the harbor of belief and reason and moving the borderline slightly forward, I can find myself again and realize the magic that dissolves identification and that re-leads to the one, inside me.

I am abandoning the illusion of "I am this or that", black or white, Christian or Muslim, right or left, rich or poor, Italian or American, in order to step into the "I Am". In this place, avoided by the small man living inside me due to the fear of responsibility and solitude, I realize that I am united with everything, accompanied by all those who began the journey towards awakening and their silent and intimately personal Revolution. Leibnitz invented a term to define the river of wisdom, in which those who leave the secure port of attachments to their own beliefs emerge, in order to begin the heroic journey towards their own Self: this is the river of *Perennial Philosophy*. The waters of all the main religions such as Christianity, Hebraism, Islamism, Hinduism, Buddhism and Taoism feed this great river. On the raft of the vision there is room for everybody, as long as you step on the raft as a free, empty and awake human being, able to see with the clear eyes of the Second Attention and ready to cross the boundaries that open in front of you. A raft ready to disappear once the river has been navigated till the end; a raft that answers, "Everything is One!" Along the river of inner experience, on the raft of the dimension, you learn to flow within existence, to stop fearing the fire from deep inside, the ardor that yearns for sexual pleasure, authentic love and spiritual ecstasy, and to draw borderlines, but at the same time to recognize their illusory nature; you learn to see beyond appearances, to understand a Further Mode[8] an experience that reveals the Truth, hidden by Reality. You take responsibility for your own deep feeling and access a sense of profound peace and tranquility that opens the door to harmony with the universe which produces a high level of comprehension of ourselves and the world that surrounds us--a world that appears closer to perfection, profoundly interconnected and populated by traveling companions en route towards themselves.

Critical Mass

The increasingly diffused possibility to access the Second Attention is the founding aspect and the operational tool of the revolution, subterranean but unrelenting. The birth of the modern self and scientific thought under the thrust of the Copernican revolution, I believe, has begun several decades ago, under the thrust of the technological and cultural post-modern revolution. Those who are over fifty years of age can easily remember their experiences with catechism at the parish or with the local doctor. The sex-phobic morality of guilt and the organismic myth of drugs reigned unopposed, weighing on our world of young teenagers in education with clouds of impotence and submission. Think about how much the globalization of information systems, the connection to the web, the ease of travel and communication has facilitated the access of millions of people in terms of religion, to ancient spiritual traditions from shamanism to Buddhism, from Sufism to Zen philosophy, from Tantra to Taoism, from Alchemy to Cabala, till the most ancient Hawaiian, Toltec, Vietnamese and Australian Aboriginal traditions.

In terms of science, even if the organismic, mechanistic, positivist and reductionist mono-thought is still dominant, we are witnessing the collateral development of multiple approaches, both epistemological and clinical, such as acupuncture, homeopathy, iridology, osteopathy, chiropractic, psychosomatic, psycho-neurological approaches by now consolidated, as well as traditional healing systems such as Ayurveda and Tibetan medicine. Who doesn't remember or know the repressive educational system our parents and sometimes even we were forced to train in?

Who could deny the brutal attitude of the previous generations towards animals, the complete disrespect towards the environment, human rights, work security and sexual habits? Who doesn't remember (if over fifty years of age) how it was normal to be slapped by our parents, teachers hitting students with a cane, animals chained up during day and night, racial discrimination towards "Southerners" or "Black people", oppression towards homosexuals, hygienic and workplace precariousness, garbage on the streets and so on?

I still remember vividly the morbid inquisition carried out by a priest during my first confession, who insisted in investigating details of possible sinful "touching", or the veto imposed on us oblivious children, by nuns, with perverse malice, of putting our hands in our pockets.

If we reflect, we can see the paradoxical aspect of things emerging again. On one hand the economic and social crisis, wars, inequality, pollution and the depletion of resources, and on the other the technological, scientific, eco-friendly, ethical and moral progress; on one hand the cultural decay and on the other the birth of a new consciousness; on one hand the persistence of fundamentalisms and xenophobic movements and on the other the liberation of sexual habits; on one hand beliefs such as the perversion of the paradigm of faith, technocracy, scientism, rationality exasperated as perversion of the paradigm of reason, and on the other the silent revolution of consciousness that slowly but inexorably is producing the awakening of awareness of multitudes without a name.

To Transcend and To Include

The Further Mode suggests considering shadows and lights as the two complementary components of an evolutionary process that transcends itself within a unity which includes and overcomes the process itself, and teaches us to see both on stage and backstage and to recognize crisis as evolution and shadow as light.

Through the unifying eye of the Second Attention we can consider the apparent crisis of modern society as a changing of the guard. The paradigms of faith and reason – typical of the culture of domination – have been sharing the same stage for centuries, whereas what we could call the paradigm of awareness – typical of *Perennial Philosophy* and the culture of sharing – has always contributed to the evolutionary day of human beings by moving backstage.

The time has come for the stage debut of the Paradigm, better known as holistic-systematic, creator of a post-conventional thought and of a transcendence and inclusion of domination and sharing. As occurring right now, this debut can only start from within, silently, progressively and inexorably, thanks to what we like to call the Revolution. A revolution that does not cut heads off, that does not throw down dictators in order to substitute them with others, that does not fight battles because it goes beyond war, that does not condemn because it goes beyond judgment. It is not resentful because it goes beyond conflict, it does not blame because it takes responsibility, it does not bury the conventional thought of beliefs and reason where it has been confined for millennia; rather, by its nature, it transcends and includes. It transcends and includes science and religion in awareness, beliefs and reason in intuition, stage and backstage in the interconnected flow of events, here and now.

Some Principles

This new vision has distinguished itself for a few decades as the most recent phase in the evolutionary process of consciousness, as a vast movement of spiritual rebirth that in a silent and perhaps underground way is growing; it is making its name both as product and creator of other small and great revolutions in different fields of science, during the past century.

To put it more simply, even if in the apparent disenchantment of this world ruled by the lust for power and domination, the number of people aware of the unity and the interconnection of all phenomena and able to behave consequently and animated by the sense of common good, is growing. Some define these people as the new man, *Homo Noeticus* (coining of term attributed to consciousness researcher, John White), to indicate its ability to conjugate body and mind, matter and spirit, emotional mastery and ethical behavior, wisdom of heart and compassionate love, mental presence and aware observation, sexuality and sacredness.

The makers of the small and great revolutions of the past century are representatives of this new thought. From the afore-mentioned archeological revolution led by archeologists such as Gimbutas, Childe and Mallory, to the quantic revolution started by physicists such as Heisenberg and Bohr, to the psychobiological revolution which took place thanks to the theories of Pert, Portmann, Lipton, Capra and Sheldrake, among others, or to the systematic revolution theorized by Ludwig Von Bertalanffy and Gregory Bateson.

Bibliography

[1] Lattuada, P.L. (2014). *Sei un genio* [You are a genius]. Milano, Italy: ITI Edizioni, p. 24.
[2] Wilber, K. (2001). *No boundaries.*ebook, Boston, MA: Shambhala, p. 9.
[3] See note 1
[4] Tarnas, R. (2012).*Cosmos and psyche.* Roma, Italy: Edizioni Mediterranee, p.17.
[5] Reich, W. (1972). *The invasion of the compulsory sexual morality.* Milano, Italy: Sugarco, p. 38.

[6] Grof, S. (1998). *Il gioco cosmico della mente* [The cosmic game: Explorations of the frontiers of human consciousness]. Como, Italy: Ed. Red, p.45.
[7] Murray, W. H. (1951). *The Scottish Himalayan expedition.* London, England: J.M. Dent & Sons Ltd., p 185.
[8] Lattuada, P.L. (2013). *Il modo ulteriore* [The further mode]. Milano, Italy: ITI Edizioni, p. 1.

PART II:

MULTIDIMENSIONAL CONSCIOUSNESS AND EXPERIENTIAL PATHS

CHAPTER FOUR

THE ANCIENT PRACTICE OF DARK RETREAT MEDITATION: AN ENDOGENOUS PSYCHEDELIC AND DIVINE FEMININE ENCOUNTER— IMPLICATIONS FROM TRANSPERSONAL THEORY, RESEARCH, AND PRACTICE

REGINA U. HESS

Abstract

An overview of the ancient high-level practice of dark retreat meditation will be described across spiritual and indigenous traditions. The goals of dark retreat practice include the enhancement of self-realization towards enlightenment through entering altered states of consciousness and the awakening of all senses. This chapter is rooted in an earth-based integrative philosophical perspective of transpersonal psychology. The neurobiological impact of prolonged darkness and the bodily release of endogenous empathogenic and psychoactive substances (Melatonin, Pinoline, 5-MeO-DMT, and DMT) will be outlined. The relevance and universal occurrence of the mythological-archetypal dimension related to darkness will be illustrated including such as examples as the creation myths, the archetypes of the trickster and the Great Mother. To provide some texture, a brief personal account of a dark retreat experience related to a prior near-death-encounter will be shared. Finally, while the potential benefits of exposure to darkness and prolonged darkness meditation will be pointed out, it will also be made clear that there is a huge gap of knowledge in this field and a need for extensive future research.

Keywords: altered states of consciousness, dark retreat, endogenous DMT, gestation, self-realization

The Ancient Practice of Dark Retreat Meditation

This book chapter is rooted in an earth-based perspective of interconnectedness drawing on an integrative philosophical framework of transpersonal psychology including and honoring the dimension of the Divine Feminine. It is recognized that each part is a fundamental part of the cosmos and each person is a fundamental part of the whole. As a result of this interconnectedness and interdependence each part impacts on every other. Through our body we connect with others and with the world. Everything is interconnected through the principle of energy. Everything is energy. Everything is interconnected through the darkness of creation – the cosmic womb.

Cave dwelling and darkness appear in every faith as a route to enlightenment.[1] Dark caves have been used for thousands of years for inner alchemy practices.[2] Dark retreats have been used by all the great spiritual traditions and indigenous shamanic traditions[3] from around the world and throughout the centuries as a higher-level practice, and even as a secret exercise in Taoism, Tibetan Buddhism and the Bön tradition.[4]

In shamanistic/indigenous practices, the initiation in the darkness of the cave plays a key role. The caves are the Earth Mother with her energy lines and contain the earliest information about life stored inside the Earth. In certain parts of the world the dark room is represented by the pyramids in Ancient Egypt, by the catacombs in ancient Rome, by the Essenes' Dead Sea caves in Israel, and in some areas by underground networks of tunnels.[5]

Ancient schools in the West used this method along with incantations, breathing, prayers, and dream practices, to create access to the awareness beyond time and space, beyond the concepts of mundane knowledge. There are many stories of wisdom seekers, prophets, temple initiates, yogis, mystics and shamans, spending extended periods in caves, where they received visions, trained their minds and senses, contacted the Divine, and mastered initiations. These were certain individuals who were able to enter another state of consciousness, had the capacity to receive the wisdom and energy of the sacred without being overwhelmed, and could express and transmit the insights and wisdom from that dimension into the sensory world of other people. In ritual initiations in all cultures around the world, including prolonged dark retreat, the initiate is thought to become a bridge to the sacred world.

The goal of prolonged dark retreat is to tap into deep clarity, accessing spiritual wisdom, connecting with the Divine, and training oneself to transform body, mind, and spirit into oneness. In the darkness, our mind and soul begin to wander freely in the vast realms of psychic and spiritual experience. In the dark, the seamless unity of space provides a seamless unity of experience in which we can recognize our true nature. By entering our primordial state through returning to the womb of darkness, one reunites with the original true self and the divinity within. It can lead to a deep presence, initial mental and emotional freedom, transformation of the ordinary into wisdom, and entrance into a state of clear light. The dark is kind of a womb in which one can grow into a new state of being.

In dark retreat the aspirant lives in complete darkness. Living in the dark changes the body chemistry, particularly the pineal, pituitary, thalamus, and hypothalamus glands. The effect of darkness is to shut down major cortical areas of the brain, depressing mental and cognitive functions in the higher brain centers. Emotional and sensory experiences are enhanced, especially the sense of smell and psychic perception. The senses of hearing and touch become more acute. Dreams become more lucid, and the dream state manifests itself in our conscious awareness. Without external light, it becomes easier to see the inner light. The darkness is intimate and boundless, full and empty at the same time. In 'clear light', a nondual awareness beyond any distinction between self and object is entered into. It is beyond experience and experiencer, beyond thinking and not thinking; all there is is, is'.[6] Eventually, one can awaken within the awareness of the Source. One can descend into the void, into the darkness of deep inner space.[7]

The dark retreat can vary from hours, to days, to months, to decades. Prolonged dark retreat is a restricted practice only to be engaged by the senior spiritual practitioner with stability in natural state and under appropriate spiritual guidance. The dark retreat will impact each person in unique ways, depending on the length of time spent in darkness, and the maturity and stage of spiritual development of the aspirant. However, it is also suggested that beginners[8] can benefit greatly from a limited dark retreat, experiencing phenomena such as relaxation of the body, mind, and spirit; balance; lucid dreams; the rise of energy and healing energy, and the perception of dreams as teachings.

A Brief Personal Account

I had a near-death experience in the major natural disaster—the devastating 2004 Asian Tsunami,[9] which was an inexpressible life-changing encounter. It took me years to integrate these overwhelming experiences of a fundamental sense of oneness, and of the exposure to mass destruction. The experiences during my dark retreat have been so far the closest I could get to my experience of near-death.

My personal practice of ceremonial meditation in darkness started some years ago in a meditation center. I participated in a 5 day long dark retreat conducted in the UK, which focused on the shamanic tradition of "seeing in the dark". One prominent scene that I received in this long period of darkness exposure was when I saw the sacred fire in my womb flowing up into my breasts, filling them up with fire, and the flames radiating to the outside world as fiery spirals. Then the fire flowed downwards and the light of the fire flashed out of my vagina. It felt ancient and archetypal. I became the illuminating flames of the sacred sexual fire. Another important scene was when I suddenly saw the light of the darkness, like a lightening within the darkness. It turned again into a fire that was transformed into a flame of darkness. So far, this 5-day exposure to dark retreat has come closest to what I can sense and can describe of my feelings in my near-death-experience during the tsunami. The literature also points out that what happens in prolonged darkness meditation can be similar to experiences during birth, death, and near-death as will be outlined in the following passages. I continue to practice darkness meditation for myself and use elements of it in my healing work and in my teaching, using blindfolds to provide at least a glimpse of the profound impact of this ancient practice.

Endogenous Psychedelic Encounter and Altered States of Consciousness in Dark Retreat

Research suggests that in prolonged darkness a biochemical reaction in the brain causes the syntheses of extraordinary molecules such as DMT, which induce altered states of perception. According to Mantak Chia,[10] the darkness actualizes successively higher states of consciousness, correlating with the synthesis and accumulation of psychedelic chemicals in the brain.

Eventually, the brain synthesizes the so-called "spirit molecules"[11] 5-methoxy-dimethyltryptamine (5-MeO-DMT) and dimethyltryptamine (DMT), enhancing the altered states of consciousness to a level of an endogenous psychedelic experience and can induce transcendental and mystical experiences such as of universal love and compassion.

Chia[12] describes the following fours stages in prolonged dark retreat:

Melatonin Stage (Day 1- 3): Complete isolation from external light causes the pineal gland to flood the brain with the neurotransmitter melatonin, manifesting itself initially into the need to sleep and rest and recuperate from the over-stimulation of the visual world. Melatonin is essential for the state of hibernation, which can facilitate the emergence of spiritual consciousness.

Pinoline Stage (Day 3 - 5): After more than three days, when the melatonin concentration reaches certain levels (15-20mg) the body begins to produce pinoline (beta-carboline). Pinoline is normally activated in the womb, in lucid dreaming, or in near death experiences. At this stage, the nervous system becomes aware of itself. Pinoline can activate clairvoyant and clairaudient experiences. Or one may see light and visions, hear music, and gain profound insights. When this primordial state is evoked, a feeling of reunion with the true Self and the divinity within can emerge, enhancing an understanding of the true meaning of existence and the order of things. It is a return to the womb, the cocoon of our material structure and Nature's original darkness.

5-MeO-DMT Stage (Day 6 - 8)- Release of Endogenous Psychoactive Triptamine: After this period of time, the pineal gland starts to produce the neurohormone 5-MeO-DMT. This psychoactive triptamine is produced endogenously and is the so-called empathogenic/entactogenic neurotransmitter that expands the experiences of emotions, feelings, and intuitions, a 'heart-opener'. When 5-MeO-DMT is released, a bright light is activated. This is often described as the darkness within the darkness, the second light, or the Divine light.

DMT Stage (Day 9 – 12 and beyond) - *Release of Endogenous Psychoactive DMT:* After some 10-12 days, N,N-dimethyltriptamine (DMT) is released. This is an endogenous hallucinogen,[13] which enables one to see in infrared and ultraviolet i.e., such phenomena, as the heat patterns of a person across the dark room. When DMT levels reach about 25mg, the sensations become intensely visual. Often it is described as an experience of clear or pure consciousness, including encountering enhanced feelings of love and compassion, and a new orgasmic-like vibration in the body. During this phase, the amount of sleep taken tends to diminish down to about 3 hours.

The 'spirit molecule' - Endogenous DMT and the Psychedelic Pineal Spirit Gland

Based on his extensive psychedelic research work, Rick Strassman coined the term 'spirit molecule'[14] for the endogenous psychoactive substance N,N-dimethyltriptamine (DMT). DMT occurs naturally in humans, animals, and plants, such as molds, barks, roots, flowers, and frogs. DMT is found most abundantly in plants in Latin America, where humans have known of its psychoactive properties for thousands of years.

DMT was first isolated in the human blood in 1965 in Germany. In 1972, Nobel prize- winner Julius Axelrod of the U.S. National Institutes of Health found DMT in human brain tissue, and later to be shown in urine and the cerebrospinal fluid bathing the brain.

DMT, produced intrinsically in the body, *became the first endogenous human psychedelic.*[15] DMT affects the receptor sites of the neurotransmitter serotonin, in a similar way such to LSD, psilocybin, and mescaline. DMT, as an endogenous psychedelic, may be involved in naturally occurring psychedelic states associated with birth, death, near-death, spiritual emergence(y), and can include psychosis. The similarities of what is experienced in these states and of external substance-induced DMT effects are striking.

Endogenous DMT is produced in the pineal gland, termed by Strassman, the "spirit gland". [16] Strassman conducted extensive research on the question of whether DMT is produced in the pineal gland during natural occurring psychedelic-like experiences such as mystical experiences.

Mystical traditions describe the experiences of a blindingly bright white light at the peak of deep spiritual experiences. The sensation has been located at the center of the skull, in an area often called the "third eye", responding anatomically to the pineal gland. The first wave of human DMT research compared DMT and schizophrenic states. Some data seem to support the hypothesis of Strassman that DMT can be produced in the pineal gland, but none has been so far conclusive and controversy remains. It is outlined here as "food for thought" – with the aim to stir up future psychedelic research into these questions by other researchers.

The Shamanic Art of Seeing in the Dark

In the western, and particularly Christian tradition, darkness is often regarded as something exclusively bad or evil, and the fertile and sacred primal quality of darkness has been lost. In this simplified view, darkness equals evil and light equals God. Western science has rejected the existence of spirits and souls, thus severely restricting our knowledge. However, when looking at other traditions and even when taking a deeper look at the full breadth of Christian backgrounds, many descriptions of the illuminating quality of darkness can be found.

In indigenous concepts, the darkness is seen as the light of the ancestors and worshipped as the power of the ancestor guides. Only in darkness can certain powerful elements be revealed.[17] Across many cultures, rituals and initiations often take place after sunset and during the night. The inner part of a temple often has a sacred space of darkness for specific initiations. It is in the place of sacred fertile darkness that the shamanic art of seeing in the dark is revealed, a seeing that is blinded by sunlight. The shaman (female or male) is assumed to be one who sees in the dark. The initiation into fertile darkness brings forth the shamanic clairvoyant abilities and specific healing powers based on a new sense of perception conceived of as seeing in the dark. The searcher in the darkness sees with the entire body and as such becomes a poet of the soul. Mystery and imagination arise from the same source. This source is called darkness, darkness within darkness, and a gateway to inclusive expanded understanding.[18]

Fertile Darkness of the Womb of Creation: The Forgotten Dimension of the Divine Feminine and the Cyclical Nature

In all parts of the Earth, the first nine months of human gestation are spent in the fertile, protective darkness of the womb of the pregnant mother.[19] Under the ground of Mother Earth, is the same darkness, where the seeds of plants grow in the soil, and develop their roots in the earth. Certain animals not only have similar gestation periods, but also have spectacular processes of metamorphoses such as from caterpillar to butterfly. Always, a process of conception is involved, a process of gestation, and birth. These are transitions of the journey into life.

Living in permanently illuminated houses, streets, and cities, we seem to have lost our primordial connection to the source, to our origin, our sense of interconnectedness with all, our belonging, our pristine ground of being, the fertile darkness where we come from. In Buddhist traditions, darkness is described as the *Void* that is full yet empty, the fertile original primordial life whence creation is born. [20] It is here that the magic of the Sacred Feminine occurs: the mysteries of life in their cyclical nature. It is in the absence of light that we humans undergo the metamorphosis into a body-mind-spirit unity before being birthed into this world of our planet.

The Mythological-archetypal Relevance of Darkness

In scientific terms, darkness is seen as primal and as such is within us all. It is known and shared independently of culture or religion. From a mythological viewpoint, the primal or primordial ground is associated with the experience of oneness with God, in the darkness where all is one as explicated in many creation myths.

In creation myths around the world[21] considerable importance is given to a phase of darkness out of which humankind is born, in different religions and animistic worldviews, the universe or cosmos is seen as God. In the darkness there exists a oneness with the cosmos as unified consciousness, an infinity. Darkness is associated with the Great Mother,[22] the spirit of the night and of giver of life. The Great Mother is assumed as "Nature itself, the great mystery of the unbroken unity".[23]

Myths and sagas from all around the world refer to the mystery of darkness. In Buddhism, practices involving darkness relate to the end of suffering.[24] The disciple who wishes to embody spiritual power must undergo extended periods of solitude in silence and darkness, seen as periods of gestation in darkness in which the mythical fruits can grow. Ancient oracle sites in Greece such as the Oracle of Delphi or the Oracle of Poseidon, also called Oracle of the Souls, used dark caves and subterranean labyrinths at temples where initiates and visitors entered altered states of consciousness. *Delphys* is a *Greek* word meaning womb,[25] and the oracle is the process of uncovering secret wisdom and knowledge. Most of the world's mythologies include at least one trickster, and this *trickster archetype* is also connected with the mysteries of darkness. The trickster is seen as a deconstructor as well as a creator of worlds such as Hermes, the Greek god of the crossroads, the messenger between worlds and the guide to the Underworld, was such a character. He dissolves all boundaries and undermines duality.

Closing Reflection

I am a forest, and a night of dark trees:
but he who is not afraid of my darkness,
will find banks full of roses under my cypresses.

Friedrich Nietzsche[26]

It seems that in our modern world with our hunger for illuminated brightness in everyday life, we have lost contact with sensual fertile pristine darkness. 'Blinded by the light', we have forgotten the power and benefits of sacred darkness, the unknown, the invisible, beyond the skin, beneath the surface of the earth. In traditional beliefs, the healing of certain wounds can only take place in the night and with the support of the ancestor spirits.[27] Darkness has been degenerated to an irritation of the modern individual often associated only with crisis, or dark forces and the bad or evil.

For the modern individual, darkness has been demoted to a nuisance, often only associated with crisis and dark forces. There seems to be an imbalance between times we spend in light and the sacred spaces of the dark. The long-term impact of living in such a dominance of light over darkness might be stimulating the development of dis-eases of a psychological and psychosomatic nature such as depression, anxiety, addictions, insomnia, and perhaps even cancer, diabetes. By contrast, research findings showed that the cycles of women sleeping in darkened rooms became more rhythmic and increased fertility.[28]

However, extensive research needs to be done on the impact of our overexposure to light. Research should focus on explorations on the fear of darkness versus light, the fear of the unknown, the fear of death, the fear of the beneficial use of altered states of consciousness, including induction through endogenous and exogenous psychoactive substances, in relation to the important and nearly forgotten dimension of the fruitful darkness of gestation in the process of creation, and integrating the Divine Feminine dimension.

Darkness meditation, including the shamanic art of seeing in the dark, can be a tool to self-exploration and self-realization and self-development. By awakening our senses and integrating the use of altered states of consciousness and their benefits into our lives, we can heal some of the 'blindness' of our modern world and become more whole again as multidimensional beings. Darkness exposure can enhance our capacity for sensory perception and the life forces, which include sensuality, sexuality, and eros.

There is something primal, primordial in darkness that connects us all that carries the mysteries of life that we all share, and which may provide a mythic quality of healing that, once remembered, provides an incredible source and potential for wellbeing and spiritual illumination.

Bibliography

[1] Chia, M. (2014). *Endless cosmic orgasm. Dark room retreat for lucid living, lucid dreaming & lucid death.* Los Angeles, CA: DolphinOlogy Inc.
[2] Lowenthal, M. (2003). *Dawning of clear light. A Western approach to Tibetan dark retreat meditation.* Charlottesville, VA: Hampton Road Publishing.

[3] Heaven, R., & Buxton, S. (2005). *Darkness visible: Awakening spiritual light through darkness meditation*. Rochester, VT: Destiny Books.
[4] Lowenthal, see 2.
[5] Chia, see 1.
[6] Lowenthal, see 2.
[7] Chia, see 1.
[8] Chia, see 1.
[9] Heβ, R. U. (2012). Beyond the abyss: Re-born out of primal waters: An autobiographical embodied understanding of the phenomenon 'surviving the 2004 Asian tsunami'. *Journal of Archetypal Studies, 2*, 121-135.
[10] Chia, see 1
[11] Strassmann, R. (2001). *DMT spirit molecule. A doctor's revolutionary research into the biology of near-death and mystical experiences*. Rochester, VT: Park Street Press.
[12] Chia, see 1.
[13] Strassman, p. 90, see 11.
[14] Strassman, p. 42, see 11.
[15] Barker, S. A., Monti, J. A., & Christian, S. T. (1976). N,N-Dimethyltriptamine. *American Journal of Psychiatry, 133*, 203-208.
[16] Strassman, p. 56, see 11.
[17] Heaven & Buxton, see 3.
[18] Lao Tzu, Tao Te Ching, *1*, "Darkness within darkness". Retrieved on Nov 2, 2016 from http://genius.com/Lao-tzu-tao-te-ching-annotated
[19] Malidome Patrice Some, in Heaven & Buxton, p. ix, see 3.
[20] Sandra Ingerman, in Heaven & Buxton, p. xiii, see 3
[21] Campbell, J. (1991). *The Power of myth.* New York, NY: Random House.
[22] Joseph Campbell, see 21.
[23] Gimbutas, M. (1991). *Civilization of the Goddess: The world of old Europe.* San Francisco, CA: HarperCollins Publisher, p. 223.
[24] Halifax, J. (1993). *The fruitful darkness. Reconnecting with the body of the Earth.* San Francisco, CA: HarperCollins Publisher.
[25] Retrieved on Nov 1, 2016 from http://www.etymonline.com/index.php?term=dolphin&allowed_in_frame=0
[26] Nietzsche, F. (T. Common, Trans.) (1978). *Thus spoke Zarathustra*. London, England: Penguin Books.
[27] Malidome Patrice Some, in Heaven & Buxton, p. ix, see 3.
[28] Dewan, E.M., Menkin, M., A, & Rock, J. (1967). On the possibility of a perfect rhythm of birth control by periodic light stimulation. *American Journal of Obstetrics and Gynecology, 99*, 1016-1019.

CHAPTER FIVE

HALLUCINOGENIC METAMORPHOSIS: AN OVERVIEW OF HALLUCINOGEN-INDUCED TRANSFORMATIVE MYSTICAL EXPERIENCE

T. J. WEISBECKER

Abstract

This chapter broadly discusses mystical experience in contexts of hallucinogen intoxication, with respect to *metamorphosis*, or self-transformation. The author provides a descriptive outline of hallucinogens in general, and of landmark research concerning hallucinogenic substances, specifically regarding efficacy as treatment in therapy, known neurological correlates, and the phenomenology of hallucinogenic experience. In addition, the author considers philosophy of intoxication for the purpose of self-realization, specifically as relates to hallucinogenic substances and the practice of modern yoga.

Keywords: experience, hallucinogen, mystical, psychedelic, yoga

Hallucinogenic Metamorphosis

For about the last 50 years in the U.S. the possession of most hallucinogenic substances has been a felony offense, even for the vast majority of researchers simply hoping to better understand these still-mystifying molecules. While it is known that hallucinogenic substances (psychedelics) can occasion visions and hallucinations, as well as transformative transpersonal states of consciousness, how and why this occurs is not well understood—even less so what it could all mean to the human person. Lacking resources and wherewithal to integrate significant psychedelic experiences, one may come to feel like a stranger to culture and to society, or even a stranger to oneself, as psychedelic music icon Jim Morrison lyrically expressed. Psychedelics should not be taken lightly, and by some maybe not at all; however, for some others—and this is the main point of this chapter—they are a *natural* and effective means of metamorphosis, or self-transformation.

A substantial corpus of psychedelic research begs for more research, and yet further experimental study for most researchers is expensive—thus impractical. Experimental psychedelic research following U.S. Congressional passage of the U.S. Controlled Substances Act (CSA) of 1970, which effectively banned psychedelic substances in the U.S., has hobbled-on for the last half-century thanks to a modest few and courageous researchers who ultimately managed to navigate U.S. Attorney General approval. The United Nations (U.N.) adopted nearly identical legislation as the CSA—the Convention for Psychotropic Substances of 1971. Psychedelics' current *Schedule I* status in the CSA—and *Schedule 1* status in the U.N. Convention for Psychotropic Substances—bottlenecks psychedelic research and leads to other negative fallout as well, written about expertly in the work of Nutt, King, & Nichols.[1]

Hallucinogenic substance-containing plants grow naturally in abundance almost everywhere on Earth. Indigenous human groups in nearly every continental region tell histories of ritual ingestion—thus the U.S. Supreme Court recognizes North-American hallucinogenic substance-containing plant-using religious groups that trace historical precedence for use.[i] As evidenced in indigenous art, architecture, music, artifacts, and design motifs around the world, familiar fractal-geometric visions associated with local hallucinogenic substance-containing plant-induced mystical experience suggest that specific psychedelic-containing plants were regarded as sacred or important cultural symbols for tens of thousands of years.

---

[i] The United States Supreme Court unanimously ruled in favor of the legal religious use of ayahuasca by the União do Vegetal, and the U.S. Court of Appeals for the Ninth Circuit has affirmed the Santo Daime Church's freedom to use ayahuasca for religious purposes.

Amateur mycologists Valentina and Gordon Wasson believed the ancient *Rig Vedas* praise the potent psychedelic *Amanitas muscaria* mushroom as a god.[2] Motifs of mushrooms and other psychedelic flowers appear frequently in ancient artifacts, and indigenous descendants from the Amazon to Siberia report their shamanic ancestors have utilized local *plants of the gods* for centuries. In many instances, local psychedelic substance-containing plants are mixed with other local medicinal plants to create a brew called *Ayahuasca*, or *Yagé*.[3] Some believe these concoctions have more desirable effects than when their constituents are ingested alone. *Neo-shamanic* groups around the world now use ayahuasca for healing and divination.[4]

The term *Psychedelic* (psyche- or mind-manifesting) is often used, however the terms *entheogen* (becoming divine within) and even psychotomimetic (psychosis-mimicking) have also been used. In medicine, they are called *hallucinogens* (hallucination-inducing). As contemporary interpretations of just what these substances are and do changes, so too do our labels for them. Likewise, depending on our point of view, as well as prospective application, they are called medicines, drugs, tools, props, et cetera. Some researchers—for example religious scholar Huston Smith—have suggested that *psychedelic* is too loaded with cultural baggage,[5] and still others believe it is a term designed to obfuscate that they are more like *suggestogens*.[ii] In other words, not only what these substances do, but also by extension just what exactly to call them is also something of an ongoing debate.

In fact, psychedelics may increase consciousness,[6] or expand the mind, or manifest more of it, enabling our brains to process information from novel, multiple, or even parallel perspectives.[7] Another view says that psychedelics expand the *sieve*, or *reducing valve,* of ordinary consciousness,[8] so that more information is received, both from within and without the sensing nervous system. Still another view says that psychedelics simply disrupt normal brain chemistry more than they actually expand consciousness[9]—that hallucinations are a natural brain

---

[ii]According to controversial work by Jan Irwin (2014), *The untold history of psychedelic spirituality, social control, and the CIA*. See: http://www.gnosticmedia.com/Entheogens_WhatsinaName_PsychedelicSpiritualiy_SocialControl_CIA

response to neurochemical chaos. Still another view says they are dangerous drugs of abuse with no scientific possibility for safe use.

Psychedelics were largely unknown in the West until the late nineteenth century. From 1901-1902, in his landmark lecture series on *The Varieties of Religious Experience*[10] American psychologist Williams James described his experience with nitrous oxide, a psychedelic compound used as a medical analgesic. Some years later, in 1954, Aldous Huxley described details of his experience with mescaline, a psychedelic substance derived from several varieties of cacti local to North America. He reported seeing a bouquet of flowers, "shining with their own inner light and all but quivering under the pressure of the significance with which they were charged."[11]

During a time when drugs such as LSD and psilocybin were legal, Harvard Professor Timothy Leary conducted experiments at Harvard University under the banner of the Harvard Psilocybin Project—resulting in the infamous Marsh Chapel Experiment. Leary famously told the world to *Turn on, tune in,* and *drop out*. In 1962, Leary, as well as Professor Richard Alpert (Ram Dass[12]), made history for being the first faculty fired from Harvard. One of Leary's students, James Fadiman, some years later, co-founded in 1975 the Institute of Transpersonal Psychology, and, in addition to conducting a number of psychedelics studies during the 1960s, authored in 2011 *The Psychedelic Explorer's Guide: Safe, Therapeutic, and Sacred Journeys*.[13]

By the 1960s, psychedelic use was more common, and a variety of substances were already being used successfully in therapy.[14] Psychedelic research was being conducted without restrictions from the CSA, which had not yet been passed into law. In spite of promising clinical results and untold questions for research, all experimental research with psychedelics stopped.

Psychedelics such as LSD and psilocybin also grew popular among 1960s progressive subcultures and counter-cultural youth. Psychedelic experiences open the brain's *doors of perception*[15] according to Aldous Huxley, or maybe also *cleanses*[16] them, to paraphrase Huston Smith half a century later—which may explain why so many psychedelic-drug users in the 1960s declined or opted out of fighting in the U.S.-Vietnam War.[17]

Western values—and particularly American values—changed significantly during the 1960's as compared with the 1950's, arguably due in large part to the infiltration of psychedelics into pop-culture.

In 1966 a landmark clinical study of the psychedelic substance psilocybin was published in the *International Journal of Parapsychology*. This study was adapted from Walter Pahnke's Harvard dissertation, which studied the effects of psilocybin on Divinity students.[18] It was the first major clinical example of a psychedelic substance definitively correlated with mystical experience. In 1991, Rick Doblin, founder of the Multidisciplinary Association of Psychedelic Studies (MAPS), reviewed Pahnke's research and found that, in spite of certain methodological shortcomings, Pahnke's conclusions were sound.[19] In 2006, Griffiths, Richards, McCann, & Jesse,[20] demonstrated in a similar landmark study that psilocybin occasioned profound mystical experiences; a 2011 follow-up study demonstrated sustained and substantial benefits from psilocybin experience months post intoxication.[21]

A number of psychologists—including Stanislav Grof and James Fadiman—had been researching psychedelic treatments in psychotherapy before research with the substances was banned in 1966. Grof alone had facilitated more than 4,000 LSD sessions—with remarkable results, which he writes about in *LSD: Doorway to the Numinous*.[22] In this book Grof describes a remarkable variety of possible transpersonal experiences under the influence of LSD.

In 1990, Rick Strassman pioneered the first new clinical research with a psychedelic substance in over 20 years. Strassman studied the effects of Dimethyltryptmine (DMT) on 60 random participants. He found that DMT occasioned profound mystical-type experiences, as well as impressions of discarnate entities that often seem to interact with users. His remarkable results are described in *DMT: The Spirit Molecule*.[23]

More recent research suggests efficacy in treatment of psychological and physiological conditions such as depression and despair,[24] anxiety,[25] alcoholism and addiction withdrawal,[26] cluster headache,[27] post-traumatic stress disorder (PTSD),[28] and even chronic allergies.[29] A variety of psychedelic substances seem to have different therapeutic applications; e.g., Iboga, a psychedelic plant from South Africa, seems particularly effective among known psychedelic substances for opiate addiction treatment.[30] Nearly every psychedelic substance seems to have slightly different effects and duration profiles—so there is much opportunity for prospective research. Exactly how much of which psychedelic substance is right for whom, and when, are questions that for the most part remain for the next generation of psychedelic researchers.

Different psychedelic substances appear to act on different regions within the brain. Just what exactly these neurological correlates mean or how these differences translate into psychedelic experiences as such is not yet known. Psychedelic substances appear to act primarily on 5HT-2A receptor sites; however, other psychedelic substances, for example DMT, also act on other regions and receptor sites—such as S1.[31] For now it is at least safe to conclude that molecular chemistry unique to each psychedelic substance gives rise to unique outcomes and characteristics.

During psychedelic substance intoxication users often report seeing visions that may include non-Euclidean hyperbolic geometric pattern formations—superimposed not only on the visual field, but also within it; and eidetic hallucinations, such as snakes, bats, figures, and other objects and figures that look like other things.[32] Psychedelic experience may also occasion non-linear information processing, so that during intoxication users report simultaneously, or parallel processing information as if from unusual, alien, or multiple perspectives.[33] For example, a user may say, *I had never thought of 'x' like that before.*[34] In his LSD therapy sessions, Grof encountered transpersonal experiences in which participants felt as if they were plants or body parts—Grof writes extensively on this topic in his book mentioned above.

Just where these hallucinations come from, how they arise, what their cognitive correlates are, and what if anything they can tell us about human nature and the nature of consciousness are all questions to explore. Mathematicians Jack Cowan, Paul Bressloff,[35] and Bard Ermentrout,[36] among others, building on pioneering work of Heinrick Klüver[37] and Alan Turing,[38] have developed a neurological-mathematical model of how the brain can produce hyperbolic fractal geometric visions—as seen not only during psychedelic intoxication, but also during other mystical states of consciousness, and during visual epilepsies of various kind.

Timothy Leary referred to experience of LSD as *modern Yoga.*[39] In fact, Patanjali's Yoga Sutras apply to the study of psychedelics—according to Sutra 4.1 *subtle attainments* are achieved by birth, *herbs*, and austerities.[40] In other words some individuals are born with natural powers for subtle attainment while others may have to work harder by means of mantra and other austerities, such as *asanas* or fasting. Still there are others who find help from the herbs.

Bibliography

[1] Nutt, D.J., King, L.A., & Nichols, D.E. (2013). Effects of schedule I drug laws on neuroscience research and treatment innovation. *Nature Reviews Neuroscience, 14*(8), 577-585.

[2] Wasson, R. G. (1968). *Soma: Divine mushroom of immortality*. New York, NY: Harcourt ace Jovanovich.

[3] (a) Burroughs, W. S., & Ginsberg, A. (1975). *The yage letters* (p. 23). San Francisco, CA: City Lights.
(b) McKenna, D. J. (1998). *Ayahuasca: An ethnopharmacologic history*. In R. Metzner (Ed.), *Sacred vine of spirits: Ayahuasca* (pp. 40-62). Rochester, VT: Park Street Press.

[4] Labate, B. C., & Jungaberle, H. (2011). (Eds.). *The internationalization of ayahuasca* (Vol. 16). Münster, Germany: LIT Verlag.

[5] Smith, H. (2000). *Cleansing the doors of perception: The religious significance of entheogenic plants and chemicals*. Los Angeles, CA: J.P. Tarcher.

[6] Schartner, M. M., Carhart-Harris, R. L., Barrett, A. B., Seth, A. K., & Muthukumaraswamy, S. D. (2017). Increased spontaneous MEG signal diversity for psychoactive doses of ketamine, LSD and psilocybin. *Scientific Reports, 7.*

[7] Kent, J. L. (2010). *Psychedelic information theory: Shamanism in the age of reason*. Seattle, WA: PIT Press/Supermassive.

[8] Huxley, A. (1954). *The doors of perception*. London, England: Chatto and Windus.

[9] For example, Tart, C. T. (1975). *States of consciousness* (p. 206). New York, NY: EP Dutton.

[10] James, W. (2015, February). *The varieties of religious experience*. New York, NY: Open Road Media. (Original work published 1902)

[11] Huxley, A. (1954). The doors of perception. London, England: Chatto and Windus, p. 5.

[12] Dass, R. (1971). *Be here now*. San Cristobal, NM: Lama Foundation; Dass, R. (2010). *Be love now: The path of the heart*. New York, NY: HarperOne.

[13] Fadiman, J. (2011). *The psychedelic explorer's guide: Safe, therapeutic, and sacred journeys*. Rochester, VT: Park Street Press-Inner Traditions/Bear & Co.

[14] For example, (a) Savage, C. (1968). Psychedelic therapy. In C. Savage & J.M. Shlien (Eds.), *Research in Psychotherapy* (pp. 512-520). Washington, DC: American Psychological Association, p. vii (papers from 3rd Conference on Research in Psychotherapy, May-June, 1966, Chicago, IL, American Psychological Association) (b) Kurland, A. A., Unger, S., Shaffer, J. W., & Savage, C. (1967). Psychedelic therapy utilizing LSD in the treatment of the alcoholic patient: A preliminary report. *American Journal of Psychiatry*, *123*(10), 1202-1209; (c) Pahnke, W. N., Kurland, A. A., Unger, S., Savage, C., Wolf, S., & Goodman, L. E. (1970). Psychedelic therapy (utilizing LSD with cancer patients). *Journal of Psychoactive Drugs*, *3*(1), 63-75.
[15] See Note 11.
[16] Smith, H. (2000). *Cleansing the doors of perception: The religious significance of entheogenic plants and chemicals*. Los Angeles, CA: JP Tarcher.
[17] Nutt, D. J., King, L. A., & Nichols, D. E. (2013). Effects of Schedule I drug laws on neuroscience research and treatment innovation. *Nature Reviews Neuroscience*, *14*(8), 577-585.
[18] Pahnke, W. N. (1963). *An analysis of the relationship between psychedelic drugs and the mystical consciousness* (Unpublished doctoral dissertation). Harvard University, Cambridge, MA.
[19] Doblin, R. (1991). Pahnke's Good Friday experiment: A long-term follow-up and methodological critique. *The Journal of Transpersonal Psychology*, *23*(1), 1-28.
[20] Griffiths, R. R., Richards, W.A., McCann, U., & Jesse, R. (2006). Psilocybin can occasion mystical-type experiences having substantial and sustained personal meaning and spiritual significance. *Psychopharmacology, 187*(3), 268-83; 284-92.
[21] Griffiths, R.R., Johnson, M.W., Richards, W.A. Richards, B.D., McCann, U., & Jesse, R. (2011). Psilocybin occasioned mystical-type experiences: immediate and persisting dose-related effects. *Psychopharmacology, 218*(4), 649-65.
[22] Grof, S. (2009). *LSD: Doorway to the numinous*. Rochester, VT: Inner Traditions.
[23] Strassman, R. (2000). *DMT: The spirit molecule: A doctor's revolutionary research into the biology of near-death and mystical experiences*. Rochester, VT: Park Street Press--Inner Traditions/Bear & Co.
[24] Yensen, R., & Dryer, D (1999). Addiction, despair, and the soul: Successful psychedelic psychotherapy, a case study. [Web Archive]. Retrieved from Etnopsico.org
[25] (a) Dutta, V. (2012). Repression of death consciousness and the psychedelic trip. *Journal of Cancer Research and Therapeutics, 8*(3), 336-342;
(b) Grob, C. S., Danforth, A.L., Chopra, G.S., Hagerty, M., McKay, C.R., Halberstadt, A.L., & Greer, G.R. (2011). Pilot study of psilocybin treatment for anxiety in patients with advanced-stage cancer. *Archives of General Psychiatry, 68*(1), 71-78.

(c) Pahnke, W., & Richards, W. (1969b). The psychedelic mystical experience and the human encounter with death. *Harvard Theological Review, 62*(1), 1-32.
[26] (a) Kolp, E., Friedman, H., Young, M.S., & Krupitsky, E. (2006). Ketamine enhanced psychotherapy: Preliminary clinical observations on its effectiveness in treating alcoholism. *The Humanistic Psychologist, 34*(4), 399-422; (b) Mabit, J. (2007). Ayahuasca in the treatment of addictions. In T. Roberts & M. Winkelman (Eds.), *Psychedelic medicine* (Vol. 2): *New evidence for hallucinogenic substances as treatments* (pp. 87-103). Westport, CT: Praeger.
(c) Unger, S. (1962). Apparent results of referrals of alcoholics for LSD therapy. Report of the Bureau, Saskatchewan Department of Public Health. p. 5. Cited in J. Fadiman & A. Kornfeld (2013). Chapter 19 Psychedelic induced experiences. In H. Friedman & G. Hartelius (Eds.), *The Wiley-Blackwell handbook of transpersonal psychology*. West Sussex, England: John Wiley & Sons Ltd., p. 366.
[27] Sewell, R. A., & Halpern, J. H. (2007). Response of cluster headaches to psilocybin and LSD. In M. Winkelman & T. B. Roberts (Eds.), *Psychedelic medicine: New evidence for hallucinogenic substances as treatments* (Vol. 1, pp. 97- 124). Westport, CT: Praeger Perspectives.
[28] (a) Catlow, B. J., Song S., Paredes D.A., Kirstein C.L., Sanchez-Ramos, J. (2013, 22 August). Effects of psilocybin on hippocampal neurogenesis and extinction of trace fear conditioning. Experimental Brain Research, *8*(4), 481-91.
(b) Mithoefer, M.C., Wagner, M.T., Mithoefer, A.T., Jerome, L., & Doblin, R. (2011). The safety and efficacy of +3,4-methylendioxymethamphetamine-assisted psychotherapy in subjects with chronic, treatment-resistant posttraumatic stress disorder: The first randomized controlled pilot study. *Journal of Psychopharmacology*, *25*, 439-452.
[29] Weil, A. (2004). *Natural health, natural medicine: The complete guide to wellness and self-care for optimum health.* New York, NY: Houghton Mifflin Company.
[30] (a) Sheppard, S. G. (1994). A preliminary investigation of ibogaine: Case reports and recommendations for further study. *Journal of Substance Abuse Treatment*, *11*(4), 379-385;
(b) Brown, T. K. (2013). Ibogaine in the treatment of substance dependence. *Current Drug Abuse Reviews*, *6*(1), 3-16.
[31] Psychedelics act on the 5HT-2A receptor site: See Carhart-Harris, R. L., Erritzoe, D., Williams, T., Stone, J. M., Reed, L. J., Colasanti, A., ... & Nutt, D. J. (2012). Neural correlates of the psychedelic state as determined by fMRI studies with psilocybin. *Proceedings of the National Academy of Sciences*, *109*(6), 2138-2143.
[32] Horowitz, M. J. (1964). The imagery of visual hallucinations. *The Journal of Nervous and Mental Disease*, *138*(6), 513-523.
[33] Kent, J. L. (2010). *Psychedelic information theory: Shamanism in the age of reason*. Seattle, WA: PIT Press/Supermassive.

[34] Erowid.org (https://www.erowid.org/); Also, William James discusses the revelatory qualities of mystical experience in Lecture XVI of *The varieties of religious experience* (James, W. (2015). *The varieties of religious experience*. Open Road Media). See Note 10.
[35] (a) Bressloff, P. C., Cowan, J. D., Golubitsky, M., Thomas, P. J., & Wiener, M. C. (2001). Geometric visual hallucinations, Euclidean symmetry and the functional architecture of striate cortex. *Philosophical Transactions of the Royal Society B: Biological Sciences, 356*(1407), 299-330.
(b) Bressloff, P. C., Cowan, J. D., Golubitsky, M., Thomas, P. J., & Wiener, M. C. (2002). What geometric visual hallucinations tell us about the visual cortex. *Neural Computation, 14*(3), 473-491.
[36] Ermentrout, G. B., & Cowan, J. D. (1979). A mathematical theory of visual hallucination patterns. *Biological cybernetics, 34*(3), 137-150.
[37] Klüver, H. (1927). Visual disturbances after cerebral lesions. *Psychological Bulletin, 24*(6), 316.
[38] Turing, A. M. (1952). The chemical basis of morphogenesis. *Philosophical Transactions of the Royal Society of London B: Biological Sciences, 237*(641), 7-72.
[39] Timothy Leary Archives (http://www.timothylearyarchives.org/).
[40] Sutra 4.1: *janma osadhi mantra tapah samadhi jah siddhyayah* (http://www.swamij.com/yoga-sutras-40103.htm)

CHAPTER SIX

INTEGRATION OF EXTRAORDINARY EXPERIENCES AND SPIRITUAL INDIVIDUATION

JOHN (SEAN) HINTON

Abstract

Integration of Extraordinary Experiences and Spiritual Individuation was the subject of the EUROTAS 2014 presentation I gave in Crete; this chapter has been formulated to capture and explore the personal meaning and integration of exceptional experiences labeled *Numinous* by Rudolph Otto,[1] given as part of the proceedings. Based on the individual narratives of 18 research subjects, who documented their experiences of transcendent events, my research illuminates the processes of working with and supporting spiritual individuation and integration of such transcendent events, particularly how art and narrative together bridge events to form meaningful presentations to the psyche and make experiences from transcendent and/or transpersonal events. Presented and illustrated are the developed themes or *bridges to meaning*, commonly emergent to the research participants' process. Material from my 2012 research study is used to illuminate the inner experiences, feelings and thoughts of the subjects that participated in the study.[2] All research participant names presented here are pseudonyms for confidentiality.

Keywords: mystical experiences, integration, extraordinary experiences, transcendent events

Study Design, Question and Method

My interest was to determine whether people that had what I considered extraordinary experiences, as defined below, felt their experiences held personal meaning or value. It was imperative that the research design ensured that each individual felt safe to disclose their experiences and that their personal experience and worth would be honored. Another critical aspect to the design was to offer a valuable experience to the participant by being part of the research. All methods used in the study design were carefully chosen not just for information gathering, but to produce a safe container in which assimilation and integration of the experience could occur for the research participant and ultimately validate their experience and its value. This process I later named the Opus favoring a Jungian process model with the alchemical and circuitousness it implied.

The basic design of the research was to have each participant write a narrative of the event they had experienced that matched the criteria of being numinous (see discussion of criteria below). The purpose of participants writing about their experience was to offer a reflexive window for them for careful recapitulation. The narrative was to be written in the present tense so participants could revive their feelings and immediacy of the experience. After the narrative was complete, the participants were asked to create an expressive art piece using clay or some form of drawing materials, again reflecting on their experience. Both a semi-structured interview and two questionnaires were given afterwards. One questionnaire measured personal feelings of meaning and purpose and the other survey measured the participants' feelings about the process they just went through as a part of the research and their current reflection of their past numinous *event.*

Discussions of the Topography of Inquiry

Numinous experiences are by definition experiences that have transpersonal import; that is, they are beyond our mundane sensing and states of existence. Numinous experiences are defined as transient (usually lasting less than an hour), with a passivity of personal volition, coming of their own volition rather than being willed. These experiences generally are thought to be impactful and profound by themselves. The numinous is presented in consciousness as a unity experience, direct knowing, the presence of the divine *other*, timelessness, infinite viewing, and/or all-knowing.[3, 4] For most of the last century such experiences were often considered a sign of psychosis and therefore pathogenic.[5] With the advent of Existential, Humanistic and later Transpersonal Psychology, researchers and psychologists became interested as Jung did, regarding his own numinous experiences and individuation processes. My research revolved around the meaningfulness of these experiences and what if any metamorphoses came about subsequent to having an experience categorized as numinous.

Obstacles to Integration

Important to consider is the foundational work on Extraordinary Human Experiences (EHEs) by Rhea White in relation to meaning. Her work as well as mine indicates that disassociation from these extraordinary experiences and lack of personal integration of such experiences often occurs. Such dissociative acts break the linkage of such events to their meaning and cause a gap in experience or, as viewed by Hillman,[6] an incompleteness of Soul. One participant explained it this way, " it almost got tucked away in this different place and I didn't think to share it in an odd way". Another said in her interview, "In writing this piece for you or for this research project I should say I just got in touch with how locked away [it felt] … mostly because I just never really knew what to do with it".

Davis, Lockwood, & Wright found that slightly over 51 percent of their 256 study participants had been reluctant to report their peak experiences for fear of having the experience devalued by others, seen as indicating imbalance, or losing the personal power of the experience if shared with others[7]. Such obstacles and closeting of these experiences have been documented by others as well as myself.[8, 9] It is therefore thought that such experiences are under reported and although non-ordinary, are not extremely rare in occurrence, as may be believed.

Meaning as Foundational

Meaning is the ever changing expanse, the ground on which personal transformations become illumined in the life of humans and thereby potentiate their higher aspirations and functional knowledge. This is an alchemical and non-causal emergence in psyche of a new personal ontology. In other words, meaning is our foundation of psychological and somatic being-in-the-world. The functional purpose of meaning is an organizing principle within a personal/transcendent world. As Capra said, "Human action flows from the *meaning*".[10]

Meaning, unlike emotion, has a deeper linkage to the human experience of being. Meaning is carried towards a future time as well as bringing forward the past and its occasioned events into the present. The epistemic nature of humans is existent as beings-in-time and is deeply rooted with meaning. The deeper personal linkage that meaning holds is the self's connection with events and the holding of those events as a part of what humans experience as the Self. Meaning is more than subjective because its qualities are both interpersonal and transpersonal.

Related to the creation of meaning are the processes of assimilation and integration. Jung's own process of working with the numinous was a circuitous progression of continual proximal movement in order to join in union with a greater wholeness of consciousness. Storr, a Jungian writer, states "There is no linear evolution; there is only the circumambulation of the self".[11] Jung in MDR (*Memories, Dreams, Reflections*) stated that the goal of psychic development is individuation, which is the fuller integration of the egoic self with the greater Self.[12] The numinous is an encounter with the greater Self. Assimilation and integration of the numinosum, or materials of such an encounter are a process of circumambulation of the Self via symbolic representation and assessment of personal meaning of the representations.

A Self, whether mythic or real, is the same for the game of identity within psyche. Psychologically, psychic wholeness must have a container that is infinite and representative of totality. Such a container is the Self. This Self is an *Imago Dei*, our natural psyche seen as transcendent and beyond human personality. The philosopher Edmond Husserl points out that our "natural being . . . continually presupposes the realm of transcendental being".[13]

Jaffe indicates that the experience of the numinous is necessary for individuation to occur in that its meaning, "flows from the numinosity of the self [and] has to be understood as the 'divine' in man".[14] It is for these reasons that the numinous is representative of a desire for wholeness and is both a state of spiritualized being and a process of self-actualization.

Design of Research Process is Meaningful

The trustworthy creation for the participants of a safe space and process, which was nonjudgmental, caring, and invited openness to explore safely, benefited many of the participants. My research was not designed to test interventions or techniques for intervention, but reports from the participants indicated that similar protocols might be useful as a therapeutic process. Lazy concluded her interview with the following comments when asked if the research had benefited her:

> I shared with you cause I trust you. You know, I feel trusted that my sharing with you is only for good ... And also I want to say that you know it's interesting because of the fact that it was beneficial.

Lazy had her experience over 25 years ago, so it was significant to me that she had the opportunity to re-explore her experience for the first time while participating in my research. Lazy further commented, as did others about the benefit of the process,

> I feel like I want to thank you for giving me that chance [to revisit her experience] . . . cause I don't usually revisit that whole thing, but revisiting it gives me a little bit of a boost . . . I have never really gone back and talked about it with anybody. So you're the number one.

Sabina Star said,

> Well. I really appreciate ... both the opportunity to share and the space to ... it was really valuable to me. And ... it seems this could be a real contribution in terms of what I got out of it ... It's just I think just researching it and writing about these experiences kind of brings more of that connection which really seems valuable.

Seeing Starz had similar thoughts and concluded, "My sense is writing about it and especially today talking about it in this way has helped me integrate it because I usually don't talk about it to anybody".

As noted by Palmer and Braud in their study of Extraordinary Human Experiences (EHE), the disclosure process itself had a positive effect on participants and, "correlated significantly and positively with personal and existential meaning in life and with psychological well-being".[15] It is interesting to note in this study what piece of the process of journaling, art, empathic listening and questioning seemed to offer the most usefulness in clarifying and integrating the participant's experience. The majority (53.8%) identified journaling of their experience as the most powerful process for growth and understanding.

Experience itself is often held Meaningful in Three Ways

The numinous experience is itself meaningful and having the experience reshapes the world view of the experiencer. As Sabrina said, "once there is a new awareness there's just a new awareness". How is this new awareness perceived in the lives of the participants? Three themes emerged as meaning integration process for the participants: *threshold, touchstone, or pivotal* to the participant's life. Not only were the experiences meaningful in themselves, but also because once assimilated, the participant could include the experience into a greater life vista and narrative. Such narratives form the ground on which integration occurs. The experience becomes part of a life story or personal narrative which is held as truthful and meaningful.

The *threshold experience* is one that leads one to a newer awareness or beyond the veil of the mundane. The experience of going beyond the veil is often described as a change that forever alters one's view of the universe or one's sense of self. Having experienced the passage through a portal in the fabric of reality, those who have numinous experiences often feel that the experience, as a given phenomenon, is itself meaningful. Being a threshold experience, once passed through, one is no longer the same as before one's passage through this veil of existence. The experience becomes an initiation into a greater possibility for existence and can be a rebirth in a spiritual sense. In Sophie's words, "as an experience without putting judgment on it, the world has opened up a different realm for me. The meaning would be an expanded experience of life".

The experience as a *touchstone* is a point of both departure and reference to return for validation. Similar to the threshold experience, the experience as touchstone is a departure point to a broader understanding. Because the experience is so powerful and embedded in the memory of the one that had the experience, it becomes a point in time and also a reference for understanding. As a reference it is used to validate future decisions or to validate beliefs about the nature of reality or metaphysical assertions about the reality of spiritual life. As a touchstone, it is the *experience itself* that is referred to over an interpretation of the meaning of the experience.

The experience as *pivotal* is a point of directional change in life's trajectory, which is distinguished from the experience of the touchstone acceptation by two factors. The first is that a change in behavior is almost immediate after the event itself or during the event, and the second is that there is an abrupt change in the direction of one's life circumstances such as profession, relationships, or social attitudes. This was expressed by the research participants stating, "It changed me" or "It changes how I look at things". Sedona was told she would be a spiritual healer though she had no idea at the time what that would mean. She found herself in a spiritual guidance class within weeks. The experience was a complete pivot or turning of her life and profession. The pivotal is a rapid integration into one's life of the numinosum.

Experience is an Ontological Shift in One's Personal State of Being

The ontological shift in being that is part of the numinous is a greater sense of one's being in the universe. Direct experience and an implicit knowledge of what is/are part of the expanded self-experience as it is given, changes the experiencer's world. This ontological shift can be profound, confusing, disturbing, and sometimes hard to assimilate and integrate. The research points to issues of how participants struggle with what they have experienced in an expanded state compared to their nominal state, which can seem very contradictory in their nature. Since the expanded self that is experienced is state specific and non-ordinary, the tendency is to relegate the experience to being anomalistic by nature, and denigrate or disassociate from the experience.

What this research concludes is that with a process for assimilation of the experience and a frame for integration of these state specific realities, one can bridge the anomalistic experience with the nominal life experience. This bridging is both the integration into one's life experience and the creation of meaning. The tendency by some that have these experiences, to place their numinous experience in a separate category is, in the prime researcher's view, a disassociation or splitting of one's experience.

Prime Question of Meaning and Purpose

The participants expressed how they learned more about themselves, more about their personal meaning in relation to their experience, and more about their purpose in life by participating in the study as co-researchers/participants. As Sophie said, "After participating in the research, I revisited my contemplation on the experiences I wrote about. Such re-visitation yielded a meaningful experience and affected my growth as a person, as well as added meaning to my life". Sedona recalled, "I gained a deeper understanding of the ancestral wounding and the healing, which took place during the experience".

What was discovered from the data collected regarding meaning and purpose was a high association between mystical experience and one's own feeling of meaning and purpose in life. This was exhibited in a couple of ways; participants who had these experiences changed their life directions and often adopted new professions, often healing professions. These were changes they felt were in alignment with what they considered their life purpose and gave their life a greater meaning as they pursued their newly chosen paths. There was also a statistical correlation with the quantitative data. The data showed a high correlation [r (16) = .503] of the Hood M-Scale (mystical experience scale) and the Hinton PPMI (Positive Purpose and Meaning Index). There is evidence from the interviews and the quantitative data of corroboration demonstrating that the numinous experience positively correlates to feelings of meaning and purpose in the participant's life.

Aspects Related to Meaning, Behaviors and Purpose

On the surface, most research participants seemed to be pursuing normal careers and conventional life styles. The experience of the numinous described by Krishna Deva was pivotal as he described it, "I don't feel like I had to change. I feel the experience had changed me".

Meaning and behavior are two separate outcomes of these experiences. Krishna Deva's statement points out that cognitively he did not need to change; however, with his depression being lifted, in terms of how he felt, he was changed. His felt sense of who he was had shifted and this held great meaning for him. This is one of the ways that the meaningfulness of the experience is felt but might not be acknowledged if looked at from the point of outward behavior or overt changes in one's life. Unless asked to reflect on feelings that are embodied, or one's ways of being, the participants may or may not say that much had been felt as being changed after their experience. Meaning is often felt as something bodily experienced rather than as a cognitive interpretation of the experienced phenomena. Ineffable senses of the experience that co-researcher/ participants reported were not expressed as thoughts. Rather, the ineffable sense is often expressed as living experience or felt. The feeling element appeared to be both memorable and meaningful yet the most difficult to communicate. Seeing Stars expressed that feeling was really what was so strong and beautiful in her experience as well as the awe of being in another dimensional world that she experienced, and this feeling part was the part of her experience that was often the most difficult to describe. If we think about the sensing part of experience we either understand, because we have experienced a similar feeling, or we do not. Anomalistically lived experiences have the difficulty of being ineffable since not all share them in common as experienced sensations. This lack of a common experience and language hinders assimilation and makes integration difficult if not consciously worked with. Maslow, in a chapter titled *Organizational Danger to Transcendent Experiences*, defines integration as what one then lives. Transcendent experiences "can be extremely important in their effects upon the person and through him [her] upon the world; this is true only if he [she] experiences them, truly lives them. Only then do they have meaning and effect".[16]

The model that this research purports is one of (a) *assimilation* or *expansion*, (b) *integration* which means that one's life is now informed by the expanded view and experience of the phenomena, and (c) *meaning,* which is defined as a negotiated collective validation of events to create experience abrim with meaning.

> The *assimilation phase* is the making of room and accommodation of the phenomena. This includes the physical accommodation of energies, newer expanded ways of being, perceiving, and thinking, which includes psychological, emotional, and cognitive boundaries that are expanded.
>
> *Integration* is the useful and purposeful action of making the assimilated material part of one's life experience. Integration is the changing of behaviors, careers, philosophical or theological references, diet, ritual, and combinations of these and more.
>
> *Meaning* is how we describe and talk about the events. How do the events fit into our current personal narrative or myth? The personal myth has a central figure, which is the self, the hero, or the victim, and describes or answers the question of, who am I?

The assimilation of these experiences as reported by participants is an ongoing process. Daadi commented, "I felt I needed to change, to practice more meditation and to live a more simple life. In terms of my values, they became more fully concentrated on a more esoteric process and self-understanding, self-actualization, that type of thing". The research indicates that assimilation is often difficult, can take years, and is a process that most participants considered ongoing. Dindale's comment indicative of the process as ongoing: "I look at it as a milestone in a process that I was going through at the time anyway and that process continued".

Integration of these experiences was predicated on a couple of elements. Assimilation of the experience successfully as well as the creation of meaning, sometimes in a life changing way that includes career or relationships, can be part of integrating the experience. As noted by Maslow (1994), those that live them, truly experience their meaning and effect. Participants who had a strong philosophical or spiritual framework, using wisdom traditions particularly, or a philosophical position of a more mystical nature, benefited from these teachings. Sabrina Star expressed this theme as, "I remember . . . I was reading Thich Nhat Hanh and I was like oooh! That is what he was talking about". She felt a meaning come alive in the connection between wisdom teachings and her own experience.

Conclusion

Preliminary thoughts and conclusions, emanating from the study were that psychological process such as holding space to explore and be reflexive is important to the work/Opus of assimilation and integration. The experiences are meaningful often in and of themselves for those that have them. Understanding the thematic patterns (threshold, pivotal, and touchstone) of meaning can aid integration and further meaning. Such integration is important to the individuation process and is foundational for meaningful and purposeful attitude towards life. Clearly, as demonstrated and measured by this research, a strong correspondence was evidenced from reports of those having had numinous experiences and how they favorably related such experiences to their feelings of meaning and purpose in life.

Bibliography

[1] Otto, R. (1923/1958). *The idea of the holy*. New York, NY: Oxford University Press.

[2] Hinton, J. (2012). *Spiritual aspects of individuation, numinous experiences and life meaning* (Doctoral dissertation). Available from ProQuest. (AAI3554711)

[3] James, W. (2002). *Varieties of religious experience*. New York, NY: Modern Library.

[4] Stace, W. T. (1960). *Mysticism and philosophy* Los Angeles, CA: Jeremy P. Tarcher.

[5] White, R. A. (1987). Dissociation, narrative, and exceptional human experiences. In S. Krippner & S. M. Powers (Eds.), *Broken images, broken selves* (pp. 88-124). Washington, DC: Brunner/Mazel, Inc. Retrieved from http://dx.doi.org/
[6] Hillman, J. (1975). *Re-Visioning psychology*. New York, NY: Harper Perennial.
[7] Davis, J., Lockwood, L., & Wright, C. (1991). Reason for not reporting peak experiences. *Journal of Humanistic Psychology*, *31*(1), 86-94.
[8] Hinton, J. (2014). Numinous experiences in the closet. *Journal of Exceptional Experiences and Psychology* (JEEP), *2*(2), 6-14.
[9] Palmer, G., & Braud, W. (2002). Exceptional human experiences, disclosure, and a more inclusive view of physical, psychological, and spiritual well-being. *The Journal of Transpersonal Psychology*, *34*(1), 29-61.
[10] Capra, F. (2002). *The hidden connections*. New York, NY: Anchor Books, p. 73.
[11] Storr, A. (Ed.). (1983). *The essential Jung* Princeton, NJ: Princeton University Press, p. 234.
[12] Jung, C. G. (1963). *Memories dreams and reflections*. New York, NY: Vantage Press.
[13] Husserl, E. (1960). *Cartesian meditations: An introduction to phenomenology*. The Hague: Martius Nijhoff, p 21.
[14] Jaffe, A. (1971). *The myth of meaning*. New York, NY: G. P. Putman and Sons, p. 79.
[15] Palmer, G., & Braud, W. (2002). Exceptional human experiences, disclosure, and a more inclusive view of physical, psychological, and spiritual well-being. *The Journal of Transpersonal Psychology*, *34*(1), 29-61.
[16] Maslow, A. (1994). *Religions values and peak-experiences*. New York, NY: Viking Press, p. 34.

CHAPTER SEVEN

BEYOND THE LABYRINTH: A TRANSPERSONAL EXPERIENCE THROUGH THE MYTH AND HUMAN CONSCIOUSNESS

ARTURO DE LUCA

Abstract

The author points out some of the fundamental aspects of the Labyrinth-Archetype arising from its universal symbolism within the conceptual system of transpersonal therapy. This experience offers new inspiration and points of reference to contemporary man that exceed the limited threshold of knowledge of conventional therapy and paradigm.

Keywords: Ariadne, consciousness, labyrinth, Theseus, transpersonal

The labyrinth, an ancient and primordial archetype, found in every part of the world, is becoming more and more relevant not only in the context of new historical and anthropological research, but also in transpersonal psychology, as a synthesis and focal point of all of man's evolutionary journeys.

The metaphor of the *entrance to the labyrinth* refers directly to the inevitable impact of new, no longer ego-centric forms of consciousness on a broader more spiritual vision of reality, as Jung described.[1] In this sense reaching *the centre of the labyrinth* corresponds with this rediscovery of consciousness no longer in an egoic and personal sense, but from the perspective of the expansion of awareness, which is the objective of transpersonal psychology. Moreover its myth of the Minotaur becomes both the liberation and integration of the Shadow, as in the unity of opposites; while the Theseus-Ariadne couple are the symbol of lost unity that is recovered and can be transformed on the return voyage through the positive function effected by this archetype, which can then re-join the sources of the Universal Conscience, as explained by Campbell.[2]

Labyrinth is a *Pelasgian* word of *pre-Greek* origin assimilated by classical Greek civilization. It is probably related to *labrys*, a word for the archaic iconic "double - edged axe", symbol of Royal power and cosmic polarity. The complex palace of Knossos in Crete is usually implicated, though the actual dancing-ground, depicted in frescoed patterns at Knossos, has not been found. According to Philostratos something was being shown to visitors as a labyrinth at Knossos in the 1st century AD.[3]

A labyrinth is a universal symbol that relates to the human psyche, wholeness, change and other dimensions of the *transpersonal* and our inner self. It combines imagery of the *circle*, human potential and the *spiral* into a meandering but unpredictable healing path.

However, according to Homer, it was originally not a maze but a dance floor inscribed with the meander, or spiral *'maze'* form. It was the floor on which the Minoan priestesses performed ritual erotic dances that led to their orgiastic rites for Dionysos.[4] The meander represented the serpentine path of underground water in Neolithic cultures. In fact, this energy, exuded by the *spiraling sacred Snake* exemplifying fertility, regeneration and the mysteries of the Great Mother (Pluto's and Dionysos' legends according to Kerenyi), was celebrated in Crete as early as 6000 BCE.

The seductive *Serpent Goddess* was discovered in the underground level of the Second Palace of Knossos (1600 BCE), according to Lapatin.[5] She depicts the benevolence of the Holy Mother and sacred power of the inner Life Force. Her ecstatic staring gaze and enigmatic inward smile, as she holds high the two serpents of healing art are particularly noticeable. The tiny panther on her headdress may indicate the goddess' connection to the fertility rites of Dionysos.

A legend tells us that Minos, king of Crete, cleared the seas of pirates and reigned over the Aegean islands and some mainland cities of Greece. Each year Athens had to send them seven youths and seven maidens, who were devoured by the Minotaur, a monster Minos had imprisoned in the Labyrinth, a structure designed and built by the architect Dedalaus.[6] The Minotaur was then killed by Theseus, son of the king of Athens, who found a way out of the Labyrinth with the help of a “guide” thread given him by Ariadne, Minos’ daughter, who had fallen in love with the hero.

The symbol of the Labyrinth is found carved on stone age megaliths in many locations distant from each other. They are found on rocks of the Atlantic coasts of Galizia, France and Cornwall, England; in India, in the Baltic, and in North America as well. These labyrinths are identical to the one found on a medallion found in Crete in the excavations of Knossos.[7] In India it is considered an object of meditation connected to the human thought process. For the Hopi Indians of North America, the Labyrinth symbolizes an initiation process of rebirth to a better world; one of the arms of the central cross shows the uterus of the mother carrying the fetus, the other her arms carrying the newborn.[8] This ancient symbol was therefore known in many places throughout the ancient world: perhaps this explains cosmic images of our deepest spiritual dimension, a transforming path transcending our limited ego through the diaspora of refugees from the cataclysm of Atlantis.[9]

We find the labyrinth in Gothic cathedrals, circular and in the form of a cross. It is one of the floor motifs and is usually found where the central nave meets the transept. Probably the name labyrinth derives from the complexity of the route. Many French churches such as those of Sens, Poitiers, Auxerre, S. Quintino, Rheims, still have the Labyrinth.[10]

The best known example of the labyrinth is embedded in the stone pavement of Chartres Cathedral. The Middle Ages was a time of pilgrimages. Since most people could not make the grand pilgrimage to Jerusalem, considered by Christians to be the center of the world and symbolizing the Kingdom of Heaven, they would make pilgrimages to important cathedrals such as Canterbury, Santiago de Compostella and Chartres. According to alchemist Fulcanelli, the bishop of Chartres in the Middle Ages is said to have conducted circular processions: probably they took place in the labyrinth.[11] The Medieval builders were careful to incorporate their understanding of sacred architecture into the design and location of the labyrinths, which were usually placed near the entrance at the west and of the nave, beside the baptismal font near the entrance of the Church. This location symbolizes our first steps on the spiritual journey with labyrinth.

In order to establish a link between the ancient symbolism of the labyrinth from Greek antiquity to Medieval culture, I will now introduce the fundamental themes of our therapeutic work in transpersonal therapy.

Accordingly, our work with the labyrinth follows two distinct yet complementary directions:

a. An *introduction* to the myth of the labyrinth which, arising from its universal symbolism, as a rite of passage, as a healing inner journey, can suggest, even to contemporary man, new inspiration and points of reference that go beyond the threshold of the limited and illusory knowledge of conventional science and paradigms.
b. An *experiential workshop* whose aim is to offer the opportunity to experience the creative and transformative dynamic of the trial of the labyrinth: an experience of self-exploration carried out using *holotropic breathwork* together with our therapeutic work methodology which also employs *transpersonal music therapy*, *humanistic psychodrama*, and *shamanism*.

We would add that the non-ordinary states of consciousness and the music that was used in the workshop are the result of our more than twenty years of research in the field of transpersonal psychology.

Moreover, the different phases of this inner journey are highlighted by four fundamental moments corresponding to the universal symbol of the *quadrant*, a metaphor for the land in synergy with the transpersonal model elaborated by Stan Grof,[12] based on our psycho physiological research on non-ordinary states of consciousness. The four phases that we have referred to are inspired by the *four matrices* of the holotropic model, demonstrating not only their scientific validity but also the possibility of further applications, which future studies can confirm.

The four phases can be summarized as follows:

Departure. Crossing the threshold; beginning the journey by emerging from the symbiotic unity and confronting life experiences and fantasies linked to the *first matrix* in a personal and archetypal way. This path is immersed in the mythological symbolism of the *Great Mother,* which not coincidentally is also the origin of the ancient myth of every matriarchal civilization and is reflected in the female figure of Ariadne, the *Lady of the Labyrinth.*[13]

Journey towards the Centre. Confronting the dynamic of descent into the depths of the subterranean world as a dimension of death or a realm of the underworld, experienced as imprisonment, can produce symptoms of fear, claustrophobia and impotence; or even just the fear of not being able to go back. This is precisely the dramatic challenge of imprisonment and the trap without escape of the *second matrix.*

Reaching the Centre. This phase, while it concerns the struggle with the Minotaur, achieves victory over the ego and signals the final conflict between death and rebirth. In accordance with Grof's *third matrix,* it simulates a titanic struggle, and, as it coincides with the final stage of birth, may cause the individual psyche to experience the most tempestuous and creative elements of nature (storms and huge battles, furious clashes and struggles between angelic and demonic entities, death and resurrection), as in the myths of Dionysus and Pluto.[14]

Return. This is demonstrated through the experience of birth, the creation of new forms of life and awareness through transcending habitual barriers (the body and the Ego). This is the experience of the *fourth matrix* marked by expulsion from the birth canal and the cutting of the umbilical cord. The return home is experienced differently by each individual. However, as is confirmed by the holographic model, even during the return, although one is aware of a real change of life and of new perspectives of existence, experiences and memories from the initial phases, both positive and disquieting, can weave together with them. This is the clearest proof that the transpersonal sources of existence intertwine with the personal story, which, as a consequence, can be fundamentally transformed.[15]

The *four phases* of the journey, which we illustrated with detailed documentation of experiments performed, concern the fundamental dynamics of the interior process of change during the journey through the labyrinth: an irreplaceable metaphor of the soul's rite of passage, as illustrated in so many poems of universal literature (the Odyssey, the Divine Comedy, etc.).

The entire path through the labyrinth is highlighted with the music of the four elements already heard during the self-exploration process of the *perinatal phase.* Our psycho-physiological studies on sound have demonstrated their effectiveness in re-awakening archetypal forces.[16] In this way the entire experience seeks to contribute not only to the development of human potential, but also to a broader conception of the

Planetary Consciousness in harmony with the actual moment of the planet's transition.[17]

On the psycho-physiological level there are numerous relationships that we have elaborated between the ancestral symbol of the labyrinth and the evolutionary development of man and consciousness. Already from observing *human embryology* and the incidence of the physiology of sound in all prenatal life one can observe that the progressive emergence of the psychic and biological identity in the embryo develops according to a "labyrinthic" experience.[18]

In fact, it is in the fetal development of the ear (the hearing organ which is completed only by the sixth month) together with the most primitive areas of the brain, such as the limbic system, that the acoustic sensations interface with the development of the fetus' image and its perception of its identity as an organism, although still not separate from the mother.[19]

This primitive phase is anterior to language, and any form of expression. However it encloses within its *protomental* awareness an immensely rich psychic content that has been identified throughout an infinite variety of Paleolithic and Neolithic cultures both in the universal symbolism of the four elements, and in the "spiral form".[20]

Thus, in this ancient labyrinthine form one perceives the diagram of the ear, just like the dance of life, and the rise of the serpent Kundalini up the tree of life and knowledge.

Our work explores the message of the labyrinth as a source of archetypal potentials developed in Greece and preserved in many other myths in order to demonstrate a comprehensive framework that bridges the gulf between conventional science and other health perspectives from the transpersonal point of view. Examining recent findings and models in light of this framework, my workshop - on which the chapter is based - also introduced a *new map* of personal life with which one can reliably plan one's future.

According to Grof's *holographic model*, using transpersonal music and not ordinary states of consciousness it is possible to restore the memory of these forgotten dimensions and to relive the cosmic experience of unity with the universal consciousness.[21]

Experiencing this voyage through the matrices, with the music of the four elements and holotropic breathwork, demonstrates that it is indeed possible to relive the most crucial phases of birth as traumatic memories and important events of prenatal existence. In so doing one can orient one's life in accordance with one's *trans-biographical* and *perinatal* level. As therapeutic experiences conducted with the music of the four elements and holotropic breathwork have shown, the transpersonal level is the most precious source of ancestral memories, both phylogenetic and collective, while all the personal mythology revealed in these experiences can effectively achieve the integration and healing of emotional wounds. From this perspective, our work with the labyrinth became a path towards transpersonal consciousness that included body, mind, spirituality and higher states of consciousness where spirituality, led to a universal dimension that is also a focus within our inner transcendent dimension. This dimension is part of *Spiritual Wisdom Philosophy* all over the world (Buddhism, Kabbalah, Christian, etc.), a perspective that Ken Wilber[22] defined as *Perennial Psychology* (1997), and *Integral Psychology* (1999), where many ancient contemplative traditions and all the spiritual dimensions of human existence join together. In this perspective, considering, moreover, that the brain is a hologram made up of all the possibilities of consciousness,[23] we have discovered within the brain's two hemispheres states of high inter-hemispheric synchronization[24] that correspond to deeper, more creative and more liberated levels of awareness. In particular, using our EEG research, our studies have identified regular recurrences of Alpha and Theta waves, well-known to correspond to states of intense quiet and the activation of the intuitive and mystic functions.[25]

Bibliography

[1] Jung, C. G., (1967). *Symbols of transformation.* Bollingen Series. Princeton, NJ: Princeton University Press.

[2] Campbell, J. (1949). *The hero with a thousand faces.* Bollingen Series. Novato, CA: New World Library.

[3] Reed, P. (1992). *The idea of the labyrinth: From classical antiquity through the Middle Ages.* Ithaca, NY: Cornell University Press.
and see Facchetti, G. M., & Negri, M. (2003). *Creta Minoica. Sulle tracce delle più antiche scritture d'Europa* [Minoan Creete. On the trail of the most ancient European writings]. Florence, Italy: Leo S. Olschki Editore.

[4] Jeanmaire, H. (1951). *Dionysos: Histoire du culte de Bacchus* [Dionysus: History of the cult of Bacchus]. Paris, France: Payot.

and see Kerenyi, K. (1976). *Dionysos: Archetypal image of indestructible life*. Princeton, NJ: Princeton University Press.
[5] Lapatin, K. (2002). *Mysteries of the snake goddess: Art, desire, and the forging of history*. New York, NY: Houghton Mifflin Company.
[6] Graves, R. (1992). *The Greek myths*. Books on Tape, Inc. New York, NY: Penguin.
[7] Guenon, R. (2010). *Symboles de la science sacree* [Symbols of the sacred science]. Paris, France: Gallimard.
[8] See Note 7.
[9] Hancock, G. (1995. *Fingerprints of the Gods: The evidence of earth's lost civilization*. New York, NY: Three Rivers Press.
[10] See Note 7.
[11] Fulcanelli, C. (1960). *Les demeures philosophales, nouvelle et augmentee*. [The philosophical remains, new and enhanced] Paris, France: Omnium litteraire.
[12] Grof, S. (1985). *Beyond the brain: Birth, death and transcendence in psychotherapy*. Albany, NY: State University of New York Press.
and see Grof S. (1988). *Human survival and consciousness evolution*. Albany, NY: State University of New York Press.
[13] Colli G. (Ed.). (1975). *La nascita della filosofia* [Birth of philosophy]. Milano, Italy: Adelphi.
[14] Kerenyi, K. (1976). *Dionysos: Archetypal image of indestructible life*. Princeton, NJ: Princeton University Press.
[15] De Luca, A. (Ed.). (1996). *Musica transpersonale* [Transpersonal music] . Milano, Italy : Xenia.
[16] De Luca, A. (Ed.). (1995a). *La psicologia transpersonale.* [Transpersonal psychology. An extended consciousness]. Milano, Italy: Xenia.
and see De Luca, A. (Ed.). (1995b). *Rebirthing. La terapia della rinascita* [Rebirthing. The rebirth therapy]. Milano, Italy: Xenia.
[17] Capra, F. (1975). *The Tao of physics*. Boston, MA: Shambhala Publications, Inc.
[18] De Luca, A. (1995a). *Rebirthing: La terapia della rinascita* [Rebirthing. The rebirth therapy]. Milano, Italy: Xenia.
[19] Benenzon, O. (2008). *Teoria de la musicoterapia* [Theory of music therapy]. Madrid, Spain: Mandala ediciones.
and see Tomatis, A. (1981). *La nuit uterine* [The uterine night]. Paris, France: Stock.
[20] Neumann, E. (1949). *The origins and history of consciousness*. Princeton, NJ: Princeton University Press.
and see Gimbutas, M. (Ed.). (2008). *Il linguaggio della Dea* [The Goddess' language]. Roma, Italy: Venexia.
[21] Grof, S. (1985). *Beyond the brain: Birth, death and transcendence in psychotherapy:* Albany, NY: State University of New York Press.
and see Grof, S., with Livingston Valier (Eds.). (1988). *Human survival and consciousness evolution.* Albany, NY: State University of New York Press.
[22] Wilber, K. (2000). *Integral psychology: Consciousness, spirit, psychology, therapy*. Boston, MA: Shambhala Publications, Inc.

and see Wilber, K. (2007). *The integral vision.* Boston, MA: Shambhala Publications, Inc.
[23] Pribram, K. (1971). *Languages of the brain: Experimental paradoxes and principles in neuropsychology*, Englewood Cliffs, NJ: Prentice-Hall.
and see Pribram, K. (1991). *Brain and perception: Holonomy and structure in figural processing,* Hillsdale, NJ: Lawrence Erlbaum Associates, Inc.
and see Bohm, D. (1980). *Wholeness and the implicate order*. London, England: Routledge Classics.
[24] De Luca, A. (Ed.). (2000). *States of high inter-hemispheric synchronization and transpersonal experience.* Roma, Italy: Dedalus.
[25] De Luca, A. (Ed.). (2010). *States of high inter-hemispheric synchronization and transpersonal experience* (2nd ed.). Roma, Italy: Dedalus.

PART III:

TRANSPERSONAL THERAPEUTIC APPROACHES AND EMBODIMENT (AND HEALING) DIMENSIONS

CHAPTER EIGHT

TRANSPERSONAL DIMENSIONS OF EMBODIMENT: EXPANDING OUR REALM OF CONSCIOUSNESS AND OUR THERAPEUTIC APPROACH

SIEGMAR GERKEN

Abstract

This chapter explores somatic aspects of transpersonal experiences and possible criteria for their subjective or objective validation. The chapter also explores the open question of how objective phenomena can become subjective events by translating neurological responses into an experience of embodiment, shaping body images, the development of mind, and the consciousness of the personality on the organismic as well as on the personal and transpersonal levels. The author proposes the use of the term *body-field* in taking the dense and more subtle levels of physical existence and its research into account, to address the unity of energy and consciousness to be acknowledged in a clinical and scientifically accepted, therapeutic approach.

Keywords: body fields, developmental, embodiment, psychology, neuroscience, love

Bridging the experience and knowledge of transpersonal dimensions with our material physical existence and its developmental unfolding of life, is a larger task than a short chapter can undertake. As an integrative, body-oriented Transpersonal Therapist, I explore how we can expand our therapeutic approach by taking somatic aspects of transpersonal experiences into account, since the transpersonal is always related to a person and a person always has a body-field.[1]

The biological evolution transcends itself in the meaning we give our search for love, truth and beauty.
Sir John C. Eccles (Nobel Laureate of Medicine)[i]

I would like to begin with a short description of a therapy session that I had with a manager who came to my office, overwhelmed by the preparations for his next teaching tour, which included a keynote for a larger congress at a university. Besides the overall stress and pressure he felt, he reported physical tension on the front and back right side of his body and around his lower neck. He shared that he felt good about his life in general. He liked what he was doing, and overall, felt supported by his partner and family.

He felt so much stress building up, that he was not able to alleviate it with yoga, meditation or other techniques. After further intake of information and touching into some emotional topics of his personal life, I first decided to invite him to do some gentle but still dynamic relaxation exercises on the structural, muscular level. I directed him to do some stretching and moving his upper torso and to make oceanic, wavelike movements with his spine. This led to a natural deepening of his breathing.

During the exercises he reported a shift of tension in the area of his solar plexus. To support him in the deepening of his relaxation, I asked him to lie down on a mattress. I guided him into further breathing exercises that helped him relieve the tension in the solar plexus. This was followed by a sense of peace flowing through his body. After some moments of silent presence and breathing, he mentioned how much he cherished this experience of a quieter inner space. At the same time, he became aware of some underlying frustration and anger, which made it difficult for him to sustain this state of flow. While he reiterated the stress that he was presently experiencing in his life, a wave of sadness emerged and expressed itself as deep crying. Images came up of the time when he was about 6 years old. It had been a difficult, emotional time for him, in which he had to leave the protection of his parental home and enter school. It was

---

[i] Quote retrieved Nov 11, 2016 from http://www.coreEvolution.com

When I refer to the body I always address the body-field—the psychosomatic unity of a human being; from its denser physical structure like bones (measured in bone-density by dual x-ray absorption), to brain waves (measured with EEG) or to its even more subtle phenomena like Bio-photon emissions (measured with a photon multiplayer in the UV range).

also the first time in his life where he felt stressed since his parents' expectations were high for him to excel at school. Later in the same year he also almost drowned in a pool and had to be resuscitated in a clinic.

He described phases that we know very well from descriptions of near death experiences (NDE); the tunnel of light and a deep surrender to a larger existence. While he was being resuscitated, though still unconscious, he described how he saw his parents caring for him in their own way. Simultaneously, he also realized that they were not able to meet him on all levels of his being–and, although he sensed the loss, in that moment he could make peace with it.

While he was in this state of deep relaxation, we took some time to explore his childhood experiences. Since we were already 40 to 45 minutes into the session, I wanted to lead it to a more emotional, physical and conceptual integration and completion. It was then that he sensed a second wave of deep sorrow emerging that was beyond any personal or biographical story–his longing for the oneness with all existence.

I gave him space to have a second wave of tears, waited until his breathing harmonized and his body fully relaxed again. When he opened his eyes and sat up, he looked at me with a grounded expression of presence, a genuine smile, good muscle tone and a clear voice. He had allowed himself to go beyond the ordinary reality of everyday life and of his personal biography. He had reconnected with a known and desired state of oneness that, over time, he had had lost contact with.

In general we would call this a "peak-experience" or transpersonal opening.[2] For me, it is the reconnection with the experience of a unity we all know, either consciously or unconsciously; a state of oneness that opens us to the extraordinary perception of all existence.

On the therapeutic level, I recognized that no therapeutic approach or modality can lead to an expanded healing or integration without recognizing and consciously addressing these expanded levels of existence--which brings me to the question: *How can I facilitate and hold this space of experience for the client? How can I support a client's inquiry into the conscious unfolding of their life? How can I recognize their process?*

Abraham Maslow formulated criteria as values for these expanded processes of self-development including: truth, goodness, friendliness and hardiness, beauty, wholeness, aliveness, uniqueness, completeness, completion and fulfillment, order, simplicity, fullness, effortlessness, cheerfulness and playfulness, and independent experience.[3]

Besides "order," I could not find any of these terms in the Oxford Dictionary of Psychology.[4] This seems to indicate that these criteria are not really taken into consideration in general psychology and, thereby, do not exist as values. Therefore, we cannot find a concept or theoretical basis to address the unity of energy and consciousness nor include these dimensions then into a clinically or scientifically accepted therapeutic approach.

Contemporary developmental psychology and affective neuroscience give us tremendous advancements in the observation and description of the developmental stages of a child, by describing the interaction with the parents or caretaker, family, and the living environment, as the basis of the forming self.[5, ii] However, we are still not able to describe the *inner awakening* of the child with each of these developmental stages.[iii, 6] When I interview clients or group members about their own remembrance of these inner awakenings,[iv, 7] their descriptions of somatic and emotional experiences are often related to a state of flow, and a sense of unity between the intra-personal, personal, inter-personal and trans-personal levels of experience. They also refer to it as being in a state of inter-connectedness, or love, in a non-romantic way.[v, 8]

[ii] In the last two decades there has been a wealth of research and books published on this topic. I refer here to some of the basic texts in endnote 5.

[iii] Daniel Stern opened the psychological mind towards an acceptance that a newborn comes with an internal knowledge into life, and is already able to initiate communication. Stern's ground-breaking observations and conclusions about this interdependency inspired further research on mother-child interactions. See endnote 6.

[iv] On a different note, the educator and transpersonal psychologist, T. Armstrong, describes the inner knowing and development of a child from a transpersonal aspect. See endnote 7.

[v] Gerken, S. Unpublished notes from ongoing interviews with workshop participants: In some workshops, I guide participants with mindful exercises into a state of relaxation. I ask them to scan through their life and connect with states of being that they have experienced as a state of love. Participants are later asked to describe this state in terms of physical phenomena and emotional feelings. Repeatedly, the answers are: heart-wide open, colorful light, feeling whole, flowing with the energy, happiness, being at ease, connectedness, warm streaming

Love is always a difficult subject for a scientific study since it seems to be elusive and difficult to measure. Although everyone acknowledges the existence of love, definitions of love are often culturally colored and difficult to understand. From my own experience and from the empirical research of the statements of clients, I propose the basic axiom: *Love is the state of resonance with the free flow of life energy in us.* In most psychological textbooks, I also do not find the child's state of love or flow recognized. The focus seems to be on defining abnormal behavior, deficits or the reasons for conflicts. Often, after I have worked with a client on moments of early neglect, mistreatments or other personal difficulties, I encounter another moment of pain. That is the pain of the rejection of the child's early love for the parent and consequently, the corresponding rejection for its own 'being' in this life.

To a certain degree we find these questions now addressed in Developmental Psychology and affective neuroscience, with the revived research on attachment styles, bonding patterns and affect attunement.[9] Not having this flow of life energy received and affirmed can lead to fear and despair. It can be perceived as an existential threat, since the inner impulse and natural stream of expression towards the realization of making contact is not really supported. This can then lead[vi, 10] to a protective withdrawal and reduction of this inner pulsation–or to the denial of it.[11]

Looking at our biological foundations, we understand that life expresses itself in pulsation and leads, on the human dimension, to embodiment. We first see this in the movement of dividing cells. They form organs in a growing organism, and this unfolding process finds its representation in a unity of body, emotions, feelings, cognition and, ultimately, to the development of the mind.[vii, 12, 13, 14]

---

and similar expressions. Most comments relate to a physical perception of an energy flow, pleasurable sense information or emotional states of lightness. There is also the feeling of openness, and forgiveness, or images of brightness, vivid colors, joyful and deeply meaningful experiences. See endnote 6.

[vi] Ed provides extensive research on the transfer of affects between mother and infant, and joint regulation of mother-infant interaction in his book. See endnote 7.

[vii] As well as any other book on embryology. Maturana and Varela (1998) describe more specifically the development of the mind. See endnote 13.

Capra (1996) and Grossinger (1986) give a detailed account from the beginning pulsation of life to the development of the mind in relation to systems theory. See endnote 14.

During different stages of this development in our continued embodiment, we form body images and neurological responses that consequently lead to a sense of self and with that, to an individuated consciousness–the consciousness of the personality. For the therapeutic context, I work with the definition that: *consciousness is the ground of experience that comes into existence when we become aware and experience that we are aware.*[viii, 15]

At about the seventh week of our gestation, we can observe that the movements are still spontaneous impulses and contractions. As development continues, the neuronal fibers from the brain and the spinal cord connect with muscle cells. That means, now muscles can contract by activation of nerve cells and vice-versa. The muscles can send information to the brain via the nerve fibers. I am addressing here the neuromuscular junction, in which the neurotransmitter Acetylcholine, induces the contraction. Here we find the first interconnection of motoric and sensory pathways; first in the spinal marrow and fluid, and later, also stabilized in the neuronal circuits.[16]

From the beginning of our early formation, learning in the brain takes place by using and practicing specific body functions. This forms inner patterns of experiences in constant relation to the further developing outer surface of the body. We call these patterns *representations*, which, on this level, are still unconscious processes. The neuroscientist Antonio Damasio called it the proto-self, a temporary coherent collection of neuronal patterns, resulting from the unconscious flow of information.[17] In the brain of the unborn child however, this process creates a complex inner picture of the body and its processes. This implies that from now on, we can approach information in the personal system, either through the body, or from cognition, to address and influence the mind.

Experiencing embodiment, therefore, provides a ground for the foundation of one's own life experience and becomes the reference system for the evaluation of these experiences. Affective neuroscience describes the development of a social brain resulting from a complex function of reactions and interactions between the caregiver and child, and its further brain development.[18] However advanced neuroscience may be, and how

---

[viii] An annual conference on Consciousness with numerous presentations ranging from Vedic philosophy to Artificial Intelligence is organized by S. Hameroff and D. Chalmers from the University of Arizona at different locations in the world; http://consciousness.arizona.edu - and endnote 15.

detailed the relation and correlation can be documented, the brain alone cannot think. The brain's role is to support and sustain a harmonious functional relationship among all body parts, and establishes a homeostasis, which is strongly influenced by physical, emotional, bodily experiences and its processes. Eric Kandel describes this in his textbook on *Principles of Neuroscience*:

> We as yet do not know how the firing of specific neurons leads to conscious perception even in the simplest cases. In fact, according to Searle, we completely lack an adequate theoretical model of how an *objective* phenomenon–electrical signal in a person's brain can cause a *subjective* experience such as pain. Because consciousness is irreducibly subjective, it lies beyond the reach of science as we *currently* practice it.[19]

In my experience, we live the duality of a spirited being in a material body. That means two developmental streams flow together to create a unity–the perpetuating, energetic, spirited principle that flows into the physical body, and the unfolding of the physical body that moves towards a spirited, larger existence.[ix, 20] The search for, and education of Tibetan Lamas is a very impressive example for this.[21]

Khalil Gibran formulated this insight:

> Your children are not your children.
> They are the sons and daughters of Life's longing for itself.
> They come through you but not from you,
> And though they are with you yet they belong not to you.
> You may give them your love but not your thoughts,
> For they have their own thoughts.
> You may house their bodies but not their souls…[22]

We know that both of these streams are necessary for this life, so that we can find a worldly existence and cultural connections. Without the cellular and conscious remembrance of this larger existence, we lose contact with these aspects in life. However, an integrated spirituality is always rooted in the consciousness of the body. This recognition is important for the therapeutic process, to prevent a state of uncontrolled dissociation and to be able to give conscious direction to life.

[ix] Armstrong (1985) addresses this topic throughout his book from the transpersonal view, including many interviews with children and parents. F. Capra (1996) describes this process based on the organismic level. See endnote 19.

Many seekers and scholars in the Western world have turned to Eastern teachings of Yoga, Buddhism, and Sufism or to Shamanic experiences to find a different framework for their embodied experiences of transpersonal dimensions.

As we can see, our fabric of life is woven by physical, social, psychological, and possibly many other energy patterns, conscious and unconscious intentions, and decision-making processes, as well as the relation we develop within these conditions.

Somatic Psychology and Trauma research describe that any chronic stress (biological, inter-relational, psychological or caused by society, environment, spiritual experiences and others) that cannot be successfully regulated and integrated in the body-field, can interfere with the free flow of energy in us. We find then, protective reactions like the control of breathing patterns. Muscles may move into hyper- or hypo-tension, which also influences circulation. Nerve endings can become stressed and sense-perception numbed or heightened, and other psychosomatic reactions. All these processes can become form-giving forces that will result in an emotional or mental attitude, which is then also mirrored in our body expression–and with that, in our expression of life. Form, then, literally influences behavior and vice versa.[x, 23]

In this process of forming our personality and under chronic stress, we may lose our subtle perception and, with that, the contact with our feeling of the larger existence. From our practice, we know that this can result in a sense of unfulfillment, emptiness, or even pushing a person toward a crisis. This is usually the moment when our clients contact us, as in the example of the manager mentioned in the case description at the beginning.

So, how can we change patterns of restrictions and limitations? We can actualize this by applying an integrative approach that is body-oriented and mindfulness-centered, which is able to facilitate an energetic and structural shift that can reach into all levels of the person's existence. This unifying experience of Being expands the perception of reality and leads the seeker as well as the researcher beyond the personal ego and its limited capacity to intellectually or scientifically formulate the experience. These integrative somatic and transpersonal dimensions add a special knowledge

---

[x] Many books in Somatic Psychology and Body-Oriented Psychotherapy describe this process. here are some of the fundamental titles. See endnote 23.

to the human experience.[xi, 24]

Karl Graf Dürkheim, a German philosopher, therapist and consciousness teacher asked over 60 years ago–what are the criteria that these moments are experiences of an expanded non-ordinary dimension?

From his observation he describes certain qualities that come into appearance:

1) The distinct quality of the experience caused by the open vibrational reality of life.
2) A special radiance, since s/he whom is touched by the experience of Being, develops another radiance. The development and projection of this special capacity of light can be cultivated.
3) The transformation–in experiencing the reality of the transpersonal nature of the world, the person rests in a deeper meaning of existence.
4) The birth of a new consciousness, which not only furthers liberation, but also understands itself as commitment.[25]

In the last decade researchers in Harvard, Stanford and other renowned institutions, became interested in documenting these expanded states of love, compassion, empathy and meditation. These are all topics that are difficult to be investigated, but neuroscience gives us new indicators.[26] By measuring brain frequencies, taking images with MRIs, or comparing heart rate-variability or other approaches, we can only document correlations–they do not really describe the complexity of this state, nor how feelings and experiences really come into existence. We need research that not only shows us correlations, which are based on a reductionist view, but research, which takes into account the larger complexities in the field of life.[xii, 27]

[xi] This is explained in detail in the training curriculum for Core Evolution and in the training handout: The Cycle of Life: www.CoreEvolution.com. See endnote 24.
[xii] For the last three decades I have been researching ways in which we can document the creation of images in our body-field. I began with medical Kirlian photography, EEA (Energy Emission Analysis). However, for the medical and psychotherapeutic documentation directly during a treatment, Kirlian photography as well as many other methods were not really practical. With the Infrared Photography and Analysis, that Dr. Schlebusch, MD, and I developed, we finally found a system with which we could continuously take pictures of the activity in the body-field during the treatment. In this way we could see immediate shifts in

Already 3,000 years ago, yoga became a well-documented discipline including multiple parameters of our human existence: the physical body, the inner experience and its formulation and, with that, the development of mind, subtle energy fields, the faculty of the will and its capacity to influence the state of mind. Yoga is possibly the first empirical research describing how energy impulses (which can also be thoughts), and how other energetic phenomena are manifested in the psyche and in the body. The developing capacity to structure thoughts allows us to reflect about ourselves and reorganize our field of experience.[28]

It is interesting how close Patanjali, the founder of the Yoga Sutras, describes the same principles of measurements that we, today, try to achieve with biofeedback, brainwave measurement and MRIs. He describes that thought waves contain emotions, memory, intuition, imagination, and conscious and unconscious impulses. Therefore, he states in the second Yoga Sutra: "*We need to practice the conscious direction of thought waves in the mind.*" [29]

This calls for a reflection about our own work: *What do we really want to achieve with our therapeutic work? How is Energy and Consciousness structured?* And: *How does Energy and Consciousness manifest in life, in general, and in the individual manifestation, specifically?*

Gautama Buddha formulated that self-realization needs the development of the qualities of the heart, which allow goodness, compassion, tolerance, empathy and wisdom. He formulated his teachings in the Four Noble Truths, The Five Aggregates and the Eightfold Path. With his detailed account about the interactions of these levels of human existence, Buddha already described principles of quantum physics and quantum biology. When we deeply inquire into the more subtle levels of our existence, nothing remains that we can still call the I, Self or Atman. The Self, or the I, is only a combination of constant changing, physical forces of energy. They interact on all levels in a momentary flow and are based on the law of cause and effect. That suggests that nothing in our existence is absolute;

---

the thermic profile according to the reaction of a client to the intervention.
Our groundbreaking documentations motivated leading international researchers to come together at the International Institute of Biophysics in Neuss, Germany under the leadership of Prof. F. Popp to share their knowledge and to elaborate on the question: How are images held in the human system? How do we attract or create them? And: What influence do they have on our state of consciousness and health? See endnote 27.

not the body, or the self, or the soul.[30]

This is one of the most threatening and, at the same time, liberating expressions for the therapeutic process, since trying to hold on to a status quo is based on an illusion and self-deception.[xiii, 31] It is liberating, in that change and opening can take place at any moment.

When Eastern philosophers, researchers and practitioners described our human experience, they, in general, did not address the social and parental influences, and with that, an individuated description of the development of the body and psyche of a person, including the topic of sexuality. Most teachers also underestimate the energy that can be held in a structural and muscular system of the body, which can resist the intentions of the mind. Yoga recognized this difficulty, and developed the Asanas to align the body and direct the mind.

The research of Wilhelm Reich opened new dimensions for medicine, psychology, therapy and social interaction. It explored the nature of the interaction of psyche and soma. Thus, the unconscious or resistance to experience the flow of life, was no longer abstract, but found its physiological understanding.[32] His further research on impulse formation has also been fundamental, since as long as we have a body, thought waves can connect with the pulsating, biological energy.[33]

In a time when we try to overcome the separation of matter and spirit, it still seems limiting that psychological and medical models are overly focused and based on the material reality like brain reactions, neurological reflexes, biochemical conditions and others. We have a wealth of research and descriptions for conditions that we call transpersonal states of our embodiment, which indicate expanded states of our reality. Research and documentations on dissipative structures,[34] morphogenetic fields,[35] quantum physics and quantum biology, photon emissions[36] as well as my own research in the field of subtle energetic dynamics during the therapeutic processes with infrared analysis, and other methods,[xiv, 37] open

---

[xiii] N. Doidge (2007) collected fascinating case studies and documented further research and the direct applications of neuroplasticity. Eric Kandel received the Nobel prize in Physiology or Medicine in 2000 for his work on Neuroplasticity. See endnote 31.

[xiv] I presented a lecture on my Biophoton Emission research and the state of coherence in a human system and how this state of coherence can be influenced by consciousness. These insights can be utilized for the therapeutic setting, since resilience and the ongoing process of integration requires a self-creation of a

our horizon about transpersonal states of embodiment. This encourages us to expand these parameters of the description of our experience, knowledge, and competence, into an integrative, experiential, and mindfulness-centered, transpersonal psychology.

Bibliography

[1] (a) Becker, R. O. M.D., & Selden, G. (1985). *The body electric: Electromagnetism and the foundation of life*. New York, NY: William Morrow, pp. 79-117.
(b) Nuneza, P. L., & Srinivasanb, R. (2006). A theoretical basis for standing and traveling brain waves measured with human EEG with implications for an integrated consciousness. *Clinical Neurophysiology, 117*(11), 2424–2435.
(c) Peacock, M., Buckwalter, K. A., Persohn, S., Hangartner, T. N., Econs, M. J., & Hui, S. (2009, August). Race and sex differences in bone mineral density and geometry at the femur. *Bone, 45*(2), 218-225.
[2] (a) Maslow A.H. (1971). *The farther reaches of human nature*. Harmondsworth: Middlesex, England: Penguin Books, pp. 128-129; 162-172 .
(b) Vrinte, J. (1995). *The concept of personality in Sri Aurobindo's integral yoga psychology and A. Maslow's humanistic/transpersonal psychology*. New Delhi, India: Munshiram Manoharlal Publishers, pp. 93-98.
[3] Maslow A.H. (1971). *The farther reaches of human nature*. Harmondsworth, Middlesex, England: Penguin Books, pp. 128-129.
[4] Colman, A. M. (2003). *Oxford dictionary of psychology*. Oxford, England: Oxford University Press.
[5] (a) Cozolino, L. (2006). *The neuroscience of human relationships: Attachment and the developing social brain*. New York, NY: W.W. Norton & Company.
(b) Schore, A. N. (1994). *Affect regulation and the origin of the self: The neurobiology of emotional development*. Hillsdale, NJ: Lawrence Erlbaum Associates, Publishers.
(c) Siegel, D. (2001). *The developing mind: How relationships and the brain interact to shape who we are*. New York, NY: The Guilford Press.
[6] Stern, D. (1985). *The interpersonal world of the infant: A view from psychoanalysis & developmental psychology*. New York, NY: Basic Books.
[7] Armstrong, T. (1985). *The radiant child*. Wheaton, IN: The Theosophical Publishing, House.
[8] Csikszentmihalyi, M. (2008). *Flow: The psychology of optimal experience*. New York, NY: Harper Perennial Modern Classics.
[9] (a) Cassidy, J., & Shaver, P. R. (2008). *Handbook of attachment: Theory, research, and clinical applications*. New York, NY: The Guilford Press.
(b) Stern, D. (1985). *The interpersonal world of the infant: A view from psychoanalysis & developmental psychology*. New York, NY: Basic Books, pp. 37-123.
[10] Tronick, E. (2007). *The neurobehavioral and social-emotional development of*

---

coherent body-field. See endnote 37.

infants and children. New York, NY: W.W. Norton & Company, pp. 206-217; 402-411.

[11] Liedloff, J. (1977). *The continuum concept: In search of happiness lost.* Reading, MA: Perseus Books, pp. 29-75.

[12] Blechschmidt, E. (2004). *The ontogenetic basis of human anatomy: A biodynamic approach to development from conception to birth.* Berkeley, CA: North Atlantic Books, pp. 27-60.

[13] Maturana, Ph.D., H. R. & Varela, F. J. (1998). *The tree of knowledge: The biological roots of human understanding.* Boston, MA: Shambhala Publications, Inc., pp. 39-52, 231-235.

[14] (a) Capra, F. (1996). *The web of life: A new scientific understanding of living systems.* New York, NY: Anchor Books, pp. 24-29, 264-274.

(b) Grossinger, R. (1986). *Embryogenesis, from cosmos to creature: The origins of human biology.* Berkeley, CA: North Atlantic Books.

[15] Revonsuo, A. (2010). *Consciousness: The science of subjectivity.* New York, NY: Psychology Press, pp. 70-73).

[16] (a) Crossman, A. R., & Neary, D. (2000). *Neuroanatomy: An illustrated colour text.* Edinburgh, Scotland: Churchill Livingstone, pp. 37-39.

(b) Rohen, J. W., & Lütjen-Drecol, E. (2006). *Funktionelle Embryologie: Die Entwicklung der Funktionssysteme des menschlichen Organismus* [Functional embryology: The development of the functional systems of the human organism]. Stuttgart, Germany: Schattauer, pp. 138-142.

[17] Damasio, A. (1999). *The feeling of what happens: Body and emotion in the making of consciousness.* San Diego, CA: Harcourt, Inc., pp. 168-179.

[18] Cozolino, L., (2006). *The neuroscience of human relationships: Attachment and the developing social brain.* New York, NY: W.W. Norton & Company, pp. 37-78.

[19] Kandel, E. R., Schwartz, J. H., & Jessell, T. M. (2000). *Principles of neural science.* New York, NY: McGraw-Hill, p. 397.

[20] (a) Armstrong, T. (1985). *The radiant child.* Wheaton, IN: The Theosophical Publishing, House, pp. 47-65.

(b) Capra, F. (1996). *The web of life: A new scientific understanding of living systems.* New York, NY: Anchor Books, pp. 157-176).

[21] (a) Golzio, K., & Bandini, P. (1997). *Die vierzehn wiedergeburten des Dalai Lama* [The 14th rebirth of the Dalai Lama]. München, Germany: O. W. Barth.

(b) Mackenzie, V. (1988). *The boy lama.* San Francisco, CA: Harper & Row, Publishers.

[22] Gibran, K. (1951). *The prophet.* New York, NY: Alfred A. Knopf, p. 10.

[23] (a) Aposhyan, S. (2004). *Body-mind psychotherapy: Principles, techniques, and practical applications.* New York, NY: W. W. Norton & Company.

(b) Heller, M. (2012). *Body psychotherapy: History, concepts, and methods.* New York, NY: W. W. Norton & Company.

(c), a. (1980). *Bioenergetics: The revolutionary therapy that uses the language of the body to heal the problems of the mind.* New York, NY: Penguin Books.

(d) Matlock, G., & Weiss, H. (2015). *The handbook of body psychotherapy and somatic psychology.* Berkeley, CA: North Atlantic Books.

[24] Gerken. S. (2008, September). *Training curriculum for Core Evolution: The*

cycle of life. Mendocino, CA: Core Evolution Publications.
[25] Dürckheim, K. G. (1994). *Vom doppelten Ursprung des Menschen* [Of the double origin of human kind] (pp. 99-111). Freiburg, Germany: Herder.
[26] (a) Center for Consciousness Studies, http://consciousness.arizona.edu.
(b) Greater Good, http://greatergood.berkeley.edu.
(c) Harvard University, http://evp.harvard.edu/mindfulness.
(d) Open Sciences, http://opensciences.org/universities-consciousness-studies University of California, Berkeley.
(e) Stanford Center for Compassion and Altruism, http://ccare.stanford.edu. Mind & Life Institute, https://www.mindandlife.org.
[27] Gerken, S., & Schlebusch, K. P. (2009). Die psychosomatische Einheit des Menschen - Eine Fallstudie [The psychosomatic unity of humankind - A case study]. *Der Freie Arzt* [*The Independent Medical Doctor*], *50*(4), 8.
[28] Rama, S., Ballentine M.D., R., & Ajaya, Ph.D., S. (1998). *Yoga and psychotherapy: The evolution of consciousness*. Honesdale, PA: The Himalayan Institute.
[29] Dass, B. H. (1999). *The yoga sutras of Patañjali*. Santa Cruz, CA: Sri Rama Publishing, pp. 5-7.
[30] Lubovsky, MD, S. (1997). *Mind-body deceptions: The psychosomatics of everyday life* (pp. 89-358). New York, NY: W.W. Norton & Company.
[31] (a) Doidge, N. (2007). *The brain that changes itself: Stories of personal triumph from the frontiers of brain science*. New York, NY: Penguin Books.
(b) Kandel, E. R. (2006) *In search of memory: The emergence of a new science of mind* (pp. 198-207). New York, NY: W.W. Norton & Company.
[32] Reich, W. (1973). *The function of the orgasm: Volume 1 of the discovery of the orgone* (pp. 268-272). New York, NY: The Noonday Press.
[33] Reich, W. (1973). *The function of the orgasm: Volume 1 of the discovery of the orgone* (pp. 286-298). New York, NY: The Noonday Press.
[34] Prigogine, I., & Stengers, I. (1984). *Order out of chaos: A man's new dialogue with nature*. New York: NY: Bantam Books.
[35] Sheldrake, R. (1981). *A new science of life: The hypothesis of formative causation*. Los Angeles, CA: J.P. Tarcher, Inc.
[36] (a) Bischof, M. (1995). *Biophtonen: Das Licht in unseren Zellen* [Biophotons: The light in our cells]. Frankurt, Germany: Zweitausendeins.
(b) Popp, F. A. (1984). *Biologie des Lichts: Grundlagen der ultraschwachen Zellstrahlung* [The biology of light: Foundations of ultra-subtle cell radiation] (pp. 100-133). Berlin, Germany: Paul Parey.
[37] Gerken, S. (2013, April). *Embodiment, personal development and the power of love mindfulness and the psychosomatic dimensions of the body-feeling-brain-mind-matrix*. Presented at Æsculap - Norwegian Medical Association meeting, Oslo, Norway.

CHAPTER NINE

MYSTERIES OF THE UNIVERSE AND TRANSPERSONAL PSYCHOTHERAPY

ZANA MAROVIC

Abstract

This chapter describes the contrast between simplicity, consumerism and the profit-driven modus operandi of the mental health industry and the fact that what we are working with – the human mind and psyche – remains mysterious and elusive with many questions unanswered. I first tackle the foundation of the mental health industry: the reductionist context of the *Diagnostic and Statistical Manual of Mental* Disorders,[1] the bio-medical model and pharmaceutical supremacy. Then I introduce transpersonal vision and review some of the unsolved and mysterious realities. In closing, I share a few thoughts on moving forward and conclude that in spite of extraordinary advances in scientific knowledge, much remains to be learned and discovered.

Keywords: consciousness, DSM-5, medicalisation, mind-body dualism, pharmaceutical industry, transpersonal psychology

In our work, we often encounter not-so-mysterious realities pertaining to medicalisation and the influence of pharmaceutical companies. We live in a consumer society that opts for a quick fix: it is no surprise that the use of anti-depressants in the USA increased by 400% during the last two decades.[2]

We face a paradoxical situation: global polls show an increase in religiousness, but psychotherapists exhibit reluctance in addressing religious and spiritual aspects and report lack of training in transpersonal aspects. For transpersonal therapists increased vulnerability to feeling displaced and isolated is the outcome of practising within the field that others seem to avoid.

One of the most important aspects of humanity and advancement is our ability to remain curious, to utilise our imagination and to probe the mysteries of life. In spite of the fact that science has made remarkable technological advances, the human body and mind remain an unsolved mystery and some controversial topics persist:

- What is consciousness and what is the relationship between consciousness and the brain?
- Gas Discharge Visualization, which I will touch upon, is a recent technologically advanced technique that yields fascinating results.
- Sleep has vast relevance for every being on earth yet there is no universal understanding of its meaning.
- Timing is present in everything we do but it remains elusive.
- Is everything interconnected as quantum physics postulates?
- Is it possible that our moods and society's transformation are connected to cosmic events?
- Are time and space travel just science fiction?

In conclusion, moving forward requires unorthodox thinking, openness to the mystery of healing, embracing the wholeness and nurturing the inner child.

Not so Mysterious Universe

Working in the health care field makes us aware of the medical and pharmaceutical reductionist approach that we health workers operate in and are limited by:

Diagnostic and Statistical Manual of Mental Disorders (DSM)

The DSM is published by the American Psychiatric Association (APA) and it is considered the most relevant authority on the diagnosis and classification of mental disorders.[3] There are numerous studies criticising and discussing the pitfalls of the DSM system, from creating public-stigma and self-stigma,[4] to dehumanisation which shrinks rather than expands opportunities for freedom, growth and dignity,[5] to the lack of clear boundaries between medical and mental health disorders[6] and finally, failure to distinguish between disorders and no-disorders.[7] A considerable controversy has arisen following the latest revised version, DSM-5, from academic articles and a public outcry to members of DSM-5 Work Groups publicly voicing doubts about DSM-5,[8,9] as well as protests from mental health professionals and organisations.[10]

Diagnosing

We use diagnostic labels daily but how useful are they? Many academics and clinicians argue that psychiatric labels serve only the interests of clinicians and their professional associations, such as the APA or the pharmaceutical industry.[11] Others point out that psychiatric labels may have devastating effects[12] and may eventually result in reduced expectations and ambitions from the person receiving diagnosis as well as from people close to the one receiving diagnosis.[13]

Medicalisation

We are faced with the daily realities of health insurance, which promotes medical over psychological treatment, dictates the type of therapy we are "allowed" to undertake and limits the number of mental health treatments. The predominant approach in medicine remains chemical treatment that emphasises biological disease, neglecting the mental, emotional, behavioural and social determinants of health.[14] Medicalisation of society comes from three driving forces: the pharmaceutical industry, consumerism and managed care.[15] Maturo[16] argues that managed care is a type of medicalisation that legitimates a treatment based on pills rather than psychotherapy, eventually leading to social problems becoming medical ones.

Pharmaceuticals

We are observing an alarming increase in drug use. Pharmaceutical companies are gaining power by selling sickness[17] whereby a lot of money is made from healthy people who believe that they are sick. Moynihan, Heath, & Henry[18] argue that pharmaceutical companies are sponsoring diseases, using the media to frame conditions as being widespread and severe and treating personal problems as medical problems to maximise potential profits. They claim that pharmaceuticals might be the driving force behind the significant increase in certain diagnoses and the use of multiple drugs. For example, diagnosing of attention deficit hyperactivity disorder increased by 66% over the past ten years.[19] The USA consumed 90% of the world's supply of Ritalin, which has been a signature pharmaceutical treatment for attention deficit hyperactivity disorder.[20] Pharmaceutical companies have stepped up their advertising efforts around the world, marketing directly to physicians and, when possible, to consumers. Conrad & Bergey[21] conclude that there is a growing influence and spread of the Americanised style of psychiatry, especially child-psychiatry that, according to them, favours biological approaches and treats psychological problems with drugs.

Transpersonal Inadequacy

In addition to dealing with widespread medicalisation and the minimisation of psychological aspects of mental health, we also face the fact that our own profession shows little interest in spiritual aspects of health, which we, as transpersonal therapists, value highly. A survey in 1991 of Psychology Internship Centers[22] reported that 83% of training directors described discussions of religious and spiritual issues in training occurring rarely or never while 100 % indicated they had received no education or training in religious or spiritual issues during their formal internship. Little change was noted a decade ago. Miller & Thoresen[23] reported that 90 % of psychologists were not discussing spiritual or religious aspects in their training. Even though number of coursework in spirituality and religion increased in the last years, still only a quarter of psychology training programs provide even one course in religion or spirituality.[24] Thus, transpersonal therapists practising within the field that others seem to avoid become vulnerable to feeling displaced and isolated.

Mysterious Universe Indeed

As we move away from medicalisation and a reductionist way of dealing with life let us look at some of the mysteries that remain unsolved in spite of advances in technology and our increased ability to research more complex and mysterious aspects of the human body and its energy.

Human Consciousness

Historically, mental health professionals treated disorders of human consciousness as biological phenomena.[25] Eaton[26] argued that consciousness cannot be treated as a product of the brain in the way that bile is seen as a product of liver or urine as a product of kidneys. The fact that science has been examining such intricate phenomena, employing reductionist methods and a restrictive focus, may explain why we still have such limited understanding of consciousness. We yet have to understand why we have feelings and awareness and how pieces and parts of the brain are connected in a way that creates private subjective experiences that you and I take for granted. Some of the questions we still cannot answer are: How early does consciousness enter the body? Where is consciousness located, and is the brain the location of consciousness? If consciousness is not only located in the brain, is it everywhere? When consciousness is gone, where does it go?

Some of the advanced technologies are providing fascinating data that are challenging our understanding of consciousness. For example, the Gas Discharge Visualization, or GDV, technique capturing electromagnetic fields[27] invented by Dr Konstantin Korotkov, was used to capture the energy of dying people. The study found that the bioenergy of people who suffer a violent and unexpected death often returns to the body in the days following death. Today, the GDV technique is being used in predictive medicine for monitoring the progress of patients treated for cancer. A fascinating study using GDV techniques measured the bioenergetics exchange between humans and found significant changes related to the intention and emotion of the sender.[28]

Another fascinating research project undertaken by a team of neuroscientists[29] deals with the presence of consciousness in braindead patients. This published study points to the ability of patients in coma to engage in mental imagery in response to simple auditory instructions. The results demonstrate the remarkable capacity of braindead patients for higher cognition, engaging in the reasoning task and deducing logical answers, hence a real indication that consciousness is not located in the brain.

Time

Timing is critical to almost every behaviour we engage in, but how time is represented in the brain is still a mystery. Eagleman, Tse, Buonomano, Janssen, Nobre, & Holcomb[30] argue that the brain exploits knowledge of elapsed time to anticipate sensory events and to prepare appropriate actions. Our auditory system processes information about 30 milliseconds faster than our visual system, while our brain employs "editing" tricks to make events feel simultaneous even when there is a different timing in processing the information. This makes us contemplate the question of whether the smooth passage of time is just one of the brain's constructions.

Sleep

One of the most astonishing facts of our lives is that we spend a third of our time sleeping yet we have little understanding of why we sleep. Newborn babies spend about twice as much time just sleeping as do adults. In humans, continuous wakefulness results in mental derangement while research on rats shows that eleven to thirty-two days of wakefulness leads to imminent death.[31] The universality of sleep, even though it comes at the cost of time and leaves the sleeper relatively defenceless, suggests the enormous relevance of sleep, yet there is no universally agreed-upon answer to the meaning of sleep. In spite of such relevance, sleep research only emerged twenty-five years ago, and worldwide there are only about twenty laboratories dedicated to sleep research.[32]

Human Creation

The content of psychotherapy conversations is affected by our beliefs. A question about human creation has a major impact on how we view the world. Were humans created by God? Are we the product of evolution? Are our ancestors from another planet as some claim? Therapists' and clients' views of these questions may have a significant impact on how well suited they will be within the therapeutic space. Clients have preferences for a specific type of therapy relevant to their beliefs and attitudes, hence therapists need to be skilled in different types of treatment.[33] For example, a therapist who follows the strictly scientific view of human creation may not be open to discussing God or to offering past life regression therapy while the client may have an interest in these. Even though skills are relevant for therapeutic alliance, the therapist's capacity to remain open and fearless in exploring "the road less travelled" may potentially be the most helpful aspect of a good therapeutic alliance.

Quantum Physics, Solar Cycles and Human Consciousness

The recent paradigm shift brought about by quantum physics indicates that everything in the universe is interconnected and through this interconnectedness everything affects everything else. This takes us to a less researched area relating to how individual and social consciousnesses are affected by elements that might be a thousand light years away. An example is Tchievsky's research[34] on the influence of solar flares on human consciousness and transformation, which after examining the histories of 72 countries from 500 BCE to the present, found that 80% of the most significant human events occurred during a five-year peak in solar activity.

Time Travel

In 1935, physicists Albert Einstein[35] and Nathan Rosen used the theory of general relativity to propose the existence of "bridges" through space-time. These paths, called Einstein-Rosen bridges or wormholes, connect two different points in space-time, theoretically creating a shortcut that could reduce travel time and distance.[36] It was postulated that these tunnels would act like cosmic shortcuts or superhighways between the stars and the planets. In 2012 the National Aeronautics and Space Administration announced the discovery of a magnetic portal between the Earth and the Sun, a path leading from our own planet to the sun's atmosphere.[37]

The discovery of magnetic portals brings the science fiction of space and time travel much closer to reality than ever before. Envision the possibility that we are able to travel to other planets using these magnetic portals. How will such advancement affect healing? Imagine a future where therapeutic intervention may include a choice of space and time that you may suggest as most useful to your client's healing. Just imagine…

Moving Forward

Understanding our humanity and our connection to the cosmos and everything around us remains the biggest challenge and deepest mystery for modern science. Progress requires moving away from familiar and dualistic thinking while engaging in unorthodox thought and a holistic paradigm but keeping in mind that life remains a mystery.

Engaging in Unorthodox Thought

In going forward, we need to keep an open mind and be prepared to engage in unorthodox and alternative thinking. David Bohm's[38] reflection yields relevance:

> So the first thing we have to do, in the long run, is to look at our way of thinking…people have to participate, to make a cooperative effort, to have a dialogue, a real dialogue, in which we will not merely exchange opinions, but actually listen deeply to the views of other people, without resistance…I think science has begun to replace religion as the major source of the world view, and therefore, if science takes a fragmentary world view it will have a profound effect on consciousness…Science is whatever people make of it, science has changed over the ages and it is different now from a few hundred years ago, and it could be different again. There is no intrinsic reason why science must necessarily be about measurement. That is another historical development that has come about over the last few centuries. It is entirely contingent and not absolutely necessary.

Mystery Prevails

Healing is a journey into the unknown, a sacred and mysterious process that we may never be able to understand completely. Einstein's words resonate[39]:

> The fairest thing we can experience is—the mysterious. It is the fundamental emotion, which stands at the cradle of true art and true science. He who knows it not, and can no longer wander, no longer feel[s] amazement, is as good as dead, a snuffed-out candle. To sense that behind anything that can be experienced, there is a something, that our mind cannot grasp and whose beauty and sublimity reaches us only indirectly and as a feeble reflection—this is religiousness.

Wholeness

As we move beyond Cartesian dualism and the mind-body split dominating Western psychology[40] we advance towards the quantum paradigm that offers a profound and cutting-edge view of consciousness.[41] The quantum model of non-locality[42] and the emerging principle of holistic interconnectedness provide a new and meaningful paradigm for health and healing. As Bohm[43] says:

> Wholeness is an attitude or an approach, but can be given a scientific realization, because of relativity and quantum theory, we can if we wish look on the world as a whole.... Wholeness is not a place you can get to, wholeness is a kind of attitude or approach to the whole of life. It's a way.

Inner Child

We have discussed how a reductionist platform leads to limiting our understanding and knowledge of complex phenomena such as the human mind and body. Keeping up with forefront research in the field of consciousness requires us to get in touch with a part of us representing an inner child: curious, open to mystery and magic, the dark side, in touch with super powers, and connected to everything.

Coleridge's poem[44] "What if you slept" hints that mystery is what remains:

> What if you slept?
> And what if,
> In your sleep
> You dreamed.
> And what if,
> In your dream,
> You went to heaven
> And there plucked
> A strange and
> Beautiful flower.
> And what if,
> When you awoke,
> You had the flower in your hand.
> Ah, what then?

Bibliography

[1] Kawa, S., & Giordano, J. (2012). A brief historicity of the Diagnostic and Statistical Manual of Mental Disorders: Issues and implications for the future of psychiatric canon and practice. *Philosophy, Ethics, and Humanities in Medicine*, *7*(1), 1-9.
[2] Wehrein, P. (2011). Astounding increase in antidepressant use by Americans, *Harvard Health Publication.* Retrieved from www.health.harvard.edu

[3] Khoury, B., Langer, E.J., & Pagnini, F. (2014). The DSM: Mindful science or mindless power? A critical review. *Frontiers in Psychology,* 5, 602.
[4] Ben-Zeev, D., Young, M.A., & Corrigan, P.W. (2010). DSM-V and the stigma of mental illness. *Journal of Mental Health, 19*(4), 318-327.
[5] Gambill, E. (2014). *The* Diagnostic and Statistical Manual of Mental Disorders as a major form of dehumanization in the modern world. *Research on Social Work Practice, 24*(1), 13-36.
[6] Kress, V.E., Barrio Minton, C. A., Adamson Matthew, N.A., Paylo, J., & Pope, V. (2014). The removal of the multi-axial system in the *DSM-5*: Implications and practice suggestions for counselors. *The Professional Counselor, 4*(3), 191–201.
[7] Wakefield, J. C. (1992). Disorder as harmful dysfunction: A conceptual critique of *DSM-III-R*'s definition of mental disorder. *Psychological Review*, 99(2), 232-247.
[8] Frances, A. (2012). One last chance for the APA to make the DSM-5 safer. *Huffington Post.* Retrieved from http://www.huffingtonpost.com/allen-frances/one-last-chance-for-the-apa-to-make-the-dsm-5-safer_b_2294868.html
[9] Greenberg, G. (2013). *The book of woe: The DSM and the unmaking of psychiatry.* New York, NY: Blue Rider.
[10] See note 9.
[11] See note 9.
[12] Frances, A. (2013). *Saving normal: An insider's revolt against out-of-control psychiatric diagnosis, DSM-5, big pharma, and the medicalization of ordinary life,* New York, NY: William Morrow, p. 109.
[13] Smith, R. (2002). In search of "non-disease". *British Medical Journal, 324*, 883-885.
[14] Clark, J. (2014). Medicalization of global health 2: The medicalization of global mental health. *Global Health Action, 7*, 1-6.
[15] Conrad P. (2005). The shifting engines of medicalization. *Journal of Health and Social Behavior, 40*, 5-14.
[16] Maturo, A. (2012). Medicalization: Current concept and future directions in a bionic society. *Mens Sana Monographs, 10*(1), 122-133.
[17] Moynihan, R., Heath, I., & Henry D. (2002). Selling sickness: The pharmaceutical industry and disease mongering. *British Medical Journal, 324*, 886-891.
[18] See note 17.
[19] New data: Medication and behavior treatment. Center for Disease and Control Prevention. Retrieved from: http://www.cdc.gov/ncbddd/adhd/data.html
[20] Conrad, P., & Bergey, M. (2014). The impending globalization of ADHD: Notes on the expansion and growth of a medicalized disorder. *Social Science & Medicine, 122*, 31-43.
[21] See note 20.
[22] Lannert, J. (1991). Resistance and countertransference issues with spiritual and religious clients. *Journal of Humanistic Psychology, 31*(4), 68-76.
[23] Miller, W. R., & Thoresen, C. E. (2003). Spirituality, religion, and health. *American Psychologist, 58*, 24–35.

[24] Schafer, R. M., Handal, P. J., Brawer, P. A., & Ubinger, M. (2011). Training and education in religion/spirituality within APA-Accredited clinical psychology programs: 8 years later. *Journal of Religion and Health, 50*, 232–239.
[25] Searle, J.R. (1980). Minds, brains, and programs. *Behavioral and Brain Sciences, 3*, 417-457.
[26] Eaton, W. W. (2012). *Public mental health.* New York, NY: Oxford University Press, p.33.
[27] Owens J., & Van De Castle, R. (2004). Gas discharge visualization (GDV) technique. In K. Korotkov (Ed.), *Measuring energy fields state of the science* (pp.11-22). Fair Lawn, NJ: Backbone.
[28] McTaggart, L. (2007). *The intention experiment: Using your thoughts to change your life and the world.* New York, NY: Free Press, p. 46.
[29] Hampshire, A., Parkin, B., Cusack, R., Fernandez Espejo, D., Allanson, J., Kamau, E., … Owen, A.M. (2013). Assessing residual reasoning ability in overtly non-communicative patients using fMRI. *NeuroImage, Clinical Volume, 2*, 174-183.
[30] Eagleman, D.M., Tse, P.U., Buonomano, D., Janssen, P. Nobre, A.C., & Holcomb, A.O. (2005). Time and the brain: How subjective time relates to neural time. *The Journal of Neuroscience, 25*(45), 10369-10371.
[31] Everson, C. A., Bergmann, B.M., & Rechtschaffen, A. (1989). Sleep deprivation in the rat: III. Total sleep deprivation. *Sleep, 12*(1), 13-21.
[32] Steury, T. (2015). Why do we sleep? *Washington State University Magazine.* Retrieved from: http://researchnews.wsu.edu/health/78.html
[33] Wamplod, B. E., & Imel, Z.E. (2015). *The great psychotherapy debate: the evidence for what makes psychotherapy work.* New York, NY: Routledge, p. 274.
[34] Rosch, P. (2015*). Bio-electromagnetic and subtle energy medicine* (p. 416). Boca Raton, FL: CRC Press (Taylor & Francis Group).
[35] Einstein, A. (1996). *The world as I see it.* New York, NY: Citadel Press.
[36] Reed, N.T. (2015, April 13). What is a wormhole? Space.com. Retrieved from: http://www.space.com/20881-wormholes.html
[37] NASA (2012, July 2). Hidden portals in Earth's magnetic field. Retrieved from: https://www.nasa.gov/mission_pages/sunearth/news/mag-portals.html
[38] Bohm, D. (1990). Documentary. Retrieved from: *Art meets science & spirituality in a changing economy*: *https://www.youtube.com/watch?v=hfHzfonAgX4*
[39] Einstein, A. (1996). *The world as I see it* New York, NY: Citadel Press, p.7.
[40] Mehta, M. (2011). Mind-body dualism: A critique from a health perspective. *Mens Sana Monographs, 9*(1), 202-209.
[41] Richards, E. (2012). Complementarities in physics and psychology. In E. Miller (Ed), *The Oxford handbook of psychology and spirituality* (pp. 62-83). New York, NY: Oxford University Press.
[42] Bohm, D. (1980). *Wholeness and the implicate order.* London: Routledge Classics.
[43] Bohm, D. (1990). Documentary. Retrieved from: *Art meets science & spirituality in a changing economy:* https://www.youtube.com/watch?v=hfHzfonAgX4

[44] Coleridge, S. T. (1985). Biographia literaria. In H. J. Jackson (Ed.), *Samuel Taylor Coleridge* (The Oxford authors; pp. 155-482). (Original work published 1817)

CHAPTER TEN

MEMORIES OF THE FUTURE: A CRITICAL INVESTIGATION INTO PRECOGNITIVE DREAMS

PAUL KIRITSIS

Abstract

The objective of the present study was to determine the empirical validity of precognitive dreams and propose underlying mechanisms of action. A total of 15 subjects participated in this study; 5 were male and 10 were female. The median age for the experimental trials was 41. They were given a three-page document detailing an effective method of dream recall and requested to record dream fragments into a diary for four to five consecutive days upon awakening. The correlational quality between the dream fragments and the corresponding waking events, or the likelihood of a precognitive episode, was determined using a categorical scale with precise diagnostic valuations for very powerful correlations (excellent), powerful correlations (good), and some correlation (average). Of the 51 dreams transcribed, 45 were of the "personal" variety and 6 of the "collective" type; the first relate to future states with implications for the receiving observer whilst the second relate to future states of other observers as well as cosmic events. The study demonstrated that precognition is a normative, distinguishable, and quantifiable activity of the human mind, most likely facilitated by transitory dissociation of neural processing systems dedicated to perception, cognition, and emotion. Looking to the future, experimental and theoretical research into mind-matter interaction (MMI) should play a critical role in the gradual shift to a postmodern worldview.

Keywords: dream, mind-matter interaction, precognition, retrocausality, telegnosis

Precognition may be defined as the intrusion of mental impressions about future events into conscious awareness through extrasensory or telegnostic means. Belief in the phenomenon has been persistent and undoubtedly ubiquitous. In sharp contrast with its disenfranchised position within the privileged epistemic frameworks of naturalistic science today, precognition was eminently woven into the ethos, the religious, and the folkloristic humus of innumerable ancient cultures.[1] It has been conceived as a form of divination and as a revelatory component of spiritual life.

Prophetic dreams are mentioned in the Bible. The most famous is one seen by the Pharaoh; a chronological rendition of seven healthy cows and seven malnourished cows emerging from the Nile waters. Joseph interprets this to mean seven wonderful years of abundance followed by seven miserable years of famine (Genesis 41). In ancient Greece people could attend oracular centres in Dodona and Delphi and have their "fate" revealed through the prophetic utterances of a priesthood acting in the service of specific divinities. Abraham Lincoln (1802-1865), who believed in the powers of prophecy, purportedly experienced a vivid dream in which mourners were engaged in heart-wrenching lamentation. Following the sound of the harrowing sobs down to the East Room of the White House he discovered a sickening surprise: "Before me was a catafalque on which rested a corpse wrapped in funeral vestments. Around it were stationed soldiers who were acting like guards." When Lincoln asked them, "Who is dead in the White House?" they responded, "The president, he was killed by an assassin".[2] The forewarning was justified; Lincoln died at 7.22 a.m. on April 15th 1865 after having been shot in the head by Confederate spy John Wilkes Booth at the Ford's Theatre in Washington, DC.

Another famous example comes from the fictional narratives of Morgan Robertson (1861-1915). In 1898 he wrote a novel entitled, "The Wreck of the Titan" about a supposed unsinkable liner that suffered the misfortune of hitting an iceberg and sinking.[3] Some interesting characteristics of the Titan are that it was a triple screw ship with 24 lifeboats; it weighed in at 70,000 tons; and it embarked on its maiden and only voyage from Southampton to New York. This sounds a lot like the Titanic, doesn't it? In fact, the details are almost identical. Weighing in at 66,000 tons, the Titanic was a triple screw ship with 20 lifeboats embarking on its maiden and only voyage from Southampton to New York in 1912. Just like its fictional counterpart, it struck an iceberg and sank.

The best evidence in support of the phenomenon comes from animal research, controlled card-guessing studies, and random number generator experiments conducted in laboratory settings.[4, 5, 6] In 1989, a meta-analysis published by paranormal investigators Charles Honorton and Diane C. Ferrari critically examined 309 studies involving forced-choice precognition tests conducted between 1935 and 1987 on a total of fifty thousand random participants by sixty-two different investigators.[7] That's an astounding two million trials all together! What they found was unparalleled and critical for any dialectical position regarding the precognitive faculty as something more than a human fabrication. The combined investigations yielded a statistical significance of thirty percent with a one to 1025 or 0.0975 percent chance that coincidence had anything to do with the descriptions of future events offered by the subjects.

The role that chance played in these experiments could be compared to bursting open a packet of M & M's and having seventy of the one hundred and five candy-coated pieces of milk chocolate land on the M side up, or to spreading seventy fans around the house and then having a breeze from the kitchen window rotate the set of propellers at precisely the same speed.

Interestingly, investigators have not limited their precognitive experiments to the wakeful state. Ullman, Krippner, and Vaughan (1973), for instance, (see Note 8) investigated the connection between REM sleep and telepathic impressions and found that it was possible for an individual's dream content to be influenced by conscious observers mentally projecting arbitrarily selected targets (art prints) from remote locations.[8] One dream percipient, a British sensitive named Malcolm Bessent, correctly identified targets on ten out of sixteen occasions—a statistically significant outcome!

Perhaps the single most important investigation outside laboratory settings, one considered a milestone in mind-matter interaction (MMI), was conducted by the aeronautical engineer and military aircraft designer John William Dunne (1866-1949).[9] After assessing the nature of his own precognitive dreams Dunne formulated a definitive hypothetical position: the precognitive faculty was not the exclusive province of genuine clairvoyants at all but a psychical ability latent in the entire population. Seeking validation for this hypothesis he set up a variable-controlled experiment with an orthodox method of dream recall (writing down dreams in as much detail as possible immediately upon awakening) for the sake of juxtaposing dream and waking consciousness, and collecting information about recurring impressions that had initially presented themselves for observation in the dreams. His data supported the idea that future impressions do seep into conscious awareness as early as a day before they're due to appear on the phenomenal plane, although most are pretty trivial and minor—phrases and words in newspaper clippings, items like stamps and seeds, the physiognomies of known and unknown individuals, and ornamental designs. Had Dunne been seeking "Big Dreams" with detailed, comprehensive content as to what would be unfolding in the immediate future, he would have surely been disappointed. Nonetheless the snippets were enough to convince Dunne that precognition was a feature of a much wider demographic than conventionally supposed.

The abovementioned data support a worldview acknowledging the premature manifestation of future, or the fact that the likely future may, to some degree, be determined. Implicit is that the cosmos cannot be causal in an absolute sense. Our ability to thwart precognitive visions from coming-to-be by consciously aborting sequential steps of our decision-making process which would have delivered such a result means we can still exercise free will. We can live in the pockets of a paradoxical world, no doubt. Save for using Dunne's experimental methodology to generate an in-depth exploration of the phenomenology, the present study also aimed to identify possible mechanisms of action for the precognitive effect.

Method and Results

Participants were given a three-page participation form which gathered personal information and detailed a set of steps for the transcription of dreams and the identification of associated waking experiences.[10] They were required to run and self-manage their own trials for four to five days and then return the results to the experimenter via e-mail. Subsequently, the correlational quality of each dream-associative waking experience set was determined using a unique categorization system with precise diagnostic valuations for very powerful correlations (excellent), powerful correlations (good), and some correlation (average). The complete dossier was then subjected to a statistical analysis.

A small sample of 15 subjects participated in this study; five were male and ten female. The median age was 41. In all there were 51 precognitive dream fragments; 33 or 65% fell into the "excellent" category, 15 or 29% into the "good" category, and three or 6% into the "average" category. Of the 51 dreams transcribed, 45 or 88% were of the "personal" variety and six or 12% of the "collective" breed. Dreams that were not retrocausally related to any waking experience were not included or analyzed.

Some overarching extrapolations were made from the 51 precognitive dream fragments.[11] The first is that precognition is a "normative" aspect of human consciousness. They do not adhere to a specific time interval; forewarnings can precede the related waking events by minutes, days, months, or years. Interestingly, precognition is not confined to altered states of consciousness; in many instances precognitive impressions were transmitted to fully conscious observers. However, their scarcity in waking states indicates intellectual conditioning may play a substantial role in the inhibition of anomalous phenomena, or phenomena incongruent with existing epistemic frameworks. States conducive to precognition, then, must be characterized by a level of detachment, the suspension of judgement, relaxation, modification of sense perception, interconnectedness, and the condensation of attention.

Just like other dream types, precognitive dreams may be experienced from a first-person or third-person perspective; sometimes the observer encounters the dreamscape from within their own body and at other times as a submissive, impartial entity looking down upon their own self. More often than not, they are found scattered within a bundle of mental impressions incorporating personal fantasies, desires, and genuine retrospection; very rarely will the associated waking experience replicate the precognitive episode in the exact same sequence and with the exact same details. The shifting perspectives may be a phenomenological expression of transitory dissociation between neural networks while the existence of precognitive fragments in dreamscapes suggests that conscious observers can scan the environment, sort through various mental patterns competing for attention, and manipulate the expression of targets away from what might be expected by mean chance.[12] In fact, experimental finds in MMI offer clear support for precognition under a conformance interplay model which fathoms the entire cluster of "psi" phenomena as unconscious data gathering processes activated by motivational salience and mediated by extrasensory means.

The study also revealed two types of precognitive dreams: the "personal" type relating to future states with implications for the observer who received them and in some instances others (analogous to Carl Jung's "Big Dreams") and the "collective" type relating to the future states of other observers as well as cosmic events. While the conformance interplay model adequately explains the existence of "personal" types, it fails to justify the existence of the "collective" variety. What would be the purpose of scouring the environment for events and objects pertaining to the survival of another organism? Absolutely none; scouring the existing

MMI theories it would appear the 'collective" type are better elucidated by the "Weak Quantum Theory" pioneered by Atmanspacher, Römer, and Walach[13]; such a correlational matrix between co-mingled particles in existence allows for the possibility that nonlocal data may be readily accessible to unconscious minds and that a filtering process prevents the data from reaching conscious awareness when it encompasses little to no survival value for the organism in question. This explanation accords well with the fact that only 12% of precognitive dreams registered were of the "collective" type.

Adopting a transpersonal stance it is feasible to conceive precognitive dreams of the "personal" variety as utilizing "percipient-active" telepathy, with the observer actively scanning and receiving information from the environment, and those of the "collective" variety as utilizing "agent-active" telepathy, a more passive, receptive process that impresses data upon the receiver's mind.[14] Hence precognitive dreams express a bidirectional orientation.

Discussion

The notion of precognitive dreams is feasible when we take into account the manner in which our neural networks have been molded by the cheap and quick mechanisms of natural selection. Extracting veridical information about the environment is costly in terms of time and energy, and so our perceptual systems have evolved to be efficient, conservative, and utility-focused. Natural selection, then, requires perceptions of our world-simulation model to be tuned to resource detection, allowing us to outsmart organisms competing for the same utilities; it cares little, if at all, for more accurate simulations or constructions of the external world.[15]

Nowhere are these evolutionary requirements more prominent than in the reflexive functions of the dominant hemisphere. With significantly looser associations to the body than its "antisocial" counterpart, the integrative properties of its language centres makes possible the organization of discontinuous, separate events into an amalgamated and continuous stream of conscious awareness.[16] Hundreds of thousands, if not millions of years of executing goal-oriented behaviours and embodying narratives that connect and present the self within a larger sociocultural context and group mind have sculpted newer additions of our cerebral hardware (the prefrontal cortex) so that they accord with these survival purposes. Foremost of demands pertaining to this mode of being is that perceptual mechanisms at the interface of inner and outer worlds should process incoming packets of information from the environment monosemantically and digitally, that is in slower, linear, sequential, and temporal fashion.[17] In so doing our brains become much more effectual at problem solving, basing our conscious decisions on whether to act or not on our learning history and appraising the likelihood of both approach and avoidance behaviors. Acquired excellence in the abovementioned areas is what separates us from the rest of the animal kingdom, and what has allowed us to subjugate and dominate Nature.

Ironically though, the same evolutionary innovations which enable us to surmount other created aspects of Nature are what stand between us, the grand intellect of the human species, and a more accurate simulation of the outside world and reality (as well as a more comprehensive understanding of the phenomenon we call 'time'). In the 0.5 seconds it takes for global discharge of neural impulses to produce conscious awareness,[18] there is room for innumerable sensory inputs not associated with self-preservation to be screened out and for internal functional modes to unconsciously modify external inputs that do make it through. Served in part by the attentional mechanism, the time-on requirement for awareness maintains the internally created coherent image of the outside world we have constructed a priori by permitting at most, several events, objects, or concerns to enter the "stream" of consciousness at once. When the duration of global neural activations diminishes (i.e., REM sleep) there is an epiphenomenal abeyance of the filter mechanism, allowing for such counterintuitive phenomena as precognitive inputs suggestive of retrocausality and telegnosis to infiltrate awareness.

What does all this mean? It means that consciousness[i] could be a form of nonphysical energy spreading across infinite wavelengths. Using our accrued neuro-phenomenological knowledge as a guide, it seems precognition, clairvoyance, and other "psi" phenomena are not contained in the neural correlates and morphological structures of the physical brain as such, but rather that underlying physical and chemical changes of brain-mind states (i.e., lucid REM-mode, REM-mode, psychosis, wakefulness, etc.) may facilitate information flow from nonconscious wavelengths and ambient fields into conscious awareness. Put another way, we might choose to regard the brain with its newly evolved prefrontal neocortex as a

---

[i] In this wider context, it may be defined as the phenomenal, nonspatial quality of all mental phenomena, as well as an extended awareness of physical, mental, and conceptual objects contained in the entire universe.

provisional transfer-and-storage mechanism for consciousness. Sometimes the interplay between neural chaos and self-organization is conducive to partial glimpses of the higher representational process and at other times it is not. Recent orthodox definitions of consciousness as a "closed-loop property" of the thalamo-cortical system[19]–meaning the neurons connecting cortical areas with the thalamus are mostly dedicated to internal functional modes–fits well with the aforesaid view. If this interpretation of consciousness were veridical, then the scarcity of precognitive experiences could be elucidated, in part, by the fact that only a small portion of thalamo-cortical connectivity encodes information coming from the external world.

At this stage, we do not quite know if precognitive fragments infiltrate conscious awareness purposely and actively or if they are simply part of a non-conscious continuum that our brain-minds access arbitrarily under certain neurophysiological conditions. This, in all honesty, remains speculative and ambiguous.

Nonetheless there is a specific brain-mind state enabling this exchange. What is its inherent nature? It is an integral state at the farthest boundary of REM-mode, experienced when we are on the knife's edge between dreaming and waking.[20] This most lucid and vivid form of dreaming cognition incorporates both internal and external stimuli, and is powered by high metabolic processes with neural activity at near-seizure levels. Acetylcholine washes over the pons in the brainstem, causing the visual brain to hallucinate; the visuo-motor and emotional circuits are buzzing like Luna Park on long weekends; and internal generation of motor programs has activated aminergic neurons about the pons.[21] This switches on the cognitive functions of the frontal cortex so that there is a reinstatement of top-down processing. However, the thalamus, a limbic system structure in which neurons of the cortex synapse, is only partly activated and cannot intercept unwanted data. These disorganized patterns of neural activity somehow enable transmission of information telegnostically.

Conclusion

The findings of the present investigation make it possible to draw a set of conclusions about the nature of mind without having to adopt a particular stance regarding the causal relationship between higher-order consciousness[ii] and the physical brain (i.e., dualism, materialistic monism, or transcendental monism).

Firstly, it should be reiterated that precognition is a typical, distinguishable, and "nonphysical" activity of the mind that cannot (as far as we know) be attributed to the complex interactions of neurophysiological networks. Some major implications here are that conscious awareness must be able to function independently of "matter", and that further, specific intracerebral conditions facilitate it.

Secondly, channels of telepathic communication are readily available to the human mind, enabling access to a vast repository of past, present, and future memories about other observers as well as to intimate details about extra cerebral phenomena co-created and/or witnessed by these observers in the social synapse. From the uneven ratio of "personal" to "collective" precognitive experiences, we can further deduce that each neurological based world simulator, each brain, is quite dexterous at filtering out information of no constructive benefit to the survival and existence of the organism as a whole.

As a final point, precognition alludes to "backwards causation" or "retrocausality", the transmission of information across time. This calls for a revision of the Cartesian-Kantian epistemological box couching the unidimensional model of time, as well as standard notions of a materialistic universe. More and more, it seems that deepening our understanding of "psi" phenomena like precognitive dreams will play a seminal role in the gradual shift to a more postmodern cosmology.

Bibliography

[1] Dodds, E.R. (1971). *The prophecies of Nostradamus*. London, England: Corgi Books.

[2] Radin, D. (1997). *The conscious universe: The scientific truth of psychic phenomena*. San Francisco, CA: HarperEdge, pp. 118, 138-142.

[3] Robertson, M., & Stevenson, I. (1991). *The wreck of the Titan: The paranormal experiences connected with the sinking of the Titanic*. Cutchogue, NY: Buccaneer Books.

[4] Rhine, J.B. (1964). *Extra-sensory perception*. Boston, MA: Branden.

[ii] Higher order consciousness may be defined as the metacognitive capacity to introspect and construct mental scenes in an imaginal mind-space, and is pervaded by an aptitude for semantic language, symbolization, and an autobiographical self.

[5] Duval, P., & Montredon, E. (1968). ESP experiments with mice. *Journal of Parapsychology*, *32*, 153-66.
[6] Schmidt, H. (1969). Precognition as a quantum process, *Journal of Parapsychology*, *33*, 99-108.
[7] Radin, D. (1997). *The conscious universe: The scientific truth of psychic phenomena.* San Francisco, CA: HarperEdge, pp. 138-42).
[8] Ullman, M., Krippner, S., & Vaughan, A. (1973*). Dream telepathy*. New York, NY: Macmillan.
[9] Dunne, J.W. (2001). *An experiment with time.* Charlottesville, VA: Hampton Roads Publishing.
[10] Kiritsis, P. (2013). *Dreamscaping without my timekeeper: A critical investigation into precognitive dreams*. Melbourne, VIC: Phantasus Publishing.
[11] See note 10
[12] See the conformance model of mind-matter interplay proposed by Rex Stanford in, Heath, P.R. (2011). *Mind-matter interaction: A review of historical reports, theory and research.* Jefferson, NC: McFarland & Company, p. 157.
[13] See note 12, p. 160.
[14] See note 12, p. 157.
[15] Mark, J. T., Marion, B. B., & Hoffman, D. D. (2010). Natural selection and veridical perceptions. *Journal of Theoretical Biology*, *266*(4), 504-515.
[16] Cozolino, L. (2014). *The neuroscience of human relationships: Attachment and the developing social brain* (Norton Series on Interpersonal Neurobiology). New York, NY: WW Norton & Company.
[17] Siegel, D. J. (1999). *The developing mind* (Vol. 296). New York, NY: Guilford Press.
[18] Libet, B. (2009). *Mind time: The temporal factor in consciousness*. Cambridge, MA: Harvard University Press, pp. 33-89.
[19] Blom, J. D., & Sommer, I. E. (Eds.). (2011). *Hallucinations: Research and practice*. Springer Science & Business Media, p. 20.
[20] Kiritsis, P. (2013). *Dreamscaping without my timekeeper: A critical investigation into precognitive dreams*. Melbourne, VIC: Phantasus Publishing.
[21] Hobson, J. A. (1994). *The chemistry of conscious states*. Boston, MA: Little, Brown, and Company.

CHAPTER ELEVEN

TRANSPERSONAL INTEGRATIVE APPROACH (AIT): COUNSELING TO PSYCHIATRIC OUTPATIENTS IN BRAZIL. CARING FOR THE SPIRITUAL NEEDS OF MENTAL HEALTH PATIENTS

MARIA CRISTINA M. DE BARROS, LIGIA SPLENDORE AND VERA SALDANHA

Abstract

This chapter presents a model of counseling in Transpersonal Integrative Approach (AIT) to outpatients at the Institute of Psychiatry, Faculty of Medicine, University of São Paulo, within the framework of the Health Program of Studies on Spirituality and Religiosity (PROSER) in that institution. PROSER is formed by a group of professionals of different backgrounds, interested in doing research and in giving assistance to patients through projects that involve spiritual practices and health care. The *Brazilian-Portuguese Transpersonal Association* (ALUBRAT) has been contributing to PROSER since its foundation in 2006, developing different assistance programs. ALUBRAT has developed a therapeutic project that explores the answers of a spiritual anamnesis developed by PROSER mapping the patient's relationship with the transcendent. The objective of the project was to stimulate religious / spiritual coping, to understand its potential therapeutic aspects, hoping for a more effective management of the mental disorder. Adult patients participated in 12 weekly individual sessions of AIT, in which they worked through AITs framework to develop better abilities in dealing with their difficulties as well as accepting them. With the sessions, patients were successful in identifying their positive personal resources by connecting with their spirituality, through specific transpersonal techniques. Besides verbal intervention, other therapeutic tools were used during the sessions, such as relaxation, meditation, active imagination, creative visualization, expressive drawing and mandalas, all of them being resources to expand awareness and facilitate access to the Transpersonal Self.

Keywords: counseling, psychiatric outpatients, Transpersonal Integrative Approach

This chapter presents a model of counseling in Transpersonal Integrative Approach (AIT) to outpatients at the Institute of Psychiatry (IPQ), of the University of São Paulo, Brazil, within the framework of the Health Program of Studies on Spirituality and Religiosity (PROSER) in that institution.

PROSER is formed by a group of professionals of different backgrounds, interested in doing research and in giving assistance to patients through projects that involve spiritual practices and health care. In 2011, PROSER developed the "Spiritual Anamnesis" (SA) that investigates how patients' religiosity/spirituality generates an impact on mental health.

The Brazilian-Portuguese Transpersonal Association (ALUBRAT) has been contributing to PROSER since its foundation, participating in different assistance programs. In the present project, the main objective is to create an intervention based on Transpersonal Psychology, more specifically on AIT, to explore the answers of the SA (spiritual anamnesis questionnaire), using them as a script in counseling. In that way, the sessions would help patients build personal resources to overcome difficulties, improving general wellbeing, self-knowledge, clarifying their vision of future and meaning of life.

Adult patients of both sexes being treated in outpatient clinics of IPQ are referred to the project by nurses, doctors or directly by the AIT psychologist, who contact them by phone. There are no impediments for adult patients to participate, other than clinical medical conditions that may interfere with their cognitive response or with the adherence to treatment. The patient is invited to participate in 12 weekly individual sessions of AIT.

Along with verbal interventions, other therapeutic tools are used during the sessions, such as relaxation, meditation, active imagination, creative visualization, expressive drawing and mandalas, all of them being resources to expand awareness and facilitate access to the Transpersonal Self.[1]

Patient and therapist evaluate the counseling project together, discussing the benefits achieved and limitations, as well as the need for other kinds of intervention or even the need for more sessions. The patient is encouraged to make a testimonial of the counseling process.

Spirituality/Religiosity and Mental Health

There has been a significant growth in the interest of health professionals to study and deal with the impact of spirituality and religiosity in patients' health. Since 1970 there has been an average of two articles per year. [2] From there, there is a jump of 10 publications in 2010 and 109 in 2011, from 1970 to 2000 there were 699 articles only. Between 2000 and 2014, the number increased to 6314 published articles.[3]

The World Health Organization states that spiritual well-being is a dimension of the state of health along with bodily, psychological and social dimensions, being one of the items that should be investigated for assessment of quality of life. [4]

In the context of health practices, the influence of spiritual and religious aspects on cure and treatment of physical and mental illnesses has been widely studied abroad and also in Brazil, which incidentally stands out as one of the places with the highest number of research publications in the area.[5,6] The vast majority of good quality studies points out that high level of religious/spiritual involvement are positively associated with psychological well-being indicators (life satisfaction, happiness, positive affect, and higher morale) and less depression, thoughts and suicidal behavior, drug abuse.

Individuals have access to spirituality through their search for meaning, through higher connection with others and with a power greater than themselves, developing resources needed for adjustment to adverse situations.[7] It is extremely important to pay attention to the spiritual identity of patients, families and caregivers, as well as their spiritual needs, which are often ignored. In a recent systematic review, Best [8] found that spiritual wellbeing and characteristics such as hope and meaning, can be positively impacted by a number of therapeutic intervention modalities; especially those that include spirituality as an integral part of daily life.

Various authors within the humanistic and transpersonal movement in psychology have written about spirituality and about the need to value the non-pathological potential in human experience.[9, 10, 11] Lukoff[12] also states that the acceptance of spiritual and religious problems as a new diagnostic category in the DSM-IV-TR and DSM V is a reflection of increased sensitivity to cultural diversity in mental health professionals and shows the impact of the clinical practice of transpersonal psychologists.

For a better understanding of this topic, it is essential to clarify the concepts of spirituality and religiosity. Religiosity refers to the extent to which an individual believes, follows and practices a particular religion. Spirituality is understood as the practice and reflection, in a specific way, of issues related to the meaning of life and reason for living. Spirituality concerns the intimate dimensions of personality and its search for serenity, not necessarily through the figure of God, but also in art, nature and in other contexts.[13] It is present in all human cultures and societies, expressed as the search of the individual for the ultimate meaning of his existence.

Today, we know that to neglect the spiritual dimension results in failure to treat the whole person.[14] However, there are still very few models in use to address these topics. In this sense, since 2011, PROSER has been using the Spiritual Anamnesis (SA), a semi structured questionnaire, as a means to know the spiritual profile of the patients of that institution. This questionnaire has not been validated yet, but is subject to ongoing research studies within the PROSER team.

The SA - spiritual anamnesis (Table 1) - allows the patient to reflect on aspects of existential quality, such as the concept of God, the meaning of life, intrinsic or extrinsic relationship with the spiritual dimension, suicide, and life after death, among others. Therefore, it opens a channel of communication with health professionals on the topic of spirituality and religiosity, which can be an important coping mechanism facing any disease.

Table 1

The PROSER Spiritual Anamnesis

1. In the difficult moments of life, what do you cling to and what makes you move forward?
2. Are you part of a religious community? YES ( ) NO ( ) Religious Denomination:
IF SO:
2A1. Do you attend congregational meetings, which activities do you participate in and, how often?
IF NOT:
2B1. What are your values in life?
2B2. How do those values influence your life?
2B3. Even without a formal religion, do you have any belief or spiritual practice?
3. What is God to you?
4. Do you ever reflect on spiritual aspects, such as the meaning of life, or life after death?
5. Have you had any spiritual experience that you consider important?
6. Has getting sick affected your beliefs, values and religious / spiritual practices? In what way?
7. About your health problems:
I) What is your vision?
II) What is your family's vision?
III) What is your religion's vision?
How does this impact you?

8. About psychiatric medical treatment:

    I) What is your vision?

    II) What is your family's vision?

    III) What is your religion's vision?

    How does this impact you?

9. About suicide:

    Have you ever considered or/and tried suicide?

    I) What is your vision?

    II) What is your family's vision?

    III) What is your religion's vision?

10. On the use of drugs and alcohol:

    I) What is your vision?

    II) What is your family's vision?

    III) What is your religion's vision?

    How does this impact you?

11. Is there any religious practice and belief that can influence your medical treatment?

12. As a health care professional is there anything I can do to help you access the resources that generally support you in these difficult times?

13. Do you think it is important to have this kind of conversation during your treatment?

The Integrative Transpersonal Approach (AIT)

ALUBRAT has been contributing to PROSER since its foundation, developing different assistance programs. The present project is an intervention that explores the individual's relationship with the Transcendent and stimulates religious / spiritual coping, hoping for a more effective management of the mental disorder.

AIT is a methodology that gathers the core concepts of the transpersonal paradigm, as proposed by Abraham Maslow,[15] Roberto Assagioli,[16] Moreno[17] and others. It has been developed by Vera Saldanha [18] during the past 20 years and today, the AIT is taught in many parts of Brazil, where more than 1600 students have taken specialization and post-graduate courses offered by ALUBRAT under the AIT methodology.

AIT understands transpersonal psychology as promoting the study and experimentation of expanded states of consciousness, which aim at the transcendence of the individual ego toward cosmic unity. These higher states facilitate the emergence of constructive and positive values in the individual.[19] For Abraham Maslow, the ignorance of such states and its vast possibilities is at the heart of human illnesses.[20] The therapist's role in this sense is to help the individual to recognize the best way to be more fully himself, awakening the forces that lead to transcendence and self-actualization. Although AIT is based on two basic sets of concepts – the structural and the dynamic aspects – for the purpose of this chapter we will briefly discuss the latter.

The Dynamic Aspect in AIT

AIT's dynamic aspect is articulated through the intersection of two-axels: the experiential axis (horizontal) and the evolving axis (vertical line). The experiential axel represents the path of one's experience in life, through four different functions of perception: reason, emotion, intuition and sensation (REIS). When a person expands and balances those functions during his life experience, he is capable of integrating its different aspects. If one does not allow the expression of any of those properties, he limits perception and feels a sense of fragmentation. In that case, coping skills are reduced and with it, the capacity of transforming difficulties into challenges.

The evolving axel is the proper connection to the Self or transpersonal dimension present in every being. This connection is facilitated through the experience of modified or expanded states of consciousness. Clinical observations show that human suffering and conflicts cannot be transformed at the same level of consciousness where they were originated. It is important that another state of mind is created, bringing with it other perceptions and less limited beliefs, more freedom and more creativity.

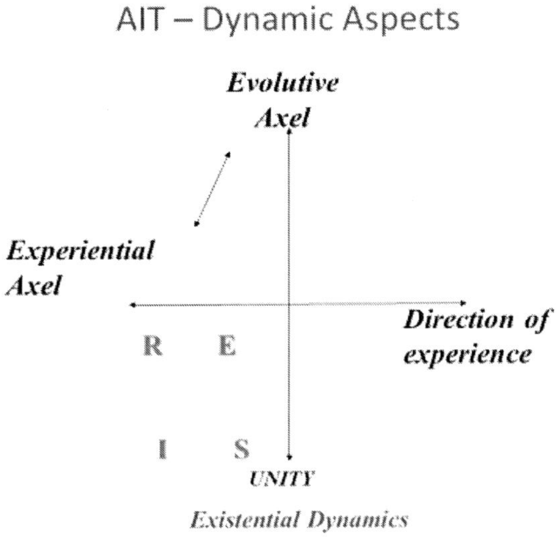

Figure 1. Dynamic aspects in AIT

The intersection between the experiential and the evolving axels take place in a dynamic way (*Figure 1*), constantly moving in a dance of life-death and rebirth, in the endless cycle of development. During this dynamic process of transformation, everyone goes through seven steps towards unity and plenitude. In the clinical context, those steps provide the therapist with a map with the stage in which the client finds himself. Therefore, the therapist is able to propose appropriate exercises for each specific stage. The "seven steps of interactive dynamics" are: recognition, identification, dis-identification, transmutation, transformation, elaboration and integration.

1. Recognition: In a counseling setting, recognition is the stage when the patient asks himself: what's going on? He senses there is something wrong, but does not know what it is. He starts asking questions and reflecting.
2. Identification: In the counseling context, this is the stage where the patient identifies what the problem or conflict he is really facing is, getting into contact with the emotions underlying his suffering and

that have somehow remained hidden. It is a difficult time for the patient and the therapist, who needs time to build confidence and be at the patient's side, to encourage the expression of any contents that need to emerge.

3. Dis-identification: In the therapeutic process, this is the time in therapy when the patient finds himself expanding his awareness of who he really is. For example, if he faces a cancer, he feels he *has* a cancer but he *is not* the cancer. He perceives that there is a healthy side and a positive part of the soul that is potentially waiting to be worked with and manifested.
4. Transmutation: This is the time in therapy when the patient comes out of duality; finds more colors between the "blacks and whites" of each polarity. He realizes that even that which he considers as a bad thing in his life, can be given a meaning or can teach him something. Every characteristic of his personality, each obstacle he encounters, can be a messenger guiding him to a better route.
5. Transformation: In this phase, the patient begins to find the exact attitudes to manifest the new insights. Internal and external behavior change, reflecting a much deeper feeling of transformation and metamorphosis from inside out.
6. Elaboration: This is a time when the patient reflects upon the meaning of all the processes he has gone through and wanders where he wants to go next. The mental elaboration is here considered important and is not only a cognitive process, but comes out of a much more complex and less fragmented state of consciousness.
7. Integration: It is the end of the therapeutic route. The patient asks himself about other circumstances in life where the new awareness can be experimented, new ways to deal with old challenges can be explored and the whole process can be integrated to other contexts in life.

In Table 2, we summarized the seven steps discussed above, giving an example of one single psychotherapy session:

Table 2
The Seven Steps within One Single AIT Session

Session 1 **Recognition**	**Establishing rapport and setting up a therapeutic contract**	**Verbal interactions and scales**	**Aiming patient´s adherence to treatment**
Recognition and Identification	Identification of the main aspects that should be worked in therapy	Verbal interaction. Reviewing the Spiritual anamnesis	Understanding patient´s spiritual profile; perceiving needs
Identification and Dis-identification	Visualization exercise	Relaxation and Visualization: the master/wise figure within	Identifying coping mechanisms and inner resources (connecting with the Sacred)
Transmutation and Transformation	Choosing a symbol and communicating with it	Drawing, coloring and verbal interaction	Enhance self-perception, facilitate the way out of polarity and the way in to a new direction in life
Elaboration and Integration	Understanding the importance of the messages	Writing down the insights and connecting them with the aim of therapy through verbal interactions	Valuing the findings and ability to work out difficulties - empowerment

The Story of Alma: A Brief Case Report

Alma is a woman of 53 years of age, diagnosed with Bipolar Disorder Type 2. She has been under treatment in the hospital for many years, but was now referred to the outpatients' clinic for psychotherapy.

She is a widow of her third husband. She has a history of many family conflicts, violence and abuse, but the relationship with the late husband was good. She has one son and one daughter, respectively, from the second and first husband and no children with the deceased. When the husband died seven years ago, her depressive symptoms aggravated and she attempted suicide.

We took her as a patient due to her interest in religious and spiritual issues. She was very helpful and hopeful throughout the counseling sessions and made a very strong bond with us. Alma was distant from work and lived by herself in São Paulo city, having a very modest lifestyle. Her family, with the exception of the daughter, lived in the south of Brazil. From our first contact, we observed feelings of loneliness and victimization: others were always responsible for her suffering.

Her husband's death by cancer seemed to be the first issue to address - her mourning and sadness. We suggested a visualization exercise, where she would imagine and hear what the late husband had to say to her (she said she used to feel his presence by her side many times in her room, before she got to sleep). In her visualization, they had a dialogue and he thanked her for her help and care during his disease. He calmed her, saying that she was not to blame for his death – something that tormented her quite a lot.

After getting some relief with that exercise, we moved on and in the following sessions we worked with mandala exercises. We wanted her to express how she saw herself and her psychological state (recognition and identification stages in the AIT). She came up with a mandala where the whole circle was filled with colored pieces and no center. It looked like a puzzle. There was life there, but there was not any direction, any focus. So, the question for her was based on some of the SA questions: What were her values in life? How did they influence her attitudes? How did her depression affect those values and attitudes?

To answer those questions, we proposed a meditation practice, always preceded by relaxation exercises. She had a tendency to dissociate, and those body relaxation exercises, combined with the meditations, were a very powerful means of raising self-awareness of the here and now of the sessions. After two meetings, she managed to draw another mandala, this time, starting with a yellow center. We then went on using that mandala to stimulate and emphasize the center in herself, asking her to continue with the meditation exercises at home, using the new drawing as a focus.

That exercise provoked many memories, bringing back the childhood and some events in her life that she related with the loss of her center and focus. She drew her refuge: a little house on a green field, with some animals, a swing on a tree branch, birds flying in a beautiful blue sky, a very yellow and big sun shining. That became her rebirth mark, the starting over point in the counseling process, when she decided to live again.

From then on, we were ready to address the Bipolar diagnosis. She had quite a hard time accepting that part of herself that pushed her down. Her first name was composed of two parts: one that she liked and the other that she hated. Obviously, the one she did not like was identified with the depressive quality of her personality. We used a dialogue exercise to make her explore those different personalities within herself. With eyes closed, she could play the roles of those characters, one at a time, trying to open up for messages and insights. As always, first she was asked to relax, go to the refuge and visualize her center, that calm center from where she could genuinely observe and know more about her different sides and aspects (dis-identification stage of the interactive dynamic).

She repeated that dialogue many times, as she was striving to accept the depressed part as the one who was responsible for giving her some sense of limits. During that phase, she was undergoing the transmutation stage proposed by AIT. When she began to understand the underlying intentions of the depressed part, she entered the transformation stage. She started to change some of her attitudes in life, as she deeply felt that the real intention of the depressive part of her personality was in fact, to protect her.

Enhancing attitudes of self-care, she started to feel the need to get closer to nature again. She had a garden with nice trees and flowers she had cultivated for some years, prior to the husband's death. Alma decided it was time to help her flowers to come back to life again. Following the same direction, she began to care for her home, repairing objects, renovating and painting walls, finding special places where she could feel comfortable again.

We were at our final sessions and it was time to think for the future. Where to go next? (Elaboration and Integration stages of the interactive dynamic in the AIT). What were her plans? How did she imagine herself in the near future? We proposed a visualization. The picture was not entirely clear for her. But some nice plans took form and by our last session, she was reconsidering returning to her previous job, where she worked as a secretary in a school. However, the dream plan was somehow touching: she imagined herself lecturing to a crowd of people about life, death and about depression. We asked her to write about this plan, which she did in detail. We also asked her to look back at all the therapeutic process we experienced. Below, we transcribe what she wrote.

> I liked it a lot, because it started to make me see things I had not seen for myself and the things I didn`t understand or accept and were hurting me a lot. As the weeks went by I began to feel increasingly motivated and happier, returned to the balls to dance, gaining more self-confidence in myself and making my life lighter and relaxed. I'm starting to learn to carry on with my life, it`s been a new beginning with many discoveries which are making me see things from different angles and ways to solve problems. I started taking more care of myself and let others go their own ways without me getting involved, just in case of need. My life has changed a lot since then and I feel very confident in saying that one day I will overcome my depression with the help of therapy.

Discussion and Considerations for Future Projects

The present work is a brief discussion and example of the application of a transpersonal approach into a mental clinical setting. The nature and format of this work is something new in the setting where it took place, because it involves the issue of spirituality and religiosity as applied directly in the assistance and care of patients with serious mental diagnoses. This transpersonal model of intervention seems to be a useful approach helping patients to find meaning and regain self confidence in themselves as well as in life. Although the format proved appropriate, we strongly recommend at least three monthly maintenance sessions after the 12 sessions scheduled. Another suggestion is the design of a new similar project for groups, therefore serving a larger number of patients at the institution.

Bibliography1

[1] Saldanha, V. (2008). *Psicologia transpessoal – Abordagem Integrativa – Um conhecimento emergente em psicologia da consciência* [Transpersonal psychology – the Integrative Approach - an emerging knowledge in psychology of consciousness]. Ijuí, RS, Brazil: Ed. Unijuí.
[2] Almeida, A.M. (2004). *Phenomenology of mediumistic experiences, profile and psychopathology of spiritist mediums* (Unpublished doctoral dissertation). Faculdade de Medicina, Universidade de São Paulo, São Paulo, Brazil. 205p.
[3] Moreira-Almeida, A., & Cardeña E. (2011). Differential diagnosis between nonpathological psychotic and spiritual experiences and mental disorders: A contribution from Latin American studies to the ICD-11. *Revista Brasileira de Psiquiatria, 33*(Suppl1), S21-36.
[4] Peres, J. F. P., Simão, M. J. P, & Nasello, A. G. (2007). Espiritualidade, religiosidade e psicoterapia [Spirituality, religiosity and psychotherapy]. *Revista de Psiquiatria Clínica, 34* suppl.1, 136-145.
[5] Moreira A.A., Lotufo, F. N., & Koenig, H.G. (2006). *Religiosidade e saúde mental: Uma revisão* [Religiosity and mental health: A review] . *Revista Brasileira de Psiquiatria*, *28*(3), 242-250.
[6] Moreira A.A. (2012). *Exploring frontiers of the mind-brain relationship*. New York, NY: Springer. Nagelshmidt, A.M. (1996). *Argonautas dos espaços interiores* [Agonauts of inner space]. São Paulo, Brazil: Vetor.
[7] Best, M., Aldridge, L., Butow, P., Olver, I., Price, M.A., & Webster, F. (2014, September).Treatment of holistic suffering in cancer: A systematic literature review. *Current Opinions in Supportive and Palliative Care, 8*(3), 308-313.
[8] See Note 7
[9] Lajoie, D.H., & Shapiro, S.I. (1992). Definitions of transpersonal psychology: The first twenty-three years. *The Journal of Transpersonal Psychology*, *24*(1), 79-98.
[10] Maslow, A.H. (1968). *Toward a psychology of Being.* New York, NY: Van Nostrand.
[11] Steele, S. (1998). Self-beyond ego: A new perspective. *Journal of Humanistic Psychology, 38*(1), 93-100.
[12] Lukoff, D., Turner, R., & Lu, F. (1992). Transpersonal psychology research review. *The Journal of Transpersonal Psychology, 24*(1), 41-60.
[13] Jawaid, H. (2014). Impact of religion/spirituality on health: What are the evidences? *Journal of Psychiatry, 17*(6), 14-111.
[14] Koenig, H. G. (2008). *Medicine, religion and health: Where science and spirituality meet.* West Conshohocken, PA: Templeton Foundation Press.
[15] Maslow, A. (1970). *Motivation and personality* (2nd ed.). New York, NY: Harper & Row.
[16] Assagioli R. (1993). *Ser transpessoal* [Being transpersonal]. Madrid, Espanha: Gaia.
[17] Moreno, J.L. (1983). *Fundamentos do psicodrama* [Foundations of psychodrama]. vol. 20. São Paulo, Brazil: Summus.

[18] Saldanha, V. (1999). *Psicoterapia transpessoal* [Transpersonal psychotherapy]. São Paulo, Brazil: Ed. Rosa dos Tempos.
[19] Weil, P. (1995). *A morte da morte* [The death of death]. São Paulo, Brazil: Gente.
[20] Maslow, A. H. (1971). *The farther reaches of human nature.* New York, NY: Viking Press.

CHAPTER TWELVE

11,000 INPATIENTS EXPERIENCE HOLOTROPIC BREATHWORK: HOLOTROPIC BREATHWORK OFFERS A NON-DRUG ALTERNATIVE FOR PSYCHEDELIC THERAPEUTIC EXPERIENCE

JAMES D. EYERMAN

Abstract

Eleven thousand (11,000) psychiatric inpatients participated in Holotropic Breathwork over twelve years. Transpersonal experiences were reported in 82% of the inpatients, biographical experiences in 16%, and no experiences were reported in 1%. Two detailed experiences are presented.

Keywords: adverse reactions, Holotropic Breathwork, inpatient, psychospiritual

This chapter is an adapted augmented version of Eyerman, J.D. (2013, Spring). A clinical report of Holotropic Breathwork in 11,000 psychiatric inpatients in a community hospital setting. *MAPS Bulletin Special Edition*, *23*(1), 24-27 (available from www.maps.org).

Holotropic Breathwork (HB) was developed by Stanislav and Christina Grof to give cathartic, therapeutic, transpersonal[1] experiences similar to the psychedelic experiences induced by LSD, DMT, Mescaline, Psilocybin, MDMA, Ayahuasca, and other entheogens. Holotropic Breathwork sessions were conducted weekly for 12 years in a community psychiatric hospital.

Methods

Holotropic Breathwork was based on psychedelic therapy principles by the Grofs.[2,3] It is an experiential therapy based on music and enhanced breathing in a non-intrusive setting. Holotropic Breathwork was offered to inpatients every Tuesday evening before dinner at the Stress Center of Hyland Behavioral Health, Saint Anthony's Medical Center in Saint Louis, Missouri, from 1989 through 2001. Twenty psychiatric inpatients were selected from several specialty units: sexual trauma, dual diagnosis, chemical dependency, anxiety, depression, adolescent, eating disorders, and the psychiatric ICU. The session filled every week, with a waiting list. The best estimate of the total number of patients is 11,200 +/- 200.

Hospital staff music therapists screened patients for exclusion criteria of severe cardiac disease, severe musculoskeletal disorders, pregnancy, and paranoid ideation. The HB session was structured for a two-hour hospital session: five minutes on the Grof map of the four perinatal birth matrices and the four realms of experience,[4] 1.5 hours of music-breathwork, then 10 minutes for mandala drawing, and 15 minutes of sharing experiences without interpretation. This 90 minute breathing format was the model used in the 1988 Holotropic Breathwork Certification in Breckinridge, Colorado.

Holotropic Breathwork experiences are unusual,[5] and participants were encouraged to not share them with others who had not been in their session. No patient reported having experienced a therapy similar to this, and no patient reported having a spiritual discipline.

During the first year, the sharing period self-reports of 482 consecutive inpatients were recorded. Their experiences were rated by the four music therapists according to the four experiential realms which Grof had identified from his prior LSD studies[6]: (a) physical-sensory, (b) perinatal, (c) biographical, and (d) transpersonal.

Results

Eighty-two percent of the 482 psychiatric inpatients had transpersonal/ archetypal experiences. 16% reported experiencing issues from their life, including perinatal experiences in two patients reported "no experiences". There were no unresolved negative outcomes or adverse reactions. Among the 11,000 inpatients, the experience was well tolerated as well. There were no subsequent reports of untoward sequelae or later complaints noted by nursing staff after the sessions during the entire 12 years. Specific DSM diagnoses and symptoms profiles were not recorded.

Two Experiential Case Reports

A 14 year-old adolescent was admitted with a severe major depression. He had attempted to kill himself twice by cutting his throat. The second time he came close to succeeding. He had a significant issue with shame and guilt over the pregnancy of his girlfriend in a small rural community. No one in the town would talk to him; nor would she. He felt rejected and isolated. In the hospital he received Fluoxetine; he breathed in the first inpatient group in 1988. He reported that he re-experienced the night when he tried to kill himself. This time he experienced death, successfully completing the suicide in his process. He then became the universe. His drawing included a bloody knife on the side with a mandala circle containing a bunch of stars. His mood had lifted. Since this was a new therapy, a guarded approach was taken to his quick remission of affective symptoms. He stayed another week and participated in the Holotropic Breathwork again. He reported that he "became the universe right away" during the second session. Then he became 'pure consciousness', in his own words. He then "became pure consciousness and the universe together". I considered this to be a significant experience of non-duality for anyone, especially a 14 year old from rural Missouri. He reported his spiritual background as "I've been to Sunday school twice!" This boy was not spiritually disciplined, but he had profound metaphysical experiences. He did well for 9 months living with his uncle in another city. When he returned to his parents' hometown, he again became dysphoric, but he was not seriously depressed nor was he suicidal.

A 31 year old woman, with suicidal major depression and a prior history of alcoholism and polysubstance abuse, admitted herself to the hospital to prevent an alcoholic relapse. She reported a history of abuse from her stepfather between the ages of 12–14. She ran away and lived on the street as a drug addict after her older brother, the main support for her in the family, died in military combat. She achieved recovery in her early 20's but continued to cycle through severe major depressive episodes on the anniversaries of the loss of her brother. As an outpatient she was being treated with Fluoxetine 60 mg and Trazodone 50 mg; she continued this treatment as an inpatient. She was in the first HB group with the boy reported above, but she refused to draw or share. Her affect, however, appeared improved. The next week, after listening to self-reports of others in the group, she agreed to share her experience: "This is too weird; in the first session my dead father and dead brother showed up. They lifted me out of my body and took me to a wonderful place full of light and joy; I was so comforted. But then they dropped me back here on the floor. I just couldn't talk about it....In my second session, my father and brother showed up again. This time they held my hands and stayed in the room. I could see them with my eyes open; I thought you could see them too". Her breathwork facilitator reassured her that he could not see them, but that did not invalidate her experience. This woman did well for over 3 years when she was lost to follow-up; by that time she had become a leader in a 12-step program in her community.

Discussion

Holotropic Breathwork allows the experience to be safe and private. The format is structured to create a supportive space. HB is non-directive and non-intrusive; and the resulting experiences are spontaneous. The patients' evaluation of HB was that it offered an opportunity for emotional expression and spontaneous internal psychospiritual exploration. No adverse sequelae were reported in more than 11,000 Holotropic Breathwork in-patients over 12 years signals that Holotropic Breathwork is a low risk therapeutic approach. Patients reported benefits across a broad range of psychological and existential life issues. These reports support the proposition that holotropic states of consciousness are safe, when done with the proper mental set in a supportive therapeutic setting. Further research on disorder specific benefits is warranted. Holotropic Breathwork and other psychospiritual experiential approaches may become a valuable therapeutic tool.

The 2% who reported 'no experience': another explanation may be proffered than an uneventful session, "No experience", or consciousness without content, is a description of the yogic state of *turiya* [Sanskrit, fourth state]. *Turiya* may occur in Holotropic Breathwork sessions with some frequency. Due to time restrictions with groups of twenty patients, there were no questions of whether turiya criteria were met. *Turiya* criteria include cessation of thought, and the suspension of breath while remaining alert, absence of sleepiness or fatigue afterwards.[7] *Turiya* is described as 'the space between thoughts' in Transcendental Meditation, mindfulness meditation,[8] and other meditation techniques. The physiology has been well described by Benson, Wallace, and Wilson as well as others.[9,10]

The inpatients' endorsement of Holotropic Breathwork, at their exit interviews, as the best therapy at the Hyland Behavioral Health Center swayed the hospital administration to assign extra music therapists to assist in the groups. The four extra music therapists allowed groups of 20 patients, with one facilitator for every four patients. The groups were oversubscribed and filled every week.

Hyland Behavioral Health Center publicly supported this work. The Hyland Center Community Training Institute sponsored Holotropic Breathwork for the professional therapists in the Saint Louis area. Some of the hospital administrators also participated in these HB sessions.

Pediatric patients: Epworth Children's Home, an adolescent residential program, began offering Holotropic Breathwork after one adolescent returned to the program from a hospitalization. During an inpatient HB session he had a transpersonal transformative experience [conscious contact with his higher power] during the inpatient sessions.[11] Epworth's music therapist, Hallie Huber, trained with me. We then offered HB to interested residents as individual sessions. Huber noted that approximately half of the 52 children-in-residence participated. She noted no adverse experiences among the adolescents.

HB may be considered similar to meditation/contemplation practices, but is much more intense. Some participants termed it a 'crash course' in spirituality. HB used enhanced breathing and evocative music to give experiences similar to LSD, and other psychedelic therapies. This may be considered remarkable; this potential is largely unknown to professionals as well as the general public.[12] The experience with the Holotropic Breathwork in 482 consecutive Saint Anthony Medical Center psychiatric inpatients was presented at the Washington University Department of Psychiatry Grand Rounds in 1991. Other presentations include the American Psychiatric/Italian Psychiatric Association in Sienna in 1997, the weekly UCSF Depression Seminars in 2007, and the EUROTAS 2014 Conference in Crete.

Bibliography

[1] Walsh, R., & Vaughan, F. (1993). Transpersonal definitions. *The Journal of Transpersonal Psychology, 25*(2), 125-182. Transpersonal experiences occur when the sense of identity or self extends beyond (trans) the individual or personal to encompass wider aspects of humankind, life, psyche or cosmos.

[2] Grof, S. MD. (1988). *The adventure of self-discovery: Dimensions of consciousness and new perspectives in psychotherapy and inner exploration.* Albany, NY: SUNY Press (Series in Transpersonal and Humanistic Psychology).
[3] Grof, S., & Grof, C. (2010). *Holotropic Breathwork: A new approach to self-exploration and therapy.* Albany, NY: State University of New York Press (Excelsior Editions).
[4] See 2
[5] See 2
[6] See 2
[7] Rhinewine, J. P., & Williams, O. J. (2007). Holotropic Breathwork: The potential role of a prolonged, voluntary hyperventilation procedure as an adjunct to psychotherapy. *The Journal of Alternative and Complementary Medicine, 13,* 771–776.
[8] Williams, M., Teasdale, J., Segal, Z., & Kabat-Zinn, J. (2007). *The mindful way through depression: Freeing yourself from chronic unhappiness.* New York, NY: The Guilford Press.
[9] Benson, H., & Wallace, R.K. (1972). The physiology of meditation. *Scientific American, 226*, 84-90.
[10] Wallace R. K., Benson H., & Wilson A.F. (1971). A wakeful hypometabolic physiologic state. *American Journal of Physiology, 221*, 795-799.
[11] Brewerton, T.D., Eyerman, J.D., Cappetta, P., & Mithoefer, M. (2012). Long-term abstinence following Holotropic Breathwork as adjunctive treatment of substance use disorders and related psychiatric comorbidity. *International Journal of Mental Health Addiction, 10*(3), 453-459.
[12] See 2, 3, 7, 8

CHAPTER THIRTEEN

MAGNOLIAS, PLUMS AND BLACK MAMBAS: FACING LIFE IN THE STAINS ON A DRESS OF WHITE ANGLAISE: A CASE PRESENTATION OF PSYCHOTHERAPY AND RESEARCH IN TRANSPERSONAL PSYCHOLOGY

MARLEEN DE VILLIERS

Abstract

This chapter is the narrative of a process of therapy and the nexus between methods of doing transpersonal research in psychology and the application of the same methods in the therapeutic process. I argue that research and psychotherapy are articulated as developmental processes. Both have the power to transform the researcher and practitioner, as well as the participants and the client. The notion of embodied development features strongly. The client in this presentation has been actively engaged in her healing process by mapping a storyline of disease and illness. In this article, I offer the story of a therapeutic journey that affirms the consciousness of transmutation: life, death and rebirth. I map the storyline of a 70–year old woman whose story becomes a narrative of shedding skin, of her eventually being compelled by life itself to experience the death of her non-authentic self. At the age of 60 she comes to a fork in the road and enters psychotherapy. Emphasis is placed on an exploration of the relational aspect of the therapist and client in the therapeutic process, which may highlight aspects of transpersonal thinking that portray that the separation between personal, therapeutic and research insights in transpersonal research is becoming obsolete. The stories of transformation in this article may lend themselves to further dialogue or research and to be written into various forms of arts-based research and art therapy.

Keywords: development, psychotherapy, research, transpersonal, transformation.

Part 1: Presenting a Case of Psychotherapy

Facing Life In The Stains On A Dress Of White Anglaise: Eliza's Timeline and Trauma Map:

Eliza was five years old when she woke up alone one morning in a room in Hotel Sarnia near Durban. Golden sunlight filtered through shuttered windows and drew song lines on the wooden floor. Her life story was forecast that day, mapping a harsh territory. Her mother had tried to commit suicide the previous night and had been taken to hospital without Eliza being told about anything...

She was born in Cape Town, South Africa as an only child to parents who got divorced when she was 5. Her childhood is marked with loneliness and isolation, fear and uncertainty. Her mother attempted suicide many times until she later died in a mental hospital where she was treated for alcoholism and severe depression. Eliza's relationship with her mother tells a painful tale, and forms an important aspect of her therapeutic journey. Her father was absent for most of Eliza's life, making awkward guest appearances from time to time. This too leaves a trace in her stories of experiencing abandonment and failed relationships with men, starting with the challenge of an unplanned teenage pregnancy.

Her adult life story is filled with experiences of poverty, abuse, trauma and divorce, illness including breast cancer, severe digestive challenges and surgery, unemployment and facing homelessness. At the age of 60 she once again experiences severe trauma and loss and finds herself at a fork in the road. Eliza embarks on a journey of healing and education, exploring various forms of therapy and training programs. She qualifies as a counselor and starts her own practice. When she turns 68 she contacts the author and a deep and profound journey starts for both of them, a journey that Eliza calls "From bag lady to butterfly"...

The Therapeutic Journey

According to Satir (as cited in Hayes, 1987)[1] the experience of therapy is deeply intimate and requires a measure of sensitivity from both therapist and client where both individuals meet the deepest part of each other. In my own experience as a psychotherapist during the process of therapy both the therapist and client are engaged in transformation, as well as transmutation. The process of the therapeutic journey echoes this as well, in that layers and layers of uncovering the wound(s) of the client takes place, much like shedding skin. As a therapist, I view therapy as a process of awakening, of healing patterns, of allowing vulnerability to be a resource, to merge with resilience and become the strength and courage to heal one's deepest wounds. I also see therapy as a deep psychological restructuring by understanding and gaining insight into the client's narrative, assisting the therapeutic process to serve the client's deep insight into herself and her story.

In psychotherapy we reconstruct our stories, we rewrite the scripts, and we dare to explore the possibilities of new ways of self-awareness, self-experience and self-expression. In the safe space, the *temenos*, that therapy provides, we can access the memories which store the wounds that for some time allowed us to form an identity, and as such also go beyond the core wound (in Eliza's case, abandonment) into exploring a process of evolution of the deeper self.

I concur with Rodrigues,[2] in my experience in working with Eliza I witnessed how Transpersonal Psychotherapy enables us to leave old structures behind, to grow into an experience of liberation, as we release/transform/transmute outdated belief systems, embracing a consciousness that encourages a death of the old self and allowing for the emergence of the authentic self.

In embracing the paradigm of transpersonal psychotherapy, Eliza and I aimed to create a space for healing that allowed her to move beyond limiting ego-beliefs such as that she is not worthy of being loved. We worked with a therapeutic view that was integrative and holistic; we worked with her body-mind consciousness and also explored the emotional, psychological, spiritual, cognitive and relational aspects of her wounding and healing. Our therapeutic sessions were a collaboration of delving into the intrapersonal, interpersonal and transpersonal realms of her being-ness. As such we aimed to enable a process of self-transformation.

The Therapeutic Relationship

Our relationship became a map for the journey while we reconstructed the past and also created pathways to explore new ways of relating and authentic self-experience and self-expression. We held the tension between the old ways of being and of walking on the wire towards embracing the authentic self as it emerged from the depths of our Being. Together we sat, silently at times, in deep waters of the therapeutic experience. We allowed and embraced the uncertainty of this difficult, mysterious process which is psychotherapy. Together we found ways of resolving challenging logistics, mostly pertaining to money, time, distance, transport, ill health and non-well-being, and so on.

The therapeutic relationship becomes an experience of relating, and it is crucial that the illness becomes the doctor: Eliza presented with deep relational trauma, abandonment wounds and co-dependent tendencies in relationships. According to Machtiger,[3] in this environment where the therapeutic relationship becomes a resource for transformation, the therapist can offer the relational space the grace of respect, belief in the process and the client, being open and non-judgmental, curious, daring, humble, fully present, accepting and sincere.

Being a Psychotherapist

As therapist, I strive to know and accept my Self, to find a still point in the therapy session in full presence, being focused, centered and grounded. In alignment with the consciousness of transpersonal wellbeing, I practice prayer, meditation, journal writing, mandala drawing, early morning walks, much solitude, art and creativity and Being in silence. I embrace the law of energy, I embrace the law of resonance and I also allow my training as Reiki Master, which heightens my capacity for sensing and witnessing energy transference in the session, to inform my transpersonal skills to be present during the therapeutic sessions. These skills are intuition, clairvoyance, clairsentience, mind-monitoring and mindfulness, self-observation and witnessing.

As a ritual to honor the therapeutic space of the consultation room, I light a candle, light a stick of incense and pour fresh drinking water for us both.

Part 2: Meeting in the Crossing Point: Exploring the Potential of Creating New Resources

A new resource can be described as interplay of initiative and active surrender, allowing for what is creatively purposeful.[4] The methodology used by the author in her doctoral study where aspects of transpersonal psychology and narrative inquiry were combined in an attempt to widen the scope of doing qualitative research, is used in the therapeutic case in this presentation. This chapter is presented in a manner of demonstrating aspects of narrative inquiry, where I give an account of ourselves and of our lives as therapist and client, our experiences and our relationship, much the same as when I was working as a researcher with co-researchers in the study.

Methods used in the Process of Eliza's Therapy and in the Research Study

Intuition

James Hillman (as cited in De Villiers, 2012)[5] describes intuition as a mode of perceiving the invisible, which includes a mythic sensibility. For Hillman intuition is fundamentally a process of immediacy, without reflective thinking. Intuition occurs we do not make it happen; it is a rapid understanding that takes place. During the process of conducting research as well as in facilitating psychotherapy, I often experienced this. It is important to be clear that intuitive insights can miss the mark.

Rosemarie Anderson[6] refers to the Latin origin of intuition, being *intuitus*, meaning the direct perception of knowledge. Anderson suggests that intuition could have a wonderful and fleeting quality of meaning being immediately interpretable and at other times elusive. William Braud[7] referred to intuition as a form of knowledge that happens rapidly without much reflection on the matter.

Intuition played an important role in therapeutic sessions when I was working with Eliza's therapy. I would often reflect on what I had intuitively 'seen' or 'known' during sessions and brought that content back into following sessions. Eliza herself is also very intuitive and as such, we could knit images, thoughts and subliminal content into content we could work with; often such content would be carried into a homework project, creative writing and so forth.

Mandala Drawings

In my doctoral dissertation (De Villiers, 2012)[8] I refer to David Fontana who says that a mandala represents that which lies all around one and deep inside oneself. Mandala means circle or circumbulation, according to Jungian texts. It is similarly described by Fincher (1991),[9] who cites Jung writing in his autobiography that the self is like a monad which is one's world. The mandala represents this monad and corresponds to the nature of the psyche. He also said that he saw the mandala as the path of individuation and very appropriate as a therapeutic method: mandala work is seen as a way of consciously creating a relationship with Self (intrapersonal)[10] (Stan Grof is known to use mandala work in an integration process in Holotropic Breathwork).

I include Eliza's mandala towards the end of her therapeutic sessions before her major surgery when her therapy was suspended, and as per my agreement with her, regarding this presentation, I also include my own mandala which I created about my experiences of her therapeutic process. This is a further example of our work as collaboration.

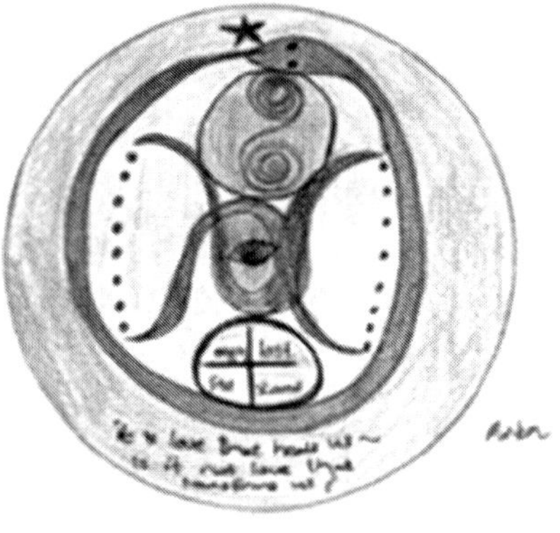

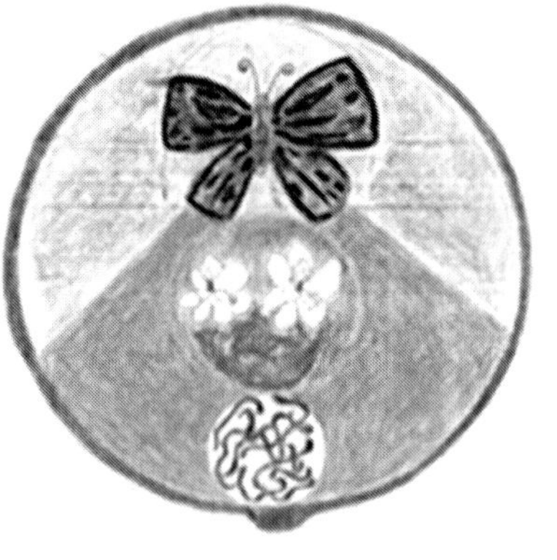

Journal Writing

Journal writing is a powerful way of documenting information.[11]

From a point of personal experience, I have been making daily entries in my personal journal since 1997 and I have come to understand that it brings a sense of meaning to my life; that the recording of events, feelings, impressions, thoughts and the like, orders the daily mundane and magical experiences of my life. It feels like having a silent witness, which gives me a sense of oneness with life.

Visual Imagery and Photographs: Making Collages

According to the New Oxford American Dictionary the word collage is derived from the French word *coller*, meaning 'glue'. Collage is a form of art in which various materials such as photographs and pieces of paper and fabric are glued together, also described as an art form consisting of an assemblage of different forms, creating a new whole.[12] Collage is an attempt to create a reality and find meaning, thus becoming a work of art as well as bearing information. I often use collage making as a therapeutic tool in my therapy practice and have had very meaningful results where clients gain deep and unexpected insight and understanding of intrapersonal experiences and of themselves.

Writing Letters

Sylvia Perera, in the introduction to a book on Jungian symbolism writes that letters are an important way to share knowledge, and that perhaps especially for women, they may enable the expression of creativity.[13]

Personal Documentation

Personal documents in the form of personal memos, newspaper cuttings cards, other items that trigger memories and reflections, all serving as a keeper of stories, were shared during our sessions. Much value was found in these rich sources of information.[14]

Dream Work

Dreams in the research process as well as the therapeutic space became very significant:[15] According to Frank,[16] dreams tell our individual stories. Dreams give voice to the existing content in the subconscious, dream images and symbolism can make the 'translation' of the transpersonal dimension possible.

Personal Mythology

Joseph Campbell became renowned for his ground-breaking work on comparative mythology. He writes that mythology is psychology that is misread or mistaken for, amongst others, anthropology or cosmology. He suggests that in the contemporary practice of psychology, much depth can be found in translating mythological figures into human characteristics. Working with personal mythology is also an important means to assist in understanding Eliza's dreams and her dream symbols. Working with the dreams of the co-researchers in my doctoral study also yielded deep, profound and useful data.

Campbell says that symbols of mythology are spontaneous productions of the psyche, while Harris says that symbols are also expressions of spontaneous experiences that point towards meaning that is only partly "conceivable". I am intrigued by the link between symbols and myths and our personal stories, and how it may perhaps create meaning in our lives. According to Stevens[17] myths are realistic expressions of life.

Other Methods and Resources in the Treatment Process

Astrology

Karen Syrett refers to the horoscope as a living mandala, in my mind a wonderfully apt description. She refers to Jung, who believed that the search for meaning is one of the human psyche's deepest and most urgent needs, and saw correlations between the therapeutic process, the alchemists' attempt to turn base metal into a pure substance and the birth-chart as a map of the psyche.

Eliza's journey changed the day when I did an astrological reading for her and revealed significant content that was written into her chart. Astrologers understand that this chart represents a picture of an individual's potential psychological and spiritual make-up. Jung said that "since an astrological constellation makes diagnosis possible, it also indicates the therapy". I do not necessarily make a diagnosis, but I can certainly read patterns, predispositions and resolutions from an astrological chart.[18]

We also worked with myths and symbols, Meditation, Reiki, Tarot and Oracle Cards, Rituals, Creative writing and other Arts-based methods such as Storytelling, Poetry, Blogging, Drawing, Crafts such as making a tapestry, knitting, sewing (anglaise), making a GOD-box, working with writing a resume and an obituary and used cross referrals using other modalities such as bodywork, homeopathy, etc.

Conclusion

Using arts-based methods in research and applying those methods in a therapeutic process became a seamless fit, bringing about development and transformation in the co-researchers and myself as researcher, as well as in my client and in myself, as therapist. An excerpt from my therapy notes,[19] taken from the final session of Eliza's therapy: "it seems that her deeper self has come to therapy, she is mindful of the smell of the flowers in the garden, she touches the leaves gently, enters the room and inhales deeply, sighs and sits herself down. She is ready to embrace what has healed her, rather than to stay in the realm of what has ailed her in the past...".

And as for me as developing researcher and psychotherapist, I am grateful to find an academic and therapeutic home in transpersonal psychology.

> I don't know any other way to live now. My dreams provide the rudder for my life. My work is to find my authenticity and then to surrender that to a higher purpose. It is at the place of wounding that we find ourselves connected to each other in love, and it is here that I open to loving other people, loving the planet, loving the cosmos. I think the future of our planet depends on human beings discovering their own light, becoming conscious of the universe as one soul (Woodman, as cited in De Villiers, 2012).[20]

Bibliography

[1] Hayes, J.A. (2014). The beneficial demands of conducting psychotherapy. *Journal of Clinical Psychotherapy, 70*(8), 716-723.
[2] Rodrigues, V. (2010). On consciousness–modifying (transpersonal) psychotherapy. *Journal of Transpersonal Research, 2*(1), 44-61.
[3] Machtiger, H.G. (1985). Perilous beginnings: Loss, abandonment and transformation. In *Chiron: A review of Jungian Analysis* (pp.101-129). Asheville, NC: Chiron Publications.
[4] Richards, M.C. (1973). *The crossing point.* Middletown, CT: Wesleyan University Press.
[5] De Villiers, M. (2012). *A transpersonal exploration of the mother-daughter relationship in transitional life cycles* (Unpublished doctoral dissertation). University of Stellenbosch, Stellenbosch, South Africa.
[6] Anderson, R., & Braud, W. (2011). *Transforming self and others through research: Transpersonal research methods and skills for the human sciences and humanities.* Albany, NY: State University of New York Press.
[7] See Note 6.
[8] See Note 5.

[9] See Note 5.
[10] Millner, D. (2005). Mandala symbolism in psychotherapy: The potential utility of the Lowenfeld mosaic technique for enhancing the individuation process. *The Journal of Transpersonal Psychology, 37*(2), 164-177
[11] Clandinin, D.J., & Connelly, F.M. (2000). *Narrative inquiry: Experience, and story in qualitative research.* San Francisco, CA: Jossey-Bass.
[12] Leavy, P. (2009). *Method meets art: Arts-based research practice.* New York, NY: The Guilford Press.
[13]Howell, A.O. (1987). *Jungian symbolism in astrology: Letters from an astrologer.* Wheaton, IL: The Theosophical Publishing House.
[14] Goldberg, N. (1986). *Wring down the bones: Freeing the writer within.* Boston, MA: Shambhala.
[15] Papadopoulos, R.K. (Ed.). (2006). *The handbook of Jungian psychology: Theory, practice and applications.* Hove: East Sussex, England: Routledge.
[16] Frank, E. (2004). *The book of dreams.* Cape Town, South Africa: Human & Rousseau.
[17] Stevens, A. (1990). *On Jung.* London, England: Routledge.
[18] See Note 13.
[19] DeVilliers, M. (2014). *Therapeutic notes.*
[20] See Note 19.

CHAPTER FOURTEEN

METAMORPHOSIS THROUGH YOGA: AN EXPRESSIVE ARTS THERAPY APPROACH TO HEALING

MILIICA ZEGARAC

Dedicated to Petra, a new light to the world.

If you bring forth that which is within you, what you bring forth will save you. If you do not bring forth what is within you, what you do not bring forth will destroy you. Gospel of St. Thomas

Abstract

The immersion into a yoga experience, openness, receptivity and surrendering to the process-oriented activities can qualify it as an expressive arts therapy. The main elements of the expressive arts therapies are the "capacity of the arts to respond to human suffering",[1] the use of play and imagination, and the collective role of arts in social change. Expressive arts therapy as a synthesis of several creative modalities (physical movement, visual arts, auditory modes, and so on) fully resonates with what authentic traditional yoga is. We will explore those theoretical assumptions and premises, as well as the attained empirical insights further in this text. The process (yoga session) may contain predominantly non-verbal and physical elements such as asana, pranayama, kriya, mudra, bandha, and so on, or constituents that refer to sensual-mental-spiritual constructs like pratyahara (withdrawal of senses), dharana (concentration), dhyana (meditation) and Samadhi (bliss of self-realization). There are also verbal components of yoga such as chanting and mantras, which can become highly emotionally charged. The visual elements of yoga imply images and visualizations. At a more global level, Karma yoga has social implications that encompass selfless service to the community and to humanity as a whole.

Keywords: Expressive arts therapy, Hatha yoga, Raja yoga, Taoist Yin & Yang yoga, yoga therapy

The topic of yoga and its healing properties in the context of the transpersonal worldview often carries a personal significance for many of us whose lives have been touched by it. There are many paths to yoga and many variants, especially in the West. Some yogic paths are similar, and some very divergent and diametrically opposite. The rivers often do not flow to the same sea, to rephrase the metaphor often used to refer to the perennial stance in transpersonal philosophy, where in general, paths may differ, but the end results (i.e., goals) are the same. In order to find what is authentic and generic, we need to go to the source and refer to historically traditional forms, Hatha yoga and Raja yoga from India, and Taoist yoga from China.

Yoga is defined as a union of polarities ("yog" means union in Sanskrit). Hatha comes from the Sanskrit words Ha (Sun) and Tha (Moon). Raja yoga or "royal yoga" is predominantly related to the classical "Yoga Sutra" text attributed to Patanjali, Indian sage of historically inconclusive origins. Taoist yoga is often called Yin and Yang yoga, and is similar to Hatha yoga with regard to postures and some other methodology.[i] All those above mentioned yogic concepts refer to transcendence of polarities and their integration into more evolved and perfect synergistic whole, self-development, healing, and further integration of body, mind and spirit as an ultimate goal.

Yoga as an Expressive and Creative Play

Most yoga classes in the West resemble Pilates or fitness sessions. Exercise as an activity entices the control of body, quick or instant gratification, separation of physical and mental, effect on mostly muscular-skeletal systems, and focus on results. Contrary to this, yoga as a therapy or practice ultimately results in control of mind, a sense of deep connection to ourselves and others, mindful awareness, a whole person view (body, breath, mind, etc.), and focus on the process.

Yogic activities do not have to be rigidly structured and follow a prescribed sequence, but strive in the direction of balance and relate to

---

[i] "Ha" corresponds to "Yang", while "Tha" relates to "Yin".

both energizing (yang), and relaxing (yin) activities, to both brain hemispheres, left (more rational and masculine), and right (more creative and feminine). According to the ancient yogic texts, there are reputedly 72,000 postures, which energetically and physiologically affect various parts of the brain. In this vein, it is advisable to introduce the whole kaleidoscope of various yogic techniques and methods gradually, so the process of learning and evolving can become more creative. Similar to the visual arts, "the rigid need to repeat recurrent creative patterns reduces the flexibility of emotional experience and prevents the growth of expression".[2] The best and most spontaneous way for a negative, subconscious and "shadow" material to come to the surface is in a nonthreatening, playful, creative and often, non-verbal way.[3]

The greatest destruction occurs when there is no outlet for creative spirit and its expression. Creativity-based processes have an innate capacity to break and deconstruct mental sets.[4] Thus, each yoga therapy class should offer a novel experience, and to a certain extent, be organic in its structure. It should also evolve through mutual interconnectedness, entrainment and sympathetic resonance between the participants and the instructor.

A great example for this creative approach to yoga therapy is the brand of Taoist Yin and Yang yoga taught by Master Paulie Zink.[5] Animal shapes and postures, the concepts of yin and yang, and five elements (earth, metal, water, wood and fire) in generative or suppressive cycles express the indigenous spirit of nature in a playful, creative and original way. Yoga becomes an art of self-expression, and these psycho-dynamic and alchemical constellations are in a constant process of transformation and playful creation. A similar view can be taken regarding Hatha and Raja yoga, allowing the participants and practitioner more freedom in expressing themselves through postures and movement, breath, visualizations, and other yogic forms, and allowing somatic, emotional and spiritual healing to occur, as an expressive arts therapy, or creative and improvisational play.

Role of Yoga in Mental and Emotional Healing

Knill[6] talks about the notion of "de-centering" as a necessary step in departure from negative, stressful experience into an environment of greater possibilities, creative unpredictability and unlimited potential. A yoga studio or any other space where the healing practice takes place must become a safe container, or what the ancient Greeks called "temenos"[7] where yoga as this intermodal activity removes the practitioner from the outside world into the "here and now". If immersed into the practice properly, it becomes possible to quiet the "monkey mind" and its fluctuations,[ii] and change the thought patterns by interrupting the negative feedback loop of "fight and flight" response, reactivity and other negative and destructive modes of being.

Clark[8] delineates three main components of asana practice, and perceives it as a process that starts with coming into a pose to a certain edge (energetic benefits), holding a pose for a certain time (physiological benefits), and a resolved attempt to stay still while holding the posture (emotional and mental benefits). This process is also analogous to remaining physically, but also mentally still during meditation, or during some yogic breathing techniques (e.g., alternate nostril breath), when we pause or hold the breath, as opposed to energizing inhale and relaxing exhale. According to the Taoist and some other forms of yoga, emotions, both positive and negative, are stored in the body, in its connective tissues, joints and organs.[iii]

The constituents or elements of yoga as expressive arts therapy can be categorized as: (a) non-verbal or physical (movement, stillness, breathing techniques, hand or body gestures, locks, and so on), (b) sensual/mental/ spiritual constructs (withdrawal of senses, concentration, meditation, and blissful self-realization), and (c) verbal, auditory or visual elements.

Non-verbal Aspect of Yoga

Expressive arts therapy, and movement/dance therapy as one of its components, addresses the importance of body, its position and locus in space, and its intrinsic capacity for self-expression, but also for self-healing (i.e., deeply rooted trauma, stored negative emotions and destructive behavioral patterns). The conventional "talk therapy" has limited success, which is substantiated by recent neuro-scientific research. The Broca area in the brain responsible for verbal communication[9] is relatively smaller and shut down in case of patients with trauma.

[ii] The main function of yoga according to Patanjali is to remove the fluctuation of the mind, "yogas chitta vritti nirodhah".

[iii] Yin organs are more receptive and hence store negative emotions: lungs store anxiety and sorrow, kidneys fear, heart excessive emotionality and excitability, liver anger, and spleen others' negative energy.

Additional research also shows that many individuals who experience traumatic experiences or emotional and physical suffering exhibit dissociation from the body. The research by Antonio Damasio indicates that insula, the part of the brain where the transmission of the physical sensations into conscious body awareness occurs,[10] is considerably reduced and with less circuit connections in people with traumatic or negative experiences. It is therefore indicative that the healing of various trauma and mood disorders must take place at the somatic and sensation level through accessing the body, and not at the emotional level.[11]

The ancient traditions of Hatha yoga, Tantra yoga, Kundalini yoga, Kriya yoga, Taoist yoga, and so on, emphasize the importance of being present here and now, and aware of our own bodies to the fullest phenomenological extent. Tantra yoga stresses the importance of relaxation as the main portal for accessing the unconscious and the superconscious. Most of those traditions hence see body as a shrine that houses dormant evolutionary energies which need to be awaken and directed, for the benefit of realizing the self.[iv]

Some other yoga traditions[v] perceive body as the bridge to higher (mental) forms of consciousness, negating the importance of the physical per se. The transpersonal view takes a position that soma and psyche are manifestations of the omnipresent consciousness, as a universal energy field of various vibrations and information. Yoga, the union of body, breath, mind and spirit, leads to expansion of consciousness, self-liberation[vi] and ultimately to the evolution of humans as species.

Nonverbal or Physical Elements of Yoga

According to yoga, body as the first and basic aspect of a person can be healed and transformed through movement and holding the postures with willful awareness and intention. In yoga, the sequence, the length of hold, and the timing of postures introduction are relatively more structured than any of the dance or movement therapies (i.e., authentic movement), but many elements are similar or the same.[12]

[iv] According to the science of yoga, Kundalini energy is an evolutionary force that lies dormant at the base of the spine.

[v] Raja yoga, Karma yoga, Bhakti yoga, Mantra yoga, Sri Aurobindo's Integral yoga mostly view body as secondary.

[vi] Self-liberation refers to becoming free from afflictions such as fear, hatred, jealousy, greed, and so on;

The kinesthetic, motoric, sensory and other forms of bodily awareness (i.e., interception, proprioception, and so on) are enhanced with both mindfulness and relaxation as two sides of the same coin. The grounding and stabilizing functions of yoga are achieved through postures that are close to the surface, while being in the supine (e.g., savasana or corps pose), prone (e.g., fetus pose), and sitting postures (e.g., forward bends). The standing postures manifest a higher level of dynamic connection between the body and mind, and its relative position in space. The inversions (e.g., headstand, shoulder stand, plough, and so on) may mean venturing into "terra incognita", and should be performed only after strengthening the physical and emotional core of the patient/practitioner (i.e., they entail the relinquishing of control and letting go). The shamanistic embodiment of animal spirits in Taoist Yin yoga serves the purpose of incarnating the strength, versatility and courage of animals and ritualistically transferring that energy into the practitioner.

Breathing techniques (pranayama), as well as hand and body gestures (mudra) and subtle energy locks (bandha) are used to transform and calm both body and mind, by means of directing energy to certain areas of the body, and enhancing the flow and utilization of prana. Spiritually, breath is a connection between the physical and transcendental, between the body and the soul, which further informs the importance of proper breathing as a way to maintain that connection. Research shows that inhalation increases the energy level, heart and respiration rate, and activates the sympathetic nervous system. Contrary to this, exhalation calms the body and mind, and affects the parasympathetic nervous system, and it is advisable to, in order to still the body and pacify the mind, extend the exhalation. Similar to Hatha yoga, Taoist yogis claim that all physical or mental disorders start with either energy blockage (too much chi) or because of its deficiency.

Sensual, Mental and Spiritual Constructs

In general, Patanjali and Raja yoga perceive the postures, breathing techniques, body locks, and body and hand gestures as auxiliary and supplemental steps that lead higher forms of yoga. Those higher forms include the elimination or withdrawal of senses (pratyahara), concentration (dharana), meditation (dhyana), and finally, the ultimate state of blissfulness and union with divine (samadhi). It is a misnomer to view meditation as separate from yoga, which is a customary thing in the contemporary research and academic circles.

The goal of those yogic concepts and their application pertain to the formation of sensual and mental constructs. This is fundamentally the process of delineating ego from the self, of becoming a silent observer or witness of our own sensations, emotions and mental processes. The ultimate goal is direct perception, higher consciousness, an ability to heal, self-liberate and self-realize oneself. The union with the divine, of Atman and Brahman, of the self with Self is attained through the state of bliss of self-realization (Samadhi), when all the boundaries are removed and the quest for being the one with God is reached. The types of yoga that predominately investigate those "higher" level yogic processes are Raja yoga and Jnana yoga.

Verbal, Auditory and Visual Constituents of Yoga

As noted before, expressive arts therapy as a compilation of several creative modalities used for therapeutic purposes (i.e., visual arts, creative writing, recitals, playing or composing music, performances, and so on) has some common aspects with yoga therapy,[13] as well as with physical, mental and spiritual aspects of authentic quotidian yoga practice.

Chanting to the imagined or concrete figures of Hindu deities or repetition of Gayatri or Maha Mrityunjaya mantras auspicious 108 times internalize as personal and transpersonal rituals and often leads to altered states. Those are also verbal and auditory aspects of Bhakti yoga,[vii] but incidentally and at the same time of yoga therapy in its broader sense of the word and the therapeutic value of auditory and verbal creative expression. Short mantras such as Aum or SoHum or personal mantras, are either integral parts of the overall yogic practice or are used in meditation (i.e., transcendental meditation).

Visual aspects of yoga entail the use of images, concrete objects, colors and forms to entice the altered states of consciousness, calm the mind, or/and engage in higher yogic practices. The initial stages of meditation may begin by focusing on an image or a flame, flower, point between the eyebrows (trikuti), and so on. Visualization of various colors as in chakra meditation aids the concrete representation of seven chakras through a variety of colors and shapes (i.e., lotus petals). In the same vein, drawing mandalas and yantras brings expressive and protective aspect to the healing process. The long "dark night of the soul" was overcome by C. G.

[vii] Bhakti yoga is a yoga of ritualistic devotion to Hindu deities.

Jung as he immersed himself into a fearless exploration of the depths of his psyche, on the "road less traveled". Jung's own metamorphosis included drawing of mandalas, as a way to bring the unconscious content of the psyche to the surface and make it understandable (i.e., active imagination method).[14]

Yoga and Social Transformation

The role that yoga plays in the social environment is two-fold. It relates to the concepts of "self-building" and "world-building",[15] as humans' innate capacity to shape themselves and their environment according to their needs. The basic premise lies in the fact that a self-realized individual, who, to paraphrase Gandhi, is the change he or she wants to see, has so much to contribute to humanity as a whole. A non-violent, peaceful and evolved person is a role model and transmitter of a higher vibration that has potential to improve social ecology in any environment. The individual traits and behaviors correspond to what Raja yoga would term niyamas, the rules of personal conduct. Those omnipresent and cross-cultural behavioral traits constitute the foundation of a healthy individual on the path to self-actualization. Purity of mind (shaucha), contentment and acceptance of what is (santosha), austerity and humility (tapas), self-development through study and personal inquiry (swadhyana) and surrender to the higher power (ishwara pranidhana) often constitute the steps and elements of several contemporary forms of individual or group psychotherapy. Those are steps away from the persona or the shadow self, towards what Sri Aurobindo calls "psychic being".

The "therapeutic community model" provides another modality for the change of global consciousness that can be done through yoga. It primarily offers the climate of mutual support, understanding, trust, and safety and enables individuals, groups and even societies to create their own, better world.

Healing emotional disorders of war veterans, teaching yoga in schools for violence reduction or to improve mental focus of vulnerable youths, and introducing yoga to prisoners, are just some of the social endeavors for a broader application of this ancient technology, as well as its world view.

"Off the Mat, Into the World" is another well -known organization and social movement with a mission to promote conscious social activism through yoga in order to enhance social sustainability and be an agent of transformation. Its global "seva" projects are in the environments where awareness and assistance are urgently needed (i.e., India, Amazon, Haiti, and so on).

The yogic rules of social behavior or yamas, such as non-violence (ahimsa), truthfulness (satya), honesty (asteya), temperance (brahmacharya) and generosity (aparigraha) instruct individuals how to find and follow their own Dharma, their destined life mission in the service of humanity. Karma yoga[viii] means paying attention to one's own thoughts, words and actions, and discontinuing the chain of reactivity, so that the suffering in the world is minimized. The personal and global metamorphosis through service, empathy and loving kindness is the goal.

Conclusion

The main thesis of this chapter, the possibility of enlisting yogic techniques, ideas and procedures as expressive arts therapy has a valid point from both theoretical and my own experiential point of view. The arguments are rooted in the recent scientific research pointing to the superiority of nonverbal therapies for healing many mental disorders, or for mere personal transformation over "talk therapies". The approach also points out to similarity of various constituents of yoga to the elements of expressive arts therapy (i.e., movement, visual, auditory, and verbal modalities). At the collective level, the role of yoga to create more peaceful, happy and evolved communities involves the application of its higher forms (i.e., personal constraints and rules of social conduct). At the global level, it is also manifested through social activism and service to humanity as a whole, and in bringing peace and saving our planet, our only home.

Bibliography

[1] Levine, S., & Levine, E. (Eds.). (1999). *Foundations of expressive arts: Theoretical and clinical perspectives.* Philadelphia, PA: Jessica Kingsley. p.11.
[2] McMurray, M. (2001). Integration and working through in art therapy. *The Arts in Psychotherapy: An International Journal, 28*(5), p. 311.
[3] Nachmanovitch, S. (1990). *Free play: Improvisation in life and art*. New York, NY: Jeremy P. Tarcher/Putnam.
[4] Amabile, T. (1996). *Creativity in context: Update to the "Social psychology of creativity*". Boulder, CO: Westview Press.

[viii] Karma yoga is a socially engaged yoga; seva, the selfless service to others without any expectations of gain.

[5] Zink, P. (2009). *Art of yin and yang yoga: Teacher training workbook*. Self-published.
[6] Knill, P. J. (2011). Communal art-making and conflict transformation.. In E. Levine, & S. Levine (Eds.), *Art in action: Expressive arts therapy and social change* (pp. 53-77). London, England: Jessica Kingsley.
[7] McNiff, S. (1998). *Trust the process: An artist's guide to letting go*. Boston, MA: Shambhala.
[8] Clark, B. (2012). *The complete guide to yin yoga*. Ashland, OR: White Cloud Press.
[9] van der Kolk, B. A. (2006). Clinical implications of neuroscience research in PTSD. *Annals of New York Academy of Sciences*, *40,* 1-17
[10] van der Kolk, B. A. (2011). Introduction. In D. Emerson & E. Hopper. *Overcoming trauma through yoga: Reclaiming your body* (pp. xvii-xxiv). Berkley, CA: North Atlantic Books.
[11] Levine, P. (2010). *In an unspoken voice: How the body releases trauma and restores goodness.* Berkley, CA: North Atlantic Books.
[12] Rogers, N. (1993). *The creative connection: Expressive arts as healing*. Palo Alto, CA: Science & Behavior Books.
[13] Kraftsow, G. (1999). *Yoga for wellness: Healing with the timeless teachings of Viniyoga.* New York, NY: Penguin Putnam.
[14] Jung, C. G. (1966). The spirit in man, art, and literature. Bollingen Series, *20.* Princeton, NJ: Princeton University Press.
[15] Levine, S (2011). Art opens to the world. In E. Levine & S. Levine (Eds.), *Art in action: Expressive arts therapy and social change* (pp. 21-30). London, England: Jessica Kingsley.

CHAPTER FIFTEEN

TRANSPERSONAL DIMENSIONS IN DANCE MOVEMENT THERAPY: EMBODIMENT AS A MEANS TO ACCESS AND INTEGRATE EXPANDED STATES OF CONSCIOUSNESS

MARIA R. SIDERI

Abstract

In this chapter I discuss aspects of dance movement therapy as a transpersonal technique. Dance movement therapy is an important instrument not only in the sense of strengthening the "ego structure" of the individual but also in transcending it, offering both possibilities in the therapeutic context. The transpersonal experience is understood as a state of expanded consciousness that goes beyond ego boundaries, includes transcendence of cultural limits and a felt sense of reciprocity with the more-than-human-world also outlined by Eco-psychology. Case experiences drawn from clients in treatment are used as illustrations.

Keywords: beyond ego boundaries, dance movement therapy, embodiment, expanded consciousness transpersonal experience.

In transpersonal literature, expanded states of consciousness are described, as non-ordinary states, altered states[1] or superior states of consciousness, as an optimum level of psychological health and wellbeing.[2] For the purpose of this chapter, an expanded state of consciousness will be considered that which includes a holistic awareness of one's mental-emotional and physical state, awareness of soul and spirit,[3] and awareness of interconnection with the external reality and global environment.

The most common cases of transpersonal experiences show short glimpses of superior realizations, followed by longer periods of draw backs. However, once a person evolves in the path of personal development expanded states and ordinary consciousness come close one to the other; "Ecstatic eruptions and regressive draw backs progressively give place to an ego experience stabilized in a superior level of mature absorption and contemplative harmony".[4]

Dance, Movement and Embodiment as Non-Ordinary States of Consciousness

Body and its movement have been used since the beginning of times as a means to represent and process both daily life and sacred experiences,[5] which at early times were not considered to be separate but belonged to the same realm. In the contemporary world, the archaic elements of dance, traditional and contemporary movement practices and modern psychotherapy, all merge in the discipline of dance movement therapy.

Dance Movement Therapy is defined by the American Dance Therapy Association[6] as "the psychotherapeutic use of movement to further the emotional, cognitive, physical and social integration of the individual" and that is based on the premise that the body mind and spirit are interconnected.

Embodiment is described as a sense of a body-based self that implies being and living through body awareness.[7]

Dance movement therapists are pioneers in the body-mind interface and the holistic vision of individuals: "Whether the issue is the will to live, a search for meaning or motility, or the ability to feel love for life, dance/movement therapists mobilize resources from that place within where body and mind are one."[8]

Given the constant focus of dance therapy and somatic psychotherapy to foster embodiment, self-consciousness and imagery, it is not uncommon that subjects in treatment will go into experiences different than their ordinary functioning,[9] feeling a qualitative shift in their overall pattern of mental, emotional and physical functioning; namely, they experience a shift in global consciousness. The therapeutic process itself trains the individual to include such experiences as part of ordinary consciousness, raising the level of one's daily awareness. Obviously, not all experiences in a dance/movement therapy session go beyond personality limits and there is information coming from different levels of personality.

The Outflow of Experiences from Deep Levels of Personality

Spontaneous movement and psychosomatic work is a powerful catalyst of mental, emotional and somatic processes activating unconscious material from various deep levels of personality. Such material matches Grof's[10] description of areas of human unconscious coming from his clinical research of the psychodynamic meaning of LSD phenomena. He describes "four major levels, or types, of LSD experiences and the corresponding areas of human unconscious: (a) abstract and aesthetic experiences, (b) psychodynamic experiences, (c) perinatal experiences, and (d) transpersonal experiences".

The following examples illustrate these levels in a somatic and movement setting:

Aesthetic/abstract experiences do not necessarily reveal the unconscious and have no psychodynamic significance: A woman in her late fifties, on her third session after being given permission to move freely, recalls, "I danced like a cloud, leaving the earth and everything behind, moving up in the sky". Deeper exploration of this experience showed no particular psychodynamic meaning.

Psychodynamic experience: A woman aged 23, after approximately a year of therapy, lying on the floor, moving her hips and legs, recalled being approached by an old man who was her neighbor, with sexual intentions, when she was about six years old. Enacting strong movements of kicking, punching and screaming she released the accumulated tension felt in the pelvic area. As a consequence, her sexual life improved considerably.

Perinatal experience: A woman aged 36, when asked to move starting from her deep physical sensation of extreme cold, realized that such feeling is recurrent in her life and goes together with a sense of anxiety and rush. Later in sessions she recalled experiences from her early life as a fetus, being born premature and left in the lonely and emotionally cold environment of the incubator.

Transpersonal Experiences in Dance/Movement and Psychosomatic Therapy Sessions

Transpersonal phenomena are very diverse and subjective but have as a common denominator a feeling that the consciousness expands beyond the usual ego boundaries and limitations of time and space;[10] when a person goes through a transpersonal experience, deeper realization and healing occurs. Such experiences in therapy are expected to take place only in advanced stages. However, as a therapist practicing in the city of Barcelona I have observed a growing interest of both clients and practitioners in transpersonal issues. I believe that this is due to a fast spreading fashion that attracts people to South-American shamanic practices, the use of psychotropic medicine plants such as "Ayahuasca" and "Peyote," the growing interest in oriental practices of Meditation, Yoga and Tai Chi, among others. Alongside these practices, there has been a shift towards the new paradigm in science,[11] with practices such as "biodescodification" and "systemic constellations" becoming very common. Another explanation can be that dance and movement by itself is an important catalyst of such phenomena.

In this context, clients approaching dance therapy and bodywork seem to be receptive to go beyond personality limits and I often come across cases where this occurs in early stages of therapy.

Fostering Insight through Direct Experience of the Transpersonal

The following examples manifest how somatic and movement work offers insight by direct experience, where action and understanding happen simultaneously:

A woman in her late twenties, exploring problems of integrating spiritual needs with demands of daily life in her seventh session, after an experience in movement reports: "My power animal, the serpent, the cobra, came and made me dance. So powerful, so joyful all obstacles where defeated by the twisting movements. I can be myself and act at the same time. Being in touch and keeping contact with what is within, I can go out there and do it anyway". In this case, embodiment of the animal allowed knowledge and understanding stemming from the animal species to be acknowledged.

A woman, in her mid-fifties, working in her discrepant tendencies says, "I am worried about my need to run and let go or stay and fight". For her treatment I used a combination of spontaneous movement and systemic representations, where cushions were used to represent the energetic field of her mother and father: Embodying the energy of her mother, represented by a cushion, her body shrinks, progressively going to the floor: "I want to disappear" she says. Embodying the energy of her father, represented by a cushion, in front of her mother´s cushion, her body inflates upwards and becomes rigid, while her arms lift up in sign of "dictating". "I feel so stiff, I will almost break. It´s horrible", she states. I guide her to experience the energy of another cushion, located in a middle point, between her mother´s and father´s cushion. She dances with strong, fast, roundabout movements, looking dizzy and needing to disgorge. I permit her to vomit and although nothing physical comes up there is energy liberation. After that, her movement progressively harmonizes while her body adopts a neither stiff nor very soft quality, accessing an optimum middle point. "It´s so good", she says, "I now understand how it should be. I feel them both, mother and father. I am none of them and both at the same time. I am something different and it feels right". In this case we can see the embodiment not only of her mother´s and father´s energetic field, but also of a new possibility, a middle point, where both realities are integrated.

A woman, in her late fifties, a meditation practitioner, reached her 12th session in an alert and confused state, due to work circumstances. When suggested to move inwards and observe present body sensations and feelings, she realized that below superficial confusion, she was at peace. Her description of the experience follows: "The peaceful feeling appeared in the form of tickling sensations on the skin that gradually expanded in the muscles and internal organs. I went on moving and dancing on these sensations until I felt my body expanding. Dance went on without me doing any physical effort. I was being moved by a field that was present in my whole body but was not my body. Some pain I normally have in my neck disappeared and although I kept moving there was no tiredness. At a certain point the dance finished and my body relaxed on the floor. My internal state was of peace and harmony. When I opened my eyes, the room and objects around seemed to have a charm I had not noticed before. This was a new experience for me. I had felt it while meditating, but it was the first time I experienced it in movement. The sensation was of being moved by something that is not my physical body, or a particular emotion, but something that is everything and nothing at the same time". Such a state is described as *"annata"* in Buddhism[12] and *"non-ego"* or absence of ego in transpersonal psychology. When asked how she now sees the difficulties with working conditions that she brought to the beginning of the session, she considered these due to her personal state of confusion and felt confident they would be surmounted if decision making happened based on her inner sensation of peace and comfort. Being in contact with what goes beyond ego, or simply the absence of ego, facilitates the inflow of deeper understanding and simplifies confrontation with life circumstances.

Transpersonal and Transcultural Embodied Pleasure

This experience took place in a dance therapy and bioenergetics workshop I led during the summer of 2014 in the Himalayan village of Vashisth in the North of India. The workshop lasted for two full days and fees were on donation, which allowed people from a variety of cultural and socio-economic backgrounds to attend. The group was a mixture of males and females, formed by western mountaineer travelers and some Indian locals. Despite these differences, participants shared a certain open mindedness and eagerness to immerse into an experience of psycho-physical liberation and expressive movement.

The description below shows the transcultural validity of non-verbal communication, dance, movement and the embodiment of transpersonal issues.

On the second day of the workshop, there was enough intimacy established in the group so as to allow experimentation with deep sensations. After a two-hour session of deep tension and emotional liberation, participants were asked to be moved from "what comes from within". A generalized sense of "looking for pleasure in movement" emerged and I felt it myself while I was moving with the group. The richness and variety of the "form" in which pleasure was being manifested reflected the cultural diversity of the group while transpersonal aspects in the experience emerged. Most westerners, males and females, adopted non-specific movements that would arouse twinkling or sparkly sensations in the body, while Indian participants realized movements related to some specific symbolism also accompanied by inner feelings. For example, an Indian middle class male danced like Krishna while another one, who was a Swami, moved intensely around the room raising his arms up and down in a gesture of "blessing everyone around". The man who danced like Krishna reported that he felt kundalini energy rising in his body just like what had happened in the past when he did yogic practices. Physical pleasure was intense and he was glad to re-connect with such sensation. A female Israeli participant trained in martial arts realized that in order to feel pleasure she had to "let go and stop fighting", which she lately related to her tendency of constant fight and mistrust towards life. A male Polish participant shared that pleasure to him relates to the feeling of having permission to "be who he really is" without judgment.

In the afternoon session the whole group moved guided by a shared sense of peaceful love and community. Two participants could not connect to this specific field, and were allowed to experience their personal journey, up until a work in couples was used to establish uniformity. Finally, the whole group moved in a circle, maintaining physical contact with each other. The initial diversity was transformed into a sense of oneness. When asked to give a single word report of inner state, verbalizations included: "at home,", "one", "tribe", "soft", "holy", "grateful", "thanks", "love", "tender", "joy". The experience ended in silence and no further verbalizations took place, apart from comments on silence and the sound of silence "like a soft vibration that leaves us speechless".

Later, on the same day, participants reported gratefulness for having had the opportunity to feel interconnected in the group and reflections took place on the reasons for such reality not being commonly present in daily life, mainly due to distractions that keeps us separated from the truth within. On the whole, participants felt comfortable enough to express inner drives and have meaningful personal and transcendental insights in a context of cultural, social and economic diversity.

Reciprocity with the More-than-human World

Eco-psychology[13] points out the importance of merging with the more-than-human world, such as animals, plants, the earth, the atmosphere and the Cosmos in order to gain consciousness of the interconnectedness of "whole there is", also described by Transpersonal Psychology. This is considered to help overcome the generalized sensation of separateness, loneliness and alienation characterized by the contemporary western world, with its inherent consequence of environmental destruction that is often due to a pathological self-destructive human tendency.

Here are glimpses of therapeutic movement experiences related to such context:

A woman, in her late thirties, reporting her experience of moving outdoors indulging in internal tension liberation: “a strong flow of oxygen came in. As I went on moving toxicity was coming out from the pores of my skin. The air, the atmosphere was receiving the toxicity and something else was coming in. There was a constant flow and interchange between me and the air, and the oxygen all around”.

A woman, in her late twenties, moving from her womb and ovaries: “my menstrual blood went down as a string, towards the center of the earth. The energy of the earth came up and filled my womb and the whole of my body. I danced frenetically, excited, powerful”.

A participant of a group moving outdoors, between trees: I connected with the trees’ sage. Like my blood - and the softness of the trunk - like horse hair - like my hair. The air was moving the branches, and it was making a noise; I moved with that sound paying attention to its meaning. The trees told me to stay calm and have faith.

In the first two cases we can see the energetic interchange between humans and the environment, while the last case shows the interconnection with non-human bodies, the trees, and the opening up to intuition and understanding through the exchange of information with the realm of plants, that fosters the sense of an ecological self.

Conclusion

The context of dance therapy allows material stemming from deep levels of personality to be worked through, including transpersonal experiences. The setting itself of bodywork and expressive movement is particularly suitable for experiences that transcend ego limits to appear and to be integrated into ordinary consciousness. Universality and the intercultural application of dance movement therapy were acknowledged, while embodiment and reciprocity with the non-human-world showed the potential for the ecological self to be developed.

Bibliography

[1] Nelson, J.E. (1994). *Healing the split: Integrating spirit in our understanding of the mentally ill.* New York, NY: State University of New York Press.
[2] Walsh, R.N., & Vaughan F. (1980). *Beyond ego: Transpersonal dimensions in psychology (*pp. 200-213). Los Angeles, CA: J.P.Tarcher, INC.

[3] Hayes J. (2013). *Soul and spirit in dance movement psychotherapy: A transpersonal approach.* [Kindle Version]. Retrieved from http://www.amazon.com/.
[4] Washburn, M. (1994). *Transpersonal psychology in psychoanalytic perspective* (p.54). Albany, NY: State University of New York Press.
[5] Serlin I. (1993). Route images of healing in dance therapy. *American Journal of Dance Therapy, 15*(2), 65-76.
[6] The American Dance Therapy Association. (2015, August 12). Retrieved from http//adta.org/About_DMT.
[7] Sletvold J. (2015). Embodied empathy in psychotherapy: Demonstrated in supervision. *Body, Movement and Dance in Psychotherapy: An International Journal for Theory, Research and Practice, 10*(2), 82-93. doi 10.1080/17432979.2014.971873.
[8] The American Dance Therapy Association. (2015, August 12). Retrieved from http//adta.org/About_DMT.
[9] Tart, C. (1980). States of consciousness and state-specific sciences. In R.N. Walsh & F. Vaughan (Eds.), *Beyond ego: Transpersonal dimensions in psychology* (pp. 200-213). Los Angeles, CA: J.P.Tarcher.
[10] Grof, S. (1980). Realms of the human unconscious: Observations from LSD research. In R.N. Walsh & F. Vaughan (Eds.), *Beyond ego: Transpersonal dimensions in psychology* (pp. 200-213). Los Angeles, CA: J. P. Tarcher, INC.
[11] Overton W.F. (2013). A new paradigm for developmental science: Relationism and relational-developmental systems. *Applied Developmental Science, 17*(2), 94-107.
[12] Fulton P.R. (2010). Anatta: Yo, no-yo y el terapeuta [Annata: Ego, non-ego, and the therapist]. In S.F. Hick & T. Bien (Eds.), *Mindfulness i psicoterapia* [Mindfulness and psychotherapy] (pp.85-109). Barcelona, España: Editorial Kairós, S.A.
[13] Cheryl, A. B. (2012). Embodiment and embedment: Integrating dance/ movement therapy, body psychotherapy, and ecopsychology. *Body, Movement and Dance in Psychotherapy: An International Journal for Theory, Research and Practice, 7*(1), 39-54. doi: 10.1080/17432979.2011.618513.

CHAPTER SIXTEEN

SEEING SPIRITS: IMPLICATIONS FOR WELLBEING AND TRANSCENDENCE— A REVIEW AND MODEL FOR PSYCHOTHERAPEUTIC TREATMENT

AIMEE V. L. HOHN

Abstract

What can a therapist do when faced with client claims of spirit activity in their lives? Claims and symptoms can seem spiritual, such as in possession, or clinical, as in dissociation. This chapter reviews some traditional and modern views about how spirits affect the human condition and discusses tools for therapeutic intervention, proposing a model for treatment that is collaborative and differentiated: the S.E.E.I.M Process. Through an iterative process of stabilization, exploration, education, integration, and maintenance, the practitioner and client are able to explore historical and cross-cultural ideas for the phenomenon they are experiencing. They may explore various modes of treatment and consult with appropriate healers, helping to integrate the experiences and forge a path for continued wellness. The collaboration of practitioner and client on this journey allows for open and safe dialogue about the reality of spirits and their effects on humans, ultimately supporting growth and wellbeing.

Keywords: entities, education, history, spirits

Definitions and Historical Overview

Throughout time and history, spirits and entities have been part of the human narrative. Recent polls in the West reveal that people believe in ghosts and their effects on humans.[1, 2] For example, 42% of Americans polled believed in ghosts and 63% of people between the ages of 18-29 believe in demonic possession.[3] Twenty-one percent of respondents believed that people can communicate with the dead, and 41% believed in extrasensory perception.[4] Over 10% of people aged 18 and over surveyed in Britain have sensed a ghost, heard voices, or seen things others cannot.[5]

Studies of experiences with various non-human entities highlight the following recurring experiences: visitation of surviving personality of a deceased person,[6] visitation by other entities, such as hauntings or poltergeist activity,[7] possession and torment,[8] and others. Explanations for such events have been categorized as glimpses into other realms through actual communication with intelligent or energetically imprinted personalities that have survived after death,[9] various forms of kinetic energy and energetic projections sourced by living human beings,[10] subconscious projections,[11] neurological impairments,[12] or legitimate possession.[13] Turner[14] surmised: "These manifestations constitute the deliberate visitation of discernable forms which have the conscious intent to communicate, to claim importance in our lives". Experiences reported are so vast and often hard to explain that current researchers seek to understand and assist those who report interaction with spirits. This paper provides a brief historical and cross-cultural review, theories about spirit entities and their effects on human life, and introduces a new model for therapeutic treatment called the S.E.E.I.M (Stabilization, Exploration, Education, Integration, and Maintenance) Process.

History

Shamanism

Historically, spirit involvement in human life has long been honored by shamanistic cultures that designated special intermediaries to handle the effects of spirit activity on human life and spent much time appeasing the souls of the departed and spirits in unearthly realms. A shaman was called—often through a physical or spiritual crisis—to spirit work to help community members in all aspects of health, healing, and social life.[15]

Other Spiritual Traditions

A variety of Eastern and Western traditions viewed spirit effect on humans similarly to that of shamanistic traditionalists, and many religious traditions stemmed from shamanic backgrounds. Various texts, such as the Egyptian Book of the Dead and the Tibetan Book of the Dead helped the living navigate the realm between life and death, infusing spiritualties with guidebooks that still influence practices today.[16] Buddhist, Hindu, Islamic, and Judeo Christian religious texts reference human interaction with spirit realms. These interactions with spirits could help or hinder the life of the human recipient, by serving as omens, reassurances, and providing a connection to the afterlife in a time when death was commonplace and unforgiving.

Modern Western View

Today, perceptions in the West about experience with spirits are varied. Seminal research starting in the late 1800s highlighted traditional cross cultural beliefs and continues to define paranormal experiences and their effects on humans and the therapeutic process today. Gurney, Myers, and Podmore[17] studied what they called *phantasms*, or apparitional experiences, attempting to define them as either projections created by the mind or actual paranormal occurrences. Based on his studies of psychic abilities and peoples' reports of apparitions, Jung[18,19] defined paranormal and occult experiences as manifestations of the collective unconscious. Jung, who came to have his own paranormal experiences that facilitated growth, started to believe there was more happening than solely unconscious stirrings and projections, and encouraged scientists to keep an open mind about paranormal phenomena. The prevalence of research on the topic validates that theorists have questioned what many indigenous cultures take for granted; what seemed to be archaic belief may have credence after all. Perhaps such researchers sought to bring back evidence for a connection to the afterlife as it was steadily ousted by science favoring empirical evidence.

In the last half of the 20th century, White[20] studied experiences with spirits or entities and found that two types were prevalent: (a) encounter experiences with spirits of the deceased or divine entities, and (b) experiences involving death such as channeling or mediumship. The author defined many of these experiences as having potential for growth, thus calling them *Exceptional Human Experiences* (EHEs); stating they were not only a normal part of human experience, but that once shared in a safe environment like therapy, can be instigators of healthy identity, healing, and spiritual growth, connecting a person with their inner and outer realms of existence and connectedness to the universe. She reaffirmed the need for human connection to the afterlife in all of its manifestations, and the benefits of these paranormal, albeit normal, experiences.

Such research provided evidence that experience with spirits, along with being normal, may be positively influential in a person's life and seemed to prove a type of human interconnectedness through either telepathy or actual contact with the deceased.[21, 22] Similar to shamanic cultures' ideas regarding mental and physical sickness prior to spiritual awakening, [23] researchers now described anomalous, or exceptional, experiences as a possible *emergence*, or having potential for psycho-spiritual growth.[24, 25] Experiences with spirit encounter can not only shake a person's paradigm, but imbue a sense of wonder and inquiry into the meaning of life and death.

Clinical Implications

In the Western clinical paradigm, clients who report experiences with spirit may be suspected as having an array of neuroses and psychoses.[26] A person claiming experience with entities may be diagnosed with a multitude of disorders such as: Schizophrenia Spectrum and other Psychotic Disorders, Bipolar Disorder, Dissociative Disorders, Parasomnias or Neurocognitive Disorders, or Personality Disorders.[27] Increasingly, Western clinicians have accepted that a person can have impactful paranormal experiences, temporary psychosis, or both, and grow from them. Some psychiatrists even argue that it seems spirit possession is possibly concurrent with certain disorders such as Dissociative Identity Disorder or Schizophrenia.[28, 29] Of treating patients with claims of spirit possession, Allison,[30] a clinically trained psychiatrist, said: "Over the years, I've encountered too many such cases to dismiss the possibility of spirit possession completely."

It is important to note that some research suggests no link between paranormal experiences and mental health disorders.[31] Western researchers continue to find that not only are experiences with spirits common, and potentially valid, but when explored, can prove non-pathological and supportive of the experiencers' growth; findings that finally connect the relatively short period of Western exploration of the psyche to its indigenous roots.

Approaches to Treatment

> . . . there are people who are having genuine psychic experiences free of pathology; there are people who are mentally ill and who may have unasked for psychic experiences; and there are those who are delusional and believe they are having psychic experiences, but are not.[32]

It is a goal of many therapists, especially transpersonal, to incorporate all traditions and ways of knowing into their practice. Like shamans, a transpersonal therapist will take into account "the nature of the ailment, the nature of the client, the nature of the setting, and the nature of the treatment" [33] before they use any specific technique. Indeed, many shamanic teachers and spiritual leaders have begun to teach therapists shamanistic and spiritual tools for working with spirit entities and the healing of self and client. Taking into account the client's phenomenology, an integrative approach is often the most logical route to treatment. In fact, practitioners theorize that Western approaches may sometimes harm treatment.[34]

Therapies that honor the validity of experiencing spirit entities and realms may be highly beneficial—not only for their record of effectiveness but due to their ability to imbue clients with a sense of empowerment, more centralized locus of control, and connection to all realms of existence and reality; it is a process. Therefore, a new therapeutic framework offering the rich history and traditions dealing with the reality of spirits and paranormal experiences would be highly beneficial to a Western practitioner. The S.E.E.I.M Process seeks to help a client integrate their experiences through such education, while helping them to incorporate newfound knowledge in support of health and wellness.

The S.E.E.I.M Process

The S.E.E.I.M Process[35] highlights five aspects of working therapeutically with a client: Stabilization and Exploration, Education, Integration, and Maintenance. *It is not limited to working with clients who have spirit experiences* and is beneficial for those wishing to include historical, cultural, and varied treatment modalities in their healing work. It is a suggested approach for all humanistic and transpersonal practitioners.

The process uses a trial-and-error approach that covers various theories. Emphasis is placed on therapists utilizing their own intuition and transpersonal training to facilitate safe environment, balance, validation, collaborative learning, and treatment. It follows the theory that collaborative, inclusive approaches are effective in treatment.[36] Additionally, early and phase-specific work may aid in the prevention of psychosis development.[37] The S.E.E.I.M Process seeks to support co-learning and exploration to facilitate wellness.

Stabilization and Exploration: Disclosure and Balance

When a client seeks treatment for experiences normally deemed pathological in clinical practice, it is important that the practitioner create a safe setting. Maintaining safe disclosure space is of paramount importance to facilitate the building or a trusting client/practitioner relationship and may help instigate healing.[38] The practitioner should acknowledge the validity of their client's spirit experiences without the need to diagnose or fit it into existing therapeutic or medical models. Whether or not the experiences contain neurotic or psychotic features can be discerned through the treatment. Neutrality is a key to success. The practitioner may provide tools for balance or anxiety control if the client needs reassurance. Balance rituals can be based on the client's spiritual traditions or history. For instance, a Catholic may find reciting the rosary to be highly effective in calming themselves. The practitioner may model balancing rituals they use, such as breathing, burning herbs or incense, or lighting candles. The goal is to create a ritual that calms in times of anxiety that can be revisited in times of need. Discussion about various traditional and cultural balancing rituals provides an educational backdrop. The practitioner is cautioned, however, that adopting cultural practices without deep understanding or guidance from coinciding spiritual teachers can become cultural appropriation—not condoned by this process. Additionally, there are instances where immediate medical attention may be necessary if panic attacks or other physiological responses are occurring that may indicate acute medical needs—in this case the practitioner should recommend clinical care and assess whether the S.E.E.I.M Process may be simultaneously effective.

As part of the diagnostic process, practitioners should use their own discernment to assess: does the person seem to have mental illness, spirit/paranormal experiences, or comorbidity? Seeking clinical and traditional spiritual opinions allows the practitioner to create a holistic opinion of the client's claims. Collaborative relationships among practitioners across all fields create multiple viewpoints on experiences and treatment options, should the client wish to explore them. Lastly, the practitioner should explain the framework, the collaborative process and various treatment approaches, as well as set benchmarks and goals.[39] This can aid in giving the client an onus of control over their work.

Education: Validation and Awareness

Validating the client's experience using similar reports of such experiences is highly effective in creating a safe disclosure space.[40] Gathering a narrative history of the client along with their spiritual and family background, as well as their boundaries for exploration into other spiritual viewpoints informs the approach. This background-gathering approach honors the validity of a person's history, relationships, and phenomenology based on their own traditions as well as Western psychotherapeutic approaches to treatment. The practitioner and client can then embark on an appropriate exploration of various historical, cultural, and spiritual views of their current life experiences such as Shamanic, Eastern, Judeo/Christian, and New Age. A client's phenomenology, relationships, and outlook may align with cross-cultural models of spiritual evolution and experience, informing the trajectory of work and helping frame their spiritual experiences.

Integration: Therapeutic Approach

As the client's phenomenology reveals itself, the practitioner may begin to align the client's exploration with Western therapeutic techniques such as Jungian, Adlerian, Art and Music Therapy, Bodywork, Cognitive–Behavioral techniques, Neuroscience, or other approaches applicable to the client's current parameters. Other techniques such as Shamanic journeying, Acupuncture, or Reiki, for example, provide alternatives that align with the research process. The client may resonate with certain treatment modalities. The practitioner should seek ongoing mentorship and training from traditional and clinical healers, where appropriate, and facilitate techniques and referrals in a culturally sensitive and respectful manner. This approach remains collaborative and transparent so clients feel an onus of control and invested in their own treatment. This approach can also help a person reconnect with their ancestral spiritual practices or resonate with new guides to wellness—a return to the transpersonal.

Maintenance

Throughout the process, it is important for the practitioner and client to take notes of their process, progress, and ideas. The S.E.E.I.M Process upholds respect for the mutual presence of client and practitioner. Approaches to work can be reassessed and aligned with the client's ongoing state. It is important for the practitioner to assess the efficacy of the trajectory and recommend options even if this means referring the client elsewhere. Ongoing research into treatment modalities, tools for balance and integration, as well as review are appropriate to sustain growth for both parties. The practitioner may also learn new views of spirit or paranormal experiences. Throughout the deep spiritual process that this framework entails, both parties may feel vulnerable and unsure; the practitioner must use best-practices by asserting boundaries to support the well-being of both client and practitioner. Both parties will find that they have embarked on a research path, imbuing the healing process with exploratory learning devoid of judgment and fostering a safe environment supportive of the discovery of the Self as connected to all.

Conclusion

According to current data, people in the West report both belief and experience with what they perceive as spirit entities.[41] Existing spiritual and cross-cultural theories about the afterlife teach that spirits can and do affect the human experience. Western scientific paradigm may assert that such experiences are products of biological or chemical events within the brain,[42] or projections of the subconscious.[43] Humanistic and transpersonal approaches to such phenomena may accept that such experiences may be both spiritual and biological, possibly instigating growth.[44, 45] This chapter provided a brief review of the history of belief in spirit effects on humans, traditional and spiritual approaches to treatment, and Western clinical attitudes and diagnostics. It makes an argument for the possible benefits of collaborative approaches to therapy and outlines a new framework for treatment: the S.E.E.I.M Process. Through an iterative process of Stabilization, Exploration, Education, Integration, and Maintenance, the practitioner and client are able to explore historical and cross-cultural ideas for the phenomenon they are experiencing. This open-minded exploration fosters an innovative safe space for growth and wellbeing.

Table 1.

The S.E.E.I.M Process Framework

	Stage 1	Stage 2	Stage 3
Stabilization & Exploration Disclosure and Balance	Safe disclosure of spirit experience. Inventory of client history is taken. Tools/rituals for balancing, decreasing anxiety, fear. Referral to psychiatrist/collaboration w/psychiatrist as needed. Therapist uses research & intuition as part of diagnostic process. Makes recommendation for S.E.E.I.M. Garners professional opinion from a variety of sources—creates collaborations.	Therapist feels comfortable with initial diagnostic ideas- shares with client where appropriate. Checks in on tools used for balancing. Makes recommendation for further therapy. Introduces collaborators if applicable.	Ongoing balancing until habituated, person feels less anxiety or fear.
Education Validation and Awareness Examples of theories	Therapist validates experience(s) by providing similar reports. Validates that in paranormal experience, physical harm is rare. Explains fear reaction (adrenaline, fight or flight, hyper-awareness). Therapist asks client to share current and prior spiritual beliefs, and parameters involving such beliefs in therapy.	Being learning about cross-cultural/spiritual/historical ideas regarding similar experiences.	**Tradition Education** *Shamanism* Collaborator (in-person meeting or assignment).
Integration Therapeutic Approach		Client gains firmer locus of control, feels invested in own healing/wellness process. Per client preference, various forms of therapy begin with ongoing education.	**Therapeutic approach** *Transpersonal*

Maintenance	Written record of interaction as well as therapist's personal process.	Progress review.	Progress review and reconfiguration, if necessary.

	Stage 4	**Stage 5**	**Stage 6**
Stabilization & Exploration Disclosure and Balance	Ongoing balancing until habituated, person feels less anxiety or fear.	Ongoing balancing until habituated, person feels less anxiety or fear.	Ongoing balancing until habituated, person feels less anxiety or fear.
Education Validation and Awareness Examples of theories	**Tradition Education** *Eastern* Collaborator (in-person meeting or assignment).	**Tradition Education** *Judeo/Christian* Collaborator (in-person meeting or assignment).	**Tradition Education** *New Age* Collaborator (in-person meeting or assignment).
Integration Therapeutic Approach	**Therapeutic Approach** *Jungian, Gestalt, etc.* Gain awareness of childhood, unconsciousness, projections. Explore client's phenomenology.	**Therapeutic Approach** *Art/Music Therapy Bodywork* Activity, expression.	**Therapeutic Approach** *Cognitive-Neuroscience* CBT Therapy to control associated thought/anxiety issues. Power of mind, neurological ideas.
Maintenance	Review	Review	Review

Bibliography

[1] Moore, D.W. (2005). Three in four Americans believe in paranormal. *Gallup*. Retrieved December 2013, from Gallup: http://www.gallup.com/poll/16915/Three-Four-Americans-Believe- Paranormal.aspx.

[2] Williams, J. (2012, October 30). Halloween poll results. *Public Policy Polling*. Retrieved August 13, 2014, from Public Policy Polling: http://www.publicpolicypolling.com/main/2012/10/halloween-poll-results.html.

[3] See note 2.

[4] See note 1.

[5] Pechey, R., & Halligan, P. (2012). Prevalence and correlates of anomalous experiences in a large non-clinical sample. *Psychology & Psychotherapy: Theory, Research & Practice, 80*(2), 150-162.

[6] Stevenson, I. (1982). The contribution of apparitions to the evidence for survival. T*he Journal of the American Society for Psychical Research, 76*, 341-358.
[7] Laythe, B., & Owen, K. (2012). Paranormal belief and the strange case of haunt experiences: Evidence of a neglected population. *The Journal of Parapsychology, 76*(1), 79-106.
[8] Betty, S. (Spring 2005). The growing evidence for ''Demonic Possession'': What should psychiatry's response be? *Journal of Religion and Health, 44*(1), 13-30.
[9] See note 6.
[10] Gurney, E., Myers, F. W., & Podmore, F. (1886). *Phantasm of the living*. London, England: Trubner.
[11] Jung, C. G. (1977). *Psychology and the occult* (R.F.C. Hull, Trans.). Princeton, NJ: Princeton University Press.
[12] Persinger, M. A. (2001). The neuropsychiatry of paranormal experience. *The Journal of Neuropsychiatry & Clinical Neurosciences, 13,* 515-524.
[13] See note 8.
[14] Turner, E. B. (1993). The reality of spirits: A tabooed or permitted field of study? *Anthropology of Consciousness, 4*(1), 9-12. doi: 10.1525/ac.1993.4.1.9, p. 11.
[15] Krippner, S. C. (2002). Conflicting perspectives on shamans and shamanism: Points and counterpoints. *American Psychologist, 57*(11), 962- 977. doi: 10.1037/0003-066X.57.11.962.
[16] Grof, S. (1994). *Books of the dead: Manuals for living and dying*. London, England: Thames and Hudson.
[17] See note 10.
[18] See note 11.
[19] Jung, C. G. (2009). *The red book = Liber novus (S. Shamdasani, Ed.*). New York, NY: W. W. Norton.
[20] White, R. A. (1995). Exceptional human experiences and the experiential paradigm. *ReVision, 18*(1), 18-25.
[21] Kennedy, J. E., & Kanthamani, H. (1995). An exploratory study of the effects of paranormal and spiritual experiences on peoples' lives and well-being. *The Journal of the American Society for Psychical Research, 89,* 249-265.
[22] Palmer, G., & Braud, W. (2002). Exceptional human experiences, disclosure, and a more inclusive view of physical, psychological, and spiritual well-being. *The Journal of Transpersonal Psychology, 34*(1), 29.
[23] Eliade, M., & Trask, W. R. (1964). *Shamanism: Archaic techniques of ecstasy*. New York, NY: Bollingen Foundation; distributed by Pantheon Books.
[24] Grof, S., & Grof, C. (n.d.). Understanding and treatment of psychospiritual crises: "Spiritual emergencies", 1-43. Retrieved July 16, 2013, from www.wisdomuniversity.org.
[25] Phillips, R., Lukoff, D., & Stone, M. (2009). Integrating the spirit within psychosis: Alternative conceptualizations of psychotic disorders. *The Journal of Transpersonal Psychology, 41*(1), 61-80.
[26] Phillips, et al. (2009). See note 25

[27] *Diagnostic and statistical manual of mental disorders: DSM-5* (2013). Washington, D.C.: American Psychiatric Association. www.behavenet.com.
[28] Allison, R.B. (March 1985). Spiritual helpers I have met. *Association for the Anthropological Study of Consciousness* newsletter, *1*(1), 4-5.
[29] Betty, S. (2005). See note 8
[30] Allison, R. B. (2000). Iin C. Wilson (2000). *After life.* St. Paul, MN: Llewellyn Publications, p. 261.
[31] Goulding, A. (2004). Schizotypy models in relation to subjective health and paranormal beliefs and experiences. *Personality and Individual Differences, 37(*1), 157-167. doi: 10.1016/j.paid.2003.08.008.
[32] Targ, R., & Hastings, A. (Spring 1987). Psychological impact of psychic abilities. *Psychological Perspectives*, *18*(1), 36-51, p. 36.
[33] Krippner, S. (2012). Shamans as healers, counselors, and psychotherapists. *International Journal of Transpersonal Studies, 31*(2), 72-79, p. 72.
[34] Pandey, R. S., Sreenivas, K. N., & Muralidhar. (1980). Sociocultural beliefs and treatment acceptance. *Indian Journal of Psychiatry, 22*, 161-166.
[35] Fig.1: Hohn, A. V. L. (2014). *The S.E.E.I.M Process Framework.*
[36] See note 25.
[37] Dein, S. (2012). Mental health and the paranormal. *International Journal of Transpersonal Studies, 31*(1), 61-74.
[38] Grof, S., & Grof, C. (1983) Assistance in spiritual emergency. In S. Grof & C. Grof (Eds.), *Spiritual emergency: When personal transformation becomes a crisis* (pp. 191-197*)*. Los Angeles, CA: Tarcher.
[39] De Rivera, J. L. (1992, January/March). The stages of psychotherapy. *European Journal of Psychiatry, 6*(1), 51-58.
[40] See note 32.
[41] See Note 1.
[42] See Note 12.
[43] See Note 11.
[44] See Note 24.
[45] See Note 20.

CHAPTER SEVENTEEN

USING TRANSPERSONAL PSYCHOLOGY AS A BASIS FOR VALIDATION AND RECOVERY FOR PEOPLE DIAGNOSED WITH BIPOLAR DISORDER

SEAN BLACKWELL AND LIGIA SPLENDORE

Abstract

Diagnosis of bipolar disorder has reached unprecedented levels[1] and yet, the potentially beneficial role of transpersonal psychology regarding this disorder is rarely recognized. In this paper, the authors will present an experimental model of a healing retreat using the theories and techniques of transpersonal psychology as a basis for validation and recovery among people labeled with bipolar disorder.

Keywords: bipolar disorder, spiritual emergency, transpersonal psychology

Background

From the perspective of some transpersonal researchers, what appears to be a "psychotic disorder" by mainstream psychiatry may also been interpreted as an opportunity for profound personal transformation. Rather than being seen as a biological disorder located in the brain, pioneers such as Dr. Stanislav Grof have interpreted a psychotic episode as an overflow of unconscious content which invades the conscious mind as a type of repressed bio-energetic material of the psyche.[2] It has been suggested that this material may be "spiritual" in nature, possibly related to our Kundalini energy, or chakra system – a spiritual dimension to our biology, which has been validated by mystics for centuries, yet remains elusive to materialist science.[3] This material itself is largely composed of emotional content from life-trauma, but may also include traumatic events from perinatal experiences, as well as energies from other more controversial dimensions of our existence, such as past lives.[4]

In other words, a "psychotic" episode could be seen as something that is completely natural, which could happen to anyone, regardless of their genetic make-up, under certain conditions. As a natural occurrence, it is believed that all people who experience a psychosis, at least have the potential to heal.

However, within today's modern culture, which is dominated by materialist science, any approach that seeks to understand the bio-energetic aspect of psychosis has enormous obstacles to confront, as this new paradigm represents a challenge to the current psychiatric model. To be blunt, mainstream psychiatry simply does not accept the possibility that psychosis could be at all beneficial. For psychiatry, any altered state of consciousness is synonymous with pathology, something that should be ceased in all cases.[5]

Based on his decades of research with people in anomalous (or 'non-ordinary state of consciousness') experiences, Grof proposes a vastly expanded cartography of the psyche, redefining our understanding of how consciousness functions and expresses itself. He postulates that we have a spiritual dimension to our psyche that, when accessed, can be very therapeutic. He refers to this dimension as the Holotropic Mind.[6] The term *Spiritual Emergency,* created by Grof, is intended to describe a condition that could be misinterpreted as psychopathology, but is, actually a difficult process of personal growth which is rooted in the spiritual (or holotropic) dimension of the psyche.[7] In his book, *The Stormy Search for the Self,* he provides differential diagnostic criteria to define what type of experience should be treated as a spiritual emergency, what should be treated as a purely spiritual experience (mostly free of psychological disturbance), and what should be treated as pathology.[8]

In addition, the work of Dr. David Lukoff is extensive with regard to the subject of spirituality and mental health. His research brings important references regarding how a psycho-spiritual crisis can manifest in different forms and also bring mixed results. Based on literature reviews and 30 years of clinical experience, Lukoff proposes the following criteria for the accurate diagnosis of a mystical experience with psychotic features: (a) phenomenological overlap with a mystical experience, (b) signs indicative of prognosis of a positive outcome, (c) no significant risk for homicidal or suicidal behavior. Along with other authors, Lukoff suggested the category of *Religious or Spiritual Problems* for the DSM-IV-TR[9] in order to help psychiatry recognize the validity of these experiences.[10]

According to Lukoff, the most common features of a mystical experience are unity: disappearance of dual perception; ineffability: the experience cannot be described with the usual semantics; noetic character: an absolute sense that what is experienced is real; transcendence of time and space; sacred sense; disappearance of the fear of death; a change in values and behavior.

Jungian psychoanalyst and psychiatrist Dr. John Weir Perry studied the potential of healing and transformation in the psychotic process in depth, bringing a visionary perspective to the crisis, which he called a Renewal Process, relating it with the mythic and ritualistic parallels of antiquity. According to Perry, this therapeutic and curative aspect of psychosis is something inherent to all of humanity – the idea that the body carries with it an innate capacity for self-healing.[11] This basic concept was the main assumption of the Diabasis Clinic, created by Perry in the 1970's to deal with patients in psychosis. Perry believed that the high state of excitement in which the Archetypical Unconscious is energized and activated within the psyche, automatically performs the healing work in its own way. The treatment involved an intimate relationship between a dedicated supporter(s) and the person going through the transformational process. The supporter(s) was trained to show empathy and encouragement towards the "patient", without interfering.

Another similar psychiatric model which is still being used today is Soteria House, created by Dr. Loren Mosher in 1971. A residence for people dealing with "first-break" acute psychosis, using an almost entirely meds-free approach with emphasis on "being with" as opposed to "doing" something to the patient, interrupting or disrupting his/her experience.[12] A space similar to that of Soteria House is considered ideal for any psychiatric clinic that intends to work with people in acute psychosis. Ciompi has described such a setting as being a small, relaxing, low-stimulus environment. In contrast to a typically cold hospital environment, a traditional house in the countryside would be ideally suited to such work.[13]

Time for a New Vision

While the pioneering theories and clinics mentioned above have shown tremendous promise, in practice they have had great difficulty taking hold within the mainstream culture. As an example Soteria Alaska, which opened in 2011, was recently closed due to cuts in government funding.[14] Being the first Soteria program on American soil in over two decades, its closing was a great disappointment to those involved. A Grof inspired project, The Fires Creek Center, also met a similar fate, going bankrupt within its first year of operation. The simple fact that the leading pioneer regarding the spiritual dimension of mental disorders, Dr. Stanislav Grof, has never created a clinic based on his own healing principles, speaks to the monumental task involved in creating one.

The obstacles to creating clinics similar to Soteria and J.W. Perry's Diabasis are many. Perhaps the most difficult obstacle to overcome is that the models mentioned above only appear to have success with people having a "first-break" of "acute psychosis". As people in their first anomalous experience (as well as their families) are generally unaware of treatment options other than psychiatry prior to any "first-break", directing these people towards any kind of alternative treatment program has proven to be a daunting challenge.[15] The only way such access can be made available is through a trusting relationship with the local mainstream psychiatric services – something which is very difficult to establish, as the underlying assumptions regarding the correct treatment modality remain in sharp contrast. However, with that said, the authors of this paper have created a healing program for people who strongly identify with the spiritual dimension of their apparent "bipolar disorder". Rather than challenging the current psychiatric system, the long term intention of this program is to work in conjunction with the current mainstream mental health model.

The Bipolar Awakenings Healing Retreat: An Experimental Model

Objective

The objective of this retreat is to provide a safe, emotionally supportive setting where people diagnosed with Bipolar Disorder are able to release the trauma which is assumed to be the underlying cause of their disorder. We do this by helping people safely access the bio-energetic material of their Unconscious Mind, releasing it through a series of powerful healing techniques. Our hypothesis is that if enough of the bio-energetic material is released, the disorder will eventually resolve itself.

Methodology

1. Evaluation of the Client's Profile

Based on years of conversations with people diagnosed with bipolar disorder, we have identified a series of criteria that we believe would characterize someone who has a high probability of healing from our program, as well as a low risk of entering into a difficult psychosis which might require hospitalization. While we remain open to considering any candidate, we believe that those who meet most of the criteria below would benefit most from our retreat:

- Can easily identify the "spiritual" aspects of their own non-ordinary experiences – feelings of oneness, heightened senses, that one is a type of messiah, social concerns, etc.
- Interested in exploring non-ordinary states in a supportive environment with open-minded curiosity.
- In good physical health, particularly with an absence of cardiac disease or musculoskeletal disorders. Women should not be pregnant.
- Good pre-episode functioning. A life history of some success in school and/or work; able to cultivate personal relationships.
- Experienced first episode after the age of 19.
- First episode occurred after experiencing a period of rapid change – many "triggers".
- Not addicted to drugs, marijuana, or alcohol. Able to completely avoid marijuana and drugs after our work together.
- Medicated for less than 10 years, or have had recent extended periods of time medication-free (6 months or more).
- Little or no paranoia to report from experiences.
- Any hallucinations (visual or audible) are considered mild, symbolic and non-threatening.
- No history of violent or suicidal behavior, or of criminal activity.
- Have friends or family who are supportive of our approach.

In order to gather information related to the above criteria, we ask each potential client to fill-out a questionnaire, which describes (a) the nature of their anomalous experiences, (b) their life history, and (c) their overall attitude regarding working through what may be very difficult spiritual/ emotional material.

2. Pre-Retreat Psycho-educational Phase

Prior to the retreat, a psycho-educational phase takes place in which individuals are introduced to the pioneering transpersonal theories of Dr. Stanislav Grof, Dr. David Lukoff and Dr. John Weir Perry, among others. This educational program brings the transformative perspective regarding anomalous experiences that could be misinterpreted as being pathological. The psycho-educational program will provide:

- A theoretical model from which to understand anomalous experiences as symbolically meaningful and potentially healing.
- Awareness of the importance of living a balanced life – having a good diet, practicing regular physical exercise, maintaining healthy relationships.
- Careful instruction in the process of medication withdrawal and why it is important to taper off medications very slowly, under the supervision of a supportive psychiatrist.
- Information on the necessity of avoiding all drug use in the future, as it is a key trigger for psychotic relapse.

3. The Role of Medication

The healing retreat can be done with clients who are currently medicated or un-medicated. Transpersonal psychiatrist, Dr. James Eyerman, conducted over 11,000 sessions of Holotropic Breathwork with patients at Washington University Psychiatric Hospital in St. Louis, over a period of 12 years, without any adverse reactions due to medication. Eyerman stated that 82% of the participants reported having transpersonal experiences during their sessions – a number similar to what you would find in an un-medicated population.[16] In addition, by working with clients while they are medicated, we reduce any tension coming from family members and health professionals who may be unsupportive towards a program which eliminates medication immediately.

If at some point after the retreat our client feels that they could benefit from a reduction in medication, we recommend discussing it with their family and psychiatrist before taking action.

4. Location

The work we do together is highly sensitive and must be done in an environment that is safe, stable and emotionally supportive at all times. It is a time where our client must be able to focus on their own personal healing, without the normal stresses of work and family interfering. As a result, a very private location, preferably a home in the countryside, is required. At this location, our client should be able to make noise without alarming the neighbors. This location should also provide private bedrooms for the client and the practitioner, as privacy and private time are required by both parties as part of the healing work.

During the retreat, contact with friends and family that are not supportive of this program should be limited, as their opinions may cause undue stress and their presence will be a distraction. In addition, although there will be plenty of time for visiting, both children and pets should be cared for by other family members at a separate location.

5. The Need for Live Support

One person close to the client should always be available at the retreat location to provide emotional support. This "supporter" will stay with us at the house where we will work with the healing techniques to be described below.

The role of the supporter is:

- To witness the healing process so that someone in the regular life of the client can have a better understanding of what is involved.
- To provide emotional support to the client as they work through what may be very difficult emotional material.
- To ensure that no inappropriate activities are taking place.
- To be a great "listener" both during and after the retreat, in order to help the client integrate their experiences.
- To keep the client company, while the practitioner gets extra rest or practices private meditation, in order to prepare for the daily healing activities.
- To help with everyday tasks such as preparing meals.

6. Healing Retreat Techniques

The techniques we use all access the unconscious; however, they vary in range of intensity. Listed below are the healing techniques that will be made available for our client as we work together:

- **Vipassana Meditation**

Vipassana meditation is a form of meditation which focuses one's concentration on the physical sensations of specific parts of the body, in order to still the mind. We use this form of meditation in order to create a sacred bond between everyone involved in the retreat. It also helps deepen the client's body-awareness as they prepare for our next technique.

- **Bipolar Breathwork**

Over the centuries, many breathing techniques have been developed in different parts of the world which have the intention of inducing spiritual states of consciousness and/or releasing painful trauma. We have found the practice of Holotropic Breathwork, created by Dr. Stanislav Grof, to be especially therapeutic. Holotropic Breathwork is a form of "over-breathing" that allows anyone to access and release the bio-energetic material mentioned above.

Because regular people have limited access to their unconscious, a typical breathwork session is quite strong, lasting up to three hours. Powerful music is also played loudly, to help encourage people to push themselves into contact with the unconscious dimension. However, based on our observations, the bio-energetic content of a person with Bipolar Disorder tends to be more sensitive and usually easier to access.

As a result, we feel that a typical Holotropic Breathwork session may be too strong for some people with Bipolar Disorder. However with a slightly modified approach, we can use breathwork in a way which is both gentle and effective. Basically, our Bipolar Breathwork sessions occur in periods of 30 to 180 minutes, depending on how our client is feeling. Music would also be more personalized, depending on the level of intensity our client feels prepared to work with. The idea is to gently access the unconscious through a series of shorter "visits" without forcing a deeper, more difficult experience. Used in this way, Bipolar Breathwork is a technique which can be used almost every day of the retreat. [It should be noted that our approach to Bipolar Breathwork is not affiliated with Grof Transpersonal Training (GTT), and that while we are working towards our GTT certification, we are currently not certified as GTT Holotropic Breathwork practitioners.]

- **Mandala Drawing**

The drawing of mandalas helps to integrate the experiences which arise from our unconscious. As a result, mandala drawings are usually done after every breathwork session, as well as at other important moments of the healing program.

- **Bodywork / Body Contact**

As the bio-energetic material releases, parts of the body may feel a variety of strong sensations such as cramping, pain, heat, cold, itching, tingling, etc. Sensations such as these should be respected as part of the healing process. As a result, the client is encouraged to stretch or contract in whatever way feels right for them, especially during breathwork. Occasionally, the client may want to feel the pressure of physical contact or simply touching of a specific part of the body. This contact can help to facilitate the release of the trapped energy.

7. Integration

As emotional issues arise, the client may realize that parts of their life are not serving their higher self. Part of our role is to help the client identify what needs to change and why, then support the process of transformation. This is a critical part of integration, as what is changing on the inside eventually needs to be manifested on the outside, in daily life and close relationships. As a result, it is important for our clients to continue with the integration aspect of their healing through regular meetings with an empathetic therapist who is supportive of our healing program. We offer online Skype support and encourage the client to speak with us a minimum of three sessions, as part of the retreat integration process.

8. Duration

Fourteen days appears to be enough time to get the most out of what this program has to offer. Regardless of its length, the last 30% of the retreat time should be reserved as an integration period, where our client simply has time to relax and share their unfolding experiences with us, in a protective setting. No deeper therapeutic techniques are used during this time.

Conclusions

The transpersonal theory of pioneers such as Grof, Perry and Lukoff are a gift to many people currently labeled with what many believe to be a permanent mental illness. Thanks to these pioneers, what most people are told is a genetic defect may now be interpreted as an opportunity for personal transformation. Our conversations with people across the globe suggest that, simply having their anomalous experiences validated in this way, could be a catalyst for deep healing to take place. However, we expect that in most cases, learning about one's disorder from a transpersonal perspective will only be the first step. For most people labeled with Bipolar Disorder, even if they identify with the concept of Spiritual Emergency, a more intensive therapeutic approach will be required.

Our limited experience to date has shown us that our two-week retreat can be very beneficial for people with Bipolar Disorder and other related disorders. In some cases, emotional issues which may have plagued someone for years can be released in a matter of minutes. However, with that said, many people have accumulated the trauma and emotional repression associated with their disorder over many decades, and it may be unrealistic to expect a total healing to take place in just one two-week retreat. As a result, additional healing retreats may be necessary for a complete resolution of the disorder.

While our retreat is still in its infancy, the possibility of healing what are thought to be permanent mental disorders in a relatively short period of time shows great promise. It is our hope that we will be able to develop a more formalized research project based on our approach in the near future.

Bibliography

[1] Moreno, C., Laje, G., Blanco, C., Jiang, H., & Schmidt. A. & Olfson, M.(2007). National trends in the outpatient diagnosis and treatment of bipolar disorder in youth. *Archives of General Psychiatry*, *64*(9), 1032-1039.

[2] Grof, C., & Grof, S. (1990). *The stormy search for the self.* Los Angeles, CA: J. P. Tarcher.

[3] House, R. (2010) 'Psychopathology', 'psychosis' and the kundalini: Post-modern perspectives on unusual spiritual experiences. In I. Clarke (Ed.), *Psychosis and spirituality: Consolidating the new paradigm* (2nd ed.). (pp.89-98). Oxford, England: Wiley-Blackwell.

[4] Grof, S. (1998). *The adventure of self-discovery: Dimensions of consciousness and new perspectives in psychotherapy and inner exploration.* Albany, NY: State University of New York Press.
[5] Grof. S. (2007). *Psychology of the future: Lessons from modern consciousness research.* Albany, NY: State University of New York Press.
[6] Grof. S. (1993). *The holotropic mind: The three levels of human consciousness and how they shape our lives.* New York, NY: Harper One.
[7] Grof. S. (1989). *Spiritual emergency: When personal transformation becomes a crisis.* New York, NY: J.P. Tarcher.
[8] Grof, C., & Grof, S. (1990). *The stormy search for the self.* Los Angeles, CA: J.P. Tarcher.
[9] American Psychiatric Association. (2000). *Diagnostic and Statistical Manual of Mental Disorders* (4th ed.), *Text Revision (DSM-IV-TR).* Arlington, VA: American Psychiatric Association.
[10] Lukoff, D. (1985). The diagnosis of mystical experiences with psychotic features, *The Journal of Transpersonal Psychology, 17*(2), 155-181.
[11] Perry. J.W. (1998). *Trials of the visionary mind.* Albany, NY: State University of New York Press.
[12] Mosher, L., & Hendrix, V. (2004). *Soteria: Through madness to deliverance.* Bloomington, IN: Xlibris.
[13] Ciompi, L., & Hoffmann, H. (2004). Soteria Berne: An innovative milieu therapeutic approach to acute schizophrenia based on the concept of affect-logic. *World Psychiatry, 3,* 140-146.
[14] Gottstein, J. (29/06/2015). *Lessons from Soteria-Alaska.* Retrieved from www.madinamerica.com.
[15] Mackler, D. (28/09/2012). *Some observations of Soteria-Alaska.* Retrieved from www.madinamerica.com.
[16] Eyerman, J. (2013, Spring). *A clinical report of Holotropic Breathwork in 11,000 Psychiatric Inpatients in a Community Hospital Setting.* MAPS Bulletin Special Edition *23*(1), 24-27 (available from www.maps.org).

CHAPTER EIGHTEEN

ON THE BENEFICIAL ASPECTS OF HUMOR AND LAUGHING

DIETRICH FRANKE

Abstract

In this chapter I emphasize that humor is an important quality not only in everyday life, but also in medicine, psychotherapy, and different spiritual traditions. Research, as discussed in the body of the chapter, has shown that humor and laughter can lead to states of greater wellbeing on the levels of body, mind and spirit. Significant aspects of humor—such as its capability to touch on the unexpected, can help you look at the world from a distance, and the fact that it has the potential to open the heart—can all provide a new frame of reference and open a door to metamorphosis.

Keywords: Humor, laughing, health, psychotherapy, transformation

Some Introductory Remarks on Humor and Laughing

> "*Heaven has given human beings three things to balance the odds of life: hope, sleep and laughter*".[1]

Smiling and laughing are universal phenomena, and isn't it remarkable that the words "laugh" and "love" sound quite similar? (This is why I began my workshop at the EUROTAS Conference entitled "*All you need is laugh*" by playing the song "*All You Need Is Love*" by The Beatles.) When I speak of "laughter" in this context, I do not mean the act of laughing *at* (which is *bad* humor that can make people feel ashamed or angry), but the act of laughing *with* (which has the potential to bring people closer together). And I also do not refer to the so-called artificial "PAN AM smile", but to the natural acts of smiling and laughing.

Let me begin with some statements:

"What water is to a flower, so is laughter to the soul" (Indian proverb).[2]

Laughing makes us feel open, light and easy. [2]

The tears that arise from laughing - you won't have to cry from sadness later. [2]

Children laugh on average four hundred times a day, adults only fifteen times. [2]

In the 1950s, adults laughed eighteen minutes per day. Today, it is only six minutes.[2]

"Laughter is the shortest distance between two people" (Victor Borge, a Danish conductor and comedian).[2]

The highest form of humor is the ability to laugh at oneself. [2]

When Do We Laugh?

Laughter is social and contagious. We laugh when we hear other people laugh, and we laugh to express ourselves. Laughter is a message we send to other people (we rarely laugh when we are alone). Laughter is not only about humor – it is mainly about relationships between people. And we laugh when we listen to funny stories or jokes, of course, or notice a slip of the tongue, or when we look at funny pictures. We also laugh when we encounter the unexpected. Here is a little example: As we were sitting on the airplane on our way to the EUROTAS Conference, I discovered a small yellow bag on the back of the seat in front of me. If a passenger was feeling sick, the bag provided space to remit; its inscription—in red letters and accompanied by a smiley face—read: "Take it with a smile". On reading it, I could not help but burst into laughter.

Why Do We Laugh?

Why did laughter develop in the evolution of mankind? There are a few reasons:

The act of smiling and laughing are gestures of peace: When we laugh, we cannot bite ("disarming laughter").

Laughter is a universal language that is understood in every part of the world. To illustrate this point, I will describe an experiment by Paul Ekman, a well-known psychologist and anthropologist, who did a lot of research on human emotions:

Two groups of people (comprised of both men and women) were asked to stand apart at a distance of approximately 100 meters. Group A's task was to enact a series of emotional expressions—without making noise—such as crying, looking furious, baring their teeth, smiling and laughing. Group B had to name the emotions that were expressed as the two groups began to approach each other slowly, until a valid statement arose. At a distance of 90 meters, it was clear that the members of Group A were laughing—no other emotional expression could be recognized at such great a distance.[3]

It seems clear that it was extremely important to our primitive ancestors to recognize if another approaching group seemed friendly or unfriendly, as soon as possible. Smiling and laughing are inherent gestures of peace.

Benefits of Laughing

Is laughter the best medicine?

> *"The art of medicine consists in amusing the patient while nature cures the disease"* .[4]

It is evident that in stressful situations, humor can be useful as an effective coping strategy and a strong resource: it reduces pain and it can bring our mind and body back into balance.[5, 6, 7] The pioneering work of Norman Cousins, who treated his own severe chronic disease by using slapstick movies and other funny material, is worthy of mention here.[8] Research proves the impact of humor and laughter on both the humoral and the cellular components of the immune system. That is why Paul McGhee, a pioneer in humor research, proposes: *Use your amuse system to boost your immune system*![8] A recent Norwegian study has shown that people who develop humorous lifestyles, have a better chance of leading a longer life.[9] And in case humor and laughter would not add years to our life they certainly add life to our years. Like yawning, laughter is contagious: the laughter of others is irresistible.

Laughter establishes – or restores – a positive emotional climate and a sense of connection between people who literally take pleasure in the company of each other. There is reason that some part of the health benefits of laughter result from the social support it stimulates. In order to foster the benefits of humor and laughter for mental health, a group of psychiatrists in Germany developed a humor-training manual for psychiatric patients.[10] As laughter has the potential to feed our inner child, it may remind us that it is never too late to have a happy childhood.

What Happens to the Brain When We Laugh?

Is there a specific center for humor in our brains? Well, the answer is no. However, there are certain areas in our brain where increased activity (measured by regional changes in blood supply) can be found when we laugh. Research has shown that during the process of hearing a joke, for instance, brain activity follows a certain course over time, and four clusters in the brain can be pinpointed.[6, 11, 12] To illustrate this process, let me first tell you a joke:

A Catholic priest, a Protestant minister, and a Jewish rabbi are discussing at what moment life begins. "Life begins," says the priest, "at the moment of fertilization. That is when the sperm instills the spark of life into an egg cell." "We believe," says the minister, "that life begins at birth, because that is when the baby becomes an individual and is capable of making its own decisions and must learn about sin." "Well," says the rabbi, "to my mind, life begins when the dog is dead and the children have graduated from college and moved out of the house".

When you hear a story like this, the first cluster of neurons that is activated in your brain is an area in the temporo-parieto-occipital region—you will find this region when you scratch behind your left ear. This region allows us to detect inconsistencies and to feel astonishment about incongruence. Secondly, an area in the left frontal lobe is stimulated, situated above the middle side of where your glasses would rest. This is a neural network that is responsible for the processing of language symbols, and assisting us recognize the punch line of a joke. The third to be activated is an area in the prefrontal part of the left hemisphere—you could reach it if you (caution!) picked your nose very deeply with your finger. This area is correlated with the regulation of our feelings, and helps us to judge the emotional content of a joke. Lastly, parts of the limbic system in the mesencephalon are included (the amygdala, hippocampus, nucleus accumbens, thalamus, and hypothalamus), which belong to the mesolimbic reward system—or "joy center"—allowing us to feel amused.

Laughter Yoga and Laughter Therapy

Besides listening to a funny joke, another practical way to encounter joy is to join a group that exercises laughter yoga, a collection of specific techniques developed by the Indian doctor Madan Cataria in 1995. One of the basic exercises in laughter yoga is the following: clap your hands twice accompanied by the sound "ho ho", then clap your hands three times somewhat faster, while uttering the sounds "ha ha ha". Performing this with a partner or in a group can be fun, so do not hesitate to try it!

Laughter therapy, also called humor therapy, is the use of humor and laughter to help relieve physical or emotional stress, reduce pain, and to promote health and wellbeing. It can help improve the quality of life for patients with chronic illnesses (cf. Paul McGhee: *Humor your tumor*[7]), and that is why many hospitals now use laughter therapy programs as a complementary treatment to illness.

Humor and Laughter in Fairy Tales

Fairytales, when used in different clinical settings such as psychotherapy, can be of great value and can touch deeper layers of patients' hearts and souls. The theme of laughter or the inability to laugh is quite common in fairy tales of many different cultures. The process of regaining the ability to laugh can be understood as a symbol of freeing oneself from rigidity and being frozen, and opening oneself up to liveliness and joy.[13]

Here is an example:

The Princess Who Never Smiled (A Russian Fairy Tale)

Once upon a time, there lived a princess. She never smiled. Her father, the King, said, "I must find a way to make my daughter happy. If only I could see her smile just once!" The King tried everything. He paid a magician to amaze his daughter. But the Princess did not smile. Next, he paid a clown to amuse his daughter. But the Princess did not smile. The King began to wonder if anything, anything in the world could make his daughter smile.

Meanwhile, a poor boy worked for a farmer. The farmer gave the boy three coins. Now, the poor boy was rich! What would he do with his coins? The poor boy went on a journey. He ran into a fish, a cricket, and a mouse. He gave them each a gold coin. Now he had none. The poor boy continued on his journey. Suddenly, he fell into a ditch. Ouch! At that moment, his friends, the fish, the cricket, and the mouse, came to save him.

The Princess saw all this from her bedroom window. She laughed and laughed and laughed at the sight. "She's laughing!" cried the King. "She's laughing! I am so happy that I am laughing, too!" And so the Princess met her true love, the poor worker. And she smiled every day from that day onwards.

The King, as we might guess, knew very well that laughing is essential for our wellbeing as humans, not only for its cathartic effects, but for its insight provoking quality, too.

The Roles of the Fool and of Clinic Clowns

In the Middle Ages at kings' courts, Fools were allowed to tell the truth, even when it was against what was commonly accepted. The Fool combines two qualities: he is both foolish and wise. In the Middle East, we find a lot of stories about Mullah Nasrudin, who is said to have lived in the 14th Century. One of his contemporaries was Till Eulenspiegel, who was born in a small village near Braunschweig in North Germany. In a lot of stories, Eulenspiegel is presented as a trickster who plays practical jokes on his contemporaries, exposing vices, greed, hypocrisy, and foolishness. There are numerous stories about Mullah Nasrudin, the most well-known being the story of his search for the key that is lost inside his house, but is outside under a lantern due to the light. I have chosen the following as an example:

Cold Day

It was a cold winter day, and a heavily dressed man noticed Nasrudin out in the cold wearing very little clothing. "Mullah," the man said, "tell me, how is it that I am wearing all these clothes and I still feel cold, whereas you are barely wearing anything, yet you seem unaffected by the weather?" "Well," replied Nasrudin. "I don't have any more clothes, so I can't afford to feel cold, whereas you have plenty of clothes, and thus have the liberty to feel cold."

A modern and professional version of the Fool in different clinical settings is the Clinic Clown. In hospitals and other clinical settings, they can help reduce anxiety related often to painful treatments, especially for children and elderly patients, by using laughter as medicine and "pain killer"[14] ("*A clown is like an aspirin, only he works twice as fast*"[15]). Another quote I overheard from Stephan Klein, a German clown with a psychotherapeutic background who works in clinical settings, may shine a light on the underlying healing power of Clinic Clowns, too: "A clown is congenial to the child, and, like a child, he still has one foot in paradise."

Humor and Laughter in Psychotherapy

As for psychotherapy, I am convinced that humor and laughter—when used appropriately—can play an important role in allowing patients to open their minds and hearts (and those of their therapist as well), which is a necessary condition for the healing process. When patients feel stuck, for instance, the cautious handling of humor can help them come out of a stagnant state. Patients with a sense of humor are capable of viewing their suffering from a distance, by laughing at themselves or by connecting with others in joint laughter. In my own psychotherapeutic work, when I am able to view my clients and myself with a sense of humor, feelings of joy and of being connected often arise in me.

Historically, other than Sigmund Freud's findings about the relation between wit and the unconscious, written one hundred years ago,[16] we have to acknowledge Viktor Frankl (he was an Austrian neurologist and psychiatrist, a holocaust survivor, a key figure in existential psychotherapy, and on the Board of Editors of *The Journal of Transpersonal Psychology*) for using what he called "paradoxical interventions" (i.e., prescribing the very symptom a psychotherapy client wants to resolve), Jacob Moreno ("the man who brought joy and laughter into psychotherapy"—as the inscription on his gravestone in Vienna informs us), and Frank Farelly, the founder of Provocative Psychotherapy, an approach that is strongly connected to a person-centered basis—otherwise it would not work as well.

Consider mindfulness, for instance, an essential quality in psychotherapy (in our context, we could perhaps call mindfulness with an added sense of humor "mindfoolness"). To combine mindfulness and humor note the following text by Jack Kornfield:

> *"If you can sit quietly after difficult news...*
> *If in financial downturns, you remain perfectly calm...*
> *If you see your neighbor travel to favorite places without a tingle of jealousy...*
> *If you can happily eat whatever is put on your plate...*
> *If you can love everyone around you unconditionally...*

If you can always find contentment just where you are...
You are probably... go to note 17, please

Laughter and Spirituality

A man dies and goes to Heaven. Frankly, he can't believe his good fortune in being there, given the life he has led. But St. Peter checks the records and says, "There's no mistake, you're supposed to be here. See, it says right here that you are scheduled for Heaven...and you are authorized for three days.

Laughter is a good medicine, and spirituality can play a key role in the coping repertoire of patients suffering from severe diseases like cancer, for instance. So why not bring spirituality and laughter together? Think of the laughing Buddha, or of the Dalai Lama, whose laughter is truly heart-opening. Here is a little Buddhist joke: a "reformed Buddhist" holds up a sign that says, *"Don't make the same mistakes twice—say 'no' to reincarnation."* I also like what John Rowan said in a workshop once when he spoke about Zen Koans: "Does a dog have a Buddha-like nature?" It is well known that there are scholars striving very hard to find an answer to this question: but in fact there is no answer. The only answer that makes sense is simply to *laugh.*

In medieval times in South Germany, namely in Bavaria, priests used to celebrate the first Monday after Easter with the "Risus Paschalis", also known as "Easter Laughter" (I would like to call it the "*Haha*leluja" here). Due to the fall in attendance following the highly attended Easter services, many pastors as well as lay people refer to the Monday after Easter as the "low Monday". Therefore, priests would deliberately include amusing stories and jokes in their sermons in an attempt to make the congregation laugh. After the service, churchgoers and pastors would play practical jokes on each other, such as drenching each other with water, telling jokes, singing, and dancing. This was their way of celebrating the resurrection of Christ—perhaps the supreme joke God played on Satan by raising Jesus from the dead. The holy "laughter Monday" was officially outlawed by Pope Clement V in the 17th Century—perhaps this was because he felt people were having too much fun.

Transformative Aspects of Humor and Laughter

Coming close to the end, I would like to point out some transformative aspects of humor and laughter. Humor and laughing can be understood as a departure from expectation, i.e., a dance between security and insecurity, between the expected and the unexpected. As it contains some elements of stepping into the unknown, you never know what comes next when you hear a joke. Furthermore, humor enables us to view ourselves from a distance, i.e., stepping back allows us to see the greater picture. We take a look at our habitual patterns, and it is the violation of our standard patterns we find funny. By allowing us to laugh at them we may step back from them a bit. Humor and laughing encourage us to open our minds and hearts, and this helps us make things easier, to relax and to let go, i.e., by clinging less to what we already know.

Last, not least, humor and laughing provide a new frame of reference to our life, i.e., by questioning our perception of how things are or how we would like them to be, our perspective may be altered. By providing a new frame of reference or a new meaning, a door to metamorphosis may be opened.

As a final remark, I would like to give a recommendation that might bring some laughter into your life:

In case (perhaps it might never happen—but just in case it does one day) you notice that you begin to take yourself too seriously (perhaps in your work as a transpersonal psychotherapist), you should take a red clown nose, stand in front of the mirror, put it on your nose, and shout, "I am a transpersonal psychotherapist!" I have personally tried this, and I can promise you, it works and helps a lot!

Bibliography

[1] Kant, I. Retrieved from www.azquotes.com/quote/1386857.
[2] Uber, H. (n.d.). All you need is love. Ein Hör-Essay über das Lachen [A Hearing Essay About Laughing]. Grünwald, Germany: Komplett-Media].
[3] Ekman, P. (2004). *Gefühle lesen* [Reading emotions]. Heidelberg, Germany: Springer Spektrum.
[4] Voltaire. Retrieved from www.brainyquote.com/quotes/quotes/v/voltaire106709.html.
[5] Martin, R.A. (2007). *The psychology of humor: An integrative approach.* Burlington, MA: Elsevier Academic Press.

[6] Wild, B. (2012). *Humor in psychiatrie und psychotherapie: Neurobiologie-methoden-praxis* [Humor in psychiatry and psychotherapy: Neurobiology-methods-practice]. Stuttgart, Germany: Schattauer.
[7] Cousins, N. (1979). *Anatomy of an illness as perceived by the patient: Reflections on healing and regeneration.* New York, NY: Norton.
[8] McGhee, P. Retrieved from www.LaughterRemedy.com.
[9] Svebak, S. et al. (2010). A 7-year prospective study of sense of humor and mortality in an adult country population. The Hunt-2 study. *International Journal of Psychiatric Medicine, 40,*125-46.
[10] Falkenberg, I., McGhee, P., & Wild, B. (2013). *Humorfertigkeiten trainieren. Manual für die psychiatrisch-psychotherapeutische Praxis* [To train humor competence. Manual for the psychiatric- psychotherapeutic practice]. Stuttgart, Germany: Schattauer.
[11] Metzner, M.S. (2013). *Achtsamkeit und humor. Das Immunsystem des Geistes* [Mindfulness and humor. The immune system of the mind]. Stuttgart, Germany: Schattauer.
[12] Wild, B. (2006). Humor and smiling: Cortical areas selective for cognitive, affective and volitional components. *Neurology, 66*, 887-893.
[13] Fink, D. (2001). *Das Wunder desLachens. Spiegelungen in Märchen und Mythos* [The wonder of laughing. Reflections in fairy tales and myth]. Stuttgart, Germany: Verlag freies Geistesleben.
[14] Wild, B. et al. (2007). *Clowns in der psychiatrie? Ein Pilotprojekt* [Clowns in psychiatry? A pilot project]. *Der Nervenarzt, 78*, 571-574.
[15] Groucho Marx. Retrieved from www.azquotes.com/qoute/568199
[16] Freud, S. (1916). *Wit and its relation to the unconscious.* New York, NY: Moffat, Yard & Co
[17] …then you are probably – a dog!

CHAPTER NINETEEN

HOW ACCOMPANIED INNER COMMUNICATION (AIC) CONTRIBUTES TO METAMORPHOSIS

MARTINE GARCIN-FRADET

Abstract

This chapter is dedicated to a new transpersonal approach, Accompanied Inner Communication (AIC), which contributes to metamorphosis and is a vector for transformation on various levels. AIC® has been conceived as much for people deprived of speech, as for those capable of verbal communication. The vision that one has of handicap is transformed through this accompaniment, which allows people deprived of speech to contribute to our own metamorphosis. AIC associates words with touch by means of speaking and supporting the hand of the person accompanied. A type of "disintegration" occurs when the repressed, lower level of the personal unconscious emerges. It includes all the neglected, undeveloped, unacknowledged parts of our personality that for the most part, originate in childhood. The "reintegration process" is permitted thanks to the mediation of the "accompanier", welcoming without judging, which allows the painful memories to be dissolved and transformed. The Self reveals itself beyond words or rather via the words that emerge from the plenitude of each person's symbolic expression. The process itself, thanks to the "heart to heart" contact guaranteed by accompanying the impulses of the hand, connects the accompanied person to his or her Essence. People who are unable to communicate verbally, seem to live in the field[1] so they are the ones, who, thanks to accompaniment, participate in changing our references, taking us higher and making us grow.

Keywords: awareness, consciousness, metamorphosis, transformation, transpersonal field

Accompanied Inner Communication is not well known, but it has proven to be very promising. It is an approach that allows the expression of a part of the self to which we do not ordinarily have access. Accompanied Inner Communication associates words through touch by means of speaking and supporting the hand of the person accompanied. This communication acts as a bridge, welcoming and listening at a deeper level, which allows each person accompanied, to structure and live his or her own life in a better way. As is the case every time a new potential arises for humanity, inner communication emerges in different places and in different ways. It is even possible that a mother who has an overwhelming need to establish contact with her child, who has been deprived of speech, can communicate spontaneously with him thanks to accompanied writing, by supporting his hand, without any prior training.

My own path has been more difficult and three encounters to this approach that was to become my own, were essential; accompanied Inner Communication was thus the meeting of three rivers that were quite distinct and yet complementary. Chronologically, the first encounter was with transpersonal psychology through Pierre Weil, the French pioneer. Accompanied Inner Communication was then elaborated within the field of transpersonal psychology combining the methods of Facilitated Communication[2] and Family Constellations, an approach initiated by Bert Hellinger.

A Unified Field Approach

This second approach showed how much everything is linked in the heart of a "knowing field."[i] Quantum physics has brought a close link between matter and the psyche to light. As the astrophysicist Massimo Teodorani[ii] explains in his book *Synchronicity,*[3] the relation between physics and psyche from Pauli and Jung to Chopra, everything is there, in the moment of the sitting, that benefits the person we are accompanying.

---

[i] Translation of the term used in German "das wissende Feld", to designate an information field which opens up in relation to the request of the person who comes to a consultation.

[ii] "The psyche is the tool which allows us at any moment to remember who we are and to what we belong, and through a strange process, it seems to coincide with matter in its most elementary forms, as the world of quantics bears witness." See endnote 3

This approach, when used as a psychotherapeutic aid, has revealed a dimension of consciousness which is not usually explored. The process can be summarized in a few words: By supporting the palm of the hand over a computer keyboard, an expression of the inner voice can emerge. The facilitator accompanies a weak, but tangible, impulse that he/she perceives from the accompanied person's arm, allowing access to the keys on the computer keyboard. From an Asian viewpoint, the palm of the hand is another centre representing the heart. We can interpret supporting the hand as a gesture connecting heart to heart; the accompanying and the accompanied persons are connected at a deeper transpersonal level. This accompaniment permits a progressive liberation from the sensation of fragmentation, which stems from repressed wounds, allowing one to experience a feeling of unity consciously. It is an approach that is aligned with the consciousness of one's heart – as an extension of the French psychoanalyst Françoise Dolto's[iii, 4] and C.G. Jung's discoveries.

Accompanied inner Communication® has been conceived just as much, for people deprived of speech, as it has been for those capable of verbal communication. The vision that one has of handicap, is transformed through this accompaniment. The texts that have been collected show that no matter what the difficulties are, preventing someone from communicating with words, an intact consciousness is deployed at a level of thought, different from one's cognitive and sensorial system in it.

Accompanied Inner Communication is related to a transpersonal type of communication; there is an expansion of consciousness during the session. The process itself, thanks to heart to heart contact guaranteed by accompanying the impulses of the hand, connects the accompanied person to his or her Essence. The accompaniment permits a progressive liberation from the sensation of fragmentation, which stems from repressed wounds, allowing one to experience a feeling of unity consciously. Painful memories emerge from the unconscious and are integrated into a consciousness that grows with each session.

[iii] Dolto's psychoanalytic approach focuses on language and is based upon the power of the spoken word.

Disintegration and Integration of the Dissociated Aspects of the Psyche

To become the being that we truly are implies integrating all of the aspects of our personality little by little, which have been dissociated from the unifying centre or centre of truth, and are leading their own existence. However, we must first be aware of those hidden and repressed aspects of the personality.

"Disintegration" occurs when these repressed, lower levels of the personal unconscious emerge. This includes all the neglected, undeveloped, unacknowledged parts of our personality that for the most part, originate in childhood.

During an AIC sitting, expression that is concerned with the repressed aspects in the psyche, is immediately reintegrated. Accompanying helps to establish contact with what I refer to as the « centre of truth » and from this centre, the accompanied person welcomes and integrates all the hidden or sometimes dissociated aspects of his or her personality. The goal is to allow a unifying process of one's being and an expansion of consciousness through the recognition and acceptance of all aspects of being, thus reconciling opposites. In fact, this approach allows for reintegration to take place because the therapist is in alignment with consciousness in the heart, while problems stem from a past that was created at a lower level of consciousness. As Einstein stressed, a problem can only be solved from a higher level of awareness than the level that created it.[5]

The "reintegration process" is also permitted thanks to the mediation of the "accompanier", welcoming without judging, which allows the painful memories to be dissolved and transformed. In the same session, buried pain and hidden resources of the unconscious can be expressed, and the AIC text acts as the unifying centre of these polarities. The process is very similar to what can be experienced during Jungian psychotherapy. What Radmila Moacanim writes in her book, *The Essence of Jung's Psychology and Tibetan Buddhism,* also applies to the process of Accompanied Inner Communication. AIC opens this communication between the conscious mind and its unconscious counterpart. As Radmila Moacanim also mentions, symbols contribute to the communication between the conscious mind and its unconscious counterpart.[iv, 6] The words which emerge with inner communication have a symbolic value and contribute to the transformation which takes place during a sitting. Based upon the Psychology of Depth initiated by Carl Gustav Jung, a symbol contains a great amount of energy that man can transform by amplifying, sublimating, and giving it a new orientation. A major function of the symbol is to allow a transformation of the psyche to take place. In general the person facilitated can easily decipher the symbol. A client in her first sitting announced "I am not well, but I have received so little love in my life". After a time of exchange and centring, I said, "We are going to ask your hand to conduct us to the key word for today's sitting". The key word was the word "Elderberry", which led her immediately to say, "Ah yes, and Elderberry preserves". Then, after a few minutes, these words were written: "man with the Elderberry loved me". Immediately the person exclaims, "Ah yes, my grandfather made Elderberry preserves, we were very close and I loved him so much, he died when I was barely ten years old".[7]

As we just noticed with the term "Elderberry", the content which a simple word may comprise, goes well beyond its usual meaning. For this client the word "Elderberry" was a symbol for love and she alone could decipher the sentence she had written. In contact with the love received from her grandfather as a child, allowed her to enter the disintegration process. It was time for the forgotten wounds to unveil themselves and become integrated. The keyword "Elderberry" and the love which the symbol carries opened the door to a possible transformation. In such a situation, the word can be seen as a sphere which covers a vast content.

Sometimes I feel almost like a "juggler" in that several words can come to mind while only one suits whatever needs to be expressed. It has to do with rooting out the essence that may be found in one word and then as the spring becomes a river, the sacred dimension of the text can be respected as it emerges from its source. The transformation of what comes to light begins in the course of the sitting and the inner work continues its action for several days. Those aspects of the personality, which could not be accepted consciously, slowly emerge bit by bit and changes word after word. An adult thus recalls his childhood in AIC:

[iv] "The process requires an open communication between the conscious mind and its unconscious counterpart, a sensitivity to the signal of the unconscious, which speaks the language of symbols." See endnote 7

> Feelings of abandonment, sadness hidden in me, mother in accusation, boundaries crossed, mother betrayed, I feel rejected, humiliation concerning mother, coat of sadness on my shoulders.

And, during the same sitting, expresses this:

> I take off the leaden covering which annihilated me, I uproot the heavy weight of sadness from my centre. The child heals in me; the path of reconciliation with myself liberates creative power. The interior sun brings, the rose of the heart to blossom. [8]

Based upon my experience, the forgotten wounds which unveil themselves through the texts only emerge at the time when the person is ready to accept them. The text, like a mirror, sends back the image of a painful experience to the accompanied person. It allows him also to get in touch with his interior force and to construct a platform where the unification of his ego can take place. Thus this client, who has great difficulties in putting himself forward, can find the force needed to get in touch again with his inner power in himself. He is discreet, the position he holds does not correspond to his competencies and, what is more, he tires easily, as though deprived of energy. From the very start of the first sitting he recalls in his text his intra-uterine life: « Coldness -placed in a stomach sack (he explains to me that his mother wore a girdle during her pregnancy), all my energy intake blocked. Utter fear of leaving the soft nest of swimming. I perceive life as a storm to be weathered. » And a little farther: « Joy to have the wind of peace blow on unrestrained swimming. In me the seed of confidence in life and in me is insinuated. » Swimming here refers to the fact that the baby was in the mother's womb. At a following sitting, after he had asked his mother what happened while she was pregnant, he explains to me the meaning of the word "storm" in his text. A part of the family house was on fire during his mother's pregnancy she had to leave the house in a hurry. He also mentions the great liberation he had felt after the previous sitting.

How People Deprived of Speech Contribute to our Metamorphosis

The content of texts emerging from people deprived of the use of speech will draw my attention very rapidly to a dominant characteristic: these beings feel in themselves that which is experienced well beyond their own individuality. The long silence that these people have experienced probably opens a path to the unconscious that we, who live in noise, no longer know how to take. People deprived of the use of speech accede not only to their own personal unconscious, but also to the collective and transpersonal unconscious. So they are the ones, who, thanks to accompaniment, participate in changing references, taking us higher and making us grow. A young woman suffering from autism shows me how much, in some ways, I am the one with the handicap. I do not always understand what she means. When I tell her this, she answers me:

> "Don't try to understand. I'm talking to you about the world within. The world that can't be seen with the eyes and that the background of the eye knows in transparency. The negative of a life photo; hassle to find a term to name the unnameable because what I feel in me, I cannot say otherwise. Find the time line, walk between the words and chose the one that goes out on the ribbon."[9]

Here again, what this young woman evokes, shows us that before being a tool for dialogue, AIC gives the floor. It is not so much about communication in the sense of an exchange, but rather about communication with oneself. Here thought and the inner feelings of this person can finally be given free course. She needs to say, for herself, what she is experiencing. She describes her world but does not really expect me to understand. When I try to understand, here is what she answers:

> You, you are still a caterpillar, stuck in the ruts, closed in by the rings of matter. I see things differently. I look from up-high, like the butterfly which has left its cocoon and flies away, there high in the sky. The butterfly flies away and leaves its envelope down below, balanced on a blade of grass.[10]

This young woman is the one, who, thanks to accompaniment, participates in changing our own references, taking us higher and making us grow.

Most people in situations of handicap allow us to make progress, by obliging us to look at ourselves and the world from a different angle. Their wounds, through their writings, invite us to look at our own wounds as trampolines towards the actualization of our potential.

Conclusion

Experience has shown how much each difficulty weathered, is in fact a bearing, indicating a way to actualization. The force, which exists potentially in each person, is often one side of a coin, of which the other is the sufferance met. Each obstacle thus contains its own solution implicitly and once the solution has been found, the obstacle can become an advantage. As a consequence of the metamorphosis that takes place through accompaniment in Inner Communication, the path of buried pain becomes the road to consciousness for the accompanied person, and thus, to awareness for the "accompanier".

Accompanied Inner Communication is still only in its infancy and many doors remain to be opened. All is consciousness and the only restrictions to communication are those that our own limitations impose upon us. As Massimo Teodorani says in his book « *Synchronicity: the Relationship between Physics and the Psyche, from Pauli and Jung to Chopra* », psychism and matter are not separated.[11, v]

The process of inner communication engages one's body in a space of unity in which the accompanied person and the one accompanying, meet during the time allotted to the sitting. A method such as this raises important questions and encourages metaphysical considerations about our origin and our destiny as human beings. Such an approach shows how much everything is linked in the heart of the Information Field surrounding us.

What emerges with AIC also shows how much our exterior experience is the mirror, of what is taking place within us. Does my interior universe determine the exterior universe in which I live? The conflicts that I experience on the exterior are in fact a barometer of my interior conflicts. Realizing that everyone is responsible for their lives, allows us to leave behind the victim role in order to take our future development in hand.

Bibliography

[1] Taylor, J.B. (2009). *My stroke of insight : A brain scientist's* personal journey. New York, NY : Viking.

---

[v] "Psychism is not separated from the world of matter. Matter, that is to say the nature of the creation as a whole, is only the lowest level of the collective unconscious. The objective reality of the universe is thus the result of an amalgamated synchrony between mind (or the psychism) and matter, of which the collective unconscious represents the common substrate. (…) One may without a doubt consider these events as an empiric proof – even if it cannot yet be tested from a scientific point of view – of the existence of an indissoluble unity which underlies psychism and matter."

[2] Crossley, R. (1994). An assistive communication technique in which the primary message receiver makes physical contact with the sender to help them overcome motor or emotional problems, *Facilitated communication training,* New York, NY: Teachers College Press. p. 131.
[3] Teodorani, M. (2010). *Synchronicity, the relation between physique and psyche from Pauli and Jung to Chopra.* Cesena Italy: Macro editions. p. 5.
[4] Walter P.F. (2010). *Francoise Dolto and child psychoanalysis.* Newark, NJ: Sirius C Media Galaxy LLC, p. 11.
[5] Einstein, A., http://www.mountainman.com.au/albert_e.html. "Problems cannot be solved at the same level of awareness that created them".
[6] Moacanin, R. (2003). *The essence of Jung's psychology and Tibetan Buddhism.* Somerville, MA : Wisdom Publications, p. 34.
[7] Garcin-Fradet M. (2014), *Du silence au verbe le chaînon manquant* [From silence to the word, the missing link). Paris, France: Dervy, p. 100.
[8] See endnote 7, p. 5.
[9] Garcin-Fradet, M. (2009). Quand la main devient messagère du cœur [When the hand becomes the messenger of the heart]. Aubagne, France: Quintessence, p. 92.
[10] see endnote 7, p. 6.
[11] see endnote 3, pp 27- 28.

CHAPTER TWENTY

COHERENCE: THE HEART OF IT ALL

DEE A. PURCELL

Abstract

As interconnected beings, the heart is the most important organ. The art and science of healing is enhanced by human interaction. When internal coherence of the heart rhythm is achieved, physiological systems become aligned and in order. When two or more heart fields resonate in coherence, a state of energetic exchange is accessible to both participants. One coherent heart rhythm can model coherence for an incoherent heart rhythm. Coherence promotes health and well-being. Through embodied, felt-sensing, emergent information can be processed, worked through, and integrated to promote health of the body, mind, and spirit. Future study of coherence has important implications for the delivery of health and wellness modalities; family and marriage therapies; workplace interactions; as well as an impact on relationships observed through cultural psychology, social psychology, ecopsychology.

Keywords: coherence, entrainment, homeostasis, healing, interconnection, resonance

We are Energetic Beings

The human body is a vast interconnected system where cells, tissues, organs and physiological systems work together rather than alone, independent, and self-sufficient. Indeed, the human body is a microcosm of the macrocosm--a compact version of the environmental and planetary system in which we exist. What happens within the human body as systems find balance is the same type of process that occurs in larger systems in nature. To briefly illustrate these connections, consider that in the whole of the Universe there is energy that expresses itself as waves and particles. As these waves and particles interact they form arrangements, and if a proper temperature is reached, the arranged energy will become matter. The observation and study of these expressions of energy is Physics. When two waves of energy have a fixed relationship between them, they are in coherence. Imagine a wave that has a peak and a valley that alternates, from peak - to valley - and back to peak again. When two waves have the same distance between peak-to-peak, or valley-to-valley, they are in coherence. If the distance between the peak phases or valley phases is random or changes regularly, then the waves are said to be incoherent. [1]

Additional interactions between energy and matter go on to form compounds and new substances, which are observed as Chemistry. Further interactions between energy, matter, and compounds lead to the organization of systems that support life, our Biology. [2] This constant, ongoing process of matter forming compounds and organizing into systems is the process of creation. As an organized biological system, the human body emits electromagnetic waves. For example, when one is focused intently on a task such as threading a needle or solving a math equation, the brain emits electromagnetic energy. Likewise, energy is emitted when trying to remember something that stays just out of conscious reach. [3] The brain is an amazing organ and yet the human heart emits an electromagnetic field that is roughly 5,000 times more powerful than the brain. The heart generates an electromagnetic field that permeates every cell in the body and extends several feet from the body at any given time. In fact, the heart may be our most important organ. It has been documented to have its own neurological function, and plays an important role in how information received from the environment interacts with human physiology to create emotion, awareness, and understanding.[4]

In other words, energetic vibrations from all matter and all living things permeate our world. What occurs in the environment affects us. How we practice self-care affects our physiologic systems. What we express or put back into the environment affects all of the other entities within the system. The sheer number of interactions and effects that take place on a daily basis--or even moment to moment--is hard to comprehend, because it is a constant way of being.

The Human Heart

The heart has been recognized as the source of wisdom, emotion, courage, and intelligence for millennia. The Chinese *Huangdi Neijing* or *Yellow Emperor's Classic of Internal Medicine* manuscript, dated 2500 BC, stated "The heart is the root of life and causes the versatility of the spiritual faculties." [5] Similarly, both Aristotle and Virgil taught that the seat of the mind and emotions could be found in the heart, rather than the cranial brain. In recent history, intense focus on neuroscience and brain function has all but ignored the impact of the heart. It seems likely however that the ancients were more correct than contemporary science has admitted.

Hold up a closed fist: this is roughly the size of the human heart. It beats approximately 100,000 times a day, supporting the flow of blood as it circulates through 100,000 miles of blood vessels in an adult body. The heart, however, is more than an efficient pump. It has an extensive system of neurons, support cells and neurotransmitters identical to those found in the brain which makes it a highly-complex information processing center in its own right. The heart has the circuitry and capability to sense, learn, and remember on its own. It is an endocrine organ that can produce and secrete powerful hormones such as the bonding hormone oxytocin, and can affect brain function as well as most of the body's major organs. The heart has its own intrinsic cardiac nervous system that has both short-term and long-term memory functions. It can influence the autonomic nervous system and brain activity, which affects psychological factors such as attention level, motivation, perceptual sensitivity, and emotional processing.[6]

It is no coincidence that feelings and emotions are felt more strongly in the heart. The heart field changes with different emotions: how one feels can affect someone who is nearby, especially if one is in physical contact with them.[7] In short, the heart plays a significant role in the emotional and mental experience and the health and wellbeing of an individual.

Health and Wellbeing

The idea that bodily systems function in order to maintain a state of equilibrium in the *milieu interieur*--the inner world--was explained by noted French physiologist Claude Bernard.[8] Harvard physiologist Walter Cannon appreciated Bernard's concept and coined the term homeostasis to further describe the principle that all cells, tissues, and organs maintain a static or constant "steady-state" condition in their internal environment. That is to say, the human body will actively work to maintain stable health to ensure its survival. These observations led to the understanding that healthy physiologic function is the result of continuous, dynamic interaction between multiple neural, hormonal, and mechanical control systems.[9] In other words, Cannon's work demonstrated that complex systems could self-regulate and organize. The goal of homeostasis can describe a variety of complex organized systems. It can apply to the delicate balance of maintaining steady-state conditions in the Earth's environment. It can apply to the social sciences as well: by demonstrating how an individual uses self-awareness and self-regulation under stress and pressure to maintain a steady psychological condition.

The heart plays a fascinating and important role in orienting the body towards homeostasis, and ultimately health. A measurement of the changes in the heart's rhythm has been shown to be an effective source of information about one's emotional states. Imagine wearing a small device on your finger that records your heart rate and projects it onto a computer screen, much like a miniature electrocardiogram. The heart rhythm will appear as a wave, with each beat as a peak on the wave. The amount of change between the peaks and valleys of each wave can indicate whether stress or negative emotions are affecting the coherence of heart rhythm. Coherence in the heart rhythm can also illustrate the effect of stress or negative emotions on cognitive processes including perception, emotion, and intuition. Emotions that are stressful such as frustration, anxiety, and grief lead to increased disorder in the autonomic nervous system and higher brain functioning, the results of which is seen in the coherence of heart rhythms. One of the ways the body can release these stressors and the system's incoherence is through the use of biofeedback. This promotes self-regulation through breathing and relaxing techniques to shift emotions. Using a dedicated computer program, the wearer of a heart rhythm measuring device can watch the waves of heart beat rhythm on a screen to conduct biofeedback. S/he can immediately implement relaxation techniques and see the effect of the adjustment in real time, as the heart rate wave comes into coherence. Research conducted by the Institute of HeartMath (IHM) in California U.S.A, has found that "coherence is a state of synchronization, entrainment, and resonance that is correlated with increased balance in the autonomic nervous system with a shift toward parasympathetic activity, heart-brain synchronization, and entrainment in other physiological systems and is measured by looking at heart rate variability." (p. 83)[10]

It is the focus on the heart's rhythm as a marker of self-regulation that motivates the internal shift towards coherence and homeostasis. When the heart is coherent with all that is, life flows. When there is frustration or resistance and the heart is incoherent, flow is interrupted. As the use of biofeedback brings the heart rhythm into coherence, the body's other internal systems begin to align into coherence as well. The heart and the brain communicate with more ease, and less dissonance. This state of coherence is associated with increased system performance that can increase an individual's resilience and accelerates recovery from stressors, which improves the individual's health and overall well-being. What takes place in the heart quite literally affects mental clarity, creativity, emotional balance, intuition, and personal effectiveness. The action of reducing stress and negative emotions produces positive changes in health, mental functions, energy levels and happiness.[11]

Energy Exchange between People

Being in coherence means that one resonates as an individual singularity and also as an integral part of the whole. If one enters a practice room where several tuned violins are stored, and plucks the A-string on one violin, the note played has coherence. Yet the A-strings on the other violins will resonate with and echo the played note. There is coherence between the two violins. Coherence can occur between two or more biological systems as well. Being responsible for and increasing personal coherence improves health and well-being of an individual, and it feeds into and influences the larger local system, and ultimately, a more global environment.[12]

The idea of an energy exchange between individuals is a component of many healing arts that involve contact with or proximity between a practitioner and client. In the field of psychology, inquiry into the sense of an energy exchange, or transmission, between a practitioner and client can be traced to Freud who observed that the sharing of information verbally served to shift awareness and bring about change in client's physical, mental, and emotional well-being. It is intriguing to consider the impact an individual's coherent electromagnetic heart field may have within a therapeutic relationship. Practitioners often form intentions and shift to a positive, caring state when working with clients. If the heart generates the strongest electromagnetic field emitted by the body, could an energetic exchange be measured through an emission of coherent heart rhythms? Initial research of two participants sitting near each other and holding hands used an electroencephalogram (EEG) and electrocardiogram (ECG) to measure the electric potential generated by the heartbeat. Results indicated that an electromagnetic signal was transferred. The signal was strongest when the participants were holding hands; however, the signal was still detected when subjects were in close proximity without contact.[13] The researchers also found that the degree of coherence within an individual's heart rhythm was an important factor in determining whether biological synchronization occurred between two participants. The researchers felt these initial inquiries provided a testable theory for more rigorous study into the observed effects of healing modalities.

One major implication of these findings is that the effects of therapeutic techniques involving contact or proximity between practitioner and patient could be strengthened by conscious introduction of increased coherence through positive affect and caring attitude into the practitioner's heart field. In this way, as a practitioner does the individual work necessary to create a state of internal coherence that is free of stress and negative emotion, s/he becomes a model for other individuals to come into coherence as well. Returning to the violin example, when one individual is in a state of internal coherence the electromagnetic field reflects this vibration. Others nearby can resonate with this vibration, and begin to come into coherence as well. The Institute of HeartMath built upon this study to explore whether individuals who had experience achieving high rates of heart rate variability coherence could increase heart rate variability coherence in individuals with no previous experience regulating internal coherence.

Results indicated that small social groups of individuals could indeed synchronize heart rhythms and find coherence. Another individual can entrain, or match this vibration and begin to resonate with the same coherence in his own body. There are meaningful implications for social sciences as the process of coherence between systems can be expanded to include other contexts such as families, workplaces, and communities.[14, 15]

Discussion

When a human is conceived, during the initial cell division and organization, a blueprint for homeostasis and health is available to the embryo. This blueprint remains encoded within each body and is accessible at any time throughout life. As life progresses, however, events happen. There are effects from the immediate environment that trigger genetic code to be activated, and parental choices and lifestyle also impact the young life. There are impacts from the greater environment--social structures within the community and nation, as well as occurrences in nature that have effects on society. All of this creates a framework, or patterns of thought, behavior, and action in the individual that pulls attention away from homeostasis and allows these stressors to have an impact on health and wellbeing.[16]

Often, those who are not living consciously find themselves overburdened and stressed, which negatively impacts their quality of life. Stress is a known precursor to illness and dis-ease and, left unchecked, becomes ingrained patterns of dysfunction leading to symptoms that are disruptive to one's life. It is well-documented that stress kills, and unresolved stress, or emotional, physical, and psychological turmoil can become patterns rooted in the body that develop into medical pathology, psychiatric disorders, and cancer.[17] Significant research has been completed showing the efficacy of mindfulness and meditation in improving health and wellbeing. [18] When practicing mindfulness individually, or working therapeutically with a practitioner, psychological and emotional material may arise for processing, release, and re-integration into the being.

At the center of conscious living is a practice of mindfulness and stillness that anchors one's awareness in the present moment. Living consciously begins to unwind one's attachment to those thoughts, behaviors, and actions which have adverse effects on health. Being a good steward of one's internal environment through good self-care, shifts awareness away from incoherence, disorder and dis-ease, toward coherence, harmony and optimal functioning. One makes choices to be attentive to something that has meaning, such as choosing a vegetarian diet, electing to develop physical fitness, adding or deepening a spiritual practice, or stretching one's intellect by challenging oneself to learn something new. There is awareness of interconnectedness between the body and the external world. As one makes positive changes within oneself, increased coherence and wellbeing is reflected to others, so that they too may move forward into health and wellbeing.

Bibliography

[1] Hecht, E. (2016). *Optics* (5th ed.). New York, NY: Pearson Higher Education.
[2] Trueman, R. (2012). *Concepts in chemistry and biology*. Dubuque, IA: Kendall/Hunt.

[3] Lipkova, J., & Cechak, J. (2005). Human electromagnetic emission in the ELF band. *Measurement Science Review, 5*(2), 29-32.
[4] McCraty, R. (2004). The energetic heart: Bioelectromagnetic interactions within and between people. In P. J. Rosch & M. S. Markov (Eds.), *Clinical applications of bioelectromagnetic medicine* (pp. 541-562). New York, NY: Marcel Dekker.
[5] Rosch, P. J. (2014). Why the heart is much more than a pump. *Neuropsychotherapist*, p. 7. Retrieved from Neuropsychotherapist.com.
[6] Shaffer, F., McCraty, R., & Zerr, C. L. (2014). A healthy heart is not a metronome: An integrative review of the heart's anatomy and heart rate variability. *Frontiers in Psychology, 5*, 1-19.
[7] McCraty, R. (2015). *Science of the heart, vol. 2*. Boulder Creek, CA: Institute of HeartMath.
[8] Bernard, C. (1974). *Lectures on the phenomena of life common to animals and plants*. (H.E. Hoff, R. Guillemin, & L. Guillemin, Trans.). Springfield, IL: Charles C Thomas.
[9] Cannon, W. (1939). *The wisdom of the body*. New York, NY: W. W. Norton & Co.
[10] Nenn, P. J., & Vaisberg, E. (2010). Translational health and wellness. *Alternative Therapies, 16*(4), 82-84.
[11] McCraty, R., & Zayas, M. A. (2014). Cardiac coherence, self-regulation, autonomic stability, and psychosocial well-being. *Frontiers in Psychology, 5*, 1-13.
[12] See note 7.
[13] McCraty, R. (1998). The electricity of touch: Detection and measurement of cardiac energy exchange between people. In K. H. Pribram (Ed.), *Brain and values: Is a biological science of values possible* (pp. 359-379). Mahwah, NJ: Lawrence Earlbaum Associates, Publishers.
[14] Morris, S. (2010). Achieving collective coherence: Group effects on heart rate variability coherence and heart rhythm synchronization. *Alternative Therapies, 16*(4), 62-71.
[15] Antonovsky, A. (1988). Family sense of coherence and family adaption. *Journal of Marriage and the Family, 50*(1), 79-92.
[16] Ridley, C. (2006). *Stillness: Biodynamic cranial practice and the evolution of consciousness*. Berkeley, CA: North Atlantic Books.
[17] Mohd, R. S. (2008). Life event, stress, and illness. *The Malaysian Journal of Medical Science, 15*(4), 9-18.
[18] Grossman, P., Niemann, L., Schmidt, S., & Walach, H. (2004). Mindfulness based stress reduction and health benefits: A meta-analysis. *Journal of Psychosomatic Research, 54*, 35-43.

CHAPTER TWENTY-ONE

EXILE AS A TOKEN OF SPIRITUAL DEVELOPMENT

UNJYN PARK

Abstract

There has been a growing awareness of the need for transpersonal psychology to expand itself both epistemologically and methodologically as a holistic discipline. This chapter attempts to respond to that need by exploring the concept of spiritual crisis in the current Tibetan socio-political context. Drawing on narrative analysis of the life-story of a contemporary Tibetan Buddhist monk, it explores how Tibetan Buddhist refugees construct the meaning of spiritual crisis and development. The emerging themes are of life as a ground of ongoing spiritual development and, in particular, the significance and complexity of the meaning of exile in the lives of Tibetan refugees in India. The chapter also demonstrates how the concept of *karma* is utilized as an interpretive framework to bring about such understandings of traumatic life experience. At the same time, it acknowledges that the transpersonal perspective expressed in the narrative cannot be generalised to that of the political understanding of collective trauma as felt by most Tibetan refugees.

Keywords: karma, political exile, spiritual crisis, Tibetan Buddhism

If we look back on the previous discussion of spiritual crisis within the field of transpersonal psychology, the concept of spiritual emergency proposed by Grof & Grof [1,2] sheds light on the potential hazard of the transformative process.[3-6] Lukoff and others[7,8] then raised sufficient awareness of the field to inform the perspective of mainstream psychiatry. Criteria were proposed to distinguish disturbingly rapid processes of psycho-spiritual transformation from cases of psychosis.[9,10] The mechanism of such a process has also been a centre of debates within the field. To mention a few prominent positions: firstly, that of a progress of deconstruction forcing one to face and integrate material (repressed and/or innate) from the unconscious, and move towards the genuine centre of the whole psyche, which occurs when the individual's ego structure reaches a certain degree of development[11,12]; or that of a disturbing process that is triggered by contact with the transpersonal beyond the ordinary consciousness, which unleashes unprecedented potential[1,13-16]; or, that of a transitory experience of becoming aware of, and free from, the attachment to a particular state of consciousness when one progresses to a higher one.[17] However, common to all these is the assumption that a psycho-spiritual transformation is an inner process confined to the individual's psyche. In the accounts of spiritual emergencies and crises,[1,3,5,6] the transpersonal realm is experienced directly without being mediated by the environment or any external event.

In this chapter, I explore the concept of spiritual crisis as life-experience in the world. For this purpose, I offer a narrative analysis of the life-story of a Tibetan Buddhist monk who lives in exile in India, as an example of such an indigenous concept of spiritual crisis. To highlight the meaning of the journey and the psychological transformation, I analyse and present the narrative according to the structure of Campbell's[18] monomyth. Focusing not upon the type of experience but upon the meaning in the concept of spiritual crisis, i.e., a crisis on the surface though with the promise of spiritual development, I demonstrate how the same meaning is generated out of an experience of imprisonment followed by exile.

Encountering Imprisonment Narrative

The current Tibetan exodus to India began at the end of the 1950's when the Chinese Peoples' Liberation Army invaded and occupied the country. In 1959, the 14th Dalai Lama fled into exile in India. Since then, major centres of spiritual gravity have moved to refugee settlements in India while the religious heritage within Tibet has been methodically undermined by the Chinese authorities. Each year, many Tibetans (anywhere between 30,000 and 40,000) cross the border between Tibet and Nepal/Bhutan, travelling 900 kilometres or so to reach the Indian town of Dharamsala where the Dalai Lama resides. In so doing, they undergo many hardships including physical injury, hunger, and the risk of encountering Chinese border police, which may result in beatings, arrest, or even death. The experience of exile therefore is typically viewed as traumatic. Refugees are often reported to suffer from post-traumatic stress disorder, anxiety, and depression.[19,20] Tibetan refugee settlements, however, have even more complicated stories to tell about the experience of exile.

In order to communicate the concept of spiritual crisis to Tibetan Buddhists, I loosely defined it as becoming spontaneously oriented towards spiritual practice or gaining spiritual insight through psychological distress. The most frequent connection they made was with that of the experience of imprisonment.

In fact, during my meeting with the 14th Dalai Lama, he also suggested that I meet political prisoners to research this idea. One of the imprisonment narratives I heard describes a master bringing an end to his life in order to stop a Chinese soldier from committing the sin of murdering him; another speaks of a youth marching to the execution ground with a smile on his face as his time in prison offered him the opportunity to complete one hundred thousand recitations of a prayer (a particularly auspicious number); or yet another of a monk who spares a portion of his daily ration to offer to a youngster as a form of spiritual practice. What is it that makes these stories a form of narrative of spiritual development amongst Tibetan Buddhist refugees?

Lobzur-la's Life-story

Let us now turn to the story of the former ritual master of Namgyal monastery. Lobzur-la, as he is respectfully referred to, was 83 years old at the time of our interviews. He is one of the few remaining survivors of those imprisoned by the Chinese army in 1959. His story is not unknown amongst Western Buddhists who have attended public teachings given by the 14th Dalai Lama, who has more than once quoted Lobzur-la as having said "The most difficult challenge in prison was that of trying not to lose compassion towards the Chinese guards". This statement, actually a misquote, is reflective of some of the many facets of the current socio-political context in which Tibetan Buddhism in exile finds itself: there is the growing emphasis on compassion in the presentation of Tibetan Buddhism both to itself and to the West and on maintaining Buddhism as the core of both national and spiritual identity--more urgently, through Buddhism as a meaningful framework of reference, Tibetans have a need to make sense of the collective trauma of losing their national independence and the resulting loss of a world which they had believed to be a genuine manifestation of the Buddhist doctrine. These in turn entwine and shape the life-story of Lobzur-la with its crises and resolutions. The following is an edited report of a conversation, via an interpreter, over the course of three interviews that I made with him.

When I was seven, I started living in Namgyal monastery, which is directly affiliated to the Wish-fulfilling Gem. Unlike other monasteries, the education in my monastery largely consisted of memorising esoteric texts and learning to chant, to play musical instruments, to dance, and to create sand-paintings for various rituals. Thanks to my good memory, I learned well and was ordained by the 13th Dalai Lama. In my twenties, I was appointed as the ritual master of the monastery, serving the Wish-fulfilling Gem (one of the Tibetan expressions to refer to the Dalai Lama). Together with my staff, I went everywhere He went. In March 1959, when His party departed for India, I was given orders to return to the Potala Palace to collect His 'personal belongings' and then to join the party afterwards. However, Lhasa was already under siege, and my staff and I were arrested by the Chinese army. I felt tremendous fear watching them coming towards us. Some days later, all of us prisoners were surrounded by Chinese soldiers who had their guns pointed at us. Everyone thought that we were going to die and began to weep. I said to them "This is our *karma*. There's nothing we can do". In prison, I endured whatever labour I was made to do. I saw the sacred objects destroyed and desecrated, but this only made my faith stronger. During the Cultural Revolution, public struggle sessions were held, where you were ordered to criticise other inmates. I staunchly refused to take part in these because one's "faults" can only be one's "illness of the mind" as a result of negative *karma*, which was my own. That's why I ended up in prison. And, obeying those orders would mean creating more negative *karma* for myself, not to mention encouraging other inmates to create more negative *karma* for themselves. Then in the end, I would be assisting the Chinese in producing yet more negative *karma*. That went against my prayers, in which I wished all beings to be happy. Whatever the consequences of this refusal, it brought me peace of mind, and confidence that my 'illness of the mind' was being cured. After I was released from prison, Lhasa was not what it used to be. I was socially ostracised and enslaved by the government. During those years, I was made to bow to children..., and to dive into the depths of a frozen dam to unblock it. In the end I was made to guard a crop field, which was far away from town. Then I received a call from the brother of Wish-fulfilling Gem, who had known me "as what I was". He offered me a large chunk of dried meat, which made me happy. Later, he reported my status to Wish-fulfilling Gem, and my visit to Dharamsala was organized by His office. So I came and finally met him in January, 1984.

Lobzur-la's Journey as an Example of the Hero's Journey

One of the striking characteristics of Lobzur-la's life-story is that it so closely follows Campbell's[18] formula of the hero's journey: separation, initiation and return. This distinguishes his story from the popular imprisonment narratives mentioned above, in that he survives the trials and returns to his community—now in exile—with a gift: a story of transcendence. Campbell describes the stages of the journey as follows. The hero receives a call, which he may not be willing to respond to immediately. In the beginning of the journey to the Unknown, he may encounter some supernatural aid. He then crosses the first threshold, and must dwell in the dark, maybe inside the belly of a whale as in the Biblical story of Jonah. This leads to the stage of Initiation, which involves various trials, temptations, reconciliation with the past, and the reclamation of one's divinity or a revelation. The hero then comes back home bearing a gift from his journey. The series of events in which Lobzur-la finds himself may be sufficient to make his life-story fit into this universal pattern.[21] The meaning of spiritual crisis, however, is constructed in the interaction between external events and the psychological process.

The Call/Departure

The description of Lobzur-la's formative years tells us that he grew up in a 'primal world' which was 'animated by the same psychologically resonant realities that human beings experience within themselves'.[22] His being embedded in this primal world is epitomized by his becoming a ritual master, i.e., his attainment of the utmost perfection of its symbolic representations of the universe. Reaching the rank of ritual master of a prestigious monastery brings him close to the centre of his Buddhist *mandala*—the Dalai Lama. To him, as to many Tibetans, the Dalai Lama symbolises both the nation and the Buddhist doctrine as representation of the universe.[23] The summoning to the journey comes in the form of the order to 'collect His (the Dalai Lama's) personal belongings', which signifies Lobzur-la's arrival at the very centre of his *mandala*, though ironically at the same time his expulsion from it and his crossing of the border into the unknown, the prison and the debris of his primal world.

Journey into the Unknown as Karmic Retribution

Lobzur-la defines his journey in terms of 'illness in [his] mind as the result of past *karma*'. The cause of this crisis, an insight into its meaning, and ultimately its resolution are all described in terms of *karma*. The concept of *karma*, which he never mentions until his arrest, provides coherence to his experience. Let us now examine this concept.

Karma is a Sanskrit term, which literally means 'action' or 'deeds' but is also understood in a Buddhist context as 'volitional intention'. The importance of *karma* is central to the concept of reincarnation. The individual is said to be the recipient of the result of his or her previous actions/intentions from the past including past lives.[24] One of the Buddhist doctrinal explanations of how *karma* is transferred from one life to another is that of the clear light mind which carries all one's *karma* as mental imprints from one lifetime to the next.[25] The nature of these imprints and the degree of transference has been subject to different interpretations.[15] Amongst transpersonal thinkers, for example, Grof [13,14,26] argues that the transpersonal realm of the psyche is constituted of systems of condensed experience (COEX), which are clusters of resonating emotional experiences and memories collected through many rebirths. On the other hand, Wilber[27] argues that it is only virtue and wisdom that are carried between lives, and denies the influence of emotions and memories on one's present psyche and life.

Whatever the nature of the karmic imprints is and however they are stored in one's psyche, the Buddhist doctrinal exposition does not explain how the psychic contents effect events in one's current life. Lobzur-la's description of *karma* explains this by adopting the popular concept of karmic retribution, in which one's deed brings the same kind of effects in return. Rather than manifesting itself as psychological experience, *karma* from his past lives forms his current life experience, manifesting itself in the form of exterior events and contexts which befall him. In Lobzur-la's account, the distinction between the spiritual and the political becomes blurred. Hence a crisis in life is by definition regarded as a crisis in the transpersonal dimension.

Accepting the Journey

Lobzur-la publicly declares his acceptance of the inevitability of karmic retribution: "It's our *karma*. We can do nothing". It should be noted that recognition of *karma* is in itself regarded as a form of spiritual awakening in Tibetan Buddhism. The first of the three stages in spiritual development according to the Tibetan Buddhist *Lamrim* system as expounded by Tshongkhapa (1357-1419 CE) begins with one's gaining assurance of the truth of reincarnation and investing one's efforts so as to achieve a better condition for one's next birth. Lobzur-la clearly, but possibly unconsciously, places himself in this category. *Karma* emerges as a means of insight into his crisis as the outcome of experiencing arrest, intense fear, and imminent death. The nature and degree of his hardships are understood as reflecting those of his past *karma*. This leads him to infer that he has the free choice to turn his experience of imprisonment into an opportunity for payback and to "mould [his] future".[28] This raised level of awareness now encourages him to avoid producing the same kind of negative *karma* (even though he could not specify its nature) and to neutralise it by creating positive *karma* both inner and outer. This defines the task/trial of his journey.

Trial/Purification/Peak Experience

For lack of space, I will focus on examining one particular event that forms both the climax of his trial and its moment of revelation—public struggle sessions during the Cultural Revolution. During these sessions, inmates were ordered to criticize and punish fellow prisoners. Not to do so could risk an attack being directed at oneself.[29] When he is pressured to join in attacks made on his fellow inmates (both physically and verbally), he refuses to "see fault in others" and goes on to declare that all he feels for them is love. However, the consequences of such an assertion (whether or not he was beaten as a result) is something he would not tell me. However, he does narrate that it brought him peace of mind, and he was confident that the 'negative karma'/cause of imprisonment had been cleansed. This compassion is a form of social act as well as one of inner realization, fashioned as a key element (force) that will enable Lobzur-la to get out of his crisis—imprisonment, and then to move on towards the ultimate goal of spiritual development, buddhahood as stipulated by doctrinal Buddhism.

Arrival of the Messenger: Synchronicity between Inner and Outer

The connection between the acquisition of inner peace and the signal for returning home has a "revelatory effect on [him] and mark[s a] decisive threshold in his psychological spiritual development".[22] Jung defined synchronicity as a meaningful pattern amongst events which have no apparent causal connection.[22] According to Jung, we live in the collective unconscious, which does not "behave merely psychologically" and the connection between inner and outer is manifested through a synchronicity.[22] As Lobzur-la told us that his "illness of the mind" created his crisis, its removal anticipates its end. In this sequence of events, synchronicity between inner and outer is implicit.

When the messenger, the brother of the Dalai Lama, arrives, Lobzur-la is living alone in the middle of a vast crop field which it is his job to guard. The psychic process has been completed. Lessons learnt from the struggle sessions have been repeatedly affirmed as he has ungrudgingly endured humiliation and forced labour. Now he is left alone in the field. The messenger, the closest blood relation of the Dalai Lama, connects him metaphorically back to the innermost circle of his Buddhist *mandala*. There Lobzur-la is given dried meat, a metaphor for the restoration of life, which brings him intense happiness as he retells it even thirty years later.

Return

Lobzur-la's flight to India as a return home is not the result of his own will as is in most exile narratives. It is rather a gift given by, and a call from, his *lama* (a respectful term for one's teacher in Tibetan). If negative *karma* manifests itself as hardship, then as long as that hardship persists, it is difficult to be assured that the purifying process is complete. Therefore for Lobzur-la, the end of hardship, and in particular, the manner of that end, i.e., being brought back to his *lama*, effectively demonstrates to him the completion of the process of karmic purification.

Lobzur-la returns to his monastery, and is finally reunited with his *lama*. He offers the 'personal belongings' the mission he was given at the beginning of his quest, now transformed into the account of his compassion to the Dalai Lama, who Tibetans believe to be an incarnation of Avalokiteshvara, the bodhisattva of compassion. To conclude his story, Lobzur-la locates his life on the path to enlightenment. As his "negative *karma*" had been cleansed, he has moved a step further on the path to enlightenment. His arrival at a new ground for further development coincides with his acquisition of the status of refugee. This paradox of returning home to a place that is not home draws our attention to the particularity of the location—India, the land where Buddhism originated.

Tibetan Buddhist history begins with stories of those who risked or lost their lives to seek Buddhist teachings. Even after Tibetans stopped travelling to India for that purpose, the mythical 'pure land' of *Shambhala*, symbol of the inner journey, was still believed to be located somewhere in northern India.[30] Such historical and mythological contexts may add a spiritual dimension to his return to his new home in exile. If so, exile as the culmination of his psychological transformation may also be understood as a type of pilgrimage. Furthermore, this may have enabled him to view and organise his life experience from a deeper and wider spiritual perspective than would have been possible had he returned to his old home.

Conclusion

We have seen how the concept of *karma* enables Lobzur-la to understand and shape his life-experience both as a crisis at the spiritual level and as an opportunity for further development drawing upon the concept of *karma*. Because he has returned and because the purification of his *karma* has been evidenced through the restoration of life, his story completes the circle of Campbell's hero, finally bringing the gift of his incredible narrative of compassion to his fellow Tibetan refugees. For Lobzur-la himself, the experience of exile is a re-integration after deconstruction in his life, an indication of rebirth and hope for the future. In accompanying Lobzur-la along his journey, I try to highlight the concept of *karma* as a dynamic experience. In discussing 'the messenger' I interpret the narrative through Jung's concept of "synchronicity". I suggest that such a connection may enable us to interpret the concept of *karma* beyond the perimeter of the individual psyche.[16] It is possible that such a connection existed in Lobzur-la's mind, if unconsciously, so helping him to produce the sequence of events in his narrative.

While Lobzur-la's story belongs to him alone, it is embedded in the cultural narrative of the bodhisattva and in the socio-political context in which all Tibetans have taken part. In return, it plays a role in future regeneration, in which the coming generations will form their own journey whether back to Tibet or still in exile. This aspect of an imprisonment-exile narrative opens a window on the collective experience of exile, and on the participation of Tibetans in a destiny greater than their own.

Bibliography

[1] Grof, C., & Grof, S. (Eds.). (1989). *Spiritual emergency: When personal transformation becomes a crisis*. Los Angeles, CA: Jeremy P. Tarcher.
[2] Grof, C., & Grof, S. (1990). *The stormy search for the self*. Los Angeles, CA: Jeremy P. Tarcher.
[3] de Waard, F. (2010). *Spiritual crisis: Varieties and perspectives of a transpersonal phenomenon.* Exeter, England: Imprint Academic.
[4] Clarke, I. (Ed.). (2010). *Psychosis and spirituality: consolidating the new paradigm* (2nd ed.). Chichester, England: Wiley-Blackwell.
[5] Lucas, C. G. (2011). *In case of spiritual emergency*. Forres,Scotland: Findhorn Press.
[6] Bragdon, E. (2013). *The call of spiritual emergency: From personal crisis to personal transformation.* Sudbury: EbookIt.com. (Original work published 1990: San Francisco, CA: Harper & Row)
[7] Lukoff, D. (1985). The diagnosis of mystical experiences with psychotic features. *The Journal of Transpersonal Psychologyy, 17*(2), 155-181.
[8] Lukoff, D., Lu, F. G., & Turner, R. P. (1996). Diagnosis: A clinical approach to religious and spiritual problems. In B. W. Scotton, A. B. Chinen, & J. R. Battista (Eds.), *Textbook of transpersonal psychiatry and psychology*. New York, NY: Basic Books.
[9] American Psychiatric Association (1994). *Diagnositic and statistical manual of mental disorders* (4th ed.) (DSM-IV). Washington, DC: American Psychiatric Association (APA). See the section 'Religious and Spiritual problems'.
[10] American Psychiatric Association (2013). *Diagnostic and Statistical manual of mental Disorders* (5th ed.) DSM-5. Washington, DC: American Psychiatric Association (APA).See the section 'Religious and Spiritual problems'.
[11] Washburn, M. (1994). *Transpersonal psychologyy in psychoanalytic perspective.* Albany, NY: State University of New York Press.
[12] Assagioli, R. (1989). Self-realization and psychological disturbances. In C. G. S. Grof (Ed.), *Spiritual emergency: When personal transformation becomes a crisis* (pp. 27-48). Los Angeles, CA: Jeremy P. Tarcher.
[13] Grof, S., & Bennet, H. Z. (1993). *The holotropic mind: The three levels of human consciousness and how they shape our lives.* New York: NY: HarperCollins Publishers.
[14] Grof, S. (1988). *The adventure of self-discovery*. Albany, NY: State University of New York Press.
[15] Grof, S. (2012). *Healing our deepest wounds: The holotropic paradigm shift.* Pagosa Springs. CO: Stream of Experience Productions.
[16] Bache, C. M. (2000). *Dark night, early dawn.* Albany, NY: State University of New York.. Bache criticises the concept of karma as being limited to the personal. However, that impression may have been due to its previous representation of in the West which has largely focused on individual spirituality.
[17] Wilber, K. (2006). *Integral spirituality: A startling new role for religion in the modern and postmodern world.* Boston, MA: Shambhala.

[18] Campbell, J. (1993). *The hero with a thousand faces.* London, England: Fontana Press. (Original work published 1949)
[19] Benedict, A. L., Mancini, L., & Grodin, M. A. (2009). Struggling to meditate: Contextualising integrated treatment of traumatised Tibetan refugee monks. *Mental Health, Religion & Culture, 12*(5), 485-499.
[20] Holtz, T. H. (1998). Refugee trauma versus torture trauma: A retrospective controlled cohort study of Tibetan refugees. *The Journal of Nervous and Mental Disease, 186*(1), 24-34.
[21] Atkinson, R. (2001). The life story interview. In J. F. Gurbrium & J. A. Holstein (Eds.), *Handbook of interview research: Context & method* (pp. 121-140). London, England: Sage Publications.
[22] Tarnas, R. (2006). *Cosmos and psyche: Intimation of a new world view.* London: Penguin Books, p. 22.
[23] Bentz, A. (2012). Symbol and power: the Dalai Lama as a charismatic leader. *Nations and Nationalism, 18*(2), 287-305.
[24] Powers, J. (2007). Introduction to Tibetan Buddhism Ithaca, NY: Snow Lion.
[25] Gyatsho, T., & Berzin, A. (1997). The Gelug/Kagyu tradition of Mahamudra. Ithaca, NY: Snow Lion Publications.
[26] Grof, S. (2009). *LSD: Doorway to the numinous*. Rochester, VT: Vermont Park Street Press. (Original work published 1975)
[27] Wilber, K. (1990). Death, rebirth, and meditation. In G. Doore (Ed.), *What Survives?: Contemporary explorations of life after death* (pp. 176-191). Los Angeles, CA: Tarcher.
[28] Schmithausen, L. (1986). Critical responses. In R. W. Neufeldt (Ed.), K*arma and rebirth: Post classical developments* (pp. 203-230). Albany, NY: State University of New York.
[29] Thurston, A. F. (1990). Urban violence during cultural revolution.Who is to blame. In J. N. Lipman & S. Harrell (Eds.), *Violence in China: Essays in culture and countercultur*e (pp. 149-174). Albany, NY: State University of New York Press. Thurston states that many Chinese took part in attacking the accused during struggle sessions as a way of self-defense because they believed that otherwise the attack would be directed at them.
[30] Bernbaum, E. (1982). *The way to Shambhala*. Boston, MA: Shambhala.

CHAPTER TWENTY-TWO

THE TRANSPERSONAL AND ESOTERIC ASTROLOGY: A SYSTEM-ORIENTED APPROACH TO TRANSPERSONAL PSYCHOLOGY

BERTIL JOHNSSON

Abstract

Transpersonalists frequently express the need for a paradigm that allows for more wholistic approaches. Openings now come from physics, where the heritage from the physicists behind quantum physics is still reverberating. New ontological and epistemological views are being presented, following the pioneers from the 20th century, among whom Wolfgang Pauli, Nobel Laureate 1945, was the most advanced. His deeply penetrating dialogue over many years with Carl Jung led to an astounding view of the world, bridging physics and depth psychology, mind and matter – a very different world view than that which prevails in normal science. This new world view confirms my observation that today's science slowly approaches an esoteric world view. This will help transpersonalists to deliver. Presenting this story of Jung's and Pauli's dialogue and parts of the new world view, in which archetypes, symbols and mythology play important parts, I exemplify what Esoteric Astrology has to offer to the transpersonal field.

Keywords: esotericism, Jung, mythology, Pauli, worldview

This chapter aims at firstly presenting the usefulness of Esoteric Astrology, including its consistent world picture, to the transpersonal community, offering new perspectives to the ongoing paradigmatic debate, and secondly showing how astrology works by presenting psychological and physical constructs indicating how cosmological factors find expression in human life. Essential here is the concept of *archetype*, defined so as to fit psychology, physics and the esoteric world view.

It is not doable in this short essay to present any detail in the different areas that combine to demonstrate the effectiveness of astrology in transpersonal psychology, as it would take a book. What I present is treated in scientific publications or extensive bodies of knowledge that cannot be cited here. I indicate the line of reasoning in big leaps, only detailing crucial arguments or unexpected facts, serving as "teasers" to motivate hesitant readers to further studies, also citing some important works.

The Line of Reasoning – Main Leaps

Starting with the *need for a new world view*, physicists today no longer agree on materialistic concepts having survived in the scientific base paradigm. Cartesianism is also being refuted. Examples:

1. Space-time does not contain all essentials for science, foci *outside of space-time* are recognized as important. This is a rule in esotericism.

2. When I studied physics in the 1970's space was completely empty, a void. Esotericism tells us that *space is an entity* [i,1] and today physicists can agree.[2] This is also connected to the *concept of ether* that is being revived.[ii, 3]

3. Cartesian objectivity is an ideal that is partly being replaced by new approaches; one of several is Dual Aspect Monism.[iii, 4]

[i] This is a recurring statement; of special interest here – see endnote 1.

[ii] A number of field-like or quantum ethers are being proposed, many sources; Why ether makes a better concept than vacuum is discussed (main theme) – see endnote 3.

[iii] Wolfgang Pauli presented this combined ontological/epistemological system together with Carl Jung; it has later been called dual-aspect monism; see endnote 4.

These examples imply a scientific approach to esotericism and has far-reaching consequences for transpersonal theorizing.

Next leap focuses on the *importance of symbols* for human knowledge, perception, language etc. In several psychological theories, as well as in esotericism, symbols result from archetypes. Wolfgang Pauli added that the physical world is also influenced by archetypes. Both new physics and psychology can thus acknowledge archetypes as "cause".

Next, we look at how *Mythology* fills the role of conveying archetypal essence of high order to symbolical forms that tell humans about creation and development of the universe, in which man plays part. This being established, the objective is near – *astrology rests heavily on archetypal understanding*, which thus connects to depth psychology, and – which is the point here – to physics and *the description of cosmos*. In this new worldview, human healing and growth come into new light. New methods, useful in transpersonal work, can be developed. Esoteric Astrology, a science in early but steady development, has this potential.

The Need for a New Paradigm

Using the world view of modern esotericism in transpersonal psychology would add to the paradigmatic discourse, already prevalent, offering a consistent world picture that is not static, nor based on ad-hoc solutions to historical problems. This could potentially clear the apparent contradictions between material and spiritual existence, between being and knowing, and straighten out anomalies. They all call for a new paradigm.
Studying the recent comprehensive *Handbook of Transpersonal Psychology,*[5] it becomes clear that many scholars experience paradigmatic problems, like obstacles within the current paradigm (whether it be called Materialistic, Reductionist or Cartesian), or dissatisfaction/worries with not being (accepted as) a "real" science, or express that the distance to real science is either a misunderstanding, or a necessity.[6]

The crucial part of the paradigm debate seems to be the underlying worldview that is necessary to go beyond to solve the current issues. Issues of objectivity, reality, and materiality need to be principally solved to open up for further research. Building on what science has so far extracted, we need to expand the perspective for future research. Esotericism seems to present plausible routes for that. Future research, including esoteric research, needs scientific rigour and prudence.

However, preconceived beliefs or creeds as within materialism/ physicalism constitute an obstacle. Charles Tart, in his book *The End of Materialism* illustrates this in an insightful way, after the long experience of a true and sincere scholar.[7]

With a background in physics/mathematics I wonder why a psychological community studying spirituality and phenomena of human experience *beyond personality*, feels bound to a paradigm of physicalistic dogma, when modern physics can no longer scientifically corroborate its basic assumptions. The disputes seem thus no longer based on findings of studies of nature, but instead on paradigmatic patterning by tradition. I believe that this has to do with being stuck in the realm of physical sense impressions, and the unreflected extrapolations thereof to phenomena that are completely out of reach for these same senses.

Walach[8] gives a brief and sensible sum-up of the history of how we got there, referring to Descartes as originator. We ended up believing in an objectivity that presupposes reductionism, and it seems we need to recover after the severing of the Subjective that Enlightenment produced. This severing created the "two cultures" and became a rule in the West.[iv, 9] Survivors, keeping to more wholistic ways, were diverse occult societies working mostly in secrecy. Some contributed to modern esotericism later on. From the esoteric perspective, this severing is a result of the workings of *lower mental* faculties, which are discriminating, analytic and lack the perspective of *higher mental* faculties. However, using what in esotericism is called "lower mind" thinking should not be blameworthy, it is just a fact we need to be aware of. People – including researchers – are different in regard to how they use their minds.

Defining science so that the delimitations of the scope of physical senses becomes a rule, as Friedman does,[10] would effectively prohibit any further scientific mapping of human expansion beyond the sense-bound consciousness, seemingly being next step on the agenda. This is not only a matter for transpersonal psychology, it is about whether science should be defined as a vehicle for confirming certain ways of experiencing an (illusive) reality, or to be a front activity to guide humanity in its further expansion of consciousness. Pauli would have disagreed with Friedman, also about conceptualization,[11] a main concern for both of them. Referring, as Friedman does, to "the physical" is esoterically correct for expressing this seclusion, but referring to "nature" in this way is very reductionist, as

[iv] For current viewpoints on the problems of Cartesianism, see endnote 9.

nature in esotericism involves non-physical planes of existence to which humans are not yet, but successively will become conscious.

Walach[12] sketches a plausible way to deal with the unbalanced heritage of Cartesian thinking and proposes a new phase of discourse that would again balance the status of mind with the matter aspect. He suggests two activities for this to happen – first, the return to *ontology*, creating balance between ontology and epistemology, and second, the *cultivation of consciousness*, where meditative practices can be used. For me ontology must rest on a clear world picture, and the epistemology in balance is best achieved by *disciplining the mind*, both main concerns for esotericists. We do not need to scrap today's scientific world view, we need to expand it and use it in wiser ways, and from a wider perspective see its limitations.

Esotericism and its Systemic World View

Study of Western Esotericism seems accepted within academia as long as recognised methods are used – mainly intellectual approaches. A wider approach is used in institutions recognizing the *esoteric traditions*. While Academia learns/teaches knowledge about esotericism, those other institutions learn and teach *how to live it*. This makes a great difference, creating a balanced living that seems to be a plausible way, somewhat similar to Walach's suggestion.

The esoteric world picture is an open system of thought and claims no absolute truths or declares no creed. It is comprehensive, complex and elaborate, and does not exclude scientific world views, but shares light on how they come about. From the point of view of knowledge, it may be considered a heuristic for learning, indicating how to proceed to expand consciousness, be part of the larger whole; a route to eventually *unifying being and knowing*.

A Brief Sum-up of the Esoteric World View

Essential reading to learn about the *esoteric world view* can be found in Theosophy, in writings by Helena Blavatsky and her colleagues. Later one finds the most comprehensive and consistent writings by Alice Bailey. She wrote for a Tibetan Master (not another "Eastern wisdom", but "ageless wisdom" adapted to the West, where a new type of mentality and thinking was evolving). The Swede Henry Laurency offers another more formal way of introducing the same system. Some Rosicrucian texts add to the above.[v, 13]

The following concepts are most relevant here.
1. The Planes. All existence takes place on different planes, from the higher most subtle, to the lower most dense. Yet the higher planes "feed" the lower planes with energy/force, but are not accessible for normal human consciousness. At the present stage humans are tuned in to lower planes. Relevant for human evolution, including the highest spiritual "post-human", are seven such planes.

The human personality, in the esoteric sense, exists on the three lowest planes, the Physical, the Astral/Emotional, and (the lower part of) the Mental. In a simplified manner, we could say that physical, biological, and sensory phenomena take place on the physical plane, while phenomena of ordinary psychology take place on the emotional and mental planes. Phenomena studied in transpersonal psychology can be found on all these planes, and higher planes where exquisite spiritual phenomena occur.

Each plane holds seven subplanes, resulting in 49 different subplanes altogether. A plane or subplane represents a certain life expression with its corresponding consciousness. The higher part of the mental plane, and those more subtle above, can be considered *outside of space-time*, leaving "true" transpersonal phenomena out of reach for methods designed to study phenomena within space-time. Higher planes hold consciousness beyond sense impressions, a fact that is highly relevant for research within transpersonal psychology.

2. All is life. There is no real consensus about a scientific definition of "life", its origin, its boundaries etc. Ecological systems thinking has given us new perspectives about life. Esotericism's view is radical – all is life!

All existing entities on the different planes are expressions of life, of *a hierarchy of lives within lives*. Life and its different life forms are ever evolving – there is a direction towards more elaborate and integrated forms, inclusive of lower plane life forms. Life (as perceived by science) evolves from lower to higher planes.

---

[v] The literature is vast, most essential works are freely available; examples, see endnote 13.

A planet is a huge systemic life, a *group* entity – the physical planet being its "body". All the kingdoms of nature, including spiritual levels, are part of this life. Humanity is one such part that can be said to be the "interface" between the coarser and the more subtle planes. The central entity, called *logos*, exists on higher planes, and needs humanity and the other kingdoms to include all the planes. The logos could not evolve planetary life if humanity was not evolving.

It is natural in this connection to discuss the concept of "God", as the higher parts of this great life are not directly within reach of normal human consciousness. Still – in numinous ways – man gets aware of something influencing conditions on the planet. Direct, or near direct, conscious contact is a potential, and when it occurs fills human history with prophetic examples.

The New Physics and Depth Psychology

The physicists behind the new descriptions of nature within the post-Newtonian paradigm were at pains in trying to *understand the reality* behind their findings. They had to become epistemologists in depth and scrutinize their own habits and beliefs. Wolfgang Pauli was seemingly the most pioneering, presenting perspectives that only today are beginning to settle in the scientific discourse.

In a parallel process psychology with its diverse background formed depth psychology studying the hidden psychic processes. The *unconscious* became a powerful factor, and Jung's unconscious, an all-encompassing polarity to the conscious, including *symbols and mythology*, a heritage of human culture.

It seems fair to say that the view of the human psyche was as shaken as was the view of matter in physics. The new realizations inferred changes within science, which are still ongoing – the potential is not yet fully explored.

Wolfgang Pauli's Dialogue with Carl Jung

Wolfgang Pauli was a key figure in the group of physicists who developed quantum mechanics, and upheld close contact with the other main actors behind this achievement; also with Einstein who saw Pauli's talent early on. Large parts of Pauli's communication took place in letter-writing, and an extensive collection of letters is kept in the Pauli-archive in CERN. It seems that Pauli played an important role as a catalyzer in establishing the new physics. Consequently, the CERN archive has become a treasure for later investigators, scholars in physics and history of science, as well as scholars of psychology and philosophy.

In 1932 Pauli consulted Jung in his capacity as a psychiatrist to get help with personal problems. After a brief contact, Jung saw Pauli's extraordinary personality, intelligent and "chock-full of archaic material".[14] He wanted to use the dream material from Pauli's analysis for his own research as objectively as possible, so he did refer Pauli's analysis to one of his pupils. After an eight-month period of analysis the two thinkers met again, their dialogue successively developing into a deep exchange on ontological and epistemological issues, bridging Psychology and Physics.

Archetypes – Symbols – Co-creative Man

The concept of archetype is central in understanding how mind and matter are related. Early on, Jung defined it as "deposits of the constantly repeated experiences of humanity".[15] Later on, after having penetrated the issue at length with Pauli, he concluded an analogy: "In physical terms, probability corresponds to the so-called *law of nature*; psychically, it corresponds to the *archetype*".[16] This came from Pauli's view that "the archetypal element in quantum physics is to be found in the (mathematical) concept of probability".[17]

In esotericism archetypes are impressed upon the human consciousness from the greater life that humanity is part of, "…the energies emanating from the *Archetypal plane*. This plane is the focus of the attention of the highest group of Intelligence on our planet."[18] This view also seems present in Jung's understanding when commenting about archetypal symbols in a letter to Pauli[19]: "…and possesses an autonomous numinosity, as if Someone had stated in advance with great authority: 'What is coming now is of great significance.'" In his reply, Pauli seems satisfied with Jung's writings, expressing his content with Jung's treatment of their common subject.[20]

Pauli studied the functioning of symbols thoroughly, specifically in language and mathematics. He wanted to create a "neutral language" in which all concepts were balanced as to their psychological and physical meanings so that the *two complementary descriptions of the same reality* became clear. He saw, with Jung, symbols occurring in a hierarchy, from the peculiar to the more encompassing and complex. He even thought of the concept of symbols as "the new fundamental unit of reality". For Pauli "reality" was not well-defined – it was formed in a quite involved process when human mind met with cosmic ordering principles.[21]

We end up with two perspectives – the archetypes express themselves *through symbols* in the life of humans, either as (a) some kind of reflection of human activity, or (b) reflecting the stage of the greater entity that humanity is a co-creative part of (esoteric view). The human kingdom is nearest to expansion of consciousness involving the Whole, outside of space-time. This is called *divine consciousness* in esotericism, and naturally extends from the human evolutionary state.

Astrology, Archetypes and Mythology

Cosmos and Psyche by Richard Tarnas was published some ten years ago.[22] Here Tarnas convincingly shows how certain planetary configurations seem to correlate with certain events and motivations among collective humanity, reflecting the archetypal qualities ascribed to these planets by modern astrology. It is an impressive work, unfortunately resting to some degree on simplifying modern astrology.

Tarnas presents his work as "archetypal" astrology/cosmology and Stanislav Grof, who took part in and promotes his work, emphasizes the archetypal aspect in his confession.[23] Mentioning astrology is taboo within science, so adding "archetypal" would avert criticism. However, from the perspective of *Esoteric Astrology*, this emphasis seems unnecessary, as *all astrology is archetypal,* especially in the wider sense presented above.

If we are to understand the *true nature* of a planet, we cannot describe that planet in terms of human reactions, we need other sources. Studying, for example, the role of Uranus, evoking what in modern astrology is called Promethean reactions among men, does not tell the truth about the planetary archetype itself, only how human beings of a certain sensitivity react to this force. Instead *mythology* can inform us.

Mythology is probably the most elaborate presentation of archetypal processes and symbols expressed by humans in historical times, *if we can read it properly*. The expression of planetary forces in the life of humans depends on their developmental stage, as in Jungian individuation. The more extended consciousness will see a more subtle expression of the archetypal function. This is where modern astrology, and Tarnas, goes a little astray.

In the myth of origin by Hesiod, Uranus is not Promethean, but constantly creates new forms in blueprint. There is nothing for Uranus to react to or against – to be "Promethean" about. He creates archetypes for successive manifestation in the form world. He entered before space-time was established. He does not need to steal fire. To understand the *archetypal essence* of planets, we need to avoid human projections; we need to *defend the integrity of the planetary lives*.

Examples of Mythological Wisdom

A more general view of mythology sums up in the following way. Myth tells us how it is to be human, where we came from and where we are going by suggesting symbolic forms to receptive human minds. Esotericism explicates the phases in human development. Simplifying, we see three main stages in man's walk "from beast to god-head": (a) Gaining experience in all walks of life in all circumstances, forming the basis for next phase: (b) Integrating the personality to make a perfect tool for the soul, a well-functioning whole for performing advanced tasks. (c) Lastly, we completely transcend the personality and fuse with the greater life of which we are part.

The Zodiac

The zodiac, as a system, is a coherent construct that tells the story of human growth and development via these stages and over the sequence of many lives. We can see the zodiac as structured space, the ordered cosmos that Pauli talked about. The geometry of the greater life in which we play but minor parts, informs and nurtures us differently in different stages.[vi, 24]

[vi] For a thorough presentation of the meaning of the twelve signs of the zodiac, based on esoteric astrology, which also connects to classical myth, see endnote 24.

Orion, the Hunter – An Example[vii]

Orion represents initially a human personality with all his vices and some virtues. He ravishes, he hunts and he mates. Desire makes him take the object of his love, Merope, by violence. Her father punishes Orion by taking out his eyes. Becoming blind symbolically represents the death of the personality, the self-sufficient earthly person. Orion gets the advice to go to where the sun rises, and seeks Vulcan's – the blacksmith of the underworld – help. He has thus to seek out the Eastern point, in astrology called *the ascendant* – in Esoteric Astrology indicating *soul potential.* Vulcan's helper guides Orion, and at sunrise he gets his eyesight back, symbolising the second phase: Orion becomes *soul-infused* – the soul controls his actions among men, and he works together with gods/goddesses. His new hunting companion is Artemis – a goddess of light, although a moon goddess, so the light is a reflection from matter and not yet from the light-source.

Orion then experiences a number of episodes which cannot be given here, but eventually he "dies" from that intermediate state too and is put in the heavens, presenting the most impressive constellation in the sky. This symbolizes the last phase of man's travel – he is made god, thus achieves the divine consciousness mentioned before.

Conclusion

The diverse field of transpersonal/spiritual psychology has seemingly much to gain from paradigmatic change, and especially an extended world-view, allowing for many concepts that are now "sensed" but not yet accepted. Focusing primarily on therapy/healing and human development/ transformation, Esoteric Astrology has much to offer. Human matters are often based on symbolic/archetypal understanding. Esoteric Astrology widens that scope considerably, compared to ordinary modern astrology, and introduces new methods to deal with questions about soul and spiritual levels. The alignment soul–personality expresses human potential, and the transpersonalist may also learn to distinguish between karmic (healing) and dharmic (potential) issues. For those who work with energy centres (chakras) in healing much is added by knowing how planetary archetypes

---

[vii] In classical mythology stories are retold in many variants. What I tell here is a sum-up from several such stories. We must know that we are trying to get near to an archetypal understanding, where expressions on denser planes of existence may vary after "receiving circumstances", and there is no absolutely right version.

work through different centres, including types of energy transmitted. Esoteric Astrology is a professional field in becoming and new methods and delineations are developed by its practitioners. New ways to work with or without horoscopes is presented. A more systemic discipline is developing where systems of horoscopes may contribute, but also the "science of triangles" that discloses energetic paths that are decisive for the functioning of human systems, whether individual, group or nation.

Bibliography

[1] (a) Bailey, A. A. (1997), *Esoteric astrology* (p. 7). London: Lucis Press, Ltd.
(b) Bailey, A. A. (1950), *Telepathy and the etheric vehicle* (p. 178). London, England: Lucis Press, Ltd.
[2] See for example: Giulini, Domenico (2009). Concepts of symmetry in the work of Wolfgang Pauli. In H. Atmanspacher & H. Primas (Eds.), *Recasting reality* (p. 52). Berlin, Germany: Springer-Verlag.
[3] Krauss, L. (1990), *The fifth essence*, London, England: Vintage.
[4] (a) Atmanspacher, H. (2014). Notes on psychophysical phenomena. In H. Atmanspacher & C.A. Fuchs (Eds.), *The Pauli-Jung conjecture*. Exeter, England: Imprint Academic.
(b) Seager, W. (2009). A new idea of reality: Pauli on the unity of mind and matter. In H. Atmanspacher & H. Primas (Eds.), *Recasting reality* (pp. 99 - 113). Berlin, Germany: Springer-Verlag.
[5] Friedman, H. L., & Hartelius, G. (Eds.). (2013). *The Wiley-Blackwell handbook of transpersonal psychology*. Chichester, England: John Wiley & Sons.
[6] See Note 5. Introduction (pp. xxv, xxx–xxxi), Foreword (p. xviii), Chapter 1 (pp. 3, 14), Chapter 2 (pp. 35, 38), Chapter 3 (pp. 53–57), Chapter 4 (pp. 68, 71, 73–74, 77, 79), Chapter 5 (pp. 92, 95–99, 103, 111–114), Chapter 10 (all), Chapter 12 (pp. 232, 234), Chapter 13 (indirectly), Chapter 15 (indirectly), Chapter 16 (pp. 302, 305, 307, 309), Chapter 17 (p.318); this list is *not* comprehensive.
[7] Tart, C. T. (2009). *The end of materialism*. Oakland, CA: New Harbinger Publications, Inc.
[8] Walach, H. (2013), Criticisms of transpersonal psychology and beyond. In H.L. Friedman & G. Hartelius (Eds.), *The Wiley-Blackwell handbook of transpersonal psychology* (pp. 64–69). Chichester, England: John Wiley & Sons.
[9] Appleby, M. (2014) Mind and matter: A critique of Cartesian thinking. In H. Atmanspacher & C.A. Fuchs, (Eds.), *The Pauli-Jung Conjecture* (pp. 7–32), Exeter, England: Imprint Academic.
[10] Friedman, H. (2013). The role of science in transpersonal psychology. In H.L. Friedman & G. Hartelius, *The Wiley-Blackwell handbook of transpersonal psychology* (p. 307). Chichester, England: John Wiley & Sons.
[11] (a) Gieser, S. (2014). Jung. Pauli and the symbolic nature of reality. In H. Atmanspacher & C.A. Fuchs (Eds.), *The Pauli-Jung conjecture* (pp. 157–160). Exeter, England: Imprint Academic.

(b) Gieser, S. (2005). *The innermost kernel* (pp. 203–205). Berlin, Germany: Springer-Verlag. (Original thesis in Swedish 1996, later revised and translated; published by Springer-Verlag in 2005.)
(c) Pauli, Wolfgang (1994). Phenomenon and physical reality. In C.P. Enz & C. von Meyenn (Eds.), *Wolgang Pauli – writings on physics and philosophy*. Berlin, Germany: Springer-Verlag, p. 128.

[12] Walach, H. (2013). Criticisms of transpersonal psychology and beyond. In H. L. Friedman & G. Hartelius (Eds.), *The Wiley-Blackwell handbook of transpersonal psychology* (pp. 74, 77–80). Chichester, England: John Wiley & Sons.

[13] (a) Henry Laurency web site: http://www.laurency.com/index.html A Rosicrucian collection: http://www.rosicrucian.org/rosicrucian-books.
(b) Lucis Trust (Bailey) web site:
https://www.lucistrust.org/store/category/alice_bailey_books_p
(all the 24 books by Bailey/The Tibetan, are available on a searchable CD-ROM)
(c) Theosophy (Blavatsky et al.) web-sites: https://www.theosophical.org/online-resources; http://www.theosociety.org/pasadena/ts/h_tsintro.htm;

[14] Gieser, S. (2005). *The innermost kernel* (pp. 143–146) Berlin, Germany: Springer-Verlag.

[15] Jung, C. G. (1998). in R.A. Segal (Ed.), *Jung on mythology*. Princeton, NJ: Princeton University Press, p. 77.

[16] Jung, C. G. (2001). In a letter to Pauli 13 January 1951. In C.A. Meier (Ed.), *Atom and archetype*. Princeton, NJ: Princeton University Press, p. 70.

[17] Pauli, W. In a letter to Jung, 12 December 1950. In in C.A. Meier (Ed.), *Atom and archetype*. Princeton, NJ: Princeton University Press, p. 64.

[18] Bailey, A. A. (1987). *A treatise on white magic*. New York, NY: Lucis Publishing Company, p. 458.

[19] Jung, C. G. (2001). In a letter to Pauli 13 January 1951. In C.A. Meier (Ed.), *Atom and archetype*. Princeton, NJ: Princeton University Press, p. 70.

[20] Pauli, W. (2001). In a letter to Jung 2 February 1951. In C.A. Meier (Ed.), *Atom and archetype*. Princeton, NJ: Princeton University Press, p. 71.

[21] Gieser, S. (2014). Jung, Pauli and the symbolic nature of reality. In H. Atmanspacher & C.A. Fuchs (Eds.), *The Pauli-Jung conjecture* (pp. 157–160, 164), Exeter, England: Imprint Academic.

[22] Tarnas, R. (2007). *Cosmos and psyche*. New York, NY: Plume, Penguin Books.

[23] Grof, S. (2013). Revision and re-enchantment of psychology. In H. Friedman & G. Hartelius (Eds.), *The Wiley-Blackwell handbook of transpersonal psychology* (pp. 115–117). Chichester, England: John Wiley & Sons.

[24] Bailey, A. A. (1992). *The labours of Hercules*. New York, NY: Lucis Publishing Company.

PART IV:

PURSUING TRANSPERSONAL THEORY AND INQUIRY

CHAPTER TWENTY-THREE

TOWARDS A VIABLE THEORY OF CONSCIOUSNESS

HARALD WALACH

Abstract

Ever since Descartes, philosophy centred around souls - minds - without bodies. With the turn of the tide the natural sciences tried to focus on matter entirely. Out came bodies without mind. It is as if the betrayal of the body, through a purely idealist philosophy that focuses only on the mind and on consciousness, is backlashing against the mind by destroying its very foundations. We therefore need a model of consciousness that allows for an integration of the great scientific success of understanding the physical-material basis of consciousness, the brain, yet understands that consciousness cannot be reduced to brain processes. The model that can achieve this and that will be presented here is the model of complementarity between material and mental processes, brain and consciousness. It hinges around the concept of a generalised entanglement correlation between two phenomenologically distinct systems that are expressions of one underlying unitary reality.

Keywords: body, brain, complementarity, consciousness, entanglement correlation, unitary reality

Short Sketch of the Problem

The scientific mainstream has developed some implicit consensus that consciousness is likely soon to be explained in physicalist terms, as a result of neuronal interactions in the brain.[1, 2, 3, 4, 5] Just exactly how this is to be conceived we do not know right now, but surely will in the near future, similar to the way lightning was explained eventually. Although no truly viable theory of this materialist-reductionist framework of conceptualizing consciousness is really available, most scientists in this field seem to be quite optimistic that there will be soon. This is what I would call the "neuroreductive credo": that all conscious activity, wanting, desiring, loving, hating, imagining, willing and avoiding, having mundane and transpersonal experiences, that all these conscious activities will be explicable in terms of neuronal, i.e., material, activity and local causality. There is only one avenue left: deep analysis of conceptual errors of the mainstream narrative, and working towards an alternative that is taking as much from the common narrative as possible into its own proposal.

Transpersonal psychology has been rather trying to set up its own academic and popular counter culture. Most transpersonalists assert that consciousness must be primary, because ancient wisdom or inner experience, or both, tell us so.[6, 7] The movement of neurocontemplative science, where neuroscientists collaborate with experienced meditators and combine their experiential-phenomenological insight, i.e., a first person, subjective view, with their neuroscientific data, i.e., a third person, objective view[8, 9] seems to be the only area where some relationship between mainstream and transpersonal experiences exists. This movement can teach us a lesson. If we want to speak to the larger scientific community, we need to speak their language.

Currently those two cultures are divided. Transpersonalists do rarely bother about scientific findings, and scientists usually ignore the claims of transpersonalists. In such a situation, it is always a good idea to ask about the history of this development.

This ancient unity between mind and body, coming out of an Aristotelian world view broke apart through increasing skepticism by such thinkers as Francis Bacon and René Descartes. Bacon voiced doubt about the security of scientific and intellectual achievements and ultimately paved the way for the experimental method of inquiry.[10] Descartes felt himself compelled to radically separate material things from mental things.[11] Descartes' ontology fixed, for the first time in intellectual history, a veritable duality between the material and the mental. Material living things, all animals and the human body, were automata, utterly different from the mind that was the only thing endowed with a principle of life and autonomy. It is an irony of history that exactly this attempt at salvaging human ownership, would in the end lead to the fact that the very mental would be conceptualized, along the same lines of material automaticity that Descartes had reserved for the biological machines. The mind has now also become a machine. Gone is the conceptual difference, and abandoned, the reservation for endangered species like the soul. We are left with a purely materialist-causal analysis of mind.

Leibniz tried to rescue the old idea of a soul-substance and to marry it with Descartes' and Spinoza's modern ideas.[12] He conceptualized soul-matter-unit-entities, whereby matter would be somehow reflective of soul and a unitary perspective. He called those entities monads.[13] The German idealist movement tried to ascertain the primacy of mind over matter by making the very simple, convincing and yet ultimately hopeless point that all knowledge about the outer world starts in the human mind, hence matter cannot be the explanatory principle. Idealism, as a movement, was unsuccessful.[14, 15] Natural science, implicitly built on Descartes' analysis, was successful. Politically and morally speaking idealism was unable to stem the power of materialist thinking that instantiated in technological progress. When this power was unleashed in the two big world wars it seemed to many intellectuals that idealism was done with.[16, 17] I am always surprised to see that people did not reach the opposite conclusion, namely that a purely materialist analysis of reality was done with.

The Great War and even more so the holocaust, seem to have contradicted an idealist analysis of reality on a grand scale. Natural sciences developed, independent and unbothered by any philosophical analysis. On the contrary, philosophy in the wake of what philosophers call the "problem of final argument" has given up on providing intellectual guidance to the sciences. Wittgenstein, Gödel, Whitehead, Russell, Collingwood and others have shown that it is impossible to find a system that is completely self-consistent. In other words: there is an element of arbitrariness to each system, and ultimately it is either success, or and common agreement, or historical developments, or political power that determines which system becomes the dominant one.[18, 19, 20, 21] As it happens, the current system that has emerged out of the crucible of history is a natural science paradigm that rests on implicit materialist foundations.

The Strength of the Current Mainstream Position

All our technology is founded on the scientific method, and the progress seems to vindicate not only the method, but also its foundation. If we can build robots that mimic human vision and action derived from principles of neuro-architecture, why would it be wrong to conceptualize the human being as a complicated biological robot that eventually can be imitated in most important aspects?[22] There seems to be no limit to the power of the analytical approach of materialism and mechanism, when it comes to consciousness. Neuropsychology has taught us how closely the destruction of certain brain areas, or the activity of them, is linked to certain mental capacities.[23] A host of neurological conditions teaches us: our psychological and mental faculties are closely linked to brain activities.[24] Each successful anesthesia demonstrates how we can pharmacologically interfere with the construal of conscious awareness. Neuroscience has provided us with a host of extremely strong and convincing correlations between brain states and experiential-conscious or behavioral states. Take away the brain-state and gone is the conscious or behavioral state. Teach the conscious or behavioral state and make it a trait and brain structures will grow and will be modified.[25, 26] Each success of the current mainstream paradigm, recursively reinforces the conceptual foundations and the presuppositions and thus strengthens the expectation that the current approach will be enough to explain consciousness.

The Problems of the Current Paradigm

Theoretical

Philosophers have pointed out that even if we knew everything about a particular brain and its states we would have no idea about the internal perspective of the person to whom this brain belongs.[27, 28] In a similar sense Chalmers argued that one could imagine complete zombie-copies of humans, where everything from the outside looked the same, except they have no inner experience.[29] They are lacking what philosophers call qualia: the feeling of what it is like to be in a state of say, tasting chocolate. In another sense, the same argument has been proposed by Hoche, arguing that every neuroreduction commits a category mistake.[30] It is like saying "The sky is painful." We are predicating something of the sky that does not belong to the sky, except in the language of poets, or in the language of schizophrenics. In the same sense a sentence like "Pain is the firing of neuron 'A'" is making a category mistake. Searle demonstrated by a famous thought experiment that a computer can never be ascribed consciousness.[31] His "Chinese Room" argument likens a computer to a man sitting in a room where Chinese symbols are handed in and he looking up a book of rules, hands them out to people who understand Chinese. Although these people might think that there is someone in there speaking and understanding Chinese, in fact there is not; because the manipulation of symbols alone does not mean the man understands Chinese. In the same way, a computer is not conscious.[32] However, history shows that theoretical arguments are likely ineffective in the face of a big, committed group with economic and political power.

Empirical

The mainstream narrative is predicated on what is technically called a sequence of local causes. By "local" we mean: only what interacts within the physical framework of special relativity with material systems can have an influence.[33] All causes are interactions of material particles or virtual particles, such as photons, that travel maximally at the speed of light and thus take time to bridge spatial gaps; because the mainstream narrative is founded on the concept of local causality, it is impossible to accept phenomena that are obviously violating local causality. Among them are practically all phenomena that have been studied by parapsychology: clairvoyance, telepathy, telekinesis, precognition. Although some parapsychologists have also tried to come up with local theories, in general they have not been successful. They would either assume that a special kind of signal is available, or that a completely different physics is assumed.[34] Meta-analyses suggest – with a very high improbability of false positives – that such phenomena as precognition and clairvoyance, telekinesis even, are possible, at least sometimes.[35, 36, 37, 38, 39, 40, 41, 42, 43] At the same time replication attempts regularly fail, if conducted as identical replications.[44, 45, 46]

The conclusion we must draw is that these phenomena are not causal in the strict local sense but that they are non-local.[47] That means they are rather like correlative regularities. Historians of science are immediately reminded of what Jung and Pauli attempted, namely to find a place for a regularity that was based on meaning, rather than the exchange of energy.[48, 49] They called this "synchronicity". Jung and Pauli conceived of a complementary structure of connectedness or regularity that would complement regular local causality as a kind of final cause. In that sense, what I have in mind is a regularity that is non-local, yet at the same time can be married to the mainstream narrative, provided one is willing to take two steps:

1. To accept that these phenomena are real, even though they are not causal, and
2. That it makes sense to conceptually accommodate them.

This is possible via a model of generalized entanglement that is derived from a generalized quantum theory.[50, 51] It is very important to understand that this is not a physical, but a systemic and general model. So, it has nothing to do with quantum *physics*, but with certain *structures of reality in general*. It seems that all instances where conscious experience is primary and non-local pose an insurmountable challenge to a neuroreductive materialist view of consciousness.[52]

Such experiences have been reported by near-death researchers, although very rarely. One instance was related by Pim van Lommel.[53] It concerns a man who was brought to hospital approximately 30 minutes after cardiac arrest, where he was resuscitated. The man later reported that he had seen his body being carried to the IC-unit, his lung intubated, and in order to be able to do this his dentures were taken out. The resuscitation was successful and when he was discharged he met the emergency nurse identifying her correctly as the woman who had taken out his dentures. Another case is the one by the neurosurgeon Eben Alexander who went into a coma as a consequence of septic shock.[54] During his time in hospital his vital signs and his EEG were recorded, suggesting that his brain was not working. Yet he described very vivid imagery in a certain time flow that is not consistent with a damaged and inactive brain.

However, a case has been made that all those so called near-death experiences are in fact awakening experiences of a brain kicking back into operation.[55] This is certainly also a viable explanation of many experiences that have been collected in the literature. The case of Eben Alexander and the one reported by van Lommel cannot be reconciled with such an explanation, as Alexander could clearly distinguish between the experiences he had shortly before and after awakening, which were unstructured and partially frightening, and those he had during the week of his coma.

A Potential Solution

We need a phenomenologically dualist model of mind-body relationship, with monist ontology. Here, the foundational stuff of the universe is neither mind nor matter but something different, unknown to us ontologically, since we only know material and mental things. However, we live in a world of phenomenological dualism. But that does neither mean that the basic ontology needs to be dualist, nor does it mean that we have to reduce this dualism to a materialist-monist position in order to salvage monism. We can assume that there is one underlying reality that is phenomenologically perceived as duality; but his duality is only in appearance and the way we and our world is made.[56, 57] One word of caution is in order here: We are not only left with a mind-body or brain-body-problem, we are left with a mind-body-spirit problem,[58] since the soul, or the Atman of Vedanta, do not fit into this model (yet). However, I think it is sufficient for the time being to have a model that is true to some extent to phenomenology and can combine some of the strengths of the current scientific approach with our experience.

The model would assume a transcendent ontological unity that breaks up into two different realms of reality that show themselves as material and mental events.[59] To borrow a terminology from quantum physics: material and mental phenomenology are complementary concepts.

Complementarity

Complementarity was introduced as a concept into quantum mechanics by Niels Bohr. Quantum entities demanded experimental set-ups for measurement of their properties, which exclude each other. The canonical example is momentum and location. It is impossible to have both measured in one and the same experimental setting at the same time. This gives rise to the famous uncertainty relationship that Heisenberg formalized. Complementarity was introduced to describe such situations. Technically these variables, also called observables, are called incompatible, because their measurement cannot be made precise at the same time.

Complementarity is a constitutive feature of quantum systems and various analyses show that one cannot get rid of it within a quantum framework.[60, 61] My proposal, following earlier ones is to see the mental and the material in a similar way as complementary attributes of reality. We cannot reduce one to the other, we cannot get rid of them, and we cannot ignore them. Yet this would salvage the underlying unity of reality, while at the same time allowing for phenomenological and systemic duality.

Entanglement

Yet, there is another step needed. For how are those two systems to be correlated, if not by a local-causal mechanism? I propose here a putative or speculative “mechanism” that is based on a generalized version of entanglement, which derives from a generalized formalism of quantum theory.[62] Now, if mind and body, or brain and mind, are conceived as incompatible or complementary, then a different type of theoretical model, namely a generalized form of quantum theory applies.

It is an interesting consequence of this model that it predicts generalized entanglement correlations in such systems. Entanglement correlations were discovered formally in quantum systems by Schrödinger in 1935,[63] and spelled out by Bell in the 60's.[64] Empirical tests were conducted since the 80's.[65, 66] Physical entanglement has been empirically shown to be existent beyond any reasonable doubt.[67] However, physical entanglement proper is a highly fragile thing. The system has to be shielded, correlations hold only for a short time, and as soon as the system interacts with other systems the correlations decay.[68, 69] However, an equivalent to quantum correlations can also be derived as potentially real from our generalized formalism. *If we have a system that combines subsystems, and descriptions pertaining to the subsystem that are complementary to descriptions that pertain to the full system exist, then there should be correlations between those subsystems* that are not causal, but non-local, entanglement-like correlations. In other words, entanglement is a special type of complementarity, namely of complementarity between global descriptions of a system and local descriptions of subsystems. Such generalized entanglement correlations would mean that those subsystems are correlated without exchanging causal-local signals. As such it introduces a new, intriguing capability, namely the feature of a non-local coordination mechanism between systems that is not built upon local signal exchange and causal interaction.

Generalised Entanglement as a Potential Coordination Mechanism between Mind and Body

There is a very generic complementarity or incompatibility that might become operative here, namely the complementarity between the whole – the organism the human being – and its parts – the subsystems of mental and physical systems.[70] If that is so, then our model would predict entanglement correlations between those systems, i.e., the mental and the physical, or mind and body. This would then be able to account for the tight and perfect correlations of two phenomenologically different, yet tightly interlinked and closely correlated systems. Such a concept would do both: it would use the strongest available theoretical model, namely quantum theory, which in its physical form has survived all experimental tests so far, and would apply it to an unsolved problem. The stipulation and justification would be that this is necessary in order to be true to the phenomenology and that it allows incorporation of empirical phenomena that otherwise have to be excluded.

There are at least two caveats in order here.

For one: entanglement correlations of a generalized type are as yet just theoretical, speculative concepts. They have a good formal foundation, but similar to Quantum entanglement correlations proper that were only taken seriously after an empirical proof of their existence, the onus of proof is now on our side. We have come up with various ideas and some empirical data are available,[71] but we are far from a definitive proof. Thus, this concept needs to be ventilated and used with due care. Neither should it be considered a cure all, nor used indiscriminately.

Apart from that, this concept cannot solve the spirit-problem in the equation. It is currently only a solution for the mind-body-duality without having to resort to a reductive materialism. The model might also be able to accommodate a spiritual reality, but then one would have to assume a phenomenological or ontological triad of physical, mental, and spiritual reality or body, mind, spirit. This might ultimately not only be necessary, but also warranted, given the phenomenology and the conceptual problems. One could assume that in a way similar to a mental and a psychological system there is also a spiritual or soul system operative in the human person. This system is in the same way non-locally correlated with the mental-physical system as they are among themselves, and that the actions, operations, and consequences we see, are at the same time expression of that spiritual or soul-system as our soul-system is impacted or correlated with our physico-mental system.

The uses of a theoretical model are not that they tell us what reality is like but that they allow us to make ourselves free from models that are restrictive. There is nothing as practical as a good theory, Einstein is credited with saying. I would not claim that this proposed model is a good theory, but I would assume that it is a reasonably good theory that can allow for some openness, and at the same time scientific viability.

Bibliography

[1] Dennett, D.C. (1991) *Consciousess explained.* Boston, MA: Little, Brown & Co.
[2] Churchland, P.S. (1986). *Neurophilosophy. Toward a unified science of the mind-brain.* Cambridge, MA: MIT Press.
[3]Nagel,T. (2012). *Mind and cosmos: Why the materialist neo-Darwinian conception of nature is almost certainly false.* Oxford, England: Oxford University Press.
[4] Metzinger, T. (2008). *The ego tunnel. The science of the mind and the myth of the self.* New York, NY: Basic Books.
[5] Metzinger, T. (2003). *Being no one: The self-model theory of subjectivity.* Cambridge, MA: MIT Press.
[6] Grof, S. (2000). *Psychology of the future. Lessons from modern consciousness research.* Albany, NY: State University of New York Press.
[7] Grof, S. (1988).*The adventure of self-discovery.* Albany, NY: State University of New York Press (SUNY Series in Transpersonal and Humanistic Psychology).
[8] Lutz, A., et al. (2015). *Investigating the phenomenological matrix of mindfulness-related practices from a neurocognitive perspective. American Psychologist, 70,* 632-658.
[9] Jo, H.-G., Hinterberger, T., Wittmann, M., & Schmidt, S. (2015). *Do meditators have higher awareness of their intentions to act? Cortex, 65,* 149-158.
[10] Bacon, F. (1990). In W. Krohn (Ed.), *Neues organon. Lateinisch-deutsch. Hrsg. und mit einer Einleitung von* [New organon. Latin-German. Editor with an introduction]. Hamburg, Germany: Meiner
[11] Descartes, R. (1954). *Philosophical writings* (E. Anscombe & P.T. Geach, Eds., Trans,). London, England: Nelson.
[12] Antognazza, M.R. (2009). *Leibniz: An intellectual biography.* Cambridge, England: Cambridge University Press.
[13] Leibniz, G.W. (1966). *Monadologie.* In A. Buchenau & E. Cassirer (Eds.), *Hauptschriften zur Grundlegung der philosophie* [Monadology. Main works for the foundation of philosophy] (pp. 435-456). Hamburg, Germany: Meiner. (Original work published 1714)
[14] Albertazzi, L. (2006). *Immanent realism: An introduction to Brentano* (Synthese Library). Heidelberg, Germany: Springer.
[15] Smith, B. (1994). *Austrian philosophy. The legacy of Franz Brentano.* Chicago, IL: Open Court.
[16] Lyotard, J.-F. (1986) *Das postmoderne wissen: Ein bericht* [Postmodern knowledge: A report]. Graz, Germany: Böhlau.
[17] Walach, H., & Stillfried, N.V. (2011). Generalised quantum theory—basic idea and general intuition: A background story and overview. *Axiomathes, 21,* 185-209.
[18] Kuhn, T. (1955). *The structure of scientific revolutions* (*reality of science studies.*) Cambridge, MA: Harvard University Press.
[19] Collingwood, R.G. (1998). *An essay on metaphysics.* Oxford, England: Clarendon Press. (Original work published 1940)
[20] Fleck, L. (1979). *Genesis and developmen of a scientific fact.* (T.J. Trenn & R.K. Merton, Eds.). Chicago, IL: University of Chicago Press.

[21] Bishop, J.P. (2010). Transhumanism, metaphysics, and the posthuman god. *Journal of Medicine and Philosophy*, *35*, 700-720.
[22] Damasio, A. (2000). *The feeling of what happens: Body, emotion, and the making of consciousness*. London, England: Vintage.
[23] Sacks, O. (2010). *The man who mistook his wife for a hat*. Oxford, England: ISIS. (Original published 1986)
[24] Driemeyer, J., Boyke, J., Gaser, C., Büchel, C., & May, A. (2008). *Changes in gray matter induced by learning - revisited.* PLoS One, *3*(7), p. e2669.
[25] Fox, K.C.R., Nijeboer, S., Dixon, M.L., Floman, J.L., Ellamil, M., Rumak, S.P. … Christoff, K. (2014). Is meditation associated with altered brain structure? A systematic review and meta-analysis of morphometric neuroimaging in meditation practitioners. N*euroscience & Biobehavioral Reviews*, *43*, 48-73.
[26] Nagel, T. (1974). What is it like to be a bat? P*hilosophical Review*, *83*, 435-450.
[27] Jackson, F. (1986). What Mary didn't know. *Journal of Philosophy*, *83*, 291-295.
[28] Chalmers, D. J. (1996). *The conscious mind. In search of a fundamental theory*. New York, NY: Oxford University Press.
[29] Hoche, H.-U. (2008). *Anthropological complementarism. Linguistic, logical, and phenomenological studies in support of a third way beyond dualism and monism.* Paderborn, Germany: Mentis Verlag.
[30] Searle, J.R. (1992). *The rediscovery of the mind*. Cambridge, MA: Massachusetts Institute of Technology Press.
[31] Maleeh, R. (2015). Minds, brains and programs: An information-theoretic approach. *Mind and Matter*, *13*(1), 71-103.
[32] Reichenbach, H. (1957). *The philosophy of space and time*. New York, NY: Dover.
[33] Alcock, J.E. (2003). Give the null hypothesis a chance: Reasons to remain doubtful about the existence of PSI. *Journal of Consciousness Studies*, *10*(6-7), 29-50.
[34] Bem, D., Tressoldi, P.E., Rabeyron, T., & Duggan M. (2016). *Feeling the future: A meta-analysis of 90 experiments on the anomalous anticipation of random future events* [version 2; referees: 2 approved]. *F1000Research* 2016, **4**:1188. (doi: 10.12688/f1000research.7177.2)
[35] Giroldini, W., Pederzoli L, Bilucaglia M., Caini, P., Ferrini A., Melloni, S. ….Tressoldi, P.E. (2016). EEG correlates of social interaction at distance. *F1000 Research*, [version 5; referees:2 approved]. *F1000Research* 2016, **4**:457. (doi:10.12688/f1000research.6755.5)
[36] Mossbridge, J., Tressoldi, P.E., & Utts, J. (2012). Predictive physiological anticipation preceding seemingly unpredictable stimuli: A meta-analysis. *Frontiers in Psychology*, *3*(Artc. 390). doi.org/10.3389/fpsyg.2012.00390
[37] Mossbridge, J. A., Treesoldi, P., A., Utts, J., Ives, J.A. Radon. D., & Jonas, W.B. (2014). Predicting the unpredictable: Critical analysis and practical implications of predictive anticipatory activity. *Frontiers in Human Neuroscience*, *8* (Articl. 146): doi: 10.3389/fnhum.2014.00146.
[38] Storm, L., Tressoldi, P.E., & Di Riso, L. (2012). Meta-analysis of ESP studies, 1987-2010: Assessing the success of the forced choice design in parapsychology. *Journal of Parapsychology*,*72*(2), online (Retrieved from www.parapsych.org)

[39] Tressoldi, P.E. (2912). Extraordinary claims require extraordinary evidence: The case of non-local perception, a classical and Bayesian review of evidence. *Frontiers in Psychology*, *2*(2):117. doi: 10.3389/fpsyg.2011.00117

[40] Walach, H., Tressoldi, P., & Pederzoli, L. (2015). *Mental, behavioural and phyisiological nonlocal correlations within the generalized quantum theory framework: A review.* Social Science Research Network. http://dx.doi.org/10.2139/ssrn.2695741.

[41] Schmidt, S. (2012). Can we help just by good intentions? A meta-anaylsis of experiments on distant intention effects. J*ournal of Alternative & Complementary Medicine*, *18*, 529-533.

[42] Schmidt, S., Schneider, R., Utts, J., & Walach, H. (2004). Remote intention on electrodermal activity - Two meta-analyses. *British Journal of Psychology*, *95*, 235-247.

[43] Walach, H., & Jonas, W.B. (2007). From parapsychology to spirituality: The legacy of the PEAR database. *Explore. The Journal of Science and Healing*, *3*, 197-199.

[44] Bösch, H., Steinkamp, P., & Boller, E, (2006). Examining psychokinesis: The interaction of human intention with random number generators - a meta-analysis. *Psychological Bulletin*, *132*, 497-523.

[45] Jahn, R. G. et al. (2000). Mind/machine interaction consortium: PortREG replication experiments. *Journal of Scientific Exploration*, *14*, 499-555.

[46] Walach, H., von Ludacou, W., & Römer, H. (2014). Parapsychological phenomena as examples of generalized non-local correlations - A theoretical framework. *Journal of Scientific Exploration*, *28*, 605-631.

[47] Atmanspacher, H., & Primas, H. (2006). Pauli's ideas on mind and matter in the context of contemporary science. *Journal of Consciousness Studies*, *13*(3), 5-50.

[48] Jung, C.G. (1952). Synchronizität als ein Prinzip akausaler Zusammenhänge. In *Naturerklärung und Psyche* [Synchronicity as a principle of non-causal connections. In Explanation of nature and psyche](C.G. Jung & W. Pauli, Eds.) (pp. 1-107). Zürich, Switzerland: Rascher.

[49] Atmanspacher, H., Römer, H., &Walach, H. (2002). Weak quantum theory: Complementarity and entanglement in physics and beyond. *Foundations of Physics*, *32*, 379-406.

[50] See Note 17, and Römer, H., & Walach, H. (2011). Complementarity of phenomenal and physiological observables: A primer on generalised quantum theory and its scope for neuroscience and consciousness studies. In H. Walach, S. Schmidt, & W.B. Jonas (Eds.), *Neuroscience, consciousness and spirituality* (pp. 97-107). Dordrecht, Netherlands: Springer.

[51] Walach, H., & Schmidt, S. (2005). Repairing Plato's life boat with Ockham's razor: The important function of research in anomalies for mainstream science. *Journal of Consciousness Studies*, *12*(2), pp. 52-70.

[52] Van Lommel, P. (2015). Endless consciousness: A concept based on scientific studies of near-death-experiences. In H. Walach, S. Schmidt, & W.B. Jonas (Eds.), *Neuroscience, consciousness and spirituality* (pp. 2017-227). Dordrecht, Netherlands: Springer.

[53] Alexander, E. (2012). *Proof of heaven: A neurosurgeon's journey into the afterlife*. London: Piatkus.
[54] Marsh, M.N. (2010). *Out-of-body and near-death experiences: Brain-state phenomena or glimpses of immortality?* Oxford, England: Oxford University Press.
[55] See Note 54.
[56] See Note 51 and
Walach, H., & Römer, H. (2000). Complementarity is a useful concept for consciousness studies. A reminder. *Neuroendocrinology Letters*, *21*, 221-232.
[57] Walach, H. (2007). Mind - body - spirituality. *Mind and Matter*, *5*, 215-240.
[58] Atmanspacher, H. (2003). Mind and matter as asymptotically disjoint, inequivalent representations with broken time-reversal symmetry. *Biosystems*, *68,* 19-30.
[59] Kim, I. , & Mahler, G. (2000). Uncertainty rescued: Bohr's complementarity for composite systems. *Physics Letters A*, *269,* 287-292.
[60] Fahrenberg, J. (1979). Das Komplementaritätsprinzip in der psychosomatischen Forschung und psychosomatischen Medizin. *Zeitschrift für Klinische Psychologie, Psychopathologie und Psychotherapie* [The principle of complentarity in psychosomatic research and psychosomatic medicine. *Journal for Clinical Psychology, Psychopathology and Psychotherapy*], *27*, 151-167.
[61] Schrödinger, E. (1979). Discussion of probability relations between separated systems. *Proceedings of the Cambridge Philosophical Society*, *131*, 555-563. (Original work published 1935)
[62] See notes 51and 56
[63] Bell, J. S. (1987). *Speakable and unspeakable in quantum mechanics.* Cambridge, England: Cambridge University Press.
[64] Aspect, A., Dalibard, J., & Roger, G. (1982). Experimental test of Bell's inequalities using time varying analyzers. *Physics Review Letter*, *49*, 1804-1807.
[65] Aspect, A., Grangier, P., & G. Roger, G. (1982). Experimental realization of Einstein-Podolsky-Rosen-Bohm-Gedankenexperiment: A new violation of Bell's inequalities. *Physics Review Letter*, *49*, 91-94.
[66] Salart, D., Baas, A., Branciard, C., Gisin, N., & Zbinden, H. (2008). Testing spooky actions at a distance. *Nature*, *454*, 861-864.
[67] Römer, H. (2012). Why do we see a classical world? *Travaux Mathematique*, *20*, 167-186.
[68] Yu, T., & Eberly, J.H. (2009). Sudden death of entanglement. *Science*, *323*, 598-601.
[69] von Stillfried, N., & Walach, H. (2006).*T*he whole and its parts: Are complementarity and non-locality intrinsic to closed systems? *International Journal of Computing Anticipatory Systems*, *17*, 137-146.
[70] Walach, H. (2014). Mind-matter interactions - On the rollercoaster from data to theory and back again. In F. Bial (Ed.), *Aquém e além do cérebro* [Behind and beyond the brain]*: 10th Symposiun of the Bial Foundation: Mind Matter Interactions* (pp. 85-114), Portugal: Fundacao Bial [Bial foundation].

CHAPTER TWENTY-FOUR

INTEGRATION OF MATERIALISTIC AND IDEALISTIC THINKING: A THREE-DIMENSIONAL MAP

REINHARD LASSER

Abstract

By constructing a non-reductionist systematisation of different fields of knowledge, big enough to include the main scientific, medical, philosophical and spiritual traditions, I arrive at a three-dimensional map of worldviews, epistemologies, methodologies and ontologies. The practical use of this meta-narrative is a transformation of controversy into contrast, of incompatible and mutually exclusive stances into an encompassing, graduated structure. This could be applied as a map to navigate the complexity of simultaneously existing narratives across individuals and cultures, thereby functioning as a "Rosetta-stone" for world views and perspectives.

Keywords: meta-narrative, medicine, non-reductionist, philosophy, science, spirituality

During the course of history many philosophies have been developed in different parts of the world that aim at explaining our own existence and the existence of the world. These explanations undergo changes and, it would seem, each idea is tested under real life conditions to a point where advantages and disadvantages become obvious. At this point they are then replaced by new ideas that become the dominant philosophical, epistemological and methodological mode of the next era, much like Thomas Kuhn describes for paradigm shifts in science.

We have come to a point in history, where seemingly mutually exclusive explanations of reality are exerted and tension between these explanations is sustained. This is undeniably happening in the sciences, which seems, in Quantum physics, to provide the most reliable explanations for our existence. Light is seen not only as a stream of particles, as Newtonian physics proposed, but also as a wave that has all of the properties of waves, such as bending at an obstacle or interference. Quantum physics also shows that there is entanglement between quanta, and that the state of one of the entangled parts is correlated directly and without delay, to the state of the other. These are facts that should not be possible according to Newtonian Physics and contradict intuitive thought. Another very important aspect of Quantum physics is that measurement influences the state of a system, so the observer becomes part of the system that is being measured which is not the case in Newtonian Physics. Thus, we must become accustomed to contradictory points of view that seem to be mutually exclusive, but are each necessary to explain the whole of existence.

The following work is based on the work of many authorities and on my personal experience in the fields of Western medicine, Transpersonal Psychology, Homoeopathy, Traditional Chinese medicine, Constellation work and my spiritual practice of Siddha Yoga, incorporating each of their respective worldviews and philosophies. Particular thanks must go to Ken Wilber, a pioneer of integration, to whom I owe many ideas and a general notion of non-exclusiveness.

Incommensurable Pairs

Two such irreducible, seemingly contradictory different realms are the pairs: consciousness/body and individual/collective. These two incommensurable pairs seemingly have been irreconcilable throughout history, although many attempts have been made to reduce them into a single concept.

Ken Wilber was the first of whom I know, who brought these four basic perspectives into one coherent system, by introducing his four quadrants of existence, also referred to as four basic perspectives:

	INTERNAL	EXTERNAL
SINGULAR	*UL - I* Individual Interiority: individual, seen from inside I feel, I think Methods: Introspection	*UR - IT* Individual exteriority: Indivudual, seen from outside Methods: Objectivation, measurment
PLURAL	*LL - WE* Collective interiority: A group or society seen from inside We feel, we think, we construct a worldview Methods: Cultural studies Deconstruction/Reconstruction	*LR - ITS* Collective exteriority: A group or society seen from outside Methods: Social studies, Archeology

Figure 1. Four perspectives (four quadrants) (based on information from Wilber, (2000). See note 4.

Upper left (UL): Individual interiority, experienced as individual, inner feelings and thoughts, through an "I-perspective" (e.g., I feel angry).

Upper right (UR): Individual exteriority experienced as individual bodies out there, from an "It-perspective" (e.g., this person is 1.82 m high).

Lower left (LL): Collective interiority experienced as collective inner feelings, notions, values etc. from a "We-perspective" that draws a border to demarcate between the "We" and "They" (e.g., we have become vegetarian because we do not want to live on suffering animals….).

Lower right (LR): Collective exteriority experienced as a system that governs individual behaviour from an "Its-perspective" (e.g., the health insurance system of this state is organised in a way that many people have to wait for their treatment for a long time).

A third pair of seemingly irreconcilable notions is the **idealistic** and the **materialistic** point of view in relation to existence as a whole. The question being: what comes first, the ideas or the material bodies? Idealistic philosophies have a notion of **involution**, of a development from mind or spirit to matter, whereas materialistic philosophies have a notion of **evolution**, of a development from matter to mind or spirit. Does the world arise from a first will, impulse or idea or is it a combination and development of a kind of material substance or energy that was there from the beginning. During history there has always been a dispute between these two convictions, which continues to be controversial. Therefore I would like to include this as a third axis in a holistic three dimensional picture of actuality, thus expanding the four quadrants of Ken Wilber by a third dimension.

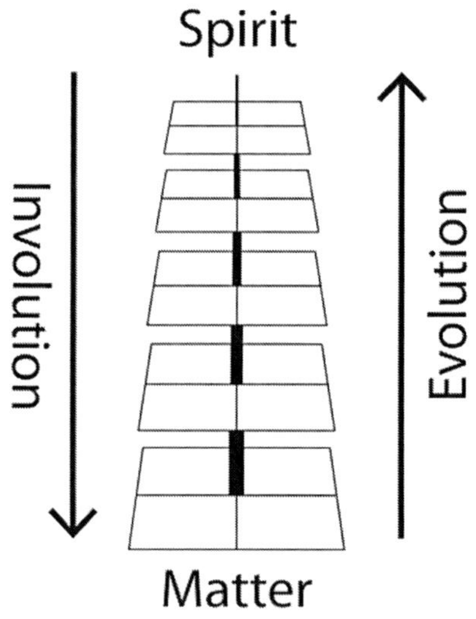

Figure 2. Developmental trajectories in idealistic and materialistic philosophies

The answer to the questions: what comes first and what is real governs our whole life and forms the most basic assumptions we build our lives on. This is not only a game of the mind but is the very question of what science is, which methods are valuable and useful and which data are produced and incorporated.

What I aim to propose, at the least a map to navigate the different worldviews and to offer a three dimensional picture or diagram to which much of the history of thought and science, inner and outer, eastern and western, northern and southern, traditional, modern and postmodern can be related.

Idealistic Worldviews

Before constructing an evolutionary, material universe I want to construct a universe of intentions and ideas, as many of the philosophical and spiritual traditions have done before. They locate the intentions, ideas and energies into a personalized vision of God, as the great monotheistic religions and indigenous religions do, they attribute it to a universal personal spirit, as the Hindu tradition does or to an impersonal force or consciousness, as Taoism or Buddhism do. There are philosophers like Plato, Plotinus, the German idealists, Alfred North Whitehead, Charles Sanders Pierce and many others, whose philosophies have in their core an idealistic worldview. This notion is supported by the direct experience of many researchers of the interior, called mystics and saints.

Meister Eckhart[1] (1260-1328) writes:

> If the soul wants to experience something, she throws out a picture of experience in front of herself and steps into it.

And Kshemaraja,[2] an Indian Sage of the 11th century A.D.:

> By the power of her own will, she [Consciousness] unfolds the universe upon a part of herself.

Involution

Philosophical traditions have termed this "throwing out" of a world emanation, involution or creation.

Ken Wilber[3] writes:

> In involution or creation, radically unqualifiable Spirit decides to play a game of hide and-seek, and hence 'forgets' itself and throws itself outward to create a manifest world of many-ness and otherness. As we saw, the first thing pure Spirit creates is soul, which then throws itself outward to create mind, which throws itself outward to create life (or prana), which then

throws itself outward to create insentient matter (quarks, atoms). At the end of that ontological sequence, matter blows into existence as a crystallization and condensation of prana.

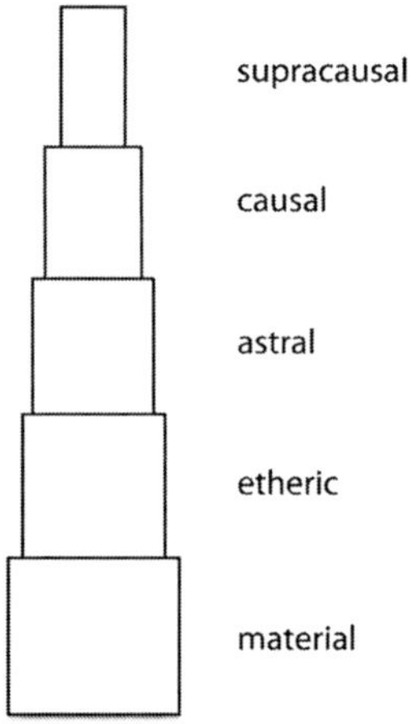

Figure 3. Sequence of involution (based on information from Wilber, 2006a). See note 3.

According to the doctrine of involution, at the moment of the Big Bang, when matter comes into existence, there is already an ordered sequence of subtle energies (*Figure 4*).

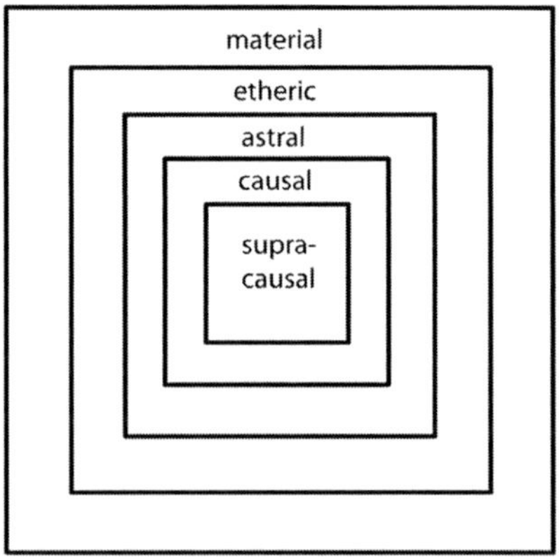

Figure 4. Implicit order at the "Big Bang" (based on information from Wilber, 2006a). See note 3.

Materialistic Worldviews

Materialistic cosmologies do not consider involution, subtle bodies or energies as real. Rather, they start with something material like some of the ancient Greek philosophers, the atomists and physicists, have done. They took undividable first building blocks, the atoms, as the basic material for existence. They see the properties of being alive, of feeling, of thinking, as emerging faculties of the increasing complexity of material bodies and systems.

In line with this view but with the perspectives of the "I", the "We", the "It" and the "Its" in mind, we can construct a material Universe. This is, what Ken Wilber did when he elaborated his four quadrants.

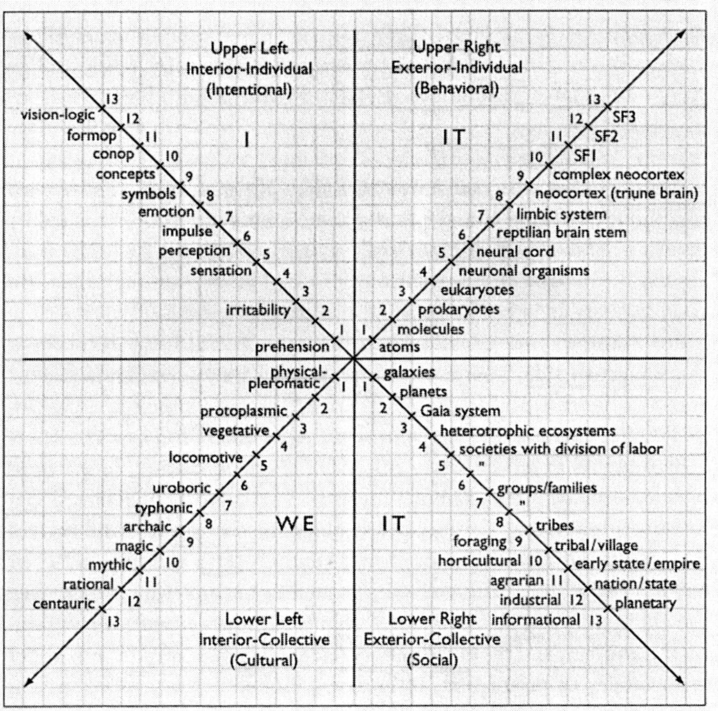

Figure 5. The four quadrants of the gross body-mind; Ken Wilber[4] (1996, 2000)
Note: From *Sex, Ecology, Spirituality,* p. 119, by Ken Wilber, Copyright © 1996, 2000 by Ken Wilber. Reprinted by arrangement with The Permissions Company, Inc., on behalf of Shambhala Publications, Inc., www.shambhala.com

This concept clearly expands the notion of Descartes and of modernity, which holds the conviction that only humans have interiority or inner experience (i.e., res cogitans). Interiority is ascribed to all of existence: physical prehension (a term used by A.N. Whitehead [5] to indicate a form of "experience" or "feeling" that he thinks to be common to all matter) to minerals, irritability to living cells, sensations to plants, impulses and feelings to animals and thoughts and higher mental faculties to humans. Each step transcends and includes his predecessors, so humans have all these kinds of inner experiences, although many of them on a subconscious level.

Subtle Bodies – Subtle Minds

Eastern and Western traditions also have experience of subtle bodies with partly well-defined systems, such as the Chakra System of India or the Meridian system of Chinese medicine. Similar orders of subtle bodies are also described in Western traditions (e.g., R. Steiner, 1980).[6]

If there are subtle individual bodies, there must be a subtle objective world and a subtle intersubjective world because individuals do not exist in a void but in community with other individuals or holons. This is expressed by the lower quadrants of our system.

Below I will present some properties of the four quadrants of the material and subtle bodies as they are represented in spiritual experiences and in healing methods, as well as in every day experience and science.

Some Characteristics of the Gross Realm

The world is experienced as consisting of material, disenchanted objects, ordered by chance and necessity or as material probability waves that collapse when they are measured or watched. Under this view, human freedom and sense of purpose are in doubt. One lives in a purposeless universe that is driven by an evolution of accidental mutations and natural selection that secures the survival of the fittest. Only what is measurable is real or worthy of scientific research. Matter is the only ontological reality; everything else is an epiphenomenon of it. God is dead. Such thinkers include Galilei, Descartes, Ockham, Darwin and many contemporary thinkers and scientists.

A natural scientist is a researcher of the gross realm whose methods include wakeful observation and **rationality**.

The following figures show the four quadrants further divided into an inner and an outer perspective of each quadrant, resulting in eight zones. This allows a finer mapping of perspectives and methods. With respect to my own work in the medical and therapeutic field I provide some examples of healing methods in the respective quadrants and zones.

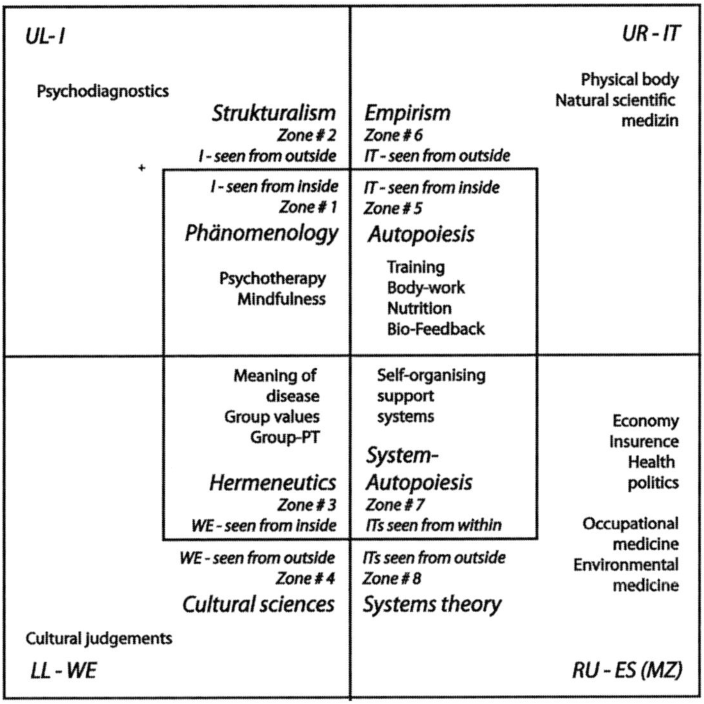

Figure 6. Perspectives and methodologies of the gross body-mind (Structure of 8 zones based on information from Wilber 2006b[7], p. 30f).

Some Characteristics of the Etheric Realm

The world is experienced as animated and living. A connectedness is felt with all living beings. Vital energy (Elan vital, Qi or Ki, Prana) may be experienced directly circulating in the body in vessels (Chinese medicine) or in nadis (Indian Chakra system).

Healers work with this energy, which can be reduced, augmented or blocked. In homoeopathy vital energy is liberated by an impulse that is working in the same direction as the disturbance of the energy and the system reacts autopoietically against this stimulus and corrects the disturbance. “Like heals like” – “Similia similibus curentur”.

Vital energy can be transmitted from one person to another by healers or by real Gurus. This can result in involuntary movements and experiences, as in Kundalini awakening. Such thinkers include Aristotle, Hahnemann and Mesmer.

A **Shaman** can be considered a scientist of the etheric realm, whose methods include **imagination.** Trance, Qi gong, Tai Chi, acupuncture, yoga, dowsing, shamanic rituals, constellation work, are methods of this realm amongst others.

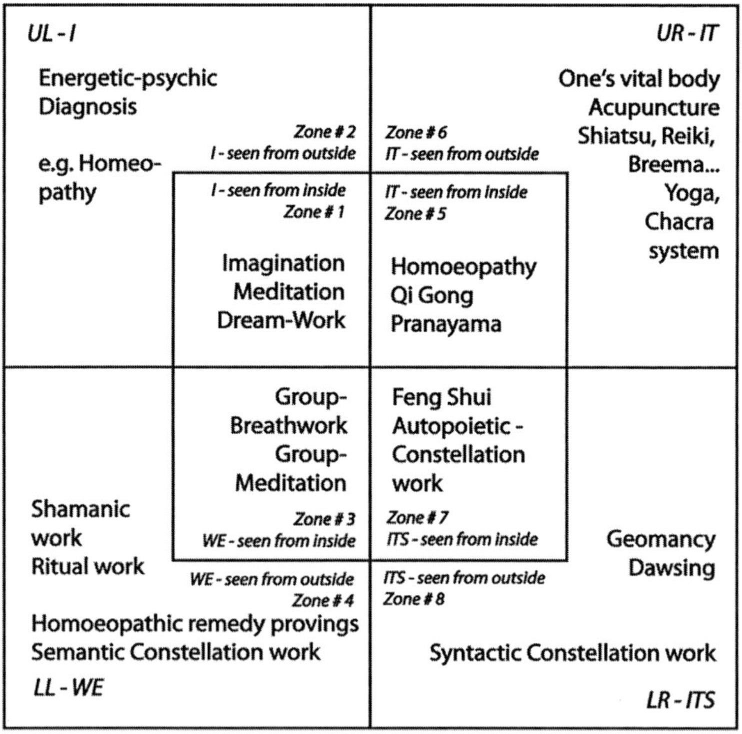

Figure 7. The four quadrants of the etheric body-mind

LL: The inner experience of a common energetic field, of an atmosphere or energy that organizes a family, group, tribe or peoples.
LR: World as animate and living "Web of Life" Energy lines, Power Places etc.

Some Characteristics of the Astral Body-mind

Archetypes and Platonic ideas may be experienced as impersonal forms, which have been termed "eternal objects" by A.N. Whitehead, or as personal Gods, Goddesses or Spirits. Plato referred to them in both ways. In meditation or during transpersonal therapies such as Holotropic Breathwork® people directly experience non material but powerful energies, which sometimes seem to be acting wilfully and personally and at other times are experienced more as abstract principles.

Archetypes often manifest in both the inner and the outer world simultaneously, as C.G. Jung has reported. Jung called this phenomenon Synchronicity.

Artists and scientists often experience themselves during moments of inspiration in such a way that they are more the tools than the originators of the creative work that they do. They often feel more as if they receive ideas from a surrounding world of ideas or from a spirit or deity than as if these ideas come out of themselves.

One cannot think of mathematical forms or laws as being arbitrary, subjective or temporarily true. The definition of a circle as all points in a plane that have the same distance to the centre will be the same in eternity for every human being. This is why A.N. Whitehead calls ideas eternal objects (See Note 5).

As the mathematician G.Spencer-Brown put it: "…we have direct awareness of mathematical form as archetypical structure."[8]

LL: The inner experience of the ideas, interests, values etc. that connects and organizes a group of people. These common constructs, narratives, myths, and paradigms are usually not questioned from inside the group.

LR: World of Ideas and Archetypes as objective reality, not only as an interpersonal social construction. This is a notion of spiritual realism in contrast to the prevailing spiritual nominalism created by William of Ockham and others. Such thinkers include Plato, Pythagoras, Whitehead and Jung.

Saints can be considered as scientists of the astral realm. The methods employed by saints and artists include **Inspiration**. Other methods are meditation with form, scriptural study, assimilation of ideas and opening up for inspiration.

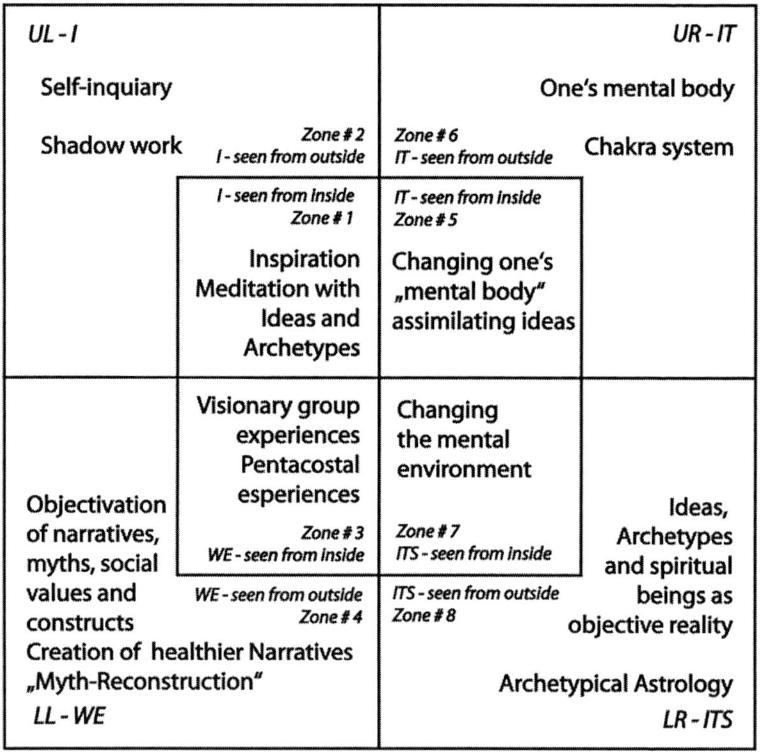

Figure 8. The four quadrants of the astral body-mind

Some Characteristics of the Causal Realm

The Causal Body is the first manifestation of Spirit. It is pure potentiality without form. Pure intentionality without objects, blackness, no experience whatsoever, deep sleep, death, annihilation and the Dark Night of the Soul.

On the other hand, if this experience is permitted and gone through, it liberates one from attachments and gives deep peace and acceptance. "Thy will be done". This is also known as Good-Friday experience, during which the fear of death is overcome. It is the first intention and will to act. Later in involution, this impulse may be clothed with ideas, vital energy and a material expression. It is the final cause in an Aristotelian sense, the goal that is created with the intention.

LL: Cultural acceptance of death and finality. Collective intentionality and a common goal.

LR: The intentionality of all sentient beings; a higher will, a higher intention as objective reality. "Not my will, thy will be done" presupposes that there is another intentionality or will, which is usually experienced as God's will. Such protagonists include Jesus, Gautama Buddha and John of the Cross.

A **Sage** can be considered a scientist of the causal, employing **intentions** and becoming silent as methods.

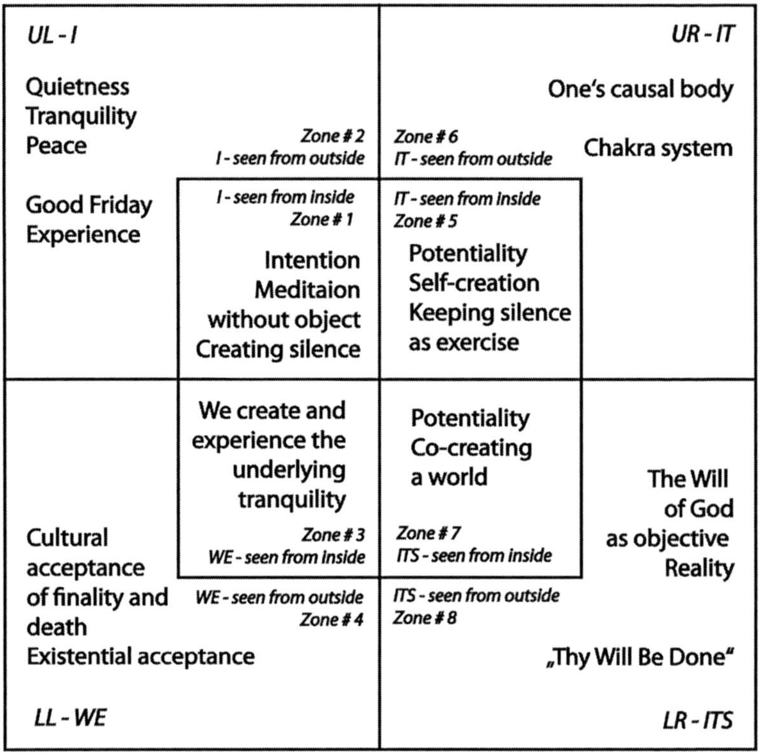

Figure 9. The four quadrants of the causal body-mind

Some Characteristics of the Supracausal

Supracausal: Turiya (Witness) and Turiyatita (Nonduality)

Opposite to the Causal the Supracausal does not have any quality, not even the quality of non-experience or potentiality nor of "no quality". All this - not; and even that – not (M. Varga v. Kybed). It is absolutely free. It is the basis of all experience, the clear light that illumines and manifests all creation. This light cannot be separated from the experiencer, which is why Ramana Maharshi calls it I-I, others call it pure I consciousness, emptiness, or clear light. The Upanishads call it "one without a second".

Turiya is known as the fourth state, because it is different from the three natural states of consciousness, waking, dreaming and deep sleep. Turiya

(Witness) can neither be experienced as an object nor as a subject with properties.

In **Turiyatita** (Nonduality "beyond Turiya") no separation is felt between the witness, the witnessed and the process of witnessing.

According to the Siddha Yoga tradition the supracausal realm also has its body (Muktananda, 2007).[9] It is the common body of all existence, which is experienced as a blue pearl with its centre in the crown of the head and in every sentient being.

Protagonists: Jesus, Ramana Maharshi, Vedanta and Vajrayana amongst others.

A **Siddha** can be considered a scientist of the Supracausal realm whose methods include self-awareness as the empty witness (Turiya) and **intuition:** knowledge through identity (Turiyatita).

One cannot talk of quadrants in respect to Turiya, because this is the basis of consciousness. You cannot witness the witness, therefore you cannot objectify it, and so there are no quadrants.

In respect to Turiyatita it is different: because Turiyatita is oneness with all of existence, it is oneness with all other sentient beings, oneness with the so called objective reality and oneness with all states and stages of consciousness. Therefore it is possible to talk about Turiyatita (nonduality) in the language of the quadrants: realising Turiyatita goes along with changes in all quadrants:

UL: The self-awareness expands and is no more identified with the own body, be it gross or subtle and therefore is no more limited. "I and the Father are one" says Jesus, because he has realised his innermost identity with God, the Self of all. And Muktananda (see note 9) says: "God dwells within you as you", which signifies the same deep identity between the individual (Atman) and the universal Self (Brahman).
LL: The community with other people and all of creation is deeper. Jesus says: "What you did to the least of my brothers and sisters you did for me", because he is aware of the one and only Self (Christ, Buddha nature, Atman, Tao) in everyone. Baba Muktananda (see note 9) teaches in Siddha Yoga: "See God in each other"[10] and means the same.

UR: Because one identifies with the Self of all of creation, the whole universe becomes one's own body.

LR: What was a system of different entities in other levels becomes one organism, as Paul says: Now you are the body of Christ, and each one of you is a part of it. (Kor 12.7) The consciousness of Christ goes along with the awareness of the universe being a whole and each of us being a limb of the body of Christ and, inasmuch as we realise Christ-consciousness, the universe becomes our body.

UL - I Intuition: knowledge through identity Experience of oneness with everything arising Atman is Brahman „ I and the Father are One"	*UR - IT* One's supracausal body, the„Blue Perl", the body-energy of Turiya and Turiyatita. Chakra system
„See God in each other" Unconditional love to all that exists. „ What you did to the least of my brothers and sisters you did for me" *LL - WE*	Everything, that is, is you. There is no difference between you and objects, between you and God. You are That *LR - ITS*

Figure 10. The four quadrants of the supracausal body-mind

Involution and Evolution in a 3-dimensional Model of Body-minds

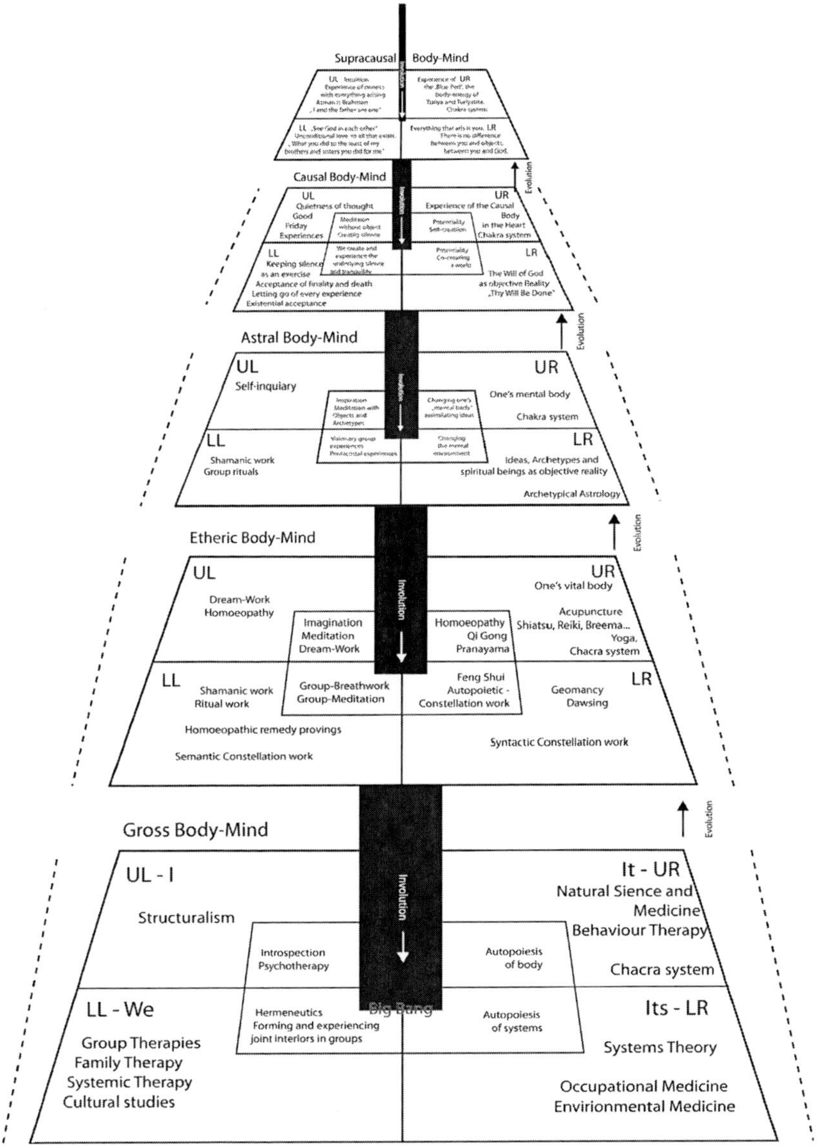

Figure 11. Involution and evolution in a 3-D model of body-minds

Figure 11 displays the central column of involution and the successive order of levels of evolution. Some methods are mentioned that are used to explore and enact the respective levels, quadrants and zones.

> Wilber: Increasing complexity of gross form (see Figure 5) is necessary for the expression or manifestation of both higher consciousness and subtler energy.[11]

Influence and Causation between Quadrants and Levels

Horizontal Influence and Exchange

There is influence and exchange between the quadrants on all levels:

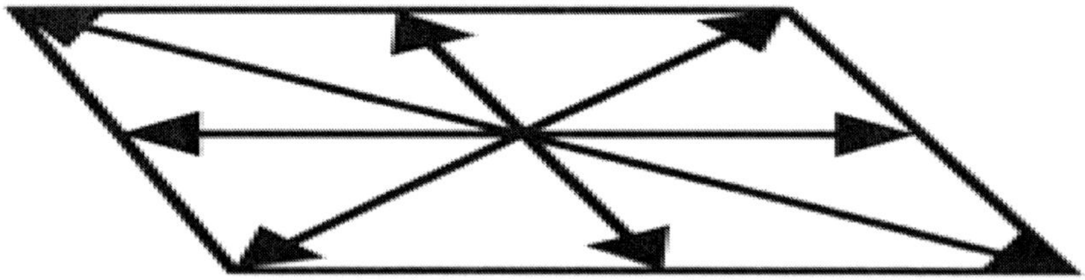

Figure 12. Horizontal interdependence and influence between the quadrants.

Vertical Causation

There is an involutionary, downward stream of causation from absolute free, nondual spirit that we are, to the causal, astral, etheric and material forms and an evolutionary, upward stream of causation. Every new creative form must deal with what is already there as (cosmic) habits in all bodies. On the other hand changes on the gross level can also cause changes in energy, attitudes and intentions. One can see the involutionary and the evolutionary stream as going hand-in-hand in an eternal pulsation.

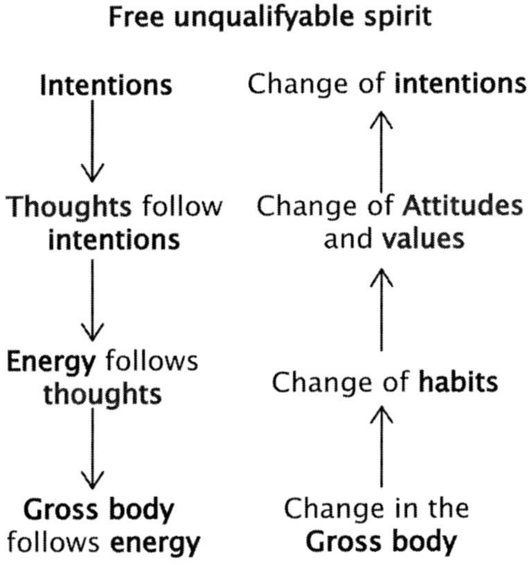

Figure 13. Vertical downward and upward causation and influence

Outlook

Here I have used the traditional concepts of subtle bodies to outline my map. I am conscious of the spiritual realism or even spiritual materialism that they suggest. Hopefully the understanding of matter in the traditional sciences will expand in a way that it will grasp the deeper layers and inner qualities of their subject.

Bibliography

[1] Eckhart, M. (1963). *Deutsche predigten und traktate* [German prayers and tracts]. Zürich, Switzerland: Diogenes.

[2] Shantananda, Swami (2003). *The splendor of recognition – An exploration of the Pratyabhijñā-hṛdayam, a text on the ancient science of the soul.* South Fallsburg, NY: SYDA Foundation.

[3] Wilber, K. (2006a). Excerpt G Retrieved from http://www.kenwilber.com/Writings/PDF/ExcerptG_KOSMOS_2004.pdf, (2015-03-19).

[4] Wilber, K. (1996, 2000). *Sex, ecology, spirituality.* Boston, MA: Shambhala Publications.

[5] Whitehead, A. N. (1978). *Process and reality* (corrected edition). New York, NY: The Free Press. (Original work published 1929)
[6] Steiner, R. (1980). *Theosophie*. Dornach, The Neherlands: Zbinden Verlag.
[7] Wilber, K. (2006b). *Integral spirituality*, Boston, MA: Shambhala Publications
[8] Spencer-Brown, G. (1999). *Laws of form* – Gesetze der Form, international edition, Lübeck, Germany: Bohmeier Verlag.
[9] Muktananda, Swami (2000). *Play of consciousness – A spiritual autobiography*. South Fallsburg, NY: SYDA Foundation. German Edition (2000). *Spiel des Bewusstseins.* Telgte: Siddha Yoga Verlag GmbH, p. 112, p. 384.
[10] Muktananda, Swami, Gurumayi Chidvilasananda, *Essential teachings.* Retrieved from http://www.siddhayoga.org/teachings/essential (8 December 2016).
[11] See Note 3.

CHAPTER TWENTY-FIVE

CONSTRUCTING AND DESTRUCTING SCIENTIFIC RESEARCH IN TRANSPERSONAL PSYCHOLOGY

HARRIS L. FRIEDMAN[1]

Abstract

Transpersonal psychology needs to rely on empiricism to discern good from not-so-good science. Observed data allow people to dispute claims based on evidence, as opposed to relying only on opinions. Transpersonal psychology differs from religion through not accepting beliefs merely on faith or authority, while it also differs from mainstream psychology by exploring areas usually marginalized or rejected as being outside of the purview of science, such as spiritual experiences and parapsychological events. Scientific discernment thus requires a reciprocal process of developing worthwhile research and discarding worthless research in order to progress rather than to stagnate. This chapter discusses the critique of two research papers relevant to transpersonal psychology for containing serious flaws requiring their being discarded, and also discusses research on self-expansiveness as an example of good scientific work within transpersonal psychology that has led to a cumulative research tradition. The scientific limits of transpersonal psychology are also discussed, as certain worthwhile questions may elude all empirical efforts and therefore be outside of the range of science to explore, such as a so-called non-dual transcendence.

Keywords: parapsychological, science, self-expansiveness, spiritual, transpersonal

The god of Judaism is often portrayed as having two figurative hands, one for justice and the other for mercy, while two of the main gods of Hinduism represent sustaining (Vishnu) and destroying (Shiva) the world. Likewise, there is a balancing process related to constructing good and destroying not-so-good science. This dynamic enables science to actively incorporate a process of change by being self-correcting, and is one of the unique aspects of science that differs it from other ways of knowing, such as religious tradition in which questioning can be seen as blasphemous. The term "fundamentalism" as used in religion involves resisting change by sticking to core belief as the bedrock of faith; religious "conservativism" literally means to conserve the past "tradition", emphasizing looking to the past to guide the present and the future, and "faith" values embracing that which is not rationally known and may not be knowable. In following these principles, religions typically resist change, whereas science has its change principles dialectically inbuilt as the interplay between destructing what no longer is seen as good understandings and constructing better, but never perfect, replacement understandings. Religion deals with so-called truth, whereas science eschews truth and instead builds models that are expected to be replaced with ever better models.[2, 3, 4]

The energy that fuels this scientific dynamo is empiricism. By allowing the world to be the teacher, and being open to discover the world through sensory data, science becomes radically open. This does not demean other ways of knowing, but is a virtue of science that allows discovery and therefore change. This does not imply a naïve materialism, as surely that which is discovered is related to the tools of discovery and shaped by the individuals and cultures involved in the discovery process. In some of my previous work, I have discussed the importance of science for transpersonal psychology (e.g., [5]), and I have also discussed how to build a strong cumulative science of transpersonal psychology in terms of constructing and testing midrange theory.[6,7] But my work is not without controversy, as some think aspects of my approach to science hamper transpersonal psychology and should be rejected (e.g.,[8]).

In this chapter, I share some of my efforts in terms of the complementary roles of construction and destruction within transpersonal psychology. I frame this as striving for balance between transpersonal psychology as a critical psychology, including as one that can be self-critical in destructing its own provisional views, with transpersonal psychology as a creative force that is needed for human adaptation and flourishing.

Transpersonal Psychology as a Destructive Critical Psychology

Critical psychologies provide perspectives that challenge many of the root assumptions and branching conclusions of mainstream psychology (Fox & Prilleltensky[9]; See also Teo, Note 14). They question conventions tacitly accepted within mainstream psychology, such as by asking who benefits and who suffers due to various power structures and ideologies? In this way, critical psychologies align with progressive causes related to social justice within psychology,[10,11,12] and can be seen as politically radical and focused on liberation in their approaches, in contrast to the mainstream that is more conservative and supports the status quo, not so dissimilar to religion. In this regard, critical psychologies are like a destructive force that reveals what may be hidden, and enables clearing away the debris so the new can flourish.

Transpersonal approaches to psychology defy many of the underlying assumptions and overlying conclusions of mainstream psychology, making it one of the critical psychologies.[13, 14] These approaches dispute conventional limitations about ontology, or what can be known, such as by challenging narrow beliefs about materialism (e.g., that everything is reducible to some inert form of matter, such as in claiming consciousness is merely brain activity when the data do not support such a sweeping reduction.[15] They dispute conventional notions about how knowing occurs or epistemology, such as by championing alternate ways to know that may surpass merely rational and narrowly empirical approaches to knowing (e.g., by providing "trans-rational" frameworks to conduct research through alternate states of consciousness, such as doing research while experiencing alternate states[16]). And they even reconsider the role of the knower within the process of knowing (e.g., by arguing against seeing individuals as isolated monads, rather than as profoundly interconnected, including in possible spiritual and even transcendent ways that can impact research, such as understood through my construct of self-expansiveness[17,18]).

Replication as a Destructive Force

One of science's greatest strengths is its emphasis on replicating findings,[19] as failures to replicate require destruction of past understandings through change, leaving behind discarded relics of what formerly was seen as good science. Without the possibility to challenge any of science's claims, science would be authoritarian and closed, as opposed to democratic and open. Anyone who disputes a scientific claim should be able to see the evidence directly, and not just rely on others. Without replication, science would not be self-correcting and would be a stagnant, rather than a dynamic, process.

However, now it is known that there is a widespread replicability crisis within all of science,[20] including within psychology.[21] In a high-profile study,[22]) over 250 scientists attempted to replicate many papers published in 2008 within three top psychology journals, but less than forty per cent of these could be successfully replicated. This gives pause to many supposedly scientific claims within psychology as, considering these papers were sampled from top journals, a much lower percentage would likely be found replicable in all published psychology studies. This demonstrates that science, including psychology, strives for an ideal, but does not always achieve its goal.

In terms of the problems specific to transpersonal psychology, I [23] have analyzed these as due to tensions between romanticism (e.g., naïve beliefs that embrace all sorts of wishful thinking) and scientism (e.g., misguided beliefs that making things merely look like science makes them in fact scientific). I described these traps as complementary problems, romanticism being prevalent in transpersonal psychology while scientism being prevalent in mainstream psychology. Consequently, I have been critical of both mainstream and transpersonal approaches to science for their respective scientism and romanticism, as both suffer from these problems. More recently, I[24,25] have explored another trap prevalent in transpersonal psychology, namely the tension between grand theories that attempt to explain everything and mini-theories that attempt to explain nothing. In these critical efforts, I see myself as working the principle of destruction, enabling new growth to emerge by destroying the old.

Criticizing Mainstream Science Applied to Transpersonal Concerns

Kok et al. (2013) [26] made a strong claim relevant to transpersonal psychology from a mainstream psychology perspective, namely that a group of people practicing loving-kindness meditation (LKM), which I see as a transpersonal practice although it was never labeled as transpersonal by this study's authors, generated an upward spiral that enhanced their physical health, positive emotions, and social connectedness. However, close examination of their claims demonstrated that their data did not actually support their conclusion.[27] In specific, I and my co-authors in our 2015 critique showed that Kok et al.'s claim of finding a significant main effect relating LKM to a physical indicator of greater health and other beneficial outcomes was based on the following errors: they seriously misinterpreted their data statistically, their main indicator for physical health was equivocal, and there were pervasive difficulties in how they defined their experimental conditions. Consequently, Kok et al.'s claim that LKM made a powerful impact for good was unsupported, as shown by critical reanalysis, a type of replication. Their claims were published in a top scientific journal that was peer reviewed, received considerable publicity and, on the surface, looked pretty impressive. However, upon closer scrutiny, it was shown to suffer from scientism, appearing to use sophisticated science, such as biomedical measures and complex statistics, but in actuality it was not-so-good research. By reanalyzing their data, as a type of replication, their unwarranted claims were challenged and, in my view, have been destroyed. To be fair, however, I want to mention that Kok and Fredrickson[28] disputed my and my co-authors' critique and defended their work, despite the many glaring problems identified. The good thing about science is that readers do not have to take anyone's word as truth, but can look directly at the evidence for themselves when there are competing claims such as in this case. I think Kok et al.'s work reflects the type of scientism that is problematic within mainstream psychology. Although I am pleased when mainstream science is applied to transpersonal concerns, it still is problematic if the science is not so good.

Criticizing Transpersonal Science

Sundararajan and Kim[29] made a claim from a more humanistic and transpersonal perspective, namely that Thomas Müntzer was not an authentic mystic. They used this historical figure as a foil in a comparative-qualitative study of several mystics, despite that many see Müntzer as a heroic figure who pioneered liberation theology and was far from being inauthentic in any way. However, Sundararajan and Kim based their claim on equivocal a priori criteria they thought characterizes authentic mystics, but which I think showed certain biases on their part, such as privileging transcendence over immanence in their definition of authentic mysticism. They then qualitatively compared Müntzer to so-called authentic mystics, whom they concluded met their criteria. In a critical paper,[30] I rejected their claim of Müntzer's inauthenticity as a mystic by challenging the historical evidence they presented, as well as by expressing conceptual concerns about the criteria they employed to classify him as being inauthentic. To again be fair, I want to mention that Sundararajan and Kim (2015) [31] in return disputed my critique and defended their work, despite the problems I identified and, once more, a good thing about science is that readers do not have to take anyone's word as truth, but can look directly at the evidence for themselves. I conclude that Sundararajan and Kim's original paper (2014)[32] and comment paper (2015)[33] on this topic reflects the type of romanticism that I see as a widespread problem within transpersonal psychology.

Transpersonal Psychology as a Constructive Psychology Creating Innovation

Transpersonal psychology is more than a critical-destructive psychology, both of the mainstream and, at least in the case of many of my critiques, of itself, because it has constructively pioneered many areas that were marginalized and even denigrated by mainstream psychology. In this way, it has created innovations adding to the reach of conventional approaches, helping mainstream psychology grow through the influence of transpersonal perspectives. Mainstream psychology now embraces much of what transpersonal psychology initially fostered, but that the mainstream at that time considered taboo. Consciousness studies were a forbidden topic to the mainstream during the advent of transpersonal psychology, yet now this is a burgeoning area of inquiry and application (e.g., mindfulness meditation is now commonplace within applied psychological practices). Similarly, transpersonal psychology initiated exploring Eastern and indigenous religious and spiritual claims with respect and admiration, while mainstream psychology long disparaged these non-Western views as primitive, shamelessly assuming that Westerners are superior to other peoples and that psychological findings are culturally universal, despite being obtained almost exclusively from Western samples. [34] This anticipated the now growing multicultural movement, which is also thoroughly in the mainstream of contemporary psychology. Transpersonal psychology also promoted insights about limitations in traditional scientific methods, which previously had excluded legitimacy from any non-quantitative approach and held the experiment on a pedestal as being the gold standard, with all else berated. Transpersonal psychology even helped pioneer the paradigm shift in psychology allowing qualitative approaches to become accepted as a legitimate approach to research that not only complements the more widely privileged quantitative approaches, but also provides uniquely well-suited tools for some tasks for which quantitative approaches are ill suited. In these and many other ways, transpersonal psychology has led in promoting the growth of mainstream psychology by not just providing critical vantages allowing deep reflection on the implicit worldview that shapes much of mainstream psychology, but through offering viable options.

However, much that transpersonal psychology can offer has still not percolated into the mainstream. Transpersonal psychology questions the hegemony of what is currently accepted as being proper science, and some of these approaches may not be easily comprehensible from the prevailing Western scientific framework. For example, some traditional meditation practices have systematically explored higher consciousness through cumulatively consensual observations that were shared, refined through community dialog across generations of teachers and students, and rigorously tested within natural-cultural contexts. These may not be considered proper science by the mainstream, yet they stem from valid empirical approaches that may simply be derived from different forms of science than are customarily viewed in the West as science. Consider that scientific Western studies of meditation typically start by teaching beginners to meditate using simple protocols that involve just a few training sessions, and contrast this to studying practitioners of many years who benefit from cumulative-cultural knowledge evolved in the context of ancient spiritual traditions. Consequently, alternate transpersonal approaches for studying these extraordinarily complex and subtle phenomena are often more appropriate than superficial conventional scientific approaches. In this regard, transpersonal psychology has pioneered various human science methods involving alternative assumptions about epistemology and ontology, as well as the self as knower, [35] and I advocate for methodological pluralism that remains congruent with a radical empiricism.[36]

Furthermore, transpersonal psychology takes much of its data from diverse spiritual, not solely Western monotheistic, traditions. In this way, it differs from the related area, psychology of religion, which is primarily derivative from monotheistic (mostly Judeo-Christian) traditions, and which focuses more on studying externalities (e.g., demographics) and less on understanding internalities (e.g., experience). The mainstream views, as reflected in the psychology of religion, has considerable cultural baggage related to its assumptions, and these taint the psychology of religion as being more parochial than universal. In contrast, transpersonal psychology shows more transcultural competence,[37] and offers creative ways to escape such cultural traps.

However, it should be noted that transpersonal psychology has often been snared in its own cultural traps, such as by deeming non-Western traditions as being superior, rather than just different. For example, many transpersonal psychologists from the West have "gone native", such as by converting to Buddhism, ignoring the rich spiritual traditions in the West for the lure of what seems an exotic tradition offering more value.[38,39] In this sense, I advocate that transpersonal psychology learn from many spiritual traditions, but through a scientific lens, albeit again in ways very broadly construed as scientific.[40, 41]

Doing Good Transpersonal Science

In criticizing these two studies (Kok et al., 2013[42]; Sundararajan & Kim, 2014[43]), I attempted to confront not-so-good science involving transpersonal concerns researched from both a mainstream quantitative and a humanistic-transpersonal qualitative approach respectively. I consider this to be an important part of science, namely to engage in critical dialog and be willing to debate differences. For good science to grow, no-so-good science needs to be confronted and, if found lacking, destroyed.

To illustrate what I think adds solidly to transpersonal psychology as a science, I present some of my work. For example, recently I and some international colleagues [44] surveyed samples from eight countries using a battery of religious and spiritual measures. We explored the hypothesis that, although religions are known to vary across cultures, spirituality might be invariant across cultures, and we found partial support for this.

This is just one stream of transpersonal research in which I have engaged, and I focus in this chapter on another research stream involving "self-expansiveness", which refers to people's willingness to conceptualize their sense of self through acknowledging interconnected with various aspects of the world. Stemming from my doctoral dissertation, I created this construct and a related measure, which I validated.[45] Self-expansiveness provides a way to understand people's sense of self or identity, including in transpersonal ways, and its measure enables this to be scientifically researched. In my initial work on self-expansiveness, I used both exploratory and confirmatory analyses on different samples, thus building an internal replication process into the research design. I also used validation samples after the confirmatory one, thus providing stronger evidence of the worth of my work. Then I hoped someone else would independently replicate my work, which did occur after a long wait.[46] Since then, I continue to extend my replications (e.g., [47, 48]) and to further bolster my findings by exploring its applications to various important problems, such as caring about the environment (e.g., [49]). I recently reviewed the research progress on self-expansiveness, looking at my own as well as many others' work on this construct and its related measure over the years (e.g., [50]). I consider my work on this to demonstrate the constructive potential of transpersonal psychology.

Conclusion

Science benefits both from weeding-out not-so-good research and sowing the seeds of good research, and that applies to transpersonal psychology as well as to all areas of science. That science allows people to dispute findings based on empirical evidence, as opposed to relying only on opinions based on authority or more idiosyncratic ways of knowing, makes it radically different from other ways of knowing. However, science can suffer various problem, such as in the two papers critiqued that I discuss in this chapter, and there are also certain questions that may be outside of the range of science to clarify and explore, such as speculations about so-called non-dual transcendence that might elude all empirical effort.[51, 52] I encourage people interested in seeing transpersonal psychology thrive as an approach to human understanding to consider the complementary constructive and destructive roles within science, and to work on discerning when to best apply either.

Some in transpersonal psychology may find my language off-putting, preferring narratives of harmony and peace, rather than a conflict approach to construction and destruction. I see this preference as contributing to the tendency in psychology, including transpersonal approaches, to ignore unpleasant aspects of the world, such as the consequences of inequality from insidious socio-political dynamics. No wonder Müntzer's revolutionary theology was seen as inauthentic by Sundararajan and Kim,[53, 54] as it challenged the then power structures and it continues to challenge contemporary injustices. Science can be seen as a battleground of ideas that are bitterly fought and won only through considerable effort. This is demonstrated by the fact that the two flawed studies I critiqued,[55, 56] are still being defended by their authors. This bias toward seeing the world as peaceful and cooperative, while ignoring the reality that lions eat lambs, is a type of romanticism that I think limits the effectiveness of transpersonal psychology.

Last, perhaps the most difficult form of romanticism to discern is "romantic scientism",[57] in which the two traps, romanticism and scientism, merge as science itself is used to promote a romantic worldview based on not-so-good science. It is important to not misuse science to advocate for any worldview, but rather to explore ourselves and the world in the deepest and most meaningful ways possible, which I think is from a transpersonal vantage. Such work is both possible and desirable, and defines my path as a transpersonal scientist.

Bibliography

[1] This chapter is an adaption and updated extension of a 2014 presentation in Crete for EUROTAS.

[2] Friedman, H. (2002). Transpersonal psychology as a scientific field. *International Journal of Transpersonal Studies, 21*, 175-187.
[3] Friedman, H. (2013b). The role of science in transpersonal psychology: The advantages of middle-range theory. In H. Friedman & G. Hartelius (Eds.), *The Wiley-Blackwell handbook of transpersonal psychology* (pp. 300-311). Oxford, England: Wiley-Blackwell.
[4] Friedman, H. (2015a). Further developing transpersonal psychology as a science: Building and testing middle-range transpersonal theories. *International Journal of Transpersonal Studies, 34*(1-2), 175-184. [note: this is a revision of Friedman, H. (2013b). The role of science in transpersonal psychology: The advantages of middle-range theory]
[5] Friedman, H. (2002). Transpersonal psychology as a scientific field. *International Journal of Transpersonal Studies, 21*, 175-187.
[6] See 3
[7] See 4
[8] Ferrer, J. (2014). Transpersonal psychology, science, and the supernatural. *The Journal of Transpersonal Psychology, 46*(2), 152-186.
[9] Fox, D., & Prilleltensky, I. (1997). *Critical psychology: An introduction.* Thousand Oaks, CA: Sage.
[10] Johnson, C., & Friedman, H. (Eds.). (2014a). *The Praeger handbook of social justice and psychology: Vol. 1. Fundamental issues and special populations*. Santa Barbara, CA: Praeger.
[11] Johnson, C., & Friedman, H. (Eds.). (2014b). *The Praeger handbook of social justice and psychology: Vol. 2. Well-being and professional issues*. Santa Barbara, CA: Praeger.
[12] Johnson, C., & Friedman, H. (Eds.). (2014c). *The Praeger handbook of social justice and psychology: Vol. 3. Youth and disciplines in psychology*. Santa Barbara, CA: Praeger.

[13] Friedman, H. (2012). Transpersonal psychotherapies: An approach critical to mainstream assumptions and practices. *Journal of Critical Psychology, Counselling and Psychotherapy, 12*(4), 199 –209.
[14] Friedman, H., & Hartelius, G. (2013). Transpersonal psychology. In T. Teo (Ed.), *Encyclopedia of critical psychology* (pp. 2036-2040). New York, NY: Springer Verlag.
[15] Krippner, S., & Friedman, H. (Eds.). (2010). *Mysterious minds: The neurobiology of psychics mediums, and other extraordinary people.* Santa Barbara, CA: Praeger.
[16] Friedman, H. (2006). The renewal of psychedelic research: Implications for humanistic and transpersonal psychology. *The Humanistic Psychologist, 34*(1), 39-58
[17] Friedman, H. (1983). The Self-Expansiveness Level Form: A conceptualization and measurement of a transpersonal construct. *The Journal of Transpersonal Psychology, 15,* 37-50.
[18] Friedman, H. (2013a). Self-expansiveness as a scientific construct. In H. Friedman & G. Hartelius (Eds.), *The Wiley-Blackwell handbook of transpersonal psychology*. (pp. 203-222). Oxford, England: Wiley-Blackwell.
[19] Pappas, J., & Friedman, H. (2012). The importance of replication: Comparing the Self-Expansiveness Level Form Transpersonal Scale with an alternate graphical measure. *The Humanistic Psychologist, 40*, 364-379.
[20] Ioannidis, J. (2005). Why most published research findings are false. *PLoS Medicine, 2*(8): e124.
Retrieved from http://www.ncbi.nlm.nih.gov/pubmed/16060722
[21] Pashler, H., & Wagenmakers, E. (2012). Editors' introduction to the Special Section on Replicability in Psychological Science: A crisis of confidence? *Perspectives on Psychological Science, 7*, 528–530.
doi:10.1177/1745691612465253
[22] Open Science Collaboration (2015). Estimating the reproducibility of psychological science. *Science, 349*(6251). doi:10.1126/science.aac4716
[23] See 5
[24] See 3
[25] See 4
[26] Kok B.E., Coffey K.A.,Cohn M.A.,Catalino L.I., Vacharkulksemsuk, T., Algoe S.B. … Fredrickson, B.L. (2013). How positive emotions build physical health: Perceived positive social connections account for the upward spiral between positive emotions and vagal tone. *Psychological Science, 24*(7), 1123-1132. doi: 10.1177/095679761247082; Kok, B., & Fredrickson, B. (2015). Evidence for the upward spiral stands steady: A response to Heathers, Brown, Coyne, & Friedman (2015). *Psychological Science, 26*(7), 1144-1146.
[27] Heathers, J., Brown, N., Coyne, J., & Friedman, H. (2015). The elusory upward spiral: Comment on Kok et al. (2013). *Psychological Science, 26*(7), 1140-1143.
[28] See 26
[29] Sundararajan, L., & Kim, C. (2014). Spiritual suffering from medieval German mysticism to Mother Teresa: A psycholinguistic analysis. *The Humanistic Psychologist, 42*(2), 172-198.

[30] Friedman, H. (2015b). Judging another's spirituality: Commentary on Sundararajan and Kim's (2014) claim that Müntzer was a false mystic. *The Humanistic Psychologist, 43,*100-102.
[31] Sundararajan, L., & Kim, C. (2015). Müntzer and mysticism: A contested connection. *The Humanistic Psychologist, 43,* 103-108.
[32] See 29
[33] See 30
[34] Glover, J., & Friedman, H. (2015). *Transcultural competence: Navigating cultural differences in the global community*. Washington, DC: American Psychological Association.
[35] Braud, W., & Anderson, R. (1998). *Transpersonal research methods for the social sciences: Honoring human experience*. Thousand Oaks, CA: Sage.
[36] Friedman, H. (2008). Humanistic and positive psychology: The methodological and epistemological divide. *The Humanistic Psychologist, 36*, 113-126.
[37] See 34
[38] Friedman, H. (2009). Xenophilia as a cultural trap: Bridging the gap between transpersonal psychology and religious/spiritual traditions. *International Journal of Transpersonal Studies*, *28*, 107-111.
[39] Friedman, H. (2010). Is Buddhism a psychology? Commentary on romanticism in "Mindfulness in Psychology." *The Humanistic Psychologist, 38*, 184–189.
[40] See 2
[41] See 30
[42] See 26
[43] See 29
[44] MacDonald, D. A., Friedman, H. L., Brewczynski, J., Holland, D., Salagame, S. K. K., Mohan, K. K., ... Cheong, H. W. (2015). Spirituality across cultures, languages, and measures. *PLOS-One*. *10*(3): e0117701.
doi:10.1371/journal.pone.0117701
[45] See 17
[46] MacDonald, D. A., Anderson, P. E., Tsagarakis, C. I., & Holland, C. J. (1994). Examination of the relationship between the Myers-Briggs Type Indicator and the NEO Personality Inventory. *Psychological Reports, 74*, 339-344.
[47] Pappas, J., & Friedman, H. (2007). The construct of self-expansiveness and the validity of the Transpersonal Scale of the Self-Expansiveness Level Form. *The Humanistic Psychologist, 35*(4), 323-347.
[48] See 19
[49] Hoot, R., & Friedman, H. (2011). Sense of interconnectedness and pro-environmental behavior. *International Journal of Transpersonal Studies, 30*(1-2), 89-100.
[50] See 18
[51] See 2
[52] See 4
[53] See 29
[54] See 30
[55] See 26
[56] See 29

[57] Brown, N., Sokal, A., & Friedman, H. (2014). Positive psychology and romantic scientism. *American Psychologist*, *69*, 636–637.

CHAPTER TWENTY-SIX

HEURISTIC AS A RESEARCH TOOL TO EXPLORE INNER STATES OF CONSCIOUSNESS

GIOVANNA CALABRESE
AND CLAUDIO CALCINA

Abstract

The focus of this chapter is about the integration of research and clinical practice using non-ordinary states of consciousness. This issue is important to improve and expand the state of the art of research in the field of transpersonal psychology and psychotherapy. We will present the dreaming body, a Biotransenergetica (BTE) practice, from a Heuristic Research perspective. Through a series of movements it is possible to enter into deep contact with the archetypal force of natural elements (i.e., the one connected with the quality of the Ocean) as source of generation and constant movement and fluidity. Entering into deep contact with the inner body, and recognizing what happens at each level, physical, emotional, energetic, mental and spiritual, will allow a process of knowledge described as second attention epistemology. This process is a kind of Heuristic Inquiry. Heuristic is an internal search for meaning of a human experience and explicitly acknowledges the researcher's involvement in the experience under investigation. The aim of this chapter is to discuss how Heuristic Inquiry can be applied, from a research perspective, to personal lived experiences of non-ordinary states of consciousness.

Keywords: Heuristic, Inner state, Consciousness, Research, Biotransenergetica.

In this chapter we would like to discuss how Heuristic Methodology can be applied to explore inner states of consciousness. Our aim is to provide a tool that can be applied in the research field of transpersonal psychology.

Inner States of Consciousness

Transpersonal psychology (TP) has built a whole new model upon the investigation of inner experience as a real, pure and powerful opportunity for renewal and healing. TP studies the person considering all the processes that are beyond inner experiences, how they arise, what triggers them, how they develop and the potential danger that might be associated with them.

TP explores those spontaneous experiences of non-ordinary states of consciousness, that are usually considered to be expressions of mental disease, discovering how they can hold information and potential utilities once their mechanism of action has been understood. Therefore, many different methods and methodologies to use inner experiences with therapeutic and developmental purposes have been developed.

Inner transformational experiences become like a gate through which it is possible to look at a wider landscape. It is a door that opens on new worlds, a powerful tool to allow the rise of those aspects of being usually disguised and not recognized in ordinary states of consciousness.

From a clinical observation we know human functions are state dependent or even state inter-dependent. This insight means that when the state changes, the functions change and their range of action, threshold of activation and possible results, all change. Furthermore, those functions can induce changes in the state of consciousness, showing that the system is much more complex than we could imagine.

TP, starting from ancient and traditional knowledge about non-ordinary states of consciousness, has developed methods and methodologies able to induce a change in the state of consciousness in a precise, sophisticated and intentional way. Going even further TP has introduced the body into the field of psychology, considering its mysterious aspect that expands the field in which the therapist and the researcher move, thus enhancing their knowledge.

Our interest as researchers is to study these non-ordinary states of consciousness from a phenomenological perspective. The term phenomenology, from the Greek verb *"phainomenon"*, or "appeared", was first used by Husserl, to indicate a method of philosophical inquiry that would lead to knowledge based on the individual's lived experience, thereby enabling the use of this method in application to the study of the dimension of consciousness.[1]

For Husserl, the phenomenon has to be considered from every angle, setting aside all the assumptions in a process that he would call *epoche*. The goal of this process is to arrive at a transcendental domain of experience where the true essence of the phenomenon would become self-evident, so that it would be possible to have knowledge of the ultimate truth.

On this theoretical ground, Heideger, Gadamer and Ricouer have developed phenomenology as a method of knowledge.[2] Similarly phenomenology applied to research, trying to describe the essence of a phenomenon, requires the investigator to bracket off his/her assumptions.[3]

The so-called process of "setting aside" is a very critical one.[4] Some authors (for example, Gadamer) say that this is not really possible and they suggest that the researcher needs to be aware and place their subjectivity in the foreground.[5] For Gadamer, as cited in McLeod, knowledge in human sciences always involves some self-knowledge.[6]

Heuristic

Heuristic is another approach to explore inner experiences. Heuristic is an internal search for meaning in human experience that explicitly acknowledges the researcher's involvement in the experience under investigation; the researcher is therefore always present and visible.[7]

Douglas and Moustakas developed Heuristic Research Methodology:

> *Heuristic research is a search for the discovery of meaning and essence in significant human experience. It requires a subjective process of reflecting, exploring, sifting, and elucidating the nature of the phenomenon under investigation.*[8]

The methodology requires an indwelling and deep engagement with the research question:

> ... *In heuristic research the investigator must have had a direct, personal encounter with the phenomenon being investigated. There must have been actual autobiographical connections.*[9]

Douglas and Moustakas[10] first described three steps of Heuristic inquiry:

immersion, acquisition, realization, further developed by Moustakas in the following seven phases.[11]

Initial engagement: The task of the first phase is to discover an intense interest, a passionate concern that calls out to the researcher, one that holds important social meanings and personal, compelling implications. The research question that emerges lingers with the researcher, awaiting the disciplined commitment that will reveal its underlying meanings.

Immersion: The research question is lived in waking, sleeping and even dreaming states. This phase requires alertness, concentration and self-searching. Virtually anything connected with the question becomes raw material for immersion.

Incubation: This phase involves a retreat from the intense, concentrated focus, allowing the expansion of knowledge to take place at a more subtle level, enabling the inner tacit dimension and intuition to clarify and extend understanding.

Illumination: This phase involves a breakthrough, a process of awakening that occurs naturally when the researcher is open and receptive to tacit knowledge and intuition. It involves opening a door to new awareness, a modification of an old understanding, a synthesis of fragmented knowledge, or new discovery.

Explication: This phase involves a full examination of what has been awakened in consciousness. Required is organization and a comprehensive depiction of the core themes.

Creative synthesis: Thoroughly familiar with the data, and following a preparatory phase of solitude and meditation, the researcher puts the components and core themes usually into the form of creative synthesis expressed as a narrative account, a report, a thesis, a poem, story, drawing, painting, etc.

Validation of the Heuristic Inquiry: The question of validity is one of meaning. Does the synthesis present the meanings and essences of the experience comprehensively, vividly, and accurately? This can be pursued returning again and again to the data to check whether they embrace the necessary and sufficient meanings. Finally, feedback is obtained through participant validation, and receiving responses from others.

According to Hiles[12] the Heuristic Approach occupies a key place in Transpersonal Inquiry where not only ordinary human experience is considered but transcendent and exceptional experiences are elicited. Braud & Anderson[13] have indicated that Heuristic Inquiry is particularly suited for research in the transpersonal field, not only for the direct involvement of the researcher into the field but even more for the recognized importance of personal knowledge and tacit knowing of the researcher.

Psycho-corporeal Practice in BTE Model

In Biotransenergetica (BTE), a transpersonal methodology founded by Pier Luigi Lattuada and Marlene Silveira, we use some psycho-corporeal practice of self-awareness, some to stimulate the inner experience.

The name Biotransenergetica explains the holistic approach to the individual: *Bio-* concerns physical aspects, *transe-* concerns spiritual and transcendental aspects, and *energetica* refers to a transcendental dimension expressing itself as energy in the physical dimension. With a holistic approach to individuals, BTE merges the physical and corporal aspects of Lowen's Bioenergetic model[14] with transcendental aspects.

Based on Reich's model[15] of an energetic aspect informing the body and influencing the psychological dimension, Lowen developed the Bioenergetic model, in which the energetic aspects were inherent in the body, in relation with the breath. BTE goes further to consider the spiritual dimension of the human being also.

From an ontological perspective, self is considered as part of the Transcendent being. In this regard BTE can be traced in the broadest field of transpersonal psychotherapy.

To describe this state of consciousness Lattuada uses the Portuguese word *Transe*, which is defined as that state allowing the individual to be in contact with the divine dimension.[16] As the concept expressed by this word is quite complex and particular to BTE epistemological bases, we prefer to use this spelling.

Transe describes consciousness through the image of a "flow of consciousness" rather than a "state of consciousness", which is an unreal and idealized crystallization. The individual flows of consciousness merge into a larger common one, in which each individual *Transe* flows, being part of it, without any interruption, realizing what Lattuada calls the "Interconnected Flow of Events" in which each *Transe* feeds the others and is fed by them, without a real separation.[17]

The term *Transe* defines the state of consciousness including also being in perennial transformation, with a high level of interweaving, both inward and outward. *Transe* is the inseparable relationship between matter, form and information, linking everything to its mode. *Transe* is, therefore, a new aspect of the threefold unity described by the triad wave, particle and their interaction.[18] Considering the material aspect it is possible to see it as a *rhythmic model*. If we consider the mental perspective we can see it as a *state of consciousness*. From the existential point of view, it is a *spiritual entity.*[19]

Existence is an endless stream in which each element and living being flows like an infinitesimal part of a much larger picture, more complex and interwoven, which he contributes to create, build and enrich with his own presence.

Flowing cannot stop to flow with all the elements in the world. It is the power of the dual mind that make us see different states as really different and unchangeable, building foolish distinctions and borders that will became our self-made cage.

Dreaming Body Theoretical Aspects

Dreaming Body (DB) is a BTE psycho-corporal practice that allows us to recognize our cage, to find some keys to open it and to live all our inner, personal talents fully. DB makes it easier to engage in different states of consciousness in which information and qualities are easily accessible.

Being in *Transe* allows us to recognize we are always in connection with the field of information that is spread through the Interconnected Flow of Events. This field is accessible just by getting in touch with what we are looking for, as it is described by Sheldrake in the Morphogenetic Fields Theory, by Jung in the Collective Unconscious, and by Lazlo's Akashic Field and many others.

The Field is not an empty place. It is a place full of vibration and all the potential information. We have to tune ourselves to those aspects in the field in which we are interested, so that we can resonate with them, arousing our consciousness and experiencing the qualities inside us.

For example we can tune to the vibration of the quality or to the information we need and let it merge from the Field. Then we can bring them into our life, from the implicit to the explicit, experiencing them on every level.

The practice is in a unique context where we can tune into a common quality, having an experience that is at the same time individual and shared. The tuning process happens progressively and at the same time on different levels, i.e., the physical, energetic, emotional, mental and spiritual ones, as they are interconnected. The various bodies are able to modulate between them through highly complex patterns of feedback between the inside and outside, adapting to the different stimulations, needs and individual yearnings. In fact, each human being is a system in which every input deeply resonates within every component mirroring their interactions. The interrelation between the different components allows each one of them to also hold the information about all the others.

Working on the physical level means to work with subtle energies. Similarly, working on the psychic level, with words, goes beyond the rational level of analytic, cognitive or other kinds of therapies.

In BTE psycho-corporal practices, the person performs the movements, paying attention to all levels, the integration of which can also be described as an integration of Mudra - Mantra - Yantra. Lattuada refers to ancient Indian culture to describe what happens at a psychic and physical level.

Mudra, in Hinduism and Buddhism, is a symbolic gesture through which the spiritual dimension interacts with the physical one.[20] Similarly Mantra is a sacred utterance having the power to connect with the spiritual dimension. Yantra, originally, referred to any instruments or machine, with mystical magic power; it is used here to refer to the level of vision or insight.[21]

Dreaming Body Practice

Dreaming Body is a complex of corporal practices that the person performs guided by the psychotherapist. It is a sequence of movements that act on the physical level like a *mudra*; this is why the structure of the movements must be followed and so, gradually, during the execution, the state of consciousness changes and contents will appear, as moods on the emotional level, as corporal sensations on the energetic level, as memories or images on the mental level, and finally as visions or insights on the spiritual level.

There are also distinct practices of dreaming body for the different natural elements, which express specific qualities on an energetic level. Vice versa the contact with the force can lead to the appearance of contents that indicate the presence of a shadow side connected to the element. In both cases, by remaining in contact with what emerges, the energy of the force becomes free to act and to liberate blocks or chronic states.

This aspect of contact with the subtle forces of the natural world differentiates between the corporal practices of BTE and Bioenergetics.

According to Lowen the interaction between *body and I* occurs through a dialectical process, in which *I* shapes the body through the control over voluntary musculature. In BTE the relationship is subtler, as if body and psyche were interconnected expressions of the same energy.[22]

This kind of interaction is stressed by the repetition of the movements and through the use of evocative words, descriptions, symbols and sounds of traditional instruments. Each of these elements allows the experience to become deeper, feeling more and more involved.

Performing the movement has a stronger power than just thinking about it, seeing them is stronger than speaking of them, so that the emotional reaction to the archetype we are working with is stressed out, and the possible traumatic experiences connected with it, can be brought to awareness more efficiently.

The DB techniques allow us to recognize the qualities inside us, favouring the enrichment of our potentialities and resources. Even more, through this practice we can get in touch, develop and express these potentialities and resources.

Before entering this archetype individuals are usually guided to connect deeply with their inner body, to recognize at each level (physical, energetic, emotional, mental and spiritual), what is happening. Then they are invited to represent how they were feeling on the five levels through the "Organismic Constellation" technique. Doing the same at the end, it is possible to match the two self-descriptions, to verify if they felt any significant and verifiable changes about their inner state and if these changes were coherent with the qualities of the archetype used for the practice; it is also important to consider if during the practice the process was somehow influenced by the non-ordinary states of consciousness.

Data collected in this way can be used for research purposes as the paper by Calabrese[23] shows.

Conclusions

In ordinary states of consciousness the mechanisms of knowledge are the ones described by Cognitive Science. From an epistemological point of view we are referring to theories that start with Aristotle and through Empiricism and Positivism lead to the modern philosophy of science. All the various theories are based essentially on perceivable data and objective knowledge processes, which can be repeated and validated.

On the other hand, when we talk about non-ordinary states of consciousness, the states described in TP, it is not possible to refer to the epistemological theories on which positivist science is based on. A new epistemology has to be considered. Two major authors, who, prior to Lattuada, addressed this issue, are Ken Wilber and John Rowan.

Wilber, talks about vision logic[24] referring to the ability to "move permanently into the higher realms", or what he would call "subtle, causal and non-dual" states of consciousness. By gaining this ability to view rationality as a whole we can now transcend it. This transcendence is no mere detachment, but a greater embrace in which the previously disassociated spheres of matter, life, mind and spirit can be integrated.

Rowan[25] talks about "Third-tier thinking". The First-tier thinking is the most common level of consciousness, being based on formal thinking (Aristotelian, Newtonian, Boolean, and Mathematical). Second-tier thinking is based on Dialectical Logic (what Ken Wilber sometimes calls Vision-logic). When we consider the spiritual dimension, we have to consider the Third-tier thinking. As Rowan says, "The essence of third-tier thinking is that we have to admit that we are spiritual beings. This recognition means that we can have steady personal experience of this great realm, which Buddhists call the *sambhoga kaya*".[25]

Lattuada talks about second attention. Whereas the first attention allows us to know the world through senses and rationality, the second attention is that modality of knowledge that allows us to understand reality, hidden behind "the Maya's veil".[26] Lattuada distinguishes between Reality and

Truth. Second attention allows access to reality, where The Science of Truth is concerned with inner experiences, which by their very nature are immeasurable and unique. Second Attention Epistemology considers that pure observation, pure sensation and pure action will allow us to transcend reality. First Attention perceives reality, with which it identifies itself; Second Attention, instead, observes and dis-identifies itself from reality.

Even if with slight differences, all these modalities of knowledge are considered more suitable to explore the world of non-ordinary consciousness and transcendence. Many different approaches have been proposed.

As Walach points out, "transpersonal psychology has simply assumed that inner experiences have some epistemological validity, without any understanding of the extremely difficult ontological ground, upon which it is marching." [27] He proposes to solve the ontological problem of consciousness appealing to Quantum Physics. Other transpersonal psychologists have taken a different direction. For example Braud[28] suggests that transpersonal experiences might be explored from four different perspectives:

- Nature of the experience itself.
- How the experience might be conceptualized.
- How the experience unfolds and develops.
- What the outcomes of the experience are.

This framework follows the line of scientific research having specific and different aims: describe, explain, predict and control the topic under investigation. Therefore, depending on the area of interest different research methods might be used. Quantitative methods are for explaining and comparing, as they are said to be nomothetic, meaning that they try to produce general laws that are universally true. Qualitative methods can be used for describing and understanding, as they are said to be idiographic, trying to capture the uniqueness and complexity of a phenomenon.

A more complex design might require a mixed method as described by Creswell and Plano,[29] like convergent design, sequential design, embedded design, and multiphase design.

Both quantitative and qualitative methods have been specially developed for transpersonal research. Quantitative methods include well-established psychometric assessments, as reviewed by Mc Donald, Friedman and

Kuentzel.[30] Anderson and Braud[31] described other qualitative methods for transpersonal research, such as Intuitive Inquiry, Integral Inquiry and Organic Inquiry.

Here we proposed a Heuristic approach, as its philosophical ground is very close to what Lattuada calls 'Second Attention Epistemology'.

The meditation practice that connects the person with the subtler planes and with spiritual levels, involves a process of self-knowledge, not only of the psychological mechanisms put in place in different situations or cognitive processes, but also expanding the boundaries of consciousness. This is the same kind of knowledge that occurs with the Heuristic method, so that we can say that the Heuristic method was already in place during the meditation practice itself.

The Heuristic could be applied to a larger field, considering not only the subjective inner experience, but also the subjective experience of the larger field in which each one of the participants is immersed, which also includes the spiritual archetypical dimension, induced by the movements, the sounds and words.

Through this discussion, we would like to show transpersonal psychologists and psychotherapists that research can be integrated in clinical practice, disintegrating any preconceived ideas of research as a unique tool for evidence based practice (EBP) and empirically supported therapy (EST) based on the "empirical myth".[32]

Bibliography

[1] McLeod, J. (2001). *Qualitative research in counselling and psychotherapy.* London, England: Sage.
[2] See note 1.
[3] Giorgi, A. (1985). *Phenomenology and psychological research.* Pittsburgh, PA: Duquesne University Press.
[4] Smit, Y., Marcus, J.H., Huibers, J., Ioannidis, P.A., van Dyck, R., van Tilburg, W., & Arntz, A. (2001). The effectiveness of long-term psychoanalytic psychotherapy—A meta-analysis of randomized controlled trials. *Clinical Psychology Review, 32*, 81–92.
[5] Colaizzi, P.F. (1978). *Psychological research as the phenomenologist views it.* In R.S. Valle & M. King (Eds.), *Existential phenomenological alternatives for psychology* (pp. 48-71). New York, NY: Oxford University Press.
[6] See note 1, p. 28.

[7] Douglass, B.G., & Moustakas, C. (1985). Heuristic inquiry: The internal search to know. *Journal of Humanistic Psychology*, *25,* 39-55.
[8] See note 7, p. 40.
[9] See note 7, p. 9.
[10] See note 7, pp. 39-55.
[11] Moustakas, C. (1990). *Heuristic research: Design, methodology and applications.* London: Sage.
[12] Hiles, D. (2001). Heuristic inquiry and transpersonal research. Retrieved from: http://psy.dmu.ac.uk/drhiles/papers.htm
[13] Braud, W., & Anderson, R. (1998). *Transpersonal research methods for the social sciences. Honoring human experiences.* London, England: Sage.
[14] Lowen, A. (1985). *Physical dynamics of the character structure* (*The language of the body).* New York, NY: Grune & Stratton.
[15] Reich W. (1994). *Analisi del carattere* [Character analysis]. Milano, Italy: Sugar Co.
[16] Lattuada, P. (2005). *Sciamanesimo brasiliano. Il simbolismo, l'iniziazione, le pratiche di guarigione dell'umbanda* [Brazilian shamanism. The symbolism, the initiation, the healing power of Umbanda]. Milano, Italy: Anima ed.
[17] Lattuada, P. (2012). *Biotransenergetica* [Biotransenergetics]. Milano, Italy: ITI Edizioni.
[18] Lattuada, P. (2008). *L'arte medica della guarigione interiore. Basi psicobiologiche e metodologia clinica* [The art of internal healing. Psycho-biological basis and clinical methodology]. Milano, Italy: Franco Angeli.
[19] See note 17.
[20] Feuerstein, G. (2003), *The deeper dimension of yoga*. Boston, MA. Shambhala Publications.
[21]Lattuada, P. (2008). *L'arte medica della guarigione interiore. Basi psicobiologiche e metodologia clinica* [The art of internal healing. Psycho-biological basis and clinical methodology]. Milano, Italy: Franco Angeli.
[22] See note 21.
[23] Calabrese, G. (2015). The therapeutic effect of Biotransenergetics (BTE) explored in a clinical study using heuristic methodology. *Integral Transpersonal Journal*, *7*, 49-69.
[24] Wilber, K. (2000). *Integral psychology: Consciousness, spirit, psychology, therapy*. Boston, MA: Shambhala Publications.
[25] Rowan, J. (2011). Dialogical self-research. *Journal of Transpersonal Research, 3*, 59-69.
[26] Lattuada, P. (2012). Second Attention epistemology: Integral process evaluation Grid (III part). *Integral Transpersonal Journal*, *2*(2), 9-25.
[27] Walach, H. (2013). Criticism of transpersonal psychology and beyond. In H.L. Friedman & G. Hartelius (Eds.), *The Wiley-Blackwell handbook of transpersonal psychology*. Chichester, West Sussex, England: Wiley Blackwell, p. 73.
[28] Braud, W., & Anderson, R. (1998). *Transpersonal research methods for the social sciences. Honoring human experiences.* London: Sage.
[29] Creswell, J.W., & Plano, C.V.L. (2011). *Designing and conducting mixed method research* (2nd ed.). Thousand Oaks, CA: Sage.

[30] MacDonald, D.A., Friedman, H.L., & Kuentzel, J.G. (1999). A survey of measures of spiritual and transpersonal constructs: Part one – Research update. *The Journal of Transpersonal Psychology*, *31*(2), 137-154.
[31] Anderson, R., & Braud, W. (2013). Transpersonal research and future directions. In H.L. Friedman & G. Hartelius (Eds.), *The Wiley-Blackwell handbook of transpersonal psychology* (pp. 241-260). Chichester, West Sussex, England: Wiley Blackwell.
[32] Elliott, R. (1998). Editor's introduction: A guide to the empirically supported treatments controversy. *Psychotherapy Research*, *8*, 115-125.

CHAPTER TWENTY-SEVEN

THE MAINSTREAMING OF TRANSPERSONAL STUDIES

PAUL FREINKEL, DAVID LIPSCHITZ AND MARLEEN DE VILLIERS

Abstract

Transpersonal thinking and research methodologies invite the researcher's whole person (body, mind, soul and spirit) to a research topic. Further, it inherently facilitates personal growth, transformation, and the development of compassion as the scholar grows in their understanding of themselves, the research topic, and the world around them. Similarly, this approach offers the same to the research participants and readers.[1] In our experience, adopting transpersonal methodologies and thinking in mainstream universities has been successful in some instances, but is stepping too far from mainstream practice in others.

Keywords: personal growth, transpersonal methodology, transpersonal research, transpersonal studies,

In this chapter we share our experiences of working with transpersonal thinking and methodologies in two mainstream academic institutions in South Africa. We focus on successes achieved, mistakes made, and possible remedies to difficulties experienced and that others may experience, should they choose to adopt transpersonal thinking and research in mainstream academic environments. We record this with the intention of offering suggestions and inspiration to those courageous enough to adopt a transpersonal approach to research and teaching. Our intention is to help foster and grow a global community of like-minded scholars.

Considering Transpersonal Thinking and Research in Mainstream Academia

We have found that mainstream academia is limited in its ability to capture the full spectrum of human experience. Transpersonal thinking is grounded in an expanded view of human experience, as emphasized by Hartelius, Caplan and Rardin.[2] They highlight three aspects of transpersonal thinking: it is pervasive, includes mind, body, soul, and spirit; beyond individual ego, and it is transformative.

In this way, transpersonal thinking adds a broader perspective to mainstream academic endeavours. This paper looks at three instances where transpersonal thinking has been integrated into mainstream academia through teaching and research.

Transpersonal research methodologies invite the researcher's, participants', and readers' whole person (body, mind, soul and spirit) to a research topic. These methodologies inherently facilitate personal development, transformation, and foster compassion as the researcher grows in their understanding of themselves, the research topic, and the world around them.[3] By introducing transpersonal research methodologies to mainstream research practices, it is not a replacement, rather an addition. We contend that transpersonal methodologies include and extend conventional research.

Our experience has shown that there are students and scholars in mainstream universities who are searching for, and in some instances adopting, transpersonal thinking and methodologies. This experience was corroborated by experiences shared at the EUROTAS Conference in Crete in 2014. In some cases this adoption has been successful, in other instances, transpersonal values and approaches have been a step too far for mainstream academia. Accusations of not being scientific enough nor academic enough were reported at the conference, by those who have taken this path. While this critique may be true for poorly conducted research, this accusation has also been levelled at rigorous research, even within the gamut of transpersonal psychology (for examples see Harris Friedman's critiques[4,5]). Surprisingly though, this has not been our experience in a business school environment, where a more expansive approach has been welcomed.

In this chapter, through sharing the experiences of the three authors working in mainstream academic institutions, the Gordon Institute of

Business Science of the University of Pretoria, and the School of Psychology, University of Stellenbosch, we consider what transpersonal thinking and methodologies can offer. We refer to three examples of teaching and conducting research at a doctoral level in mainstream South African universities. These examples include lessons learned, mistakes made, and successes achieved.

Example 1: Applied Personal Transformation: A New Kind of Leadership Studies

Lipschitz and Freinkel were invited to teach an elective course on a newly constituted doctoral studies programme at the Gordon Institute of Business Science (GIBS), University of Pretoria. The brief was to develop something fresh, innovative and relevant to assist in establishing GIBS as the premier business school focusing on Africa.

With this in mind, we recognized that Africa needs a different kind of leadership. Business leaders in Africa carry the burden of responsibility for far more than merely generating profits for shareholders. They are faced with issues such as civil war caused by political, religious and ethnic affiliation, pandemic illnesses such as AIDS and Ebola, and natural disasters such as floods and famine. Our colleagues and clients who are business leaders in Africa are forced to deal with poverty, with fragile and draconian political systems, with globalization and the need for pan-African infrastructure development. In order for these leaders to navigate successfully through the myriad of these turbulent and uncertain times, we recognized they required an understanding and mastery of transpersonal leadership. This transpersonal leadership we characterize by a willingness to not only focus on the external world, but to also focus on their internal world, examining issues such as authenticity, humility and a willingness to tap into something that is greater than themselves.

We designed a course in transpersonal leadership, which we called Applied Personal Transformation. Our intent was to offer students both a theoretical understanding as well as the practical skills to expand their own awareness, thereby embracing the essence of this aspect of leadership. Specifically, the six-week elective examined leadership and personal growth through the lens of transpersonal and integral developmental theory. The key elements of the course included:

1) Examining the full spectrum of human potential, and its implications for leadership.

2) Various frameworks for expanding leadership consciousness.
3) Two particular pathways for development, those described by Susan Cook-Greuter and Hillevi Ruumet.
4) Processes and techniques for personal transformation.

In addition, to a variety of applied leadership articles, the students were prescribed the following authors, which none of them had been exposed to previously: William Braud,[6] James Hilman,[7] Ken Wilber,[8] Susan Cook-Grueter,[9] Hillevi Ruumet.[10.]

Six months after the completion of the course, we ran a focus group to assess the impact of the course on the students. The following themes emerged:

1) *The newness of integral and transpersonal thinking in a business school environment.* This newness was met by a range of reactions from intrigue, to mistrust, to irritation.
2) *An expanded perspective of leadership.* The students generally integrated an additional perspective on the roles and responsibilities of African leaders.
3) *Finding and validating an authentic voice as scholars and personally.* For many students, it was a surprise to be encouraged to share their own views and experiences as well as their reaction to the literature.
4) *Examining deeply held beliefs.* A number of students felt challenged to examine their own deeply held beliefs. These included religious beliefs, beliefs around race, gender, culture, and sexual orientation.
5) *Developing tolerance and curiosity.* Students reported that through understanding the developmental principles informing the human narrative, they developed a tolerance for, and a curiosity in, the richness of the diversity of the expression of humanity.
6) *A respectful approach by faculty (Lipschitz and Freinkel).* This was a surprising outcome. The students noted that because they experienced us as present, engaged and respectful, they were more willing to take risks, and express their views, even if it left them feeling vulnerable.

We concluded that the infusion of transpersonal thinking into a leadership curriculum at a mainstream business school positively contributed to the experience of the students, and in some cases facilitated personal growth. We published our findings in the *Journal of Integral Leadership.*[11]

Example 2: Infusing Qualitative Research Methodology with Transpersonal Values

Example 2 demonstrates how Freinkel and Lipschitz infused a conventional course in qualitative research methodology with transpersonal research values in the doctoral program at GIBS, and how it was received. This compulsory 6 week course consisted of online learning and a two day face to face seminar. Our brief was to ensure that all students understood the fundamentals of qualitative research.

We developed the syllabus to include the philosophy and application of Case Study research, Narrative Inquiry, and Grounded Theory. We wanted the students to understand that qualitative research is rigorous and nuanced, useful when exploring issues that are personal and ideographic, investigates phenomena in their depth and diversity, and that it can be transformative.

We felt it important for students to learn qualitative research methodology by doing it, rather than reading about it. To this end, we immersed students in an experiential qualitative research process that they could build from week to week, to teach the skills appropriate to the prescribed reading. We asked the students to research the life of one of their grandparents.

Our particular bias as transpersonal researchers, clinicians, and teachers, is to help people to see more of themselves. We viewed teaching qualitative research as an opportunity to supplement a conventional course in research methodology with transpersonal research values, although we deliberately never mentioned the word transpersonal. We felt researching the life of a grandparent would be an opportunity to infuse the syllabus with these values, because it would engage the students emotionally, integrate the researcher personally with the research, and bring students insight into themselves, their families, their personal history, and in some instances their chosen areas of research.

We encouraged self-reflection throughout the research process. The following themes emerged.

Students reported developing insight into their family history and culture. Students also, through understanding the socio-political context of their grandparents' lives, came to understand how they (the grandparents, their families, and consequently the students) came to construct their ethnic identities. They also noted coming to an understanding of the causes of their parents' choices and actions with which they had previously struggled.

Some students came to an appreciation for the values that their grandparents had lived by, especially the value of education in extricating themselves from poverty. Some realized that these values, passed down by their parents, had led the students to enroll for this doctoral programme. In some cases, the life experiences of their grandparents had influenced their choice of dissertation research. Many reported an appreciation for the struggle their grandparents went through to survive, and often through self-sacrifice, bettered the lives of their offspring primarily through education. Some, through gaining insight into the historical dynamics of their family, came to places of forgiveness and healing.

Students realized that there was a remarkably similar human story, across cultural narratives that pervaded the lives of their grandparents, regardless of ethnicity or religion. Despite different backgrounds, students identified with the common innate values and drive for betterment of their conditions for which their grandparents strove. They discovered there was much that bound them together; perhaps more so than separated them.

We were surprised at how receptive students were to our novel approach. Students in personal letters and in the course evaluation, remarked that not only had the process deepened their appreciation for the potential richness and depth of qualitative research, but they had grown personally from the course. This affirmed our belief that transpersonal values can offer an expanded view to research methodologies even in the context of teaching the fundamentals of conventional research methodology.

Example 3: Doing a Transpersonal Research Doctorate in a Mainstream Psychology Department

De Villiers was inspired by Pelias, cited by Leavy,[12] to conduct heartfelt research: "the heart is never far from what matters. Without the heart pumping its words, we are nothing but an outdated dictionary, untouched". Her study adopted research practices that fell outside the norm of traditional inquiry - *A Transpersonal Exploration of the Mother-Daughter Relationship in Transitional Life Cycles.*[13]

De Villiers strove towards creating methods whereby meaning could be found in a creatively intricate, relational way with subtle expression of information. She merged the inquiry of transpersonal research with Narrative Inquiry. A major difficulty she experienced was the issue of validity, trustworthiness, and scientific rigor. Traditional conceptions of validity and reliability, which developed out of positivism, are considered narrow, and inappropriate to evaluate artistic inquiry. To address this, De Villiers adopted a poststructuralist critique to deconstruct the positivist lenses with which her research was viewed by the examination board, and to some degree, the faculty.

The examination board struggled to accept transpersonal thinking. For example, she was told to replace the term "meditation", a central process of the research, with the word "reflection" which was not an accurate reflection of the process. The dissertation had to be re-written three times before the examination committee was satisfied that transpersonal methods were indeed "scientific enough"; that the researcher had adhered to rigor, and acceptable forms of reliability and validity, trustworthiness and integrity.

Discussion

Lipschitz and Freinkel's endeavours to introduce transpersonal thinking and research values were well received, De Villiers struggled. It is possible that the business school environment is more open to new ideas than a mainstream psychology department. Further, Freinkel and Lipschitz were faculty whereas De Villiers was a student. It may be that this power dynamic allowed freedom to faculty and limited a student's choice.

Transpersonal thinking and research methodologies remain on the fringes of mainstream academia. For students interested is pursuing transpersonal studies, there seem to be two options, to remain within transpersonal educational structures; or to find transpersonal supervisors within mainstream academia. Where the second option is chosen we advise discernment; similar wisdom is advised to faculty looking to do same.

Our experience in the business school indicates that language plays a critical role. When motivating to pursue transpersonal studies, whether as student or faculty, we advise that the language adopted is palatable to that audience. Furthermore, we have found that one of the risks of transpersonal research is that the scholarship becomes self indulgent, ungrounded, and ill-disciplined. For transpersonal thinking to be accepted in mainstream, the scholarship must adhere to academic rigor and integrity. It must be defensible and internally consistent as is the case with all research. Poor scholarship should not be confused with alternate forms of rigor, and never excused.

Conclusion

In this article we have recorded our experience with the intention of offering suggestions to those adopting a transpersonal approach to research and teaching. We hope it helps foster and grow a global community of like-minded researchers whether they are embedded in the field of transpersonal psychology, operating from within mainstream universities, or working as independent scholars.

Bibliography

[1] Anderson, R., & Braud, W. (2011). *Transforming self and others through research: Transpersonal research methods and skills for the human sciences and humanities*. Albany, NY: State University of New York Press, p. xvii.
[2] Hartelius, G., Caplan, M., & Rardin, M.A. (2007). Transpersonal psychology: Defining the past, divining the future. *The Humanistic Psychologist, 35*(2), 1–26.
[3] Anderson, R., & Braud, W. (2011). *Transforming self and others through research. Transpersonal research methods and skills for the human sciences and humanities*. Albany, NY: State University of New York Press, p. xvii.
[4] Friedman, H. (2002). Transpersonal psychology as a scientific field. *The International Journal of Transpersonal Studies, 21*, 175-187.
[5] Friedman, H. (2013). The role of science in transpersonal psychology: The advantages of middle-range theory. In H. Friedman & G. Hartelius (Eds.), *The Wiley-Blackwell handbook of transpersonal psychology*. Chichester, England: Wiley-Blackwell.
[6] Braud, W. (2011). *Seeing with different eyes: On the varieties of ways of knowing*. Retrieved December 2, 2012, from Inclusive Psychology: http://www.inclusivepsychology.com/uploads/Seeing_With_Different_Eyes_final.pdf
[7] Hillman, J. (1996). *The soul's code. In search of character and calling*. London, England: Bantam.
[8] Wilber, K. (2000). *Integral psychology. Consciousness, spirit, psychology, therapy*. Boston, MA: Shambhala.
[9] Cook-Greuter, S. (2002). *A detailed description of the development of nine action logics in the leadership development framework: Adapted from ego development theory*. Retrieved December 2, 2012, from Cook-Greuter and Associates: http://www.cookgreuter.com/Detailed%20descrip%20ofaction%20logics%20updated.pdf
[10] Ruumet, H. (2006). *Pathways of the soul. Exploring the human journey*. Victoria, BC, Canada: Trafford.

[11] Lipschitz, D., & Freinkel, P. (2014). A case for integral developmental psychology in leadership education: Perspectives from teaching integral and transpersonal psychologies on the doctoral programme of a premiere African business school. *Integral Leadership Review,* January – February 2014. Downloaded 31 August 2015 from http://integralleadershipreview.com/11231-case-integral-developmental- psychology-leadership-education/

[12] Leavy, P. (2009). *Method meets art: Arts-based research practice.* New York, NY: The Guilford Press, p. 2.

[13] De Villiers, M. (2012). *A transpersonal exploration of the mother-daughter relationship in transitional life cycles* (Unpublished doctoral dissertation). Stellenbosch University, Stellenbosch, South Africa.

AFTERWORD

BERNADETTE BLIN

Metamorphosis, death and rebirth are the movement of life. In the middle of the 20th century, the awakening of the transpersonal vision emerged simultaneously with the new paradigm, making old patterns and thoughts of the materialistic paradigm obsolete. This development, however, does not mean that all scientists, researchers, teachers, politicians, economists amongst other, have accepted to question their backgrounds. Each evolution or revolution creates resistance. A metamorphosis rarely happens without some resistance and resistance creates opposition, conflict and suffering.

We live at a special time when we have the results of an old paradigm in front of us. We know we are facing the greatest risks of the extinction of humankind. This is a serious challenge and it is unbelievable that this question is not the first concern of our politicians! What is being done to other human beings, animals and nature, is beyond understanding. We need change and to engage in the real transformation of every aspect of our lives. This is not a superficial question, but a calling out for the survival of our species; we can also see it as an opportunity for evolution. Metamorphosis is not an option but it is an obligation if we want to survive. With higher states of consciousness and the opening of the heart, the vision of our true nature and understanding of our infinite potential and the realization of our interconnectedness, we are like messengers pointing out what kind of development we could achieve and offering alternatives to the model of our consumer society. Our world is run by an ego state, and people run by their egos.

The transpersonal movement (through individuals and associations) has a role to play in supporting the process of awakening consciousness, to actualize our unity rather than our separateness. Destroying the environment is like destroying ourselves, harming others is like harming ourselves. Transpersonal psychology teaches us that our deepest reality is beyond the ego and is based on the Self as Jung or Assagioli expressed it.

Access to other states of consciousness is one way of showing us the limitations of the ego state and opening paths to experience our true nature. If we do not accompany metamorphosis consciously and voluntarily, then we'll have to face extremely difficult challenges, as is already the case for millions of people suffering from war, famine and displacement amongst other hardships; transformation will be more like a tsunami that sweeps everything away. The transpersonal community aims at helping people realize they are more than what they are aware of. It aims at supporting the individual and global process of awakening which will inherently facilitate the emergence of real solidarity and brotherhood. As Gandhi said "be the change you want to see in the world," therefore change starts with the self. This is a huge responsibility but one that must be taken on, as it is vital to stay connected as a community, to inform and educate so our works affects the collective.

As president of EUROTAS, this is one of the first concerns. How can we help the world to make the big shift before it is too late? We are a small group of people but everything starts inside us and together, we can make a difference. There is no pride, arrogance or ignorance in this statement. We can be humble and determined at the same time and with faith, like the humming-bird in the African legend, "do our part". The Crete conference on Metamorphosis opened a window and now with this book, a doorway opens. It is a contribution to the world, which is in need of personal and collective action.

Bernadette Blin
EUROTAS President

EPILOGUE

REFLECTING ON THE PAST – TENDING TO THE PRESENT – LEARNING FOR THE FUTURE

MARCIE BOUCOUVALAS

This book has come together in honor of humanity, to catalyze the further collective development of the human species, and propelled by the sustained belief in the powerful potential of humanity to transform. We have experienced an extended and multi-faceted history on this planet. As bio-psycho-socio-spiritual inhabitants, how will we now proceed into our future, a time when ecological, economic, ethical, social, political, and other crises and urgent societal issues, including terrorism, abound and when world systems are changing—some might even venture to say collapsing around us. It is a time period as well, however, when renewed respect for ancient wisdom is being complemented by an expanded broadened worldview of modern science, both of which are converging and balancing, especially within the transpersonal perspective that undergirds this book.

A core foundation of the transpersonal orientation is the recognition of a sacred center within. Likewise acknowledged is humanity's capacity for an expanded deeper broader consciousness that connects to others and to the cosmos, enabling one to recognize and transcend the potentially limiting perception of one's own ego, or other collective identities, yet simultaneously honor and celebrate the diversity of individual, group, national, and other identities.

The transpersonal orientation, however, also includes awareness of and concern with the "shadow" (á la Jung) aspect of humanity—matters not expressed, not even consciously recognized, often due to inconsistency with perceived self-image, that can be harbored within individuals or group identities, or in society as a whole. These matters can sometimes manifest as hate groups and what has been termed collective evil, perhaps even masquerading as a commitment to a larger cause, transcending one's ego, and connected to a "higher" purpose.

Appropriately, therefore, *Metamorphosis*--as the book is entitled--applies not just to individuals (including one's inner work and understanding one's consciousness in all its levels, states, and structures) but also to the macro-context. Equally important are the quality and kind of relationships we develop (intimate and professional), the organizations we create, the nature of communities and societies in which we live, and how we treat our mutual home, planet Earth--and beyond.

The future calls upon us to collaborate in a multi and trans-disciplinary manner. The voices, in the array of chapters--in their richness and depth--are many and varied. Some authors have offered visions, others specific pathways for this pursuit in the human quest; some are therapeutically oriented, yet others pave ways of pursuing inquiry, theory, model-building, and research that involve the whole person (body, mind, spirit) in all the nuances and many ways of knowing.

Metamorphosis through Conscious Living: A Transpersonal Psychology Perspective is the book's clarion call. What may be or seem (both for individuals and collectives) as a dis-integration--where one's ways of living and perceiving may be shattering--is often a pathway for a renewed awareness that leads to re-integration and more mindful conscious living.

Understanding the process by which one's socially constructed reality can become deconstructed such that one perceives a deeper, broader, higher sense of selfhood is fundamental. Such a feat is sometimes incremental—evolving gradually and naturally over one's lifetime. After much societal success one might even ask "Is that all there is"? Other times one might embrace a path of disciplined practice. Yet for others, a more immediate tragedy or life-threatening situation or catastrophe might impel one to re-examine one's life and emerge with a transformed perspective. Then too there are those who catch glimpses from a young age. Some continue on that path, some abandon it to adjust to societal expectations, yet others return at a later age and re-integrate.

May this volume inspire and enrich you and perhaps create an aperture for further metamorphosis in your own context. We welcome your comments and queries, as well as conversations, with the authors, editors, or with each other—perhaps in educational institutions, in community groups, in informal gatherings, in relationships, or other venues and contexts.

Toward that end, some authors have shared their contact information for further dialogue. May we move onward into a fresh future for humanity. Much awaits our efforts.

List of Contributors

Rosemarie Anderson, PhD, is Professor Emerita of Psychology at Sofia University USA, author, and an Episcopal priest. In 1998, she authored *Celtic Oracles* and co-authored, with the late William Braud, *Transpersonal Research Methods for the Social Sciences,* the book that established the field of transpersonal research methods. In 2011, Rosemarie co-authored *Transforming Self and Others through Research* with William Braud and co-authored *Five Ways of Doing Qualitative Research: Phenomenological Psychology, Grounded Theory, Discourse Analysis, Narrative Research, and Intuitive Inquiry.* In 2014 she co-founded the Transpersonal Research Network (www.transpersonalresearchnetwork.com) with several European colleagues. In 2017, Rosemarie was awarded the Abraham Maslow Heritage Award by Division 32 of the American Psychological Association.

Anne Baring, MA, (Oxon) is a Jungian analyst, author and co-author of 7 books. Her recent book, *The Dream of the Cosmos: a Quest for the Soul,* was awarded the Scientific and Medical Network Prize 2013. The ground of all her work is a deep interest in history and the spiritual, mythological, shamanic and artistic traditions of different cultures. Her website offers a new vision of reality and includes her talks and interviews on YouTube. It is devoted to the affirmation of a new vision of reality and the challenges facing us at this crucial time of choice. www.annebaring.com

Bernadette Blin, MA, is a psychologist, transpersonal psychotherapist, Gestalt therapist, teacher and supervisor. She holds certification in Holotropic Breathwork and Transpersonal Psychology from Stanislav Grof and has been initiated by shamans from different traditions. Founder of IRETT in France (Institute of Training in Transpersonal Psychotherapy) and co-founder and Vice-President of GRETT (Group of Research and Studies in Transpersonal Therapy), Bernadette is the current president of EUROTAS. Author of many articles on Transpersonal Psychotherapy, she is co-author of *Healing the Ego, Revealing the Being, the Challenge of Transpersonal Therapies* (Tredaniel), *Manual of Transpersonal*

Psychotherapy (Interéditions) and *When Consciousness Will Awaken* (L'Harmattan).

Marcie Boucouvalas, PhD, Professor Emerita of Human Development (Virginia Tech/National Capital Region) and editor of *The Journal of Transpersonal Psychology,* has a lifelong, life-wide, and life-deep interest and involvement with the transpersonal terrain. Her background in psychology and sociology and further specialization in adult development/learning (broadly defined), led her to work with diverse cultural groups, urban and rural poor, in an array of community contexts, including as delegate to major UNESCO World Assemblies. Her publications and professional practice are framed by her foundational inquiry on the multi-layered nature and scope of the transpersonal movement as it applies to development not only of individuals, but to relationships/groups, organizations/society, and the planet/cosmos.

Sean Blackwell has been researching the spiritual dimension of bipolar disorder for over eight years. Since 2007, he has been producing videos for his YouTube channel, BipolarORwakingUP. His book, *Am I Bipolar or Waking Up?* describes his own bipolar awakening, subsequent hospitalization and complete recovery, which happened in 1996. Together with his wife, Ligia Splendore, Sean has been leading private healing retreats for people diagnosed with bipolar disorder since 2013. www.bipolarawakenings.com, bipolarawakenings@gmail.com.

Giovanna Calabrese, MD, PhD, is a medical doctor specialized in psychiatry and transpersonal psychotherapy, with a strong background in research in the field of neuroimaging, applied to psychiatric and neurological diseases, and in qualitative methods applied to transpersonal psychotherapy. She is co-founder of the Transpersonal Research Division of EUROTAS, EDTR.

Claudio Calcina, PhD, is a psychologist and transpersonal psychotherapist in training to become an official trainer of the Biotransenergetic transpersonal approach. A philosophy graduate, he has studied many traditional and modern body-mind techniques. Practices include Craniosacral, Shiatzu, Reiki, Overtone singing, Denthosophy and Shorei-kan. In 2009 he qualified in body-mind practices of Corpo del Sogno and Arte del Dono di Sé of Biotransenergetic.

Maria Cristina M. de Barros is a clinical psychologist with an MSc in Development Psychology at the Institute of Psychology of the University of São Paulo. She has a post graduate certificate in Transpersonal Psychology from ALUBRAT and is vice-president of the association. Cristina integrates the Board of the International Transpersonal Association and the Board of the Asociación Transpersonal Iberoamericana. She is currently studying the interface of mental health and spirituality at PROSER (the program of health, spirituality and religiosity of the Institute of Psychiatry- USP) and at GEALTER (Institute of Psychology USP), searching for new clinical models of intervention.

Arturo De Luca, PhD, is a transpersonal psychologist and psychotherapist, who teaches at the Faculty of Psychology, University of Rome La Sapienza, and at the Faculty of Medicine of Perugia. Former contract researcher for the National Research Council (CNR), he holds the ECTP award (European Certificate) of Transpersonal Psychotherapy. He is a graduate in Psychology, Philosophy, Law and Naturopathy, and is also teacher/trainer for the postgraduate training of the Transpersonal Psychotherapy School OM of Milan and author of several publications on transpersonal psychology, rebirthing, shamanic practices, traditional medicine and music therapy. He is publisher of the scientific magazines *Samsara* and *Rivista di Psicologia Transpersonale.*

Marleen De Villiers, PhD, is a psychotherapist in private practice in Cape Town, South Africa. She works with transpersonal psychotherapy and arts-based therapy methods. She is an independent researcher, with her current research interest being the process of psychotherapy and the continuous development of the inner life of the psychotherapist. She also pursues research in mindfulness practices for psychotherapists with a particular focus on arts-based practices. Marleen is an artist, making and exhibiting jewelry and creating mandalas for healing and rituals. She is a member of EUROTAS and one of the founding members of EDTTF.www.tamar.co.za, drmarleendevilliers@gmail.com.

James Eyerman, MD, AHIHM, DFAPA, had his first major transpersonal experience at age 16 in a NDE, when he was involved in a car-accident. Within the year, Thomas Merton, an anti-war activist poet turned Trappist monk, sent him a note a few weeks before his untimely death, to read Jung and learn to meditate. Krishnamurti's lovely poetic diary, *The Only Revolution*, brought an immense epiphany and gave him a taste of non-duality. The LSD psycholytic therapy papers by Stanislav Grof helped psychologically frame these experiences. His life's focus has been on Meditation, Ayurveda, Yoga, Jyotish, Dreamwork, Transpersonal Psychology, Psychopharmacology, and Holotropic Breathwork.

Dietrich Franke, MD, is a medical doctor and clinical psychologist with a psychotherapeutic practice in Freiburg/Germany. He is married, has one daughter and one grandson. Dietrich is a certified psychotherapist of the European Transpersonal Association (EUROTAS), a member of the Spiritual Emergence Network (SEN) Germany, a member of the International Institute for Consciousness Exploration and Psychotherapy in Wittnau, Germany, and a member of the Swiss Medical Society for Psycholytic Therapy (SÄPT). He takes care of the monthly joke on the EUROTAS website. www.dietrich-franke.de.

Paul Freinkel, MB BCh, PhD, is a medical doctor, researcher and entrepreneur. He is faculty on the Alef Trust MSc program awarded through Middlesex University, and adjunct faculty for the doctoral program of the Gordon Institute of Business Science, South Africa. His research includes mainstreaming transpersonal values and research methodologies, spirituality and classical singing, and transpersonal development theory, and its multiple applications. He is a trained singer and exhibiting fine art photographer. As an entrepreneur, Paul is co-founder of the StarTraq Group - a global leader in traffic offence processing, and an executive director of LatestSightings.com, a world-wide social media community.

Harris Friedman, PhD, is Research Professor (retired) of Psychology at University of Florida, Professor Emeritus of Saybrook University, and currently teaches at Goddard College. He has over 200 professional publications, and his recent books include *Transcultural Competence* (2015), *The Praeger Handbook of Social Justice and Psychology*, Vols. 1-3 (2014), and *The Wiley-Blackwell Handbook of Transpersonal Psychology* (2013). He is senior editor of the *International Journal of Transpersonal Studies* and Associate Editor of *The Humanistic Psychologist.* He is principal investigator on several research grants, and consults as an organizational and clinical psychologist. harrisfriedman@hotmail.com.

Ashok Gangadean, PhD, is a world renowned global philosopher, author and spiritual activist. He is the Margaret Gest Professor of Global Philosophy at Haverford College (USA) where he has taught for the past forty-eight years. He is author of several books, including *Meditations of Global First Philosophy, Quest for the Missing Code of Logos* and the audio book *Awakening the Global Mind, A New Philosophy for Healing Ourselves and Our World (with Sounds True)*. Ashok is also the Founder-Director of the (Global Dialogue Institute) which introduced the *Seven Stages of Deep Dialogue*, an innovative technology of deep dialogue between worlds in the art of being an awakened human. www.awakeningmind.org, www.globaldialogueinstitute.org.

Martine Garcin-Fradet, MA, is a EUROTAS certified transpersonal psychotherapist and teacher of *Transpersonal Inner Communication* practitioners. She also conducts systemic constellations and is a certified member of DGfS. She created and developed *Accompanied Inner Communication*, as a direct result of her life's path. Years spent in foreign countries and ten years in Japan gave her a belief system that benefits the vision of a human being able to integrate various representations of the world and life. She has published a number of books about her work, her latest one *From Silence to the Word, the Missing Link.*

Siegmar Gerken, PhD, ECP, HP, is therapist, trainer and supervisor in integrative, body-oriented, mindfulness-centered therapy, somatic, humanistic and transpersonal psychology. Faculty member at JFK, Esalen and former SBGI, he teaches world-wide on the interconnectedness of psychosomatic processes, as they manifest on the levels of body, emotions, mind, will and consciousness. His research in energy field documentation of psycho-emotional states has opened new horizons for scientists and practitioners. www.CoreEvolution.com, info@CoreEvolution.com.

John (Sean) Hinton, PhD, is a professional consultant in private practice, author, researcher, and professor. He currently teaches in the graduate school of psychology at Capella University. He studied Depth Psychology at Pacifica Graduate Institute, and received a PhD in Transpersonal Psychology from the Institute of Transpersonal Psychology, and also received an MBA from the Graziadio School of Business and Management Pepperdine University Malibu, California. Sean Hinton has researched extraordinary experience that related to the phenomena of the numinous, as well as imaginal realms. Interests include philosophy, consciousness studies, neurobiology and writing poetry.

Regina U. Hess, PhD, is a clinical psychologist, transpersonal psychotherapist and researcher. She is founder of the *Ase World Forum* for the investigation of ancient transcultural healing modalities and their integration into modern intervention and research. She is faculty at international educational institutes, and is editorial member at the *Integral*

Transpersonal Journal and the *Forum Qualitative Social Research*. Regina is on the Board of Directors of EUROTAS and of the International Transpersonal Association. She is co-founder of the Transpersonal Research Network and the EUROTAS Division for Transpersonal Research. She is a member of the Swiss Medical Society for Psycholytic Therapy (SÄPT). E-Mail: dr.reginahess@gmail.com
www.drreginahess.com, www.eurotas.org

Aimee V.L. Hohn, MA Ed., MA T.S., received her Master's degree in Transpersonal Studies as part of a Doctoral track in transpersonal psychology at the Institute of Transpersonal Psychology/Sofia University (USA). She also has a Bachelor's degree in history and American Indian studies and a Master's degree in Social Studies Education. For over ten years, she has worked as an educator in a variety of environments, from the classroom, to state and tribal government. She also has an intuitive counseling practice. Working with people of all ages and abilities, she has innovated strategies for learning and wellness.

Tanna Jakubowicz-Mount, MA, is a clinical psychologist and a psychotherapist. She is president of the Polish Transpersonal Forum, Warsaw, Poland and has been plenary presenter at European Transpersonal Conferences. From 2000-2015, Tanna led the Polish Transpersonal Forum which prepares the ground for humankind's reunion with self, other people and the whole of creation. She leads therapeutic and educational workshops based on her own transpersonal approach, practices Buddhism, Shamanism and Jewish Mysticism. She is a member of the Circle of Women Elders and founder member of the EUROTAS Council of Elders.

Bertil Johnsson is an independent consultant/coach and organizer of personal and team development, also doing independent research in systemic areas of human integration. He has worked as a human resource specialist in R&D management, Nokia Data & Ericsson Information Systems. Additionally he has worked with and taught counseling in internal programs at Stockholm University and the Royal Institute of Technology (KTH). He studied the MSc program in Electronics at KTH as well as the MSc program in Esoteric Astrology at the University of the Seven Rays, USA. www.innocation.se, bertil.johnsson@innoaction.se.

Paul Kiritsis, PhD, is a scholar and professional writer with interests in cognitive neuroscience, clinical psychology, the philosophy of mind, esotericism, comparative religion, and mythology. He holds a Bachelor of Behavioural Science, a Graduate Diploma in Professional Writing and Speech; a Master of Western Esotericism and a BA/MA in Metaphysical Science and a PhD. He is currently completing a doctoral degree in Clinical Psychology. Academically he wishes to harness a more adequate view of the nature of mind and is immensely interested in the link between creativity and schizophrenia, a neurological model for Julian Jaynes' Bicameral Mind theory, and visual hallucinations and the construction of visual reality.

Les Lancaster, PhD, is Professor Emeritus of Transpersonal Psychology at Liverpool John Moores University, and an Honorary Research Fellow in the Centre for Jewish Studies at Manchester University. He is a past Chair of the Transpersonal Psychology Section of the British Psychological Society, and currently chairs the International Transpersonal Association Board. He is Director of Programming at the Alef Trust (www.aleftrust.org). In addition to many journal articles, Les' published works include *Mind Brain and Human Potential*, winner of a Science and Medical Network Best Book Award, *Approaches to Consciousness*, *The Marriage of Science and Mysticism*, and *The Essence of Kabbalah.*

Reinhard Lasser, MD, lives and works as a general physician in free practice and in two facilities for addicts in Graz, Austria. Trained in western medicine, he came across Homoeopathy, Acupuncture, Holotropic Breathwork® and constellation work amongst others with their respective world views and philosophies. Siddha Yoga is his spiritual path and has enriched his life deeply and helped him understand his own tradition from a different perspective. His work aims at the integration of different approaches of eastern and western medicine, different forms of therapies, philosophies and spirituality into a comprehensive world view.

Pier Luigi Lattuada, MD, PhD, is director of the Integral Transpersonal Institute in Milan and an adjunct faculty professor of Sofia University. He is a medical doctor, has a PhD in Behavioral Studies and a PsyD in Clinical Psychology. He is also a psychotherapist and founder of Biotransenergetics. Pier Luigi is director of the Transpersonal Psychotherapy and Counselling School in Milan and faculty and chair, of BA for Integral Transpersonal Psychology at Ubiquity University. Scientific Director of the *Integral Transpersonal Journal*, he serves as co-Vice-President of EUROTAS. Pier Luigi has published sixteen books, more than 30 articles, and presented Biotransenergetics at more than 50 International Conferences worldwide.

David Lipschitz, PhD, is a clinical psychologist engaged in a variety of fields. He is adjunct faculty at Gordon Institute of Business Science, South Africa and teaches on the Alef Trust MSc course in Consciousness, Spirituality and Transpersonal Psychology through Middlesex University, UK. David's interests include psycho-spiritual development and its application to personal, leadership and team development. He consults to diverse organizations in this field. David runs an independent, private psychotherapy practice and has initiated a fathers and daughters program at Roedean School in Johannesburg. He has two Psychology honors degrees (Industrial and Applied); two master's degrees (Management, and Clinical Psychology); and a PhD in Transpersonal Psychology.

Zana Marovic, PhD, works in private practice in Johannesburg, South Africa. She is a clinical psychologist, transpersonal therapist, hypnotherapist, supervisor, yoga teacher and published author. Zana has published in international academic journals, presented workshops and papers at congresses around the world and published a book on clinical supervision. She is an executive member of The International Transpersonal Association and accredited trainer for transpersonal psychology in South Africa. In her practice and training she integrates Western traditional psychology techniques with Eastern philosophy, hypnotherapy, yoga and African indigenous cosmology.
www.drzana.co.za, www.transpersonalpsychology.co.za.

Lindy McMullin, PhD(c), was Founder and President of the Hellenic Association for Transpersonal Psychology and Research, and Director of the XVI EUROTAS conference in Crete. Author of *A Soul's Journey,* she lectures and runs workshops locally and abroad and is in private practice as a therapeutic consultant. Lindy uses art and drama in her work with both adults and children, and is particularly interested in re-visioning ancient techniques for self-actualization and self-transcendence. Certified by EUROTAS as a transpersonal psychotherapist and supervisor, Lindy also works as editor of the EUROTAS newsletter and is core team member of EDTR. www.quantumgreece.com, www.eurotas2014.com.

Judith Miller, PhD, is professor of Human Development at Columbia University, where she teaches Spiritual Development across the Lifespan. She is also a faculty member of the International Institute for Consciousness Exploration and Psychotherapy in Freiburg, Germany. She facilitates training programs in Transpersonal Breathwork and Spiritual Guidance internationally and supports and guides people on their psycho-spiritual journeys, individually and in groups for over 25 years. She is the author of numerous articles as well as *Healing the Western Soul, A Spiritual Homecoming for Today's Seeker* (Paragon House, 2015). She is a professional member of the Spiritual Emergence Network in the US, and a regular contributor to Psychology Today's Online Blog.

Unjyn Park is a PhD candidate at Leeds Beckett University, UK. She lived in a Tibetan settlement in India for several years, where she studied Buddhist philosophy and meditation techniques. Her PhD research centers on voicing the lived experience of indigenous Buddhists and their individual interaction with Buddhism, drawing on Buddhist history and doctrinal studies, contemporary qualitative research methods, and transpersonal theories. u.park@leedsbeckett.ac.uk, neantise@gmail.com.

Dee Purcell is a spiritual mentor and guide in private practice focusing on self-actualization and individuation. She is a PhD(c) in Integral and Transpersonal Psychology. Her research interests include nonverbal communication, nonlocality, and heart-centered healing modalities. An international speaker, she travels the world to study spiritual and healing traditions. She holds certification in Dynamic Stillness-Biodynamic cranial sacral practice. Her passions include embodied awareness of an integrated mind-body-spirit for health and wellness; creative expression therapies; empathy, compassion and mindfulness; and traditional healing modalities.

Vitor Rodrigues, PhD, was the president of EUROTAS, 2004-2009, and the coordinator of the EUROTAS Committee for Certification and Accreditation, 2000-2013. He is a practitioner in transpersonal psychotherapy and a writer, having published 12 books from Sci-Fi to social criticism to self-help manuals. He uses Regression Therapy, Hypnosis, Guided Imagery, Psychic Defence and other procedures in his practice and is currently working on his own model for psychotherapy, named *Awakening Transpersonal Psychotherapy*.
www.vitorrodriguespsicologo.weebly.com, psicosophos6@gmail.com.

Vera Saldanha, PhD, is president of the Portuguese-Brazilian Association of Transpersonal Psychology (ALUBRAT) based in Brazil and Portugal, the first association to offer post graduate courses in Transpersonal Psychology in Brazil. She has a PhD in Transpersonal Psychology (FE Unicamp) and is author of *Transpersonal Psychology: An Emerging Knowledge of Consciousness*. She has developed a methodology called the Integrative Transpersonal Approach (AIT) and has taught courses in Transpersonal Psychology throughout Brazil for over 25 years. She works in the clinical area and is a founding member of the Asociación

Iberoamericana Transpersonal and member of the International Transpersonal Association.

Maria R. Sideri, MSc, MA, is a psychologist, transpersonal body psychotherapist and dance movement therapist. She is a professional member of the European Transpersonal Association (EUROTAS), of the Spanish Association of Dance Movement Therapy (ADMTE), and director and co-founder of the Spanish Association of Psychosomatic and Energetic Therapy (PSIQUESOMA). She works in private practice, offering psychotherapy and professional training in Transpersonal Dance Therapy and Psychosomatic Movement in Barcelona, Spain. www.danzaterapia.org, mariarossisideri@gmail.com.

Ligia Splendore is a graduate of Santos University in Clinical Psychology and has a post-graduate degree in Transpersonal Psychology from ALUBRAT. She has experience with the mental health system in Trieste, Italy and, over the past eight years, has been studying the relation between Bipolar Disorder and Spiritual Emergency. Together with her husband, Sean Blackwell, Ligia created AlmaBipolar.org (Bipolar Soul), an online social network for people diagnosed with bipolar disorder in Brazil. www.ligiasplendore.com, ligiasplendore@gmail.com.

Harald Walach, PhD, is director of the Institute of Transcultural Health Sciences at the European University Viadrina in Frankfurt (Oder), Germany, and director of a postgraduate program on Cultural Sciences and Complementary Medicine. His research interest is in Methodology and Evaluation of Complementary Medicine and the Impact of Consciousness.

T. J. Weisbecker, PhD(c), is founder and co-chair of the Southern California Psychedelics Research Society, Founder, CEO, and Senior Designer at ZenVector Graphics Art & Design Studio in Los Angeles, yoga Instructor with Chandrana Yoga, and executive minister of the Southern California Transpersonal Fellowship. Weisbecker completed postgraduate studies in psychology with the Institute of Transpersonal Psychology (Sofia University) and is currently conducting dissertation research into mystical experiences in the contexts of hallucinogen intoxication. In addition, Weisbecker holds an MA in Theology from Loyola Marymount University, and a Certificate in Religious Studies from the University of San Francisco.

Milica Zegarac is a PhD candidate at Sofia University (formerly the Institute of Transpersonal Psychology) in Palo Alto, with a concentration in Consciousness and Creativity. She has an MBA in marketing from the University of Illinois in Chicago and has also taught undergraduate marketing and advertising. She holds multiple certificates from various yoga schools in India and the USA and is a registered yoga teacher (RYT500). With a passion for everything transpersonal, her diverse travels and research has taken her to diverse parts of the world, including extended stays in Indian ashrams and Brazilian spiritual healing centers. She is also trained in several somatic modalities, energy healing and yogic breathwork.